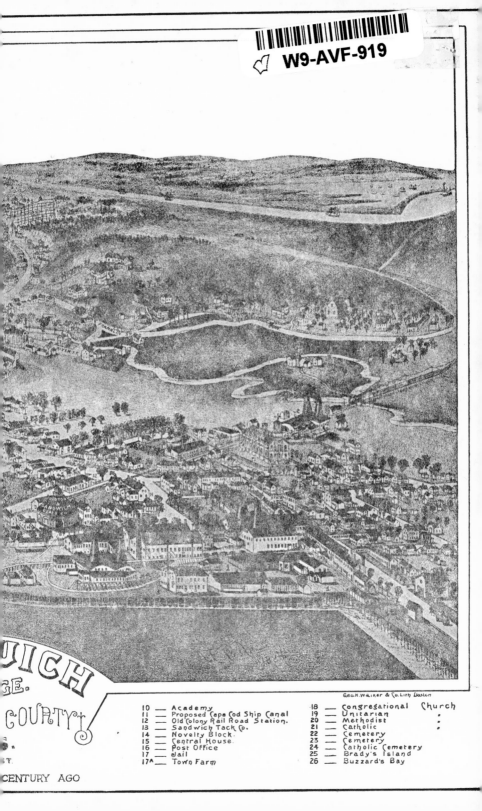

Geo.H.Walker & Co.Lith Boston

DICH
GE.
COUNTY

CENTURY AGO

10 — Academy	18 — Congregational Church
11 — Proposed Cape Cod Ship Canal	19 — Unitarian
12 — Old Colony Rail Road Station.	20 — Methodist
13 — Sandwich Tack Co.	21 — Catholic
14 — Novelty Block.	22 — Cemetery
15 — Central House.	23 — Cemetery
16 — Post Office	24 — Catholic Cemetery
17 — Jail	25 — Brady's Island
17ᴬ — Town Farm	26 — Buzzard's Bay

SANDWICH GLASS

BOOKS BY RUTH WEBB LEE

EARLY AMERICAN PRESSED GLASS
Enlarged and Revised

HANDBOOK OF EARLY AMERICAN PRESSED GLASS PATTERNS

SANDWICH GLASS
Enlarged and Revised

SANDWICH GLASS HANDBOOK

VICTORIAN GLASS

VICTORIAN GLASS HANDBOOK

ANTIQUE FAKES AND REPRODUCTIONS
Enlarged and Revised

PRICE GUIDE TO PATTERN GLASS

A HISTORY OF VALENTINES

NINETEENTH-CENTURY ART GLASS

CURRENT VALUES OF ANTIQUE GLASS

LEE AND ROSE

AMERICAN GLASS CUP PLATES

Rare opaque blue Sandwich glass flower pot and tray. Period 1830—1840.

SANDWICH GLASS

The History of the
Boston & Sandwich Glass Company

Enlarged and Revised

By RUTH WEBB LEE

LEE PUBLICATIONS

WELLESLEY HILLS ⚹ MASSACHUSETTS

REVISED AND ENLARGED

ISBN 0-910872-04-X

TO

MRS. HENRY H. FREEMAN

OF

BOSTON AND SANDWICH, MASS.

WHOSE INVALUABLE CONTRIBUTIONS FORMED MUCH
OF THE NECESSITY FOR THIS REVISED EDITION.

ACKNOWLEDGMENTS

Without help promptly and cheerfully given it should have been impossible for me to overcome the many obstacles that stood in my way while preparing this book. Friends lightened a heavy burden by sharing it with me. I cannot adequately convey my sense of gratitude, however graceful the words I might select to express it. But my thanks are heartfelt, and I am sure my friends know it.

At first it was planned to do a handbook devoted exclusively to lacy glass, but on second thought I considered that too much of that type of the Sandwich output was in the hands of private collectors and antique dealers to be readily available for thorough study by less fortunate collectors or by lovers of fine early American glass. It was therefore decided to treat the Sandwich product in general, since I am convinced that collectors of any one of the many Sandwich lines would welcome a more comprehensive account of the achievements of a great concern.

To the Sandwich Historical Society and, in particular, to its former Curator, Mrs. Henry H. Freeman, I am indebted for the loan of photographs, specimens of Sandwich glass, and quantities of historical material. Mrs. Freeman has been helpful in innumerable ways and never left unheeded my frequent appeals for her advice and assistance. The unfailing courtesy and sympathetic understanding of the reasons for my many requests which she displayed are deeply appreciated. Indeed, much of the data which have formed the justification for the revision of this edition have come through her efforts. For these reasons I must pay special tribute to Mrs. Freeman and her most important contributions.

Mr. Francis Wynn, of Sandwich, Mass., is entitled to public acknowledgment of my appreciation of the work he has so painstakingly carried on at Sandwich. To his co-operation and steadfast devotion to the cause of factual data concerning Sandwich I owe a considerable portion of the material printed in this book. His excavations in the site of the old factory have brought to light not only fragments of glass but clues which have led to a more complete knowledge of the marvelous output of what was, I believe, the foremost glass house in America during the second quarter of the nineteenth century or longer. Many doubts have been settled by Mr. Wynn's finds.

All collectors of glass should, at least once annually, return a vote of thanks to the late Mr. Harry Hall White for his researches in an important field. His excavations at old factory sites contributed more than any other man's work to our knowledge of this early industry. He was forever digging up treasures, both in the field and in books. He was most helpful to all writers on glass, generously placing at their disposal the results of his work.

Mr. James H. Rose cheerfully contributed much time to my problems about cup plates, on which he is a well known authority. I am indebted to him for the photographs of the Curling creamer and the "glassed-in-pastes." His patience in discussing the more intricate details of cup plates and his conclusions about their "greatest density of distribution" was inexhaustible and is to the same degree appreciated.

Mr. Albert C. Marble, whose collection of cup plates is one of the greatest in this country, is a Stoic philosopher as well as a great gentleman. Not the faintest murmur came from his lips when I removed from his cabinets the twenty-one rarest cup plates to photograph for illustration in this book. They are among the choicest of the hundreds of items in his collection and their loss or damage by careless handling would have been irreparable. It is difficult to know which to admire the more, his trustfulness or his optimism. It is a pleasure to acknowledge my indebtedness to him and his disposition.

Mr. George L. Tilden was helpful with freely expressed views on the rarest cup plates and kindly allowed me to photograph many beautiful pieces from his shop. They were appreciated at their full value, for, after all, pictures help collectors to identify their specimens far more than the most careful verbal descriptions.

Mr. James Gillinder, an active glass manufacturer of today, is the descendant of a famous family that has been identified with the glass industry in this country since 1854. He was most helpful whenever technical questions required the advice of an expert. Moreover, I may add that he is one of the very few present-day manufacturers who are keenly interested in what was done by our early glassmakers.

Mr. Albert E. Shaw supplied me with his notes and photographs of his collection of perfume bottles and jars. Much painstaking and systematic work was involved but, fortunately, Mr. Shaw is a systematic and painstaking person, who derives a keen and highly intelligent pleasure from his hobby. I am greatly indebted to him for his help. I may say the same of Mr. Channing Hare who kindly sent me the photograph of his rare and charming pair of amethyst compotes.

The following owners allowed me to photograph some of their specialties, often at considerable inconvenience to themselves but always graciously. They are true collectors and co-operate gladly in whatever is done to advance the "cause"! Mr. Edwin Lefevre— now deceased, Mr. W. Colston Leigh, Mrs. C. C. Nitchie, Mrs. William Greig Walker, Mrs. Austin Chilson, Mr. B. H. Leffingwell, Mrs. Edgar I. Lefavour. My thanks are due, also, to Mr. George E. Burbank and Mrs. Raymond D. Van Name for interesting letters pertaining to Deming Jarves; to Miss Flora Jarves for data about her grandfather, Deming Jarves; to Mr. Clarence Haines for the loan of William Stutson's memo book; to Dr. Edward Hashinger for many photographs of his interesting collection, only a few of which were used because many of his rare pieces had already been pictured. The *American Collector* was also helpful, as well as many courteous assistants in libraries in Boston and elsewhere where necessary research work had to be done. I am particularly indebted to Mr. H. M. Lydenberg, formerly director of the New York Public Library, and to his courteous and efficient staff.

All of the photographs of lacy glass, with those exceptions as noted on the illustrations, were taken from the superb collection assembled by Mrs. Charles W. Green. Having access to such a nearly complete collection of the best in lacy glass, shortened the writing time of this book considerably and was appreciated in proportion to its great value.

INTRODUCTION

It is a curious commentary on the capriciousness of human events that some three years after the first appearance of this book, and fifty-three years after the closing of the factory, there should be delivered into my hands all of the recorded minutes of the meetings of the Boston & Sandwich Glass Company, from the date of its incorporation in 1825 until the factory closed in 1888 and the last account was settled. All of the Company correspondence deemed of sufficient importance by the executives to be preserved was among the papers, thereby comprising the most complete and valuable set of records known to be extant, to document authoritatively the history of any old glass factory in America. In the first edition of *Sandwich Glass,* the history and products made at the Cape factory were covered and sound conclusions drawn which stand up well under the floodlight of this new factual evidence. The only sins are those of omission, which can now be supplied to fill those gaps. Subsequent years of exhaustive research, collation and organization of data have resulted in this greatly revised and enlarged volume.

*

Whoever in these United States has felt the inescapable thrill at the sight of a collection of objects that sing in colors, the glittering marvel of the survival, through the years, of such fragile creations, has perforce heard of Sandwich glass. More books have been written and articles printed, more human-interest stories told— and more misinformation circulated—about the Boston & Sandwich Glass Company than about any other glass factory in the United States, and, perhaps in the world. For many years "Sandwich," applied to glass, has meant much more than the product of the factory that, beginning in 1825, operated at Cape Cod for over three score years. It is today a generic rather than a specific label and explains the popular division of collectors into those who "collect glass" and those who "collect Sandwich." The word is applied to a recognized American Institution. Its eight letters spell for us the saga of a factory, of a period and of a genius.

True Sandwich collectors do not ride a hobby, not even when they hunt for specimens in attics and shops. They assure you they really fulfill a patriotic duty and, in so doing, earn the right to be enrolled among the elect of the earth; that is to say, among those for whom Keats' line has been amended——and greatly improved—to read: "Sandwich glass is a joy forever!" And you cannot criticize the Sandwich devotee for a fervor that would put halos on cup plates or creamers. If they do not genuflect daily before their lacy dishes, it is probably because they fear to shake the shelf on which the treasures rest. If you will stop, look and listen, you are almost certain to become a Sandwich collector yourself, for it must be admitted that there are sound reasons why an avocation which turns collectors' cabinets into veritable shrines should be encouraged.

The tale of Jarves' achievements, revealed by our collections, merely gives to us, to have and to hold, the glory of his glass. Knowing little as we do of the real Deming Jarves, the animating spirit of the Boston & Sandwich Glass Company, the true romance of Sandwich is, for most of us, dimly outlined. The quiet streets of a quaint little town in Cape Cod or the records of a factory operating at a period of our history when industrial triumphs were rare and drab in hue are but unimportant facets of the still incomplete romance of Sandwich.

The many-sided Deming Jarves, for all his dreams of an enduring glass empire, could not possibly have foreseen that the ware he made and sold would, within a century of its manufacture, occupy a place of honor in the front rank of American collectibles. And even had he foreseen it, he still could not have realized the intensity of the interest that his fellow countrymen would feel in his theories and practices, in his improvements in methods and technique, in the dates and lists of his creations.

No satisfying portrait of Deming Jarves, not even of his physical self, exists. His descendants have been unable to find for us any paintings or drawings or silhouettes that could show us how he looked as a child, as a lad, as a young man, or as a leader in his prime. The likeness in the possession of the Sandwich Historical Society, donated by his granddaughter, Miss Flora Jarves, shows us a septuagenarian. To sketch a likeness of him as he probably was at the various stages of his career only one method is left to us, which is, to reverse the usual procedure: Begin at his 75th year, and then walk backward to his 35th. No really revealing anecdotes are available. There is no one to tell us how he looked or how he talked or what he had in mind when he was making the rare lacy pieces that we so treasure today.

The very glass we prize most highly is the glass produced when the factory was all Jarves and not when it made the most money. In Appleton's "Encyclopedia of American Biography," there is no mention whatever of Deming Jarves, but his son, James Jackson Jarves, has 36 lines. The list of the younger Jarves' books and papers is given, but the name of his father is not. In the "Dictionary of American Biography," Deming Jarves is presented too sketchily and in a rather unfavorable light, but not as the result of new discoveries. We know much of the history of the town of Sandwich itself, from its founding in 1637 to 1946, but of Deming Jarves, who made the place famous, we know little. The annals of the little town have been carefully preserved; the year-by-year history of this great man has not.

Where much has been written in the past, very little of which is the result of careful research, discouraging inaccuracies may be expected, as well as deliberate misinformation. The task of the historian is thereby made doubly difficult, since he must toil tirelessly to unearth facts and fragments and at the same time expose myths and legends that have sprung from the desire of well-meaning souls to please collectors with agreeable answers to their questions, or, as it unfortunately cannot be denied, from the efforts of many who would use apocryphal stories to help the sale of an eagerly sought American glass.

It was not that what has been printed gives a wrong picture but that it leaves too much ground uncovered. As most of us see it, "Sandwich" means more than fine glass, more than a superlative "collectible," more than early craftsmanship, more than an American industrial triumph. It connotes so much more that the calm consideration of all that should be adequately treated in the unwritten book and the difficulties of securing the needed data, have discouraged attempts to undertake its writing. There are no survivors of the Golden Age of Sandwich from whom we might obtain anecdotes of the key men and their idiosyncrasies; or the shop gossip at the various periods of the factory's existence; or more illuminating glimpses of the experiments and the industrial philosophy of the genius who created it. Single articles may disclose much that never before has appeared in print, but they usually contain material written by earlier writers that is not checked for errors. Absurd mistakes have been perpetuated, particularly in the case of attributions, for it had become the usual practice to call all glass, good, bad, and indifferent, Sandwich. Some of it did not add to the reputation of the Cape factory but, on the other hand, fine work by certain glassmakers was credited to the genius of Deming Jarves.

The variety and extent of the factory's output in its sixty-three years of operation is incredible. Sandwich offers to the antique-loving public more desirable collectibles than any other early American glass factory—blown, pressed and molded glass in all sorts of forms, colors and designs. There are objects for everyday use, like tableware and superb vases, decorative ornaments, playful trifles, animals, candlesticks, lighting fixtures, etc. You can specialize in one Sandwich line and still be able to spend years in forming your collection. You may go in for blown glass and nothing else and Sandwich will fill your cabinet with glorious specimens. You may decide to collect Blown Molded glass exclusively and become too proud for the comfort of your listening friends. You can discern the difference between the best Sandwich pressed glass and stop amassing less fine Midwestern patterns. And of course, there is Lacy Sandwich—the royal family of American glass.

But, if you collect Sandwich you must be sure that what you acquire is in reality Sandwich. It is always difficult to authenticate the product of a particular glass factory. In the case of Sandwich you must exercise even greater care, for much harm was done by allowing misattributions to go unchallenged too long. Only recently have students of Sandwich been able to turn into certainties what for years had been merely suspicions—or wishful thinking. Excavations carried on at the site of a building erected in 1849 have brought to light fragments of pieces made prior to that year. It was only after the brick floor had been torn up that it was possible to treasure-hunt there. It has been a mine, for the findings have settled many hitherto unanswered questions and have at last established the Sandwich origin of many fine pieces, as well as their particular period.

Some effort should be made to do away with the confusion inseparable from the lack of some sort of classification. In the case of lacy glass, which leads all others in popularity, it is suggested that the numbers of the Plates in this book be utilized. Specific names cannot be given to all the patterns and designs. Wherever custom and usage have fixed upon a designation by which collectors now know or recognize a certain form or item in lacy glass, I have used it. It is too much to hope that *every* specimen of lacy glass that was made at Sandwich has been found and photographed, but all the important collections have been drawn upon for the hundreds of illustrations in this book. Collectors need merely specify the particular piece and the number of the Plate when it is pictured.

In Blown Molded glass, it would be wiser to adopt designations by which individual patterns might be known. To classify this kind of glass in such vague and general terms as "Baroque, Arched, Geometric, Quilted," etc., is as much to be deprecated as the failure to adopt a genuine name by which this line should be known. When you consider that no one has to date found an illustrated catalogue in which trade names are given, it merely shows how little the old makers dreamt of the exasperation of collectors in later years.

It is not necessary to treat here at length the unfortunate habit of attributing the work of other factories to Sandwich. It is the motive that must be condemned. All collectors, the world over, are afflicted by a mania for attributions. With many it becomes an obsession, for which they apologize by calling it a laudable desire for accurate classification. If they can establish the origin and the period they can "date" their specimens. Naturally, the authenticated work of a Master does all that, besides enhancing the market value, since it is reasonable to assume that a famous maker's handiwork must be of the highest class. The value-making factor of rarity enters also into the craving for the label. It is an exceptional collector who prefers to own a fine work of art, "artist unknown," rather than an inferior piece to which a famous signature may be attached. Hence the fakes and the forgeries. The blue ribbon of an "attribution" is nothing to be either sure or proud of, unless it hangs on a really fine work. The day has fortunately gone by when everything that glittered was Sandwich in the antique shops.

Our collectors were too long the victims of our national ailment—*labelitis Americana*—which is a near blood relation of our fondness for slogans. The phrase almost supersedes the fact. We have much to learn from the European collectors who as a rule go about their hobbies far more intelligently. They take more pains to be better informed about the origin and characteristics of their glass. They study it in books and check up in museums. They swap not only duplicates but also information, with brother collectors. They know the traditions and legends and also the facts. But with us there are a hundred "antiquers" to one antiquarian. Fortunately, the number of serious research workers and investigators grows daily.

Ruth Webb Lee

CONTENTS

ILLUSTRATIONS

Rare opaque blue Sandwich flower pot and tray, period 1830–
1840 . . . . *Frontispiece*

xxi

xxiv *Illustrations*

SANDWICH GLASS

Chapter I

DEMING JARVES

It is always difficult to define human greatness and still harder to describe it. It may consist of what a man has done or what he has said or what he has thought. Perhaps most of us really have in mind an unusual man when we speak of him as being great; that is, the possessor of a single abnormally developed faculty or of a rare combination of normal traits. The handy receptacle to which nearly all definitions of greatness find their way is the word "genius," which seldom completely satisfies; for a genius, to be conceivable, must be plainly seen in the act of being a genius. If the known facts are not presented with the particularity needed to give a clear mental picture, the average man builds his own bridges across the gaps that check the progress of his curiosity. Hence, hero-myths and legends are born, that die slowly and hard.

Over a century ago a man lived whose handiwork today delights thousands of Americans, an unusual man of whom we would know more, the better to evaluate his remarkable achievements. His greatness has been assumed without really adequate corroborative pictures. When a man becomes a legendary figure without the help of a well-constructed legend, he is apt to turn into a man of mystery. Such a man is Deming Jarves. There is no "living likeness" of him, in print or on canvas. He was too aggressive and adventurous a man to have been particularly secretive or, for that matter, of a particularly retiring nature. But, seek where you will and you will find neither enthusiastic panegyrics nor red-hot philippics from the pens of Jarves' contemporaries; too few revealing flashes in letters or private journals or unpublished memoirs. He should have had a Boswell—and unlimited funds for his experiments!

3

Tradition transmitted by word of mouth seldom serves the needs of the realistic portrait painter. Even so, I regret to have heard so few really illuminating anecdotes handed down from generation to generation, about Deming Jarves. We cannot effectively analyze his achievements to find therein the master key to his psychology. But we may read between the lines of his own "Reminiscences" and fit items from his company's old account-books, minutes of business meetings, and correspondence, into a human pattern, picture-puzzlewise. After all, it is not the "Reminiscences of Glass Making" that collectors would like to read today but his "Confessions"!

The first and most important thing that a man usually does in this life is to be born. It is significant of the obscurity that hovers over Deming Jarves' entire career that notwithstanding all the researches of innumerable writers on Sandwich the date and place of his birth were not definitely established until 1939. In the magazine *Antiques* the author of a long and carefully compiled article on Jarves, states that "he was born abroad where his parents were travelling." The day of his arrival on earth was not recorded though the date of his christening day was. Precisely which place "abroad" can claim the credit of being his birthplace was not revealed. Another writer, in a previous article in the same magazine, gives the date of his nativity as 1791 and a footnote informs us that "Deming Jarves is said to have been born in Boston but he is not listed on the city records." In the *Dictionary of American Biography* the year is given but not the month or day. It is clear that these writers were not aware that "facts" about Deming Jarves are apt to elude investigators with the ease born of long practice. Assuming that an independent search by me of the Boston birth records also would prove futile, I called on his granddaughter, Miss Flora Jarves. She is my authority for the statement that Deming Jarves was born in Boston on November 21, 1790. On December 9th he was baptized in the New South Church, Boston. His parents may have been travelling abroad when he was born. If so he still could not have crossed the Atlantic in 1790 in a sailing ship in the winter time and been baptized on December 9th—unless he was born before the date taken from the family records. And if, on the other hand, he was born in 1791, the christening must have taken place months before he arrived in Boston—or, for that matter, anywhere "abroad" or at home.

It may be perceived from the foregoing that all the important Deming Jarves career-dates were difficult to fix from the very first. This fact should convey to the reader some of the difficulties that attend the task of writing the definitive biography of Deming Jarves.

He was buried in Mt. Auburn Cemetery, Cambridge, Mass. A picture of his tombstone is shown on Plate 7. There his admirers may read: "Deming Jarves. Died April 15, 1869: Aged 78 Years and 5 Mos."

There can be no wisdom in going back of this undisputed Jarves "fact."

The historian who could trace back Deming Jarves' ancestry four or five generations might uncover interesting hereditary tendencies. We know only that he was descended of a Huguenot family—*Gervais*—that left France after the revocation of the Edict of Nantes in 1685 and settled in Jersey, the largest of the Channel Islands, which were a favorite refuge for Huguenots, for they lie closer to the mainland of France than to the English coast. Moreover, no change of language was involved by settling where everybody could talk French. The Islands were occupied by Rollo and his Northmen and became a part of the Duchy of Normandy. After William the Conqueror the group—Jersey, Guernsey, Alderney and Sark—belonged at different times to the King of England, when he happened to be also Duke of Normandy. In reigns when the two crowns did not rest on one head the Islands were Norman. Since Henry II, in 1154, the Channel Island group has been English. But the inhabitants did not become thoroughly Anglicized for centuries. They were not of Anglo-Saxon stock but of Celtic and, to this day, the French Celts (Bretons) are not like other Frenchmen. The laws of the Channel Islands were not, and still are not, those of England and the inhabitants have enjoyed a distinct political existence and observe curious traditions. They are still subjects of the Duke of Normandy and not the King of Great Britain. In the course of centuries of uninterrupted English sovereignty the racial differences naturally became less pronounced. The infusion of Anglo-Saxon blood into the Celtic strain through intermarriage and the gradual preponderance of the official language, could not but be felt. But it is not unreasonable to assume that a Jersey family, 150 years ago, might still show characteristics both of Anglo-Saxons and of Celts.

In Deming Jarves we find more than a slight trace of the French temperament. It shows in his love of beauty and his fondness for brightness and color. From his English father, he may have derived his courage and his commercial venturesomeness. From the Seabury strain, through his mother, the tenacity of purpose, independence of mind and disregard of non-essentials, which so characterized his maternal grandfather Samuel Seabury, who was the first American Episcopal Bishop. He had to go to Scotland to be ordained because the English Bishops, resenting America's secession from the mother country, obstinately refused salvation to the Rebels, *via* an American Bishop. They would not ordain him in England; but he had his way in the end. His life seems to have been one of active opposition to whatever he did not like. He was a Tory, served against the Americans, was imprisoned and came back to become a kindly priest, unaffected by tradition.

John Jackson Jarves, Deming's father, left his native Jersey and came to America in 1787, with his wife, Hannah Seabury. *À propos* of the Anglicization of the original family name, Miss Flora Jarves, Deming's granddaughter, wrote me from her home in Kingston, R. I., that her brother and her uncle always told her that the name was originally Gervais, which explained the "e" in Jarves. Some of the family at times expressed a preference for the French spelling; but it had been Jarves too long. "And so, it sticks!" wrote Miss Jarves.

John Jackson Jarves—the middle name may indicate the latest

admixture of English blood—came to America in 1787. A writer in the magazine *Antiques* asserts that the Jarves family was prominent in England for their wealth and their Whig affiliations. If true, America naturally would be selected by an English Whig as the best country in which to settle. Whatever the Jarves family's standing was or was not in England, John Jackson Jarves had no aristocratic inhibitions. He may well have been a man of means and culture and taste. What his occupation was in his own country is not known to me but he had not been long in Boston before he embarked in a business that required not only some capital but a practical knowledge of cabinetmaking.

His name appears for the first time in the Boston Directory in 1789, as "Jarves, John, Cabinet maker, No. 76 Newbury Street." A clipping of a newspaper advertisement, owned by the Massachusetts Historical Society, reads:

JARVES

Cabinet, Chair, & Clock Case Maker from London
No. 76 Newbury Street, Boston

Respectfully informs Gentlemen and Ladies that he makes the following Mahogany Furniture on reasonable Terms, viz.: Library Book Cases, Desks & Book Cases, Chests & Book Cases, Double Chest of Drawers with Desk Drawers, single Chest of Drawers, Desks, Gentlemen's Portable Writing Desks, Counting House Desks, Ladies Commode Dressing Tables with furniture Drawers, Library Tables, Dining Tables in sets, round & square Card Tables, Pembrook, Claw, China, Chamber, Toilet & Night Tables, convenient Stools, China Shelves & Brackets, Balance, Pole, Face, and Hand Fire Screens, Side Boards, Cellerets, Butler's Treys, Knife Treys, Oval Tea Treys, Tea Chests & Cadys, Sconce & Swing Glass Frames, Ladies Urn Stands, Gentlemen's Wardrobes, Sophas, Easy Chairs, carved & plain, Chairs, four post, Field Bureau & Common Bedsteds, Weight & Spring Clock Cases, Watch Cases, & all kinds of Picture Frames.

In the 1796 Directory he is listed as "Jarves, John, Cabinet maker, No. 76 Newbury St. House, Beach Street." In 1798, and until 1813, he is still listed as a cabinetmaker, at Beach Street. The house number was probably No. 6 for it is so printed in 1823, the year of his death. In the 1816 book John Jarves' occupation for the first time was not given, although the address remained the same. It meant he was no longer a cabinetmaker.

It is clear, however, that John Jackson Jarves prospered in his business, for at his death in 1823 he bequeathed $25,000 and six buildings to his wife and their children, Deming and Sally (Hastings), the bulk of the estate going to the son. It is equally plain that the elder Jarves entertained for his only son not only a deep affection but a firm confidence in his business ability and his character. He must have been certain that Deming would deal lovingly as well as wisely with his mother and sister and their affairs. A clannish family, the Jarveses! It is the common trait of families and communities that have suffered cruel religious persecution.

John Jarves is referred to as "gentleman" in his will. It was the custom in this country, derived from the English, so to style men who were no longer actively "in trade." The omission of "cabinetmaker" in the Directory after 1813 makes his retirement from business a reasonable assumption. He made money and kept it, during the war and after. It may possibly have helped to raise his social rank but it certainly must have given him broader views on business in general, from which his son duly benefited.

The importance of the need of more definite information on this particular point lies in its bearing on the career of Deming Jarves. In 1813 he is listed as "Jarves, Deming, dry goods, 11 Cornhill" but we are left in the dark as to the precise nature of his "dry goods" enterprise. He was 22 years old when he was so listed. In 1815 and 1816 he was a partner of "Henshaw & Jarves, dealers in crockery ware, Belknap St." In 1818 he appears in the directory as a "glass factor," still at Belknap St. Deming's name does not appear again in the Boston Directory until 1826, when he is listed as "agent" for the Sandwich Glass Company, Phillips Building. The absence of his name from the directory covers the period when he was at Cambridge with the New England Glass Company. Incidentally, the "agent's" address in the early advertisements is given as at "Henshaw & Jarves, 20 Broad St.," although one writer has it that the firm was forced to close its business in the hard times after the close of the War of 1812.

Now, John Jackson Jarves, a shrewd business man and a loving and admiring father, must have concerned himself with his only son's future. Successful men are usually anxious to have their sons inherit their profession or business, together with their name and their reputation for integrity, which are their most valued assets. Did John Jarves see no future for his son as a high-class cabinet-maker in Boston as early—or as late—as 1813? It is certain that Deming did not go into the dry goods business against his father's wishes. Had he done so, Jarves, Sr., would not have made him the principal legatee. Similarly, had John Jarves disapproved of the glass venture at Cambridge he would not have advanced money to the New England Glass Company, for among the assets he left was a note of the company for $1,900. Perhaps he early fell under the spell of Deming's eloquence as others did, and saw the future success of the glass enterprise with his son's eyes. Whatever the reason, he did not urge Deming to carry on the business that had enabled "Jarves John, Cabinet maker" to retire in well earned comfort.

It is, of course, possible that during the War of 1812 the cabinet-maker may have suffered reverses, as so many other Boston merchants did, sufficient in themselves to discourage Deming. Then, too, another line of business may have appealed more strongly to the alert 22-year old lad. In any event, it is not known that Deming was seriously engaged in cabinetwork, though he must have found something to do with his time between his sixteenth year and his twenty-second, when he entered the dry goods business. His was too active a mind—and too vigorous a body—to have simply idled away those years.

Why did not Jarves, père, send his son to Harvard? Was it because there was too much theology in the curriculum, too heavy a stress upon Scholasticism to please an independent-minded son-in-law of Bishop Seabury, who was a chronic oppositionist where non-essentials were involved? It is obvious that letters written by Deming Jarves in his early manhood are not the epistles of a man with the education, or, if you prefer, the book knowledge that we would expect of one so richly endowed mentally as Jarves. Who was responsible, since the economic need was lacking, for compelling Deming Jarves to become, as he did, a self-educated man? There is so much we do not know about him that we despair of ever knowing the real Deming Jarves intimately.

A few points, however, stand out clearly when we consider his life in connection with the character of his later achievements. Whether or not he ever engaged in the making or selling of fine furniture, it is at least probable that he must have learned, in his father's place of business, much that was to prove of value to him afterward at Sandwich. During his most impressionable years, the fashionable furniture, fortunately for him, was in the best of taste. The designs of Chippendale, Sheraton, and Hepplewhite were greatly admired. America had not yet "gone Empire." Deming Jarves could and, in all likelihood, did learn to appreciate the beauty of line, of contour and color, of decorative values. The high quality of the merchandise he saw and the admonitions he heard in his father's shop probably sowed the seeds of the unfailing insistence on using the best obtainable materials and the passion for good workmanship that governed his glass operations years later.

Of his dry goods experiences it is impossible to learn much. We may assume, of course, that his father helped him financially and gave him sound advice; but Deming's own personality, you may be sure, was already vigorously asserting itself. He was a marked man in Boston business circles even then. Before he was 28 he had all that it takes to make a successful promoter who, after all, must be a super-salesman, for he must sell himself and his visions. He inspired confidence in his abilities, which, I take it, consisted even then of clear-sightedness, hard sense, persuasive eloquence, business shrewdness and very quick apperceptions. It is logical to assume also that in his dry goods business he could and did indulge his love of color and design—sanely controlled by his recognition of the exigencies inseparable from the business of selling and by the need of wise selection in the business of buying. He might indulge his own inclinations, and at times, perhaps his dreams; but he also keenly studied his clients' tastes and habits. It was the only way of anticipating their needs and he well knew that it pays to "beat the gun" in selling the sort of merchandise which, while primarily useful and practical, must also appeal to the eye.

Later, long years of industrial and financial success probably inclined him somewhat to that form of wishful thinking in which the hardest-headed businessmen paradoxically indulge as they grow old. It consists of reversing the tried-and-true mental telescope of commerce so that the dollar profits in the distance shrink to negligible dimensions while the desired triumph of a theory or a whim magnifies itself into mountain size. It is neither megalomania nor stubbornness but that deafness to warnings which grows into a habit, after hundreds of similar disregarded warnings have been followed by dazzling success. Jarves, in his lifetime, probably made and also lost fortunes by his "experiments." But today we see his triumphs collected while his failures find no place in our curio cabinets, not even to remind us that the race is not always to the swift nor the battle to the strong.

His experience in the crockery and glass business, also, must have played an important part in his later success at Cambridge and at Sandwich. Unfortunately, it is only another surmise, unsupported by documented "facts" but, I think, difficult to dismiss lightly because there is no other logical way of accounting for the development of the son of a successful cabinetmaker so quickly into the financially successful producer of some of the finest and most beautiful glass ever manufactured in America. We cannot tell for a certainty that he inherited his undoubted artistic temperament from the Huguenot strain in his Channel Island father but we know that he had it and that he, in turn, transmitted it to his own son, James Jackson Jarves, who, as a famous connoisseur, collector, critic and writer on art, earned a place in a standard American biographical dictionary which, ironically, does not even mention the name of his father.

Knowing so little of the Jarves family history we cannot envisage Deming's early home influence. In his "Reminiscences" he has so little to tell about himself that I regard his mention of Robert Hewes as an unconscious revelation. Moreover, it significantly suggests that his interest in glass began at a very early age. On page 54 of the 1864 edition of his "Reminiscences," you will find:

Shortly after the close of the Revolutionary struggle, we think about the year 1785, the late Robert Hewes, a well-known citizen of Boston, made, probably, the first attempt to establish a window-glass manufactory on this continent. This manufactory was modelled upon the German system. Mr. Hewes carried his works to the fuel, and erected his factory in the then forest of New Hampshire. The writer well remembers, when a boy, hearing Mr. Hewes relate that when building his glass-works the tracks of bears were frequently seen in the morning in and around his works.

The time was to come when Deming Jarves also would find it expedient to carry his works to the fuel, for it was that, more than water transportation to Boston, which took him to Sandwich. He did not need to see bear tracks to pick the spot for his factory but it is significant that he remembered Mr. Hewes' story all his life. He was highly susceptible to the romantic thrill of adventure, which his incessant experimentation and innovations bear out, as well as to the appeal of commercial profit, as his earned fortune attests. Glassmaking in America in 1818 was precisely that—an adventure which promised dividends in a day when the bold gambler and the shrewd trader often were united in one person. And if he did not find bear tracks about the factory grounds at Sandwich, we are told by Mr. George E. Burbank, the painstaking historian of the old town, that:

"In July of this year, 1847, the last wolf in Sandwich was killed by George Brailey, a teamster of the Boston & Sandwich Glass Company; was brought to the Town Hall and hung up between the columns for exhibition. The bells were rung and there was much rejoicing among the farmers. The loss of their sheep had been great."

Deming Jarves made glass for twenty years, within the sound of the eerie ululation of wolves!

At the age of 25 he married. The Boston *Independent Chronicle* of May 29, 1825, printed under "Marriages": "In this town (Boston) Mr. Deming Jarves, mar. to Miss Anna Smith Stutson." It proved to be a successful marriage. Nine children were born to them. Deming's devotion to his family went, if anything, beyond the limits laid down for busy American industrialists in the first half of the 19th century. But we know they were a clannish family, those Jarveses, and Deming's later dynastic dreams are comprehensible in a man of his temperament and ancestry.

In 1818 he was listed in the Boston directory as "glass factor," which merely tells us that he acted as agent for unnamed glass firms; but in 1817 he is said to have been a "clerk" of the Boston Porcelain & Glass Company of East Cambridge. His old firm, Henshaw & Jarves, was not in the 1818 directory, though the name continued to appear in newspaper advertisements at least as late as September of the same year as a place (20 Broad St.) where orders for glassware might be left for Deming Jarves, "agent" of the New England Glass Company. It has been intimated that Henshaw & Jarves wound up their affairs during the troublous times that followed the close of the War of 1812. If so, it seems curious that Jarves should engage in a far more important enterprise at about the same time. There is no knowledge of precisely what his "clerkship" at Craigie's Point (East Cambridge) consisted but his name was signed to a call for a meeting to wind up the affairs of the Boston Porcelain & Glass Company. The sort of "clerk" he may have been probably meant more then than the same word means today, just as the "agent" of the New England

Company really meant that he was the general manager and sales agent.

Carefully omitting, as usual, all personal details, he tells the story of his new venture in his "Reminiscences":

Contemporaneous with the South Boston enterprise (a flint glass factory operated by Thomas Caines) a company was formed and incorporated under the title of the Porcelain and Glass Manufacturing Company. Their factory was located at East Cambridge, then called Craigie's Point. Their china department was directed by a Mr. Bruitan, but for want of proper materials it proved an entire failure. Their glass works were under the direction of a Mr. Thompson, who built a small six-pot furnace, similar in size to the one at South Boston. Thompson brought out a set of hands, at a heavy expense, to work the furnace, but the result proved he was in no way qualified for the task, nor possessed of the least practical skill or knowledge of the business, and, of course, proving an entire failure. The attempt to make porcelain and glass was abandoned by the company.

In 1815, some of the workmen left the South Boston Factory and hired of the Porcelain Company their six-pot furnace, and commenced the making of flint-glass under the firm (name) of Emmet, Fisher & Flowers. They succeeded for a time very well, and turned out glass suitable for the trade; but want of concert of action prevented a successful result, and they dissolved without loss. The Porcelain Company, discouraged by so many failures, agreed to wind up their concern, and in November, 1817 they disposed of their entire property at public auction.

As one manufactory dies out only to give place to another, so the present New England Glass Company was formed, and became the purchasers of the Porcelain Works. The company, from 1817, to the present time, (1854) have pursued the business with signal success; beginning with the small capital of $40,000, they have from time to time increased it, until it amounts at the present time to $500,000. They commenced business with a small six-pot furnace, holding seven hundred pounds to each pot; employed, all told, about forty hands, and the yearly product did not exceed $40,000. They now run five furnaces, averaging ten pots to teach, capacity of two thousand pounds to each pot. They employ over five hundred men and boys, and the yearly product is not less than $500,000.

That is all that Deming Jarves has to say about his own connection with the formation of the New England Glass Company—his first really important step. The company was organized by shrewd men, experienced in business and banking, but he was concededly the moving spirit. He was not then a practical glass man but he had both the commercial vision and, necessarily, the magnetic personality and persuasive eloquence that made him the successful promoter we know him to have been. We must think of him as he was then, not quite 28 years old, active, resourceful, undoubtedly possessing that acute perception of "possibilities" that we, not always flatteringly, call "Yankee gumption." He had a highly developed acquisitiveness, not only financially but mentally. He may have dreamt his dreams even then but, if he did, it was not during business hours! He could not have had obfuscating illusions about himself at a period of his life when he was keenly aware of what he did not know and, more important, of what he needed to know, about glassmaking. That knowledge he was sure he would one day possess in full measure, given his type of mind; but since the business in hand could not wait for him to educate himself he made use of the most competent men obtainable in this country and abroad. He had the gift of a quick and accurate grasp of character, which he kept throughout his life, though with age came the enemies that the years bring to all born leaders of men—impatience with opposition and, possibly, indulgence in personal prejudices.

At the time of the organization of the New England Glass Company he was at the beginning of the formative period of his career as a manufacturer and salesman of American-made glassware. While little is known of his personality and previous history he seems to have had the gift, not only of turning his hand to all sorts of constructive work but of selecting the right men to work under him.

Jarves indeed had that gift in a superlative degree, together with the courage of his convictions. A story of how he secured the services of a highly skilled engineer, James B. Barnes, is revealing. He, Barnes, was taking a stroll in the Common with his children, when Jarves, who undoubtedly knew all that he needed to know about Barnes, approached him and in a short talk convinced Mr. Barnes that a golden opportunity was before him. All Barnes had to do to grasp it was to enter the employ of the New England Glass Company.

As a salesman, Deming Jarves had all the necessary qualities. In his five years in dry goods, pottery and glass, he learned more than most salesmen do because he combined business sagacity with an alert imagination. He made use of well-tested bridges to cross rivers. That was wise and in accordance with prudent business methods; but, knowing his strength, he also could leap across gullies, and for years could convince his associates that it was not only a safe operation but bound to be profitable. In no other way can the rapid success of his enterprises and the co-operation of his associates be explained.

He has been called a many-sided genius, which he undoubtedly was, but we lack the human details. He probably was not an inventor of the first magnitude nor a great innovator, although he was both to a marked degree, but he had a lightning-quick grasp of possibilities in the way of improvements in both methods and machines—for some of which he has perhaps received more credit than he could justly claim. In this connection, when you read about the denial or disallowance of some of his claims for patents and his acquisition of color formulas or utilization of others' patterns and designs, it would be well to remember what were the common business practices of his day.

He must have had social gifts of a high order that won for him the friendship of all sorts and conditions of men. Whether or not he was a prodigal giver or an easy person to wheedle out of money he seems, at least, never to have attached excessive importance to fortune-winning or to the advertising value of ostentation. Per-

haps his New England environment and early home training may
have restricted an innate tendency to reckon costs as of secondary
importance and the quality of the finished product as the main ob-
jective. Whatever consideration he showed at Sandwich for his
workmen or for his stockholders, we know he was able to win the
good will of all manner of people without having to buy it with
favors. At Cambridge he was known and esteemed by the voters.
He was an assessor in 1822–1823, a selectman in 1823–1824 and a
representative to the General Court from that district in 1824.
Whatever his motive may have been in accepting these offices at
times when it is reasonable to assume his New England Company's
"agency" must have kept him extremely busy, it at least shows one
of his many good sides. And it may be said here that there is no
credible record that he was a particularly vain man. That he knew
his capacities, and perhaps made clear to others that he was fully
aware of possessing them, was natural and proper. An egocentric
man is not necessarily a megalomaniac and Deming Jarves had too
many children and was too devoted to them to ever have been
exaggeratedly egotistical. His mind was geared to a much higher
rate of speed than the average man's. It probably made him impatient with slower understandings.

Mrs. Watkins in her *Cambridge Glass* wrote: "It was said by
a contemporary [William Cains] that he [Jarves] left Cambridge
on account of a difference of opinion with the directors of the
[New England] company." This may well have happened but it
would be interesting to know the exact nature of the difference.
Probably Deming Jarves was keen about certain innovations or
improvements that did not appeal with equal force to his more
conservative associates. I have read, without being able to substantiate it, that Jarves was at one time the largest individual holder
of the stock of the New England Glass Company. In any event
he, together with his relatives and intimate friends, controlled a
very large block. That it was not a bitter quarrel which caused the
parting may be assumed, for we have the evidence of the first
account book of the Sandwich Company to show that the relations

of the two companies were friendly. They often called on each other for supplies or ingredients and they bought from and sold to each other without hesitation.

It is altogether likely, however, that Deming Jarves was not happy during his last year or two at Cambridge. After several years of managing the New England Company's business he had acquired a fuller practical knowledge of glassmaking. He had secured the services of expert workmen from whom he learned much. But it was only after his father's death, in 1823, that he could carry out wishes that he had long cherished. Among these was a trip to Pittsburgh to round out his glass education. He had already developed a new and cheaper method for making red lead which was of immense benefit to the industry but he was of the type that must know every detail of the business and seek to lower costs and improve the quality. He was much impressed by what he saw at the Bakewell-Pears works. Incidentally, Jarves' account of the demands of labor in the early days reads almost word for word like the news printed daily in our newspapers today.

He regarded Mr. Bakewell as the father of the flint glass business in the United States. He learned much that he never forgot from the story of the great Pittsburgh manufacturer's long fight with unskilled and unreasonable workmen and inferior ingredients and his final triumphs over almost insuperable obstacles. When Jarves went back to Cambridge he was unquestionably a much better-informed glassmaker and he probably perceived the need of making certain changes. He saw more clearly than ever and with keener eyes than most of his associates possessed, the industry's vast possibilities and new openings for the New England works. His restless mind urged him onward possibily at a more rapid pace than seemed safe to them. It is easily conceivable that the brakes the other directors sought to apply irked him. No man of his temperament and disposition is ever really the "lone wolf" of romance but Deming Jarves, after six years of discussions with his business associates, visualized a happier state of affairs for himself, in a factory where he could do, unhampered, what he wished. There would be less friction with Jarves working for Jarves and for no one else. A family business would be best. He therefore organized the Sandwich Manufacturing Company. The early operations of the works are treated more fully in other chapters.

He saw what could be done in Sandwich and wasted no time. There was an abundance of timber for fuel and easy transportation by water. There was a little town, already close to two centuries old, in that state of chronic somnolence that results from the absence of important industrial plants and regular payrolls. The temptations of a larger town did not exist there, which was an important factor in connection with glass blowers who, as a class, were well paid and reputed to be convivial. He roused the native sleepers of Sandwich with his glowing promises of steady wages. Perhaps he fixed them lower than the wage level of other places, but they seemed high enough to the jobless inhabitants. He made staunch friends of them and unhesitatingly used them to his own advantage whenever necessary; but he also brought them steady work and a living and helped the town in so many ways during so many years that their relations were never deemed unfairly one-sided.

The Deming Jarves who started to make glass in Sandwich, Mass., in 1825 was not the "Jarves Deming, dry goods, Cornhill," of 1813 nor the "Jarves Deming, glass factor, Belknap St.," of 1818. He was now 35 years of age. Being in his very prime, he was spurred by his faith in the certainty of success. He was blue-eyed and fair-haired, "the perfect type of an Englishman," very tall and strong. His affection for his children, which so characterized him in later years, found expression in his concern for the children of his workers.

I suspect it was at Sandwich that his dynastic dreams began to crystallize into a policy. He would now work for Jarves; not for *Deming* alone, be it understood, but for every Jarves in Boston— for his family; that is, for his *name*. It was the germ of a new industrial philosophy for him. His factory should be operated always by his own flesh and blood and by workers who automatically would become relations-by-adoption. He planned to do so from the first, either from kindliness or because local conditions necessitated it; or it may be that his dream made him see the wisdom of providing homes and comforts for his help. Since a Jarves would always be at the helm and Jarves men always at the oars, he must build a seaworthy family boat.

One man's life is not long enough to finish the colossal monument to his name that grows in his mind the more he thinks of it in terms of decades of labor! He must have realized that the only immortality a man may achieve, when the thinks only of a dream that must come true, is to build the edifice with an eye to permanence. He would lay the foundations and perhaps live to half finish it. To complete it would be the work and, above all, the duty of his heirs. They must make sure that the Jarves banners waved forever over it: Banners of smoke; always more banners; always more smoke; always more glass; the best, the most beautiful glass in America—made by a Jarves so that Deming the First might dynastically continue to live on!

It is not rhetoric that you have just read but a Jarves trait that is demonstrably justified by what we know. From the day that Deming Jarves decided to go on his own, the more he thought about the future the more he planned as I have written. In one of the few self-revelatory observations in his disappointing "Reminiscences" he wrote of Mr. Thomas Bakewell, whom he admired and desired to emulate: "He lived to realize an ample fortune as the fruit of his industry and his sons still carry on a profitable business on the premises originally occupied by their father. By father and sons this has covered a space of forty-four years, a length of time rarely finding a business in the same family in America. *May the factory be always occupied and conducted by a Bakewell!*"

For "Bakewell" read "Jarves." It will not be a wild guess at his real meaning. He made his brother-in-law, William Stutson, his superintendent. Edmund H. Munroe, a wealthy relative of his wife, was the treasurer. He sought, years later—unfortunately, in vain!—to have his sons succeed him. He built glass works for them to conduct and develop. But he could not read the future. While his sons were too young, he contented himself with educating his other boys, the sons of the workers. Sandwich must be more than a glass factory: It would be the Jarves Training School for Jarves men.

And so he formed his own company, the *Sandwich Manufacturing Company*. Why was the word "glass" not used in the corporate title? Had Jarves in mind to do more than make glass at Sandwich? Was he thinking of possibilities in other manufacturing fields? Probably not. But the enterprise was to be, as nearly as he could make it, a personal venture. He and a few relatives would own it and direct it. He could count on their support, for he firmly believed that blood is thicker than water and that friends are loyal and grateful. His relatives not only loved him but admired him intensely. For years he had been their pride and their boast. They trusted him as implicity as he relied on them. He had every proof of this and felt safe in assuming that so long as he did his best for them and the business prospered he could count on them not to oppose his policies or his plans.

He was what today would be called a dynamic hustler. Nothing was done except by his orders and under his personal supervision. He did everything. He acquired the timber lands and the factory site; he secured in divers ways the help and co-operation of the population of Sandwich; he raised, in Boston and Cambridge, the capital needed; he engaged his lieutenants, planned the works, improved methods, hired the workers, built cottages, planted trees, looked after everything. Of course, he was ably aided by men he had picked out for their abilities and for their personal devotion to him. A many-sided man, indeed; jovial here; coldly businesslike there; firing all hands with his enthusiasm and, probably, with his promises—which he duly carried out, as his associates felt sure he would, with a pat on the shoulder for one or a frown of disapproval for another. He was at all times Deming Jarves to his men,

the trusted leader, concededly the superior of everybody in everything, for when he had to use a man better qualified than himself
for a particular task, he himself picked him out, and told him why.
Did not that very selection prove his genius? The man he picked
was sure of it. The others, who saw the results, also voted yes.

The unusual diversity of his activities did not fluster him. For
this statement we have "documented facts"—unfortunately only in
skeleton form and therefore not sufficiently picturesque to drama-
tize vividly—a line here and there in the first account book of the
Sandwich Company; a sentence or two in a letter; a paragraph in
his "Reminiscences"; a surviving fragment of some contemporary
rumor. But all these must be treated almost paleontologically in
reconstructing the man that he undoubtedly was.

In his "Reminiscences" he is guilty not so much of chronic understatement but of an indifference to "human" details. He devoted page after page to information about glass and glassmaking,
from 1500 B.C. to his own day, dealing, literally, in glittering gen-
eralities and in mechanical or technical particularities. The personal factor in such a book may have seemed to him incongruous
rather than offensively obtrusive. Whatever the reason, his own
account of his own work at Sandwich is irritatingly typical of the
entire book. For example, he merely tells us that "in 1825 a flint
glass manufactory was established by individual enterprise in
Sandwich, Mass." He does not give the name of the company,
which surely would not have made him appear egotistical; nor
admit that he himself was the "individual" of the enterprise. Then
he writes that "ground was broke in April, dwellings for the workmen built, and manufactory completed; and on the 4th day of
July, 1825, they commenced blowing glass—three months from
first breaking ground." That told for him the entire story of
three months of grueling work, of hundreds of problems met and
solved, of incredible speed and accomplishment. It was all in the
day's work and he so treated it.

"In the following year," he goes on to say, "it [the individual
enterprise] was purchased of the proprietor and incorporated

under the title of Boston & Sandwich Glass Company." The "proprietor," being himself, was not named. Was it a morbid dislike of the personal pronoun or could he have thought that everybody in the world knew, of course, that the proprietor was Deming Jarves? Why did he not tell, one almost might say, in self-defense, that the reason why he gave up his first agency was that he had found the interference of fellow directors an intolerable annoyance at Cambridge? If he discovered, a few months later, as it has been reported, that he lacked sufficient capital to carry out all his plans at Sandwich, in part because an overzealous agent had bought much more timber land than Jarves could conveniently pay for, he could have called the operation a far-sighted, sagacious purchase and not have unduly stretched the truth. Or was he importuned by relatives and friends to be allowed to share the dividends they knew he would earn for them until he good-naturedly abandoned his plan for an "individual enterprise"?

He picked his associates as cannily as before. Edmund H. Munroe, his wife's rich relative, a banker, broker and ship owner, who because of him had gone into the New England Glass Company, now invested in the new company, of which he also would become the treasurer. And, even more, a few days before the Boston & Sandwich Glass Company was incorporated, Munroe and Jarves organized the New England Glass Bottle Company to manufacture black and green glasswares in Boston and Cambridge. Corporate "affiliates" were even then in the making. The company did a successful business for years.

The history of the Boston & Sandwich Glass Company, from 1826 to 1854, when the first pamphlet edition of the "Reminiscences" appeared, is told by Jarves as follows:

Like their predecessors, they commenced in a small way, beginning with an eight-pot furnace, each holding eight hundred pounds. The weekly melts at that period did not exceed seven thousand pounds, and yearly product of seventy-five thousand dollars; giving employment to from sixty to seventy hands. From time to time, as their business warranted, they increased their capital until it reached the present sum (1854) of four hundred thousand dollars. Their weekly melts have increased from seven thousand pounds to much over one hundred thousand pounds; their hands employed from seventy to over five hundred; their one furnace of eight pots to four furnaces of ten pots; and yearly product from $75,000 to six hundred thousand dollars.

The inadequacy of the Deming Jarves personalia recorded in the numerous books and articles about the Boston & Sandwich Glass Company has been a source of disappointment not only to collectors but to all students of the early glass industry of New England, for, however excellent may have been the product of the various other glassworks, it is only Sandwich that cannot be dissociated from its founder in the popular mind. Other concerns that produced fine glass are recognized as worthy of notice but there is little curiosity about the men at their head. But "Deming Jarves" and "Sandwich" remain interchangeable terms. For a man as averse to self-advertisement as he was, to become so identified by the present generation with his factory's products is a remarkable instance of what may be described as posthumous ballyhoo. In the history of the American glass industry, Stiegel alone occupies a place close to Deming Jarves. In lesser degree Wistar and a few of the Western makers may be included. If, however, we reckon by numbers of collectors and admirers, the genius of Sandwich leads all others by many lengths. It is a remarkable, perhaps unique, example of the force of personality, almost incredible when it is recalled how very little we know of that personality.

To describe in detail Deming Jarves' work in Sandwich as it deserves would require a large volume by itself. From the time ground was "broke," as he wrote in his "Reminiscences," he adhered to his steadfast policy of hiring the most competent workers, using the best materials and forever seeking not alone better color formulas but more efficient methods, aiming to reduce cost without impairing quality. It would be a tragic blunder to think of him as dangerously "erratic" or "temperamental," when he was, on the contrary, an intensely practical manufacturer, whose unusualness consisted of combining imagination and the appreciation of beauty with great shrewdness and a distinct flair for machinery. Not having grown up in the glass manufacturing business, he did not fall into ruts, as men are apt to do who have followed a trade or a profession too long. Glass-makers were notoriously conservative and for centuries they did no more than they had been taught to do. But tradition did not touch Jarves. Because a certain thing had always been done in a certain way was no reason for him not to try to find a better way; and as a rule he succeeded. He realized, without the slightest pang, our ignorance of important processes used by foreign makers. Glassmakers from time immemorial had been superstitiously secretive. Each had his particular secret formulas for color and pet mixtures and tried ways of making glass. Jarves imported experts from abroad. He even sent some of his men across the Atlantic to learn how to do what American glass companies had never done before. He developed a considerable export trade to various countries, at the expense of European competitors. He had the curiosity about their product and methods which is always alertly utilized by great business men in all ages. And if he needed excuses for his quest of perfection he found them by visioning future markets that would increase the profits. Having been for years a salesman of the first rank he could easily convince himself that he knew the buying public better than his associates.

His decidedly practical side is shown in his patents and inventions. They are fully treated in another chapter. Perhaps he did not "originate" as much as he "improved." For example, when he saw the commercial possibilities of pressing glass he saw also that the real problem consisted of improving the pressing machine. So he promptly improved it and promptly developed a business in pressed ware that made him rich and famous and charms millions today, more than a century later. If he sought patents to which he was not fairly entitled, it may be said that it was part of the then usual business routine—to claim as much as possible when there was much to gain and little to lose by such claims. In any event, he certainly improved the pressing machine to make it serve his purpose, which was to make good glassware more cheaply. He had secured earlier patents that proved profitable because his inventive mind was strictly businesslike. Altogether, irrespective of dates, priority of claims, etc., it cannot be denied that he did more than any other man to revolutionize the pressed glass industry of America.

He was versatile to a remarkable degree. Perhaps the very many-sidedness of his genius is what has kept us from having a clear-cut portrait of him. He was too many men in one for a single presentment of him to show him in all his capacities. It was precisely because he happened to be at once a shrewd and resourceful manufacturer and a lover of quality, that he found a way of making the red lead so urgently needed at Cambridge to produce the finest quality of flint glass. Aided by a director of the New England Glass Company, he built the first American lead furnace in 1818. Of the lead, a costly but necessary ingredient of flint-glass, Jarves knew that it should be perfectly pure because the presence of any other substance of metal would be shown in the color of the glass. Consequently, the purity of the latter depended mainly on the quality of the metallic lead and on its being well manufactured.

His only guide was a volume of "Cooper's Emporium of Arts & Sciences" which "furnished a plan on a very limited scale." Again the story of a very important event is told with the same omission of personal details. All he thinks it necessary to tell is:

The furnace proved successful, and enabled the Company to continue their manufacture of glass at a period when no foreign red lead was to be procured. They enlarged their works, until they have become the most important in the country; while for over thirty years they monopolized the business in all its branches, from the highest qualities of pure Galena and painter's red lead to common pig lead.

Only a few years before, young Deming Jarves had been in the dry goods business, then bought and sold glassware and pottery and then acted as glass factor. As "agent" of the New England Glass Company, and still very young, he was in complete charge of the factory. He not only managed the business end but even superintended the making of the glass. His ability to learn quickly showed both remarkable powers of absorption and an instinctive elimination of non-essentials. They won for him hard-headed associates, whom he later frightened because their vision could not encompass what Jarves saw so plainly. Undoubtedly his experience at the New England Glass Company's works proved to be the best possible training for his next venture. What he had done at Cambridge and what he had wished to do after his return from Pittsburgh were reflected in his work at Sandwich.

A picture is shown on Plate 2 of what he called an American model glass factory in 1854. By comparing it with early Venetian and French factories, the great improvements over the old plants may be seen. He writes of it in his book:

Thirty years have passed in its development, during which many difficulties arose from the conflicting opinions of the English and German glass-makers; and, in fact, it was not until the proprietors [he means his company] boldly separated themselves from the current and influence of old and almost fixed opinions, that any decided progress was shown in manufacturing efficiency or in any plan contributing to the health and comfort of the workmen.

It is to be borne in mind that the first glass works in this country were established by the Germans, who used no other fuel than wood, the furnaces for window-glass constructed under their directions being for that fuel only; on the other hand, the English workmen who introduced the making of flint-glass, had made use of no other fuel than coal, and the English were therefore obliged to adopt (for the want of coal) the German plan for furnaces, half-English and half-German, and from the year 1812, for thirty years, little or no improvement was made in this particular, until necessity paved the way for new plans in the effort to secure a less expensive mode of melting glass.

The result has been that more than one half has been saved in the melt, annealing leers, and working places, yielding the workmen greater space and facilities in performing their work, and no longer exposing them to the discomfort of extra heat, smoke and unhealthy gases. These improvements have enabled the American manufacturer to sustain his business in the severe and trying competition with foreign manufacturers.

There was no department of the industry to which he was a stranger, none in which he did not find ways and means of bettering in sundry ways.

A very early letter of Deming Jarves' is reproduced in facsimile on Plate 4 through the courtesy of the present owner, Mr. James Gillinder. It was written by Jarves to William Stutson, his superintendent, and is dated November 23, 1825, less than five months after operations started at the glassworks. Believing that a skilled graphologist might find in the handwriting interesting traits or characteristics, I submitted it to an expert. In including it herewith I permit myself the liberty of stating that one should not make light of what may be learned of a person's character by expert graphological analyses. Considering that he had never even heard of Deming Jarves, the findings are nothing short of remarkable. The graphologist's report follows:

"General 'competence' perhaps best sums up the characteristics of this writer. His handwriting evidences a sound education in the elementals, with a streak of aesthetic sensitivity; this, however, rigidly subordinated to 'practicality,' in meeting the needs of 'business.' He was a clear-headed, observant, orderly person, with a nice balance of logic and intuition (former predominates) and his judgment was on the whole apt to be good. Self-control was undoubtedly as nearly complete as could be wished. He seems to have enjoyed a full measure of physical strength, and a fully normal capacity for the ordinary human emotions, but will-power was strongly developed and—probably—in full dominance. He was on the whole a sociable person; certainly *not* on the introvert side. Normally cautious in speech he was quite frank when occasion demanded, and quite decided in his opinions when once he had formed them, which he did *not* do hastily. He was active both physically and mentally. I suspect that he had a good many friends, although he did *not* wear his heart upon a sleeve. He was but little troubled by internal tensions and was without any trace of neuroses. He was also devoid of pose or pretensions of any kind and probably addicted to understatement. His temper was under thorough control at all times, and his disposition was not of the kind that seeks to dominate others, but firm in resisting attempts to dominate him. He seems to have had a good sense of rhythm in general; I suspect that there was no 'jerkiness' about him either mentally or physically. He had his ideals too, whatever they were; he might have been a church-goer but no fanatic, nor was he troubled by 'doubts' or speculations in these matters.

"On the whole, a steady, stable, normal citizen who would have been one of the 'solid' men in his community."

To his uncanny ability to pick the right helpers Deming Jarves undoubtedly owed much of his success. It is a temptation which, unfortunately, must be resisted to include in this chapter a dozen short sketches of his chief lieutenants. Some of them have left a few anecdotes about their leader, none of them particularly striking, the shining exception being William E. Kern. Nearly all the stories, however, make clear Jarves' amazing resourcefulness and his sure grasp of the innumerable minor and even major problems that daily arise in a busy factory. He solved them without resort to complicated devices or appliances, so frictionlessly indeed that his contemporaries scarcely realized the degree of ability required to state a problem accurately enough for the solution almost automatically to suggest itself. They had to carry freight from the harbor to the plant, so he built a horse railroad—a tramway. It was a novelty, perhaps the first in America. And he had a car built to carry passengers to and from the packets. In 1848 the Old Colony Railroad extended its line to Sandwich but its charges were too high. Deming Jarves asked for lower transportation rates and was refused. He threatened to build a steamer to carry his product to Boston and the railroad men laughed at him. One of the officials told him: "The acorn from which will grow the oak that will provide the lumber for your ship has not yet been planted!"

"Wait and see!" said Jarves. He had a model made to suit his needs and a small steam propeller was built for him in Philadelphia. He christened it *Acorn* and it carried freight for the company from Sandwich to Boston, until the railroad gave in. Incidentally the acorn was one of his favorite pattern designs. The company from the first had used sloops, some of which he built when the business justified it and not before.

A new harbor was needed. The old was filling up. He needed to build channels and ditches for barges. He convinced the residents of Sandwich that his troubles were their troubles and that what benefited the company necessarily benefited the town. He talked the townsmen into giving him one day of labor. It was co-operation, the recognition of mutual benefits. His oratorical gifts saved the company money. But after all, whatever meant more business, meant in turn more wages for more men. He even built a lock to impound the water at high tide. It was all part of his business.

He was considerate of the welfare of the men. He built them houses, helped them to furnish them on easy terms and planted rows of elms which still stand. He did not misuse the company store. His interest in the children of the workers never slackened. Child labor was still accepted as an economic necessity but he and his successors also, insisted the the boys attend the village school in the morning or the afternoon, according to their shifts. He encouraged them to learn the trade in their spare time. If a boy made a worthwhile piece, the older men finished it and the piece was given to the youngster, to treasure for years. Every Fourth of July the boys received a half dollar for firecrackers. Patriotic American boys would develop into conscientious American glass workers, and how could they help becoming Jarves men if they had been Jarves boys?

His charities were what would be expected of a Christian gentleman who also happened to be the town's first citizen. During the hard times of 1840, his tenants occupied their homes rent free. He opened a store where the necessities of life were supplied to the needy. In 1857, it is recorded in the "History of Sandwich" that he gave much assistance to poor widows and others. For years his Christmas gift to the widows of former workers was a barrel of flour.

He encouraged his best men to experiment with mixtures and colors and rewarded them liberally for their successes. The men appreciated his encouragement. It might be pointed out that by these researches the company spent less than a laboratory or experimental shop would have cost. The real accomplishment in his mind was the communicating to his trusted men of his industrial ideals, his regard for fine workmanship and his love for beautiful color.

How successful Deming Jarves was in his experiments is borne out by Prof. Alexander Silverman, head of the department of chemistry at the University of Pittsburgh, who made an exhaustive study of Sandwich formulas and published a series of articles on the results of his research for *The Glass Industry*. I quote him as follows:

From the first installment on Sandwich glass it was evident that the glass makers in this factory had a remarkable knowledge of crystal glass for their time. The borosilicate glasses were not yet known, but with this exception and the use of compounds of the rarer elements, practically every type was made at Sandwich. We are similarly impressed with their knowledge of opal and alabaster glasses. Of course, the borosilicate opals and the newer zinc-aluminum alabasters, had not yet come into being. The only one of the old alabaster glasses which seems to be missing in the Sandwich records is that which utilized Federweiss, a natural magnesium silicate. This was employed in Germany.

Deming Jarves has left many detailed accounts of mixtures and color formulas, some of which were not original with him but were printed in his "Reminiscences" without credit to the originators. He was thoroughly familiar with everything connected with glassmaking as practiced in his time. His written directions for making all kinds of glass and for every operation in connection with various types of ware and with cutting, etching, overlay, etc., show this. He experimented with sand, not only from various parts of the country but from France and British Guiana. He was mad about color. His granddaughter tells me that he loved to draw and paint. Of the opaque shades which are so "typically Sandwich" his favorite was a beautiful opaque blue.

He organized the Mt. Washington Glass Works in South Boston for his son George, then a young man in his 20's. But George did not take a very keen interest in glass. The Mt. Washington factory was operated for a short period by Capt. Luther Russell. It reverted to George Jarves after two years. He formed a partnership with one Labree. The firm, Labree & Jarves, is listed in the Boston Directory for 1846. In 1850 the firm became Jarves & Cormerais who enlarged the business by additional furnaces. W. L. Libbey purchased the works in later years and for a short time was sole owner.

Deming Jarves, Jr., who is reported to have been the most brilliant of the children, showed many of his father's characteristics but did not like glassmaking. He wanted to be a sailor. There is no question that Deming's hopes for a successor were almost an obsession but he was a loving father and, even more, a wise father. He sent Deming, Jr., as the lone passenger of a clipper ship on a long voyage. The young man rounded the Cape of Good Hope in the dead of winter, ran into a typhoon in the China Sea, arrived in India at the height of the Mutiny and finally returned to Boston, a sadder but a wiser man, not in a sailing vessel but in a Cunard steamer. He had lost all ambition to be a blue-water sailor. He served as a clerk in his father's store in Boston, enlisted in the Civil War, fought throughout the four years and after his discharge settled in New York, where he sold glass for various concerns. Later, he went to Michigan where he made a fortune in manufacturing bone-black, fertilizers—and glass! He retired to

PLATE 1

Deming Jarves, founder of the Boston & Sandwich Glass Company.

PLATE 2
Deming Jarves' Model Factory.

PLATE 3

John Jarves (left), for whom the Cape Cod Glass Works was built by his father, Deming Jarves.

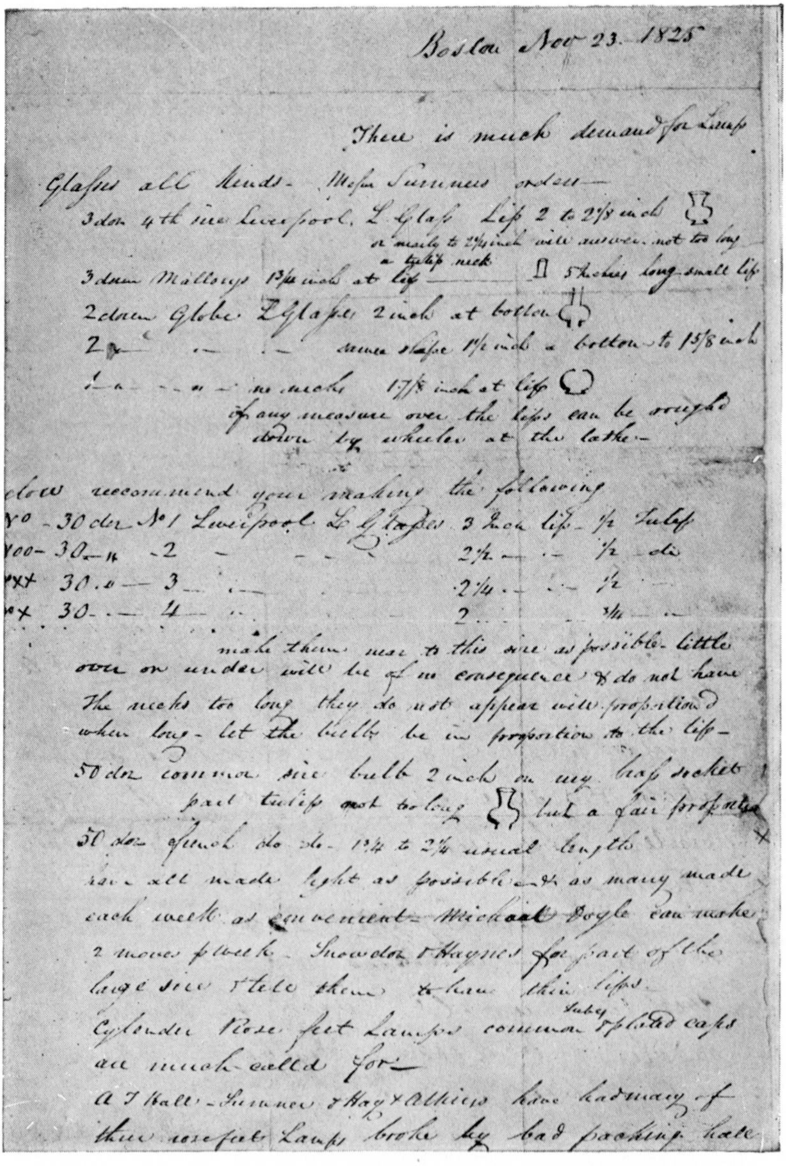
Boston Nov 23 1825

There is much demand for Lamp
Glasses all kinds — Messrs Sumners order —
3 doz 4th size Liverpool L Glass Lip 2 to 2 7/8 inch
or nearly to 2 3/4 inch will answer not too long
a tulip neck
3 doz Mallongs 1 3/4 inch at lip — 5 inches long small lip
2 doz Globe L Glasses 2 inch at bottom
2 — — same shape 1 1/2 inch a bottom to 1 5/8 inch
1 — — no necks 1 7/8 inch at lips
if any measure over the lips can be roughed
down by wheeler at the lathe —

[illegible] recommend your making the following
No — 30 doz No 1 Liverpool L Glasses 3 inch lip — 1/2 tulip
[illegible] — 30 — 2 — 2 1/2 — 1/2 do
[illegible] 30 — 3 — 2 1/4 — 1/2
[illegible] 30 — 4 — 2 — 3/4

make them near to this size as possible — little
over or under will be of no consequence & do not have
the necks too long they do not appear well proportioned
when long — let the bulb be in proportion to the lips —
50 doz common size bulb 2 inch on my brass socket
part tulips not too long but a fair proportion
50 doz French do do — 1 3/4 to 2 1/4 usual length
[illegible] all made light as possible & as many made
each week as convenient — Michael Doyle can make
2 moves p week — Snowdon & Haynes for part of the
large size & tell them to have thin lips
Cylinder Rose feet Lamps common & plated caps
are much called for —
A T Hall — Sumner & Hay & Atkins have had many of
their rosefeet Lamps broke by bad packing [illegible]

PLATE 4

Specimen of Deming Jarves' handwriting, written with a quill pen, in 1825.

Collection of the author

PLATE 5

DEMING JARVES' LETTER OF RESIGNATION

It is dated May 7, 1855, and states that his health requires a release from the cares and anxiety attending his situation. He actually left the company in June, 1858.

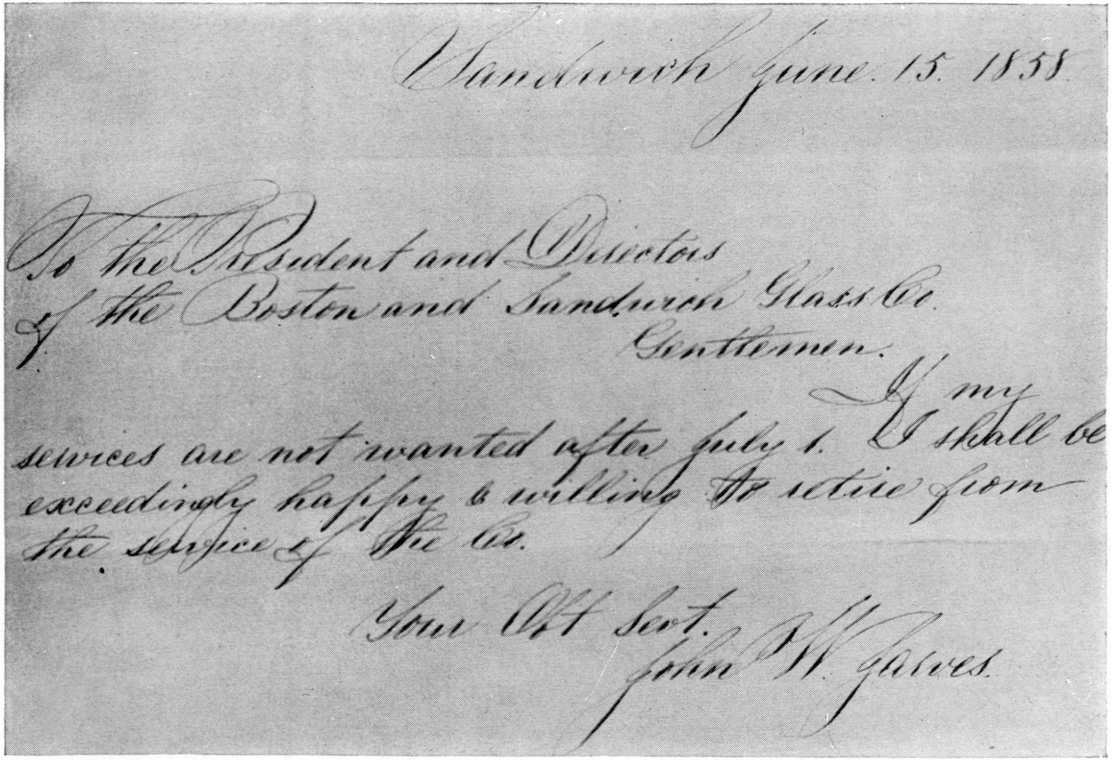
Sandwich June 15. 1858

To the President and Directors
of the Boston and Sandwich Glass Co.

Gentlemen.

If my services are not wanted after July 1. I shall be exceedingly happy & willing to retire from the service of the Co.

Your Obt Sert.
John W. Jarves.

Collection of the author

PLATE 6

RESIGNATION OF JOHN W. JARVES

It was for this son that Deming Jarves organized the short-lived Cape Cod Glass Works after both had severed their connection with the Boston & Sandwich Glass Company.

Courtesy of Robert W. Lee

PLATE 7

Deming Jarves' Tombstone. Mt. Auburn Cemetery, Cambridge, Mass.

France and there he intelligently collected antiques. He was made a Chevalier of the Legion of Honor for his services during the First World War.

The best known of Deming's sons was James Jackson Jarves, who became famous as a collector and critic of art. His health and eyesight were too delicate for him to go to Harvard as had been planned, so he travelled all over the world and wrote many books on art and other subjects.

He became very much interested in works of art and was an ardent admirer and collector of old Venetian glass. He once asked his father why he did not make glass like the old Venetians instead of "that awful pressed stuff."

"I don't at all like the idea of your making it," James told his father, who retorted: "But you like spending the money it makes, don't you?"

James in the end succeeded in inducing his father to try making Venetian glass at Sandwich but it is reported that the first piece that they attempted blew up. It has been insisted by some writers that Deming was very keen in experimenting with that style of glass but there is no evidence that it was ever produced in noteworthy quantities at Sandwich while he was in charge.

Deming Jarves organized the Cape Cod Glass Works after he severed his connections with the Boston & Sandwich Glass Company. He hoped to see his life-long dreams fulfilled at last by his son John W. Jarves, but unfortunately the son died in 1863 and the father's life ambition was frustrated. He could not have been a domineering parent for he did not force his children to go against their inclinations if it made them unhappy. He would do the suffering for the family.

Nobody would dream of writing about the Boston & Sandwich Glass Company without reading Deming Jarves' "Reminiscences," and nobody can read them without regretting their sad inadequacy as a source of the sort of information that collectors of Sandwich would give much to possess. The full title of the little book, to be sure, is "Reminiscences of Glass Making," and it is only fair

to admit that Jarves had no intention and, perhaps, no desire to
tell the story of his own career and experiences as the foremost
glassmaker in New England. Today we feel that he owed such an
account to his family, to his friends and associates and even to the
inhabitants of the town of Sandwich, whose chief asset he still is.
To have recorded in detail the part he and his workmen played
in the development of a great and successful enterprise and in the
American glass industry in general, would have been of incalcula-
ble value to historians of our industrial expansion after the War
of 1812. The growth of the Sandwich factory, the volume of its
output and its nature, the improvement in methods and plant
equipment, the innovations that earned for Sandwich its wide fame,
the designing of "typical Sandwich patterns," the changes in the
popular taste and the growing demand for a greater variety of
more sophisticated glassware by a nation growing in population
and wealth, the many problems met and solved, how it became
possible to find and develop markets at home and abroad for
American glass in the '30's and '40's—all these were assuredly
worth recording, without fear of incurring the reproach of excessive self-advertising. It needed a garrulous old man to write
the sort of "Reminiscences" that we would read with avidity and
profit today and Deming Jarves unfortunately was not the type
of whom it could be expected.

The preface, as printed in the second edition is as follows:

The articles upon the history and progress of Glass Manufacture
herein presented to the public were originally published in the columns of a village newspaper.

They are the result of investigation upon these topics made in the
few leisure moments gained from the engrossing cares of business,
and consequently make no pretension to anything of literary character
or execution.

The object of the writer has been to gather, in a condensed form,
whatever of interesting information could be gained from authentic
sources, in regard to a branch of manufacture which has attained a
position among the useful and elegant arts scarcely rivalled by any

other of those which mark and distinguish the progressive character of our country.

It is believed that they present, in a condensed and convenient form, much valuable information, useful alike for reference and instruction. Aside from historical or mechanical facts, there is much of romantic interest attaching to the progress of this department of art. The partiality of friends interested in the topics herein presented, rather than his own opinion of their value, has induced the writer to present the articles in a more permanent form.

Boston, March 17, 1854.

———

The above was the Preface to a small pamphlet in 8vo of the "Reminiscences of Glass Making," printed for private circulation in 1854, and now enlarged into a more permanent form, and brought down to the present year, in order to meet the demand for information which has unexpectedly sprung up from those interested in the manufacture of Glass in America.

Boston, January, 1865.

The most significant parts of the prefaces are: First, his recognition of the "romantic interest" attaching to the art of glassmaking, which implies to me, at least, that he must have had in mind his own "romantic" rôle as a glassmaker. Second, his remark about "the demand for information which has unexpectedly sprung up from those interested in the manufacture of glass in America." To reconcile these expressed views with his literary performance one must believe that if he kept himself out of the picture, it was not because he was unaware that a more personal record would have been appreciated by the public. He surely knew how much he had accomplished at Sandwich by being very "personal." To be sure, when he started the articles in the village newspaper, he did not anticipate their publication in book form. He was writing for small-town readers.

He had access to Apsley Pellatt's and other English books and encyclopedias and he had read much about glassmaking. There is no evidence of any original historical researches of his own. His descriptions of ancient glassmaking undoubtedly interested his village readers; and the technological passages, color formulas, mixtures, etc., were undoubtedly welcomed by other glass men. The book clearly shows that he knew his trade thoroughly but, unfortunately, that is something everybody expected of him. It imparts no thrill to those collectors whose interest centers exclusively on what Jarves himself did at Sandwich and how and why he did it. Every detail of his operations in designing and manufacturing, of the nature, forms, purpose and trade names of the amazingly varied Sandwich product, is what collectors and students of our early glass crave to know. His over-condensed versions of the organization and growth of his companies are an exasperation to the non-technical reader who is proud of his collection of Sandwich glass, knowing that he owes it to the too-reticent genius who was "Sandwich" for many years as much as "Elizabeth" was "England" or "Napoleon" was "France" during the years of their dominance.

Perhaps it is what one reads between the lines that makes the book indispensable to writers on American glass. The first edition of the "Reminiscences," consisting as it did of the collected newspaper articles, differs in important respects from the 1865 edition. In the latter, there is much to ponder because there is much that he probably would not have written before 1858, when he severed his connection with the Boston & Sandwich Glass Company. Having ceased to be the directing spirit of the company he created, his attitude toward it, logically, changed. Being human we find him going out of his way, at the age of seventy-five, in 1863, to bestow warm praise on the most active of all the competitors of the Boston & Sandwich Glass Company. He was striking at the child he had been forced to disown! And more significant still are his remarks about the pressing of glass and the pressing-machine, to this day identified with some of his most notable work. If he did not invent it, he surely improved it to the point where it revolutionized the industry. The subject is treated fully in Chapter IV.

There can be no question about the importance which the Bos-

ton & Sandwich Glass Company and its salesmen attached to Sandwich pressed ware and to the claim of being the first factory in the
world to turn out a first-class product. It must have been a standard
"selling point." Many old stories are still heard of how the agents
boasted of the company's long record of achievement in that line
of glassware, in the main fully justified.

But in 1865, when the second edition was published, other pilots
were steering the ship he had launched and, apparently, steering it
with success. A few excerpts from his book clearly indicate a desire
to make little of the Sandwich claims, which he once had been the
loudest in proclaiming:

The ancient glass-makers excelled the modern ones in fine fancy
work, in colors and in the imitation of gems. They were also acquainted with the art of making and using moulds for blown and
pressed glass, and forming what in England is now called patent
pillar glass. All these operations, however, were directed mainly to
the production of small but costly articles. And while they possessed
the knowledge of the use of the moulds to press and blow glass by
expansion, it does not appear that they produced any articles for
domestic use.

This important branch of glass-making (pressed glass) demands
more than a passing notice. Although it is commonly believed here
that the invention originated in this country, the claim cannot be fully
sustained. Fifty years back the writer imported from Holland salts
made by being pressed in metallic moulds, and from England glass
candlesticks and table centre-bowls, plain, with pressed square feet,
rudely made, somewhat after the present mode of moulding glass.
From 1814 to 1838, no improvement was made in Europe in this
process, which was confined to common salts and square feet.

America can claim the credit of great improvements in the needful
machinery which has advanced the art to its present perfection. More
than three quarters of the weekly melt is now worked up into pressed
glass. With us there is active competition for excellence. It is, however, conceded that James B. Lyon & Co., of Pittsburgh, stand first.
To such a degree of delicacy and fineness have they carried their
manufacture, that only experts in the trade can distinguish between

their straw stem wines and other light and beautiful articles made in moulds, and those blown by the most skilled workmen. When we consider the difference in the cost between pressed and blown ware, this rivalry in beauty of the former with the latter becomes all the more important to the public, as it cheapens one of the staple necessaries of civilized life.

Great credit therefore is due this firm for their success in overcoming difficulties well understood by glass-makers, and doing away with the prejudice of the skilled blowers, who naturally were not inclined to put the new and more mechanical process of manufacturing glass on a par with the handicraft of the old. Lyon & Co. also excel all other American firms in large ware for table services, as well as in the more delicate objects of use.

In speaking of the improvements in glass-making in America, we must not overlook what has been done by the New England Glass Company.

Convinced of the importance of scientific skill in their business, they secured some years ago the services of Mr. Leighton and his three sons, at a liberal compensation. Besides possessing the best practical knowledge, they had also artistic taste, which enabled them to give elegant finish to their workmanship and to introduce new and more beautiful patterns into it.

They did not neglect, however, the more homely but useful articles; but executed orders for large and heavy objects, for druggists and chemical wares and philosophical apparatus, so satisfactorily as to secure a monopoly in them. Their richly cut, gilded, colored, and ornamental glass is considered equal to European work.

The foreging extracts are given in full simply to stress the significance of the obviously deliberate omission of the name of the Boston & Sandwich Glass Company from the 1865 edition and the contemptuous minimizing of its claims to priority of manufacture and excellence of its pressed product. He would not glorify his own work because it bore the Sandwich label *minus* Jarves. The praise lavished on Sandwich's chief competitors, of course, could come from a lofty spirit; but also from a man with a grievance that had rankled for years.

Deming Jarves' resignation from the company which he founded, and served so well for thirty-two years, seemed on the surface to be a management problem such as has occurred time and again in other American manufacturing enterprises. It appeared to be a struggle within the board of directors for control of the company in which members sought to displace the founder. But company records never before available to the writer for study, disclose that there was a different complexion to the matter.

Jarves had submitted letters of resignation as far back as the early 1830's, but he was always prevailed upon to continue his association with the Company. Most significant of these was his resignation of 1844, wherein the recorded minutes state the committee was awaiting word from Mr. Jarves as to what the conditions of his stay with the Company would consist in. They were as follows:

That it is to be understood that he shall have the entire control of the Factory, subject only to the advice and direction of the Board of Directors and when there is any complaint to be made with regard to his doings, it must be laid before the Board at its earliest meeting.

That he shall have the liberty to sell the goods of the Company when and to whom he thinks proper according to his best judgment, and to give any extension of credit to customers when he considered it for the interest of the Company, charging interest for the time allowed, beyond the usual credit—it being understood that the Agent in this particular shall act in concert with the New England Glass Company Agent.

That a store be procured suitable to carry on the business of the Company and Mr. Jarves will let the Company one of the stores now being built on Federal Street, with a privilege in the store adjoining at a rent not exceeding $1,600 per annum.

These conditions appear merely to be a definitive statement of his position. Apparently, clarification was called for in order that Jarves might proceed efficiently, and without hindrance in the discharge of his widespread responsibilities. We may readily imagine that the founder of Sandwich, as we know him, was wont to take matters in his own hands, was impatient of petty carping and opposition to his acts, which were already clear and resolved soundly in his mind. Obviously such a man would call for a formal statement of his responsibilities, once doubt had been cast as to their scope and discharge.

The partnership of George D. Jarves, Deming's son, and Henry Cormerais as sales agents in the store on Federal Street in Boston for the Company proved one more contentious point, which, together with certain other factors, culminated in Deming Jarves' severance from his thirty-two year association. R. S. Fay, one of the Directors, charged that the connection between the company and the partnership of G. D. Jarves and Cormerais had, since 1854, cost the former "upwards of $50,000 per year." From letters which will be quoted in the chapter dealing with the middle years, it is evident that both Deming Jarves and his son, as well as Henry Cormerais bitterly resented this unjust accusation, and failing to readjust his relation with the Board of Directors, Jarves resigned from the Company in 1858, once and for all.

Unpleasantness still lingered, for within a few months after Jarves' abdication, Messrs. G. D. Jarves and Cormerais, after a heated dispute, relinquished their store and the partnership was dissolved. And so ended the association of the Jarves, "père et fils" with the Boston & Sandwich Glass Company.

But this is not the whole story. It is further complicated by the fact that the Company was not operating at a profit. Competition with the more cheaply operated Western factories was taking its toll, forcing curtailed production and reduced salaries. These factors consequently led to dissatisfaction among the employees, and here we have the signal inception of labor trouble which, many years later, resulted in the final shut-down and cessation of the Boston & Sandwich Company's operations.

Whatever may be said of the merits of either side in these disputes, it cannot be denied that through this man's enterprise, expressed in terms of equipment, artistic taste, and industrial philosophy, the Sandwich Company owed its fame and its past profits. Stockholders, workmen and buyers of fine glassware had benefited by his genius. Under his successors, the Sandwich Company for a time made money and glass. But ask collectors which period is represented in their cabinets.

Mr. J. N. Leonard has some interesting comments on the Cape Cod Glass Company which Deming Jarves organized and operated later: "The nucleus of the new factory (situated within a half mile of the Sandwich works) was a moderate-sized but very up-to-date furnace, holding ten pots. There had been certain important discoveries about draughts, firing and other technical details, and so the furnace of the Cape Cod was much superior to any other then operating. It worked excellently from the first firing-up and burned soft coal more efficiently than the furnace of its rivals.

"The new factory was successful from the first. A second furnace was built and a cutting plant erected. No etching or engraving was done, although glass was made for these processes and sold to outside shops. With these exceptions the Cape Cod made pretty nearly every kind of glass in general use. The highest class work was done in the shop of Thomas Williams, an expert who had come over with Deming Jarves from the old factory. . . . The Cape Cod gave a great deal of attention to colored and opaque glass. "Sandwich alabaster" was one of its discoveries, and for a long time the formula was known only to Jarves and James Lloyd. Peachblow and gold-ruby were other specialties. . . . At no time could the Cape Cod compare in size with the Boston & Sandwich. It employed at maximum only some fifty men. But it was prosperous and in constant operation. Jarves paid higher wages and attracted the most skillful workers. The factory itself was very efficient. Its pressing machines and cutting equipment were especially good."

And we have the last paragraph of William E. Kern's own *Reminiscences,* which, despite much exhaustive research, I still consider most appropriate: "After Deming Jarves retired from the

Boston & Sandwich he started the Cape Cod Company with a factory in Sandwich. I was superintendent of this factory at the time it was closed in 1869. Mr. Jarves' son, John, for whom chiefly he had built it, was dead, and Mr. Jarves himself was seriously ill at his home in Boston. The family did not care to continue the plant in operation, and I received instructions to draw the fires on a certain date at midnight. As I was returning from the factory after attending to this last service, some boys who were congregated in the village street shouted: 'There he goes; he's gone up!' I paid little attention to the words at the time, but they came back to me the next morning when I received word that at the very moment when I had drawn the fires in the glass factory, Deming Jarves had passed from this world into the world beyond."

The Boston newspapers were searched for the obituary notices of the man to whom his State and his country owed so much. In the *Evening Transcript* for April 16, 1869, under "Deaths" one may read:

"On the 15th inst. Deming Jarves, Esq. 78. Funeral services will be held at 64 Boylston Street on Monday, April 19th at 12 o'clock."

Such was the importance of the news in the opinion of the Boston papers.

But the dreams came true, after all, and no lover of our best early American glass can forget what he owes to Deming Jarves.

Chapter II

FOUNDING OF THE BOSTON & SANDWICH GLASS COMPANY

Sandwich, Massachusetts, in Barnstable County is located on Cape Cod near the point where that arm of the old Bay State is all but separated from the mainland by the waters of Buzzards Bay on the one side and Cape Cod Bay on the other. While it is a shore town, it had not developed harbor facilities in 1825 and, of course, there was no thought of a railroad at that time. What we see today is not what Deming Jarves saw. We might wonder why a site for a glass manufactory should have been chosen so far from the beaten paths of travel and the centers of population but in 1825 that part of the Cape abounded in pine forests, which meant an adequate and cheap supply of fuel and that in turn was of the first importance. Land was cheap, and moreover a navigable stream was near at hand. Boston lay fifty miles distant by water, supplies could be brought in cheaply, and the output of the factory could reach the Boston market by boat.

In speaking of the founding of the *Sandwich Manufacturing Company* which was later developed into the famous *Boston & Sandwich Glass Company,* Deming Jarves sums it all up, briefly, as was his custom, in his "Reminiscences of Glass Making." He states:

"In 1825 a Flint-Glass Manufactory was established by individual enterprise in Sandwich, Mass. Ground was broke in April, dwellings for the workmen built, and manufactory completed; and on the 4th day of July, 1825, they commenced blowing glass—three months from first breaking ground. In the following year it was purchased of the proprietor, a company formed, and incorporated under the title of Boston & Sandwich Glass Company.

Like their predecessors, they commenced in a small way; beginning with an eight-pot furnace, each holding eight hundred pounds. The weekly melts at that period did not exceed seven thousand pounds, and yearly product seventy-five thousand dollars; giving employment to from sixty to seventy hands. From time to time, as their business warranted, they increased their capital until it reached the present sum of four hundred thousand dollars. Their weekly melts have increased from seven thousand pounds to much over one-hundred-thousand pounds; their hands employed from seventy to over five hundred; their one furnace of eight pots to four furnaces of ten pots; and yearly product from seventy-five thousand dollars to six-hundred-thousand dollars."

The Sandwich Manufacturing Company was a private enterprise owned by Jarves. In the company account book, under date of July 1826, I find this record: "Real Estate. To Deming Jarves for all the real estate and wood lots, transfer by deed dated April 3, 1826"—the amount being duly entered in this ledger for $31,-125.00. Directly underneath this entry appears the following: "Deming Jarves by E. M. (Edmund Munroe) for transfer of his factory, etc. April 3, 1826, as per voucher accepted by the company, for the sum of $62,713.68."

The Act of Incorporation under the Acts of 1825, Private and Special Statutes of the Commonwealth of Massachusetts, for the Boston & Sandwich Glass Company, reads as follows: "That Deming Jarves, Henry Rice, Andrew T. Hall, Edmund Munroe, and such persons as may become associated with them and their successors and assigns be and hereby are made a corporation by the name of the Boston & Sandwich Glass Company for the purpose of manufacturing glass in the city of Boston and town of Sandwich, in the County of Barnstable, and for that purpose shall have all the powers and privileges, and shall be subject to all the duties, requirements and disabilities prescribed and contained in an act defining the general powers and duties of manufacturing corporations and several acts in addition thereto.

"That the said corporation in their corporate capacity shall and may lawfully hold and possess such real estate not exceeding $100,000 and personal estate not exceeding $200,000, as may be necessary and convenient for carrying on the manufacture of glass in the place aforesaid. As of February 22, 1826."

There are several reasons why Deming Jarves may have decided to abandon his original individual enterprise. Perhaps he saw greater possibility of developing a larger business than he had foreseen, for which a greater capital than his own was needed. The incorporation of a second and larger company followed. He had rich relatives whose faith in him and his abilities made them anxious to invest in his new venture. The War of 1812 had awakened Americans to the need of industrial independence. There would be money in glass. There is a story that the agent Jarves sent to Sandwich to purchase timber lands and the factory site exceeded his orders and bought 20,000 acres in all, which hampered the proprietor of the Sandwich Manufacturing Company. In any event, the men who now were associated with him had means and business sagacity and were his devoted friends.

Edmund H. Munroe was born in Lexington, Mass., October 29, 1780. He was descended from the Lexington Munroes of Revolutionary fame and was well educated. His activities were many and varied. He was a banker, a director of the Boston Porcelain & Glass Company, and treasurer of the New England Glass Company. He became treasurer of the Boston & Sandwich Glass Company on May 12, 1826, a month after its organization. An item is entered in the first company ledger which reads as follows: "E. Munroe—Treasurer to Capital Stock—For 150 shares of said stock at $500. per share, in his hands, to be issued under the company certificate and seals to the respective stockholders—$75,000.00." The original capital stock of the company was, as Jarves stated in his book, $75,000.00. It was gradually increased to $400,000.00.

Captain William Stutson, brother-in-law of Jarves, was the first superintendent and metal maker at Sandwich. It is recorded of him that he was an energetic youth, who, at the age of nineteen, had been in full command of a ship. During the War of 1812 he held the rank of captain and commanded a privateer which was later captured by the British. He was succeeded in his position as superintendent, in 1830, by Theodore Kern, who served as manager until 1866, a period of thirty years. Captain Stutson remained at Sandwich, in the capacity of "resident agent."

Andrew T. Hall, another one of the founders of the Boston & Sandwich Glass Company, was president of the New England Glass Bottle Company (another of Jarves' ventures) and for many years was also treasurer of the New England Glass Company. Deming Jarves was the first agent of the company and remained in charge until 1858. He was succeeded by Sewell H. Fessenden, who in turn was succeeded by Henry F. Spurr in 1882.

The Sandwich Manufacturing Company lasted from the day it began work, July 4, 1825, until April 3, 1826, when the Boston & Sandwich Glass Company was incorporated. The officers first in charge of the new company were Samuel P. Fay, president; Edmund Munroe, treasurer; Andrew T. Hall and Benjamin Sewall, directors; Samuel Hurst, clerk.

Since the writing of *Sandwich Glass* in 1939, an extensive array of documentary evidence has come into my possession. Fortunately, this new material which consists largely of the actual business records of the Boston & Sandwich Glass Company has served to substantiate many of the assertions made previously. However, many gaps existing heretofore can now be closed, which is a source of considerable satisfaction to the writer in the never ceasing search for data.

The first ledger displays evidence of the high importance, esteem and affection with which the new enterprise was regarded by its officers and stockholders. It is bound in light brown leather, embellished with a delicate hand tooling and stripes of gold, and is boldly lettered on the cover, also in gold, "BOSTON & SAND-WICH GLASS CO." The back spine is simply marked "Records" and at the bottom "L. W. Goodrich, Maker." The Goodrich name is inscribed in much smaller lettering than the word "Maker," so he must have been proud of his handiwork!

The pages of this volume are delicately lined and beautifully written in a fine Spencerian script. The opening page is entitled, "Act of Incorporation, Commonwealth of Massachusetts." There follows: "In the year of our Lord one thousand eight hundred and twenty six, An Act to Incorporate the Boston and Sandwich Glass Company." Each sentence is carefully underlined. The first two are in very heavy ink, as is also "An Act" and "Boston and Sandwich Glass Company." From these opening sentences written in 1826, until the fires of the old factory were ordered drawn at once, at a meeting held on February 13th, 1888, there unrolls from the penned lines in now faded ink, the drama of one of the most interesting old glass factories in America.

The record book contains, besides a copy of the Act of Incorporation, the by-laws of the company. The original capital stock was one hundred and fifty shares at $500. each. Stockholders were to meet annually on the first Monday of June at a time and place appointed by the directors. At these annual meetings there would be chosen, by written votes, the officers for the following year. These included a clerk, a treasurer and five directors, who should be stockholders at the time of their election. Whenever any of them ceased to be a stockholder, his office terminated. Each share of the stock entitled the owner to one vote, but there was also a provision that no one stockholder would be entitled to more than twenty votes.

It was the duty of the clerk to record in the books kept by him all the "Acts and doings of the stockholders and Directors," register and certify all certificates of the shares, and all transfers on sales thereof. The treasurer was required to give bonds of $5,000 to the company, with one or more sureties. Among the other stipulations of the treasurer's duties was that he should "settle with the agent at least once in each year, and exhibit at the annual meeting a true statement of all the money dealings transacted of the company."

The directors had their work laid out for them, too. The by-laws stated that they must choose one of their own members to

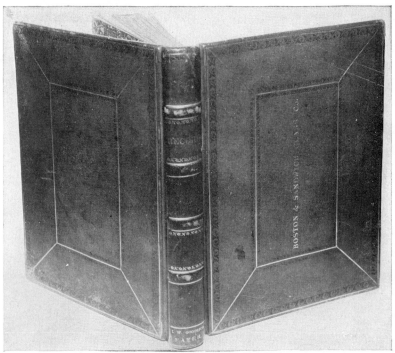

Collection of the author

PLATE 8

THE ORIGINAL RECORD LEDGER

In it, handwritten, are the Act of Incorporation of the Boston & Sandwich Glass Company, its by-laws, and the directors' meetings from the start in 1826 until May 22, 1851. Continuity is preserved in other books until the close of the factory.

Memorandum
Transfers of Stock up to the
Wooden Agenwich (John)
Company

Collection of the author

PLATE 9

THE STOCK TRANSFER RECORDS

In these two books are written the names and number of shares of the original stockholders, and the transfer of

be the president of the company. They could also fill any vacancy of clerk, treasurer, or director that might occur in the interval between stockholders' meetings, or call special meetings for that purpose. They must employ such agent or agents and such artisans or workmen, as they deemed proper and necessary for the discreet, faithful and economical management of the affairs of the company and prescribe their power and duties and compensation.

The directors were also empowered to remove any workmen, according to their discretion. They were to direct the clerk to notify all concerned of stockholders' meetings "when such meetings became necessary or when thereto required to do so in writing, it must be signed by any one or more stockholders owning twenty shares." They should declare dividends of the profits of the company and order the treasurer to pay the same, when it could in their opinion be done "with propriety." They were to examine the account of the agent at least once in six months and make a full settlement with him and also with the treasurer once in each year. Any two directors who might meet in pursuance of a notice of the whole, were declared competent to transact business.

The duties of the president were the usual formal ones, such as presiding at the meetings and the like. He was also to hold the bonds given by the treasurer and agent for the faithful discharge of their respective duties!

The office of agent was in many ways the most important, as he was general manager. Deming Jarves was the company's agent. His duties were manifold. According to the by-laws, "With the advice of the directors, he was to make all necessary contracts and bargains for labor, stock, and material; negotiate for the disposition of the sale of the glass to be manufactured and subscribe all obligations in behalf of the company, for every transaction of purchase and sale, subject to such order and regulating as the directors from time to time should make or prescribe, and [be responsible] for the general superintendence and management of the Manufactory. He should keep the necessary books for the faithful entry and record all of his transactions both of money and as general superintendee and the same always to be open to the inspection of the directors and stockholders. . . . Once in each quarter of a year, he was to make a full statement thereof for settlement with the Treasurer. He should make no obligations or contract in behalf of the company exceeding the amount of four hundred dollars and issue no negotiable paper, unless approved by the president or treasurer of the corporation by their written approbation."

The by-laws also stated that there could be no alteration of them except at a regular meeting at which at least two-thirds of all the shares entitled to vote were represented.

On April 26th, 1826, the directors of the Boston & Sandwich Glass Company met at the office of Edmund Munroe in State Street, Boston. Present were Samuel Fay, Benjamin Sewall and Deming Jarves. (In the ledger his name is sometimes spelled Jarvis.) Samuel Fay was unanimously elected president. Deming Jarves was appointed agent (according to articles of agreement on file), and at this time it was also voted that "the committee take an account and estimate the value of the stock and materials, utensils, tools and manufactured goods, of Mr. Jarves', for the purpose of being transferred to the Boston & Sandwich Glass Company."

The directors then voted to pay Mr. Jarves, in money and notes for his Sandwich real estate and personal property, "deducting and reserving the amount of the mortgages on the estate estimated at $2,540.00 and also $300.00 for the deficiency of the measure of wood land, according to Mr. Jarvis' agreement."

Mr. Jarves was directed to proceed on a southern tour, as soon as convenient and make such arrangement for the sale of the company glass as he deemed necessary.

The agent, Mr. Jarves, was also voted to proceed with the erection of four cottages on company land, to be rented to the workmen as soon as finished. Also a horse mill and a room for cutting glass adjoining the present ware room. This was all under date of April 26, 1826.

A special meeting was called on July 25th, 1826, which included the president, Samuel Fay, and Henry Rice, Benjamin Sewall and Andrew T. Hall, at which time Mr. Jarves was authorized to employ a suitable agent for the sale of the company glass in Baltimore, for a term of one year and at a salary not exceeding $500.00 per year.

In a separate account book, is shown how the original stock of the company was subscribed to, as follows:

Deming Jarves	71 shares	(Agent)
Edmund Munroe	12 "	(Treasurer)
Samuel Hunt	5 "	(Clerk)
David Hill	7 "	(Director)
Benjamin Sewall	5 "	(Director)
Samuel Fay	6 "	(President)
Henry Rice	5 "	(Director)
Andrew T. Hall	— "	(Director)

At a meeting held on November 16, 1826, a dividend of five per cent was declared, payable in December. Thus, in less than a year after this new venture was under way, the profits were such as to warrant dividends.

Apparently the officers of the company sold stock outside their official circle, as the amount they took themselves totalled only $55,500. There is a notice to the treasurer to sell six shares, which had been subscribed to by one Rufus Webb, but never taken.

Thus the Boston & Sandwich Glass Company was a paying enterprise from the beginning The officers were all shrewd business men. Some were men of wealth and all were in more than comfortable circumstances. As the story of this venture unfolds, there is much of interest which has never been told before concerning both the years of adversity and the years of tremendous prosperity.

Chapter III

EARLY DAYS AT SANDWICH

(1826–1840)

No one can write about the early days at Sandwich without making use of the paper read by William E. Kern, nephew of Theodore Kern, before the American Association of Flint and Lime Glass Manufacturers, Inc., at Atlantic City, N. J., on July 20, 1906. Mr. Kern began work at Sandwich in 1843 and stayed with them until 1867. At the time he died, at the age of over ninety, at New Bedford, Mass., he was the oldest workman still living from that factory. That the trade held him in high esteem was made clear by the manufacturers at their convention. They heard him with keen interest and deep respect. No one is in a position to question his sincerity or the accuracy of his statements, and his address is still an important source of information concerning the early days at Sandwich. I have found it expedient to quote from his speech in this chapter, even though some of his comments do not precisely tie in with facts and figures as noted in extracts from the recorded minutes of the Company's meetings, or personal letters, which must be considered accurate documentary proof. Mr. Kern was an elderly man and lapses in memory may be readily excused. The excerpts taken from the Boston & Sandwich Glass Company books constitute a valuable supplement and will also be quoted extensively.

With the factory in running order, it is interesting to note what made up a factory day. The workmen were divided into four shifts or turns. According to William E. Kern, who entered the employ of the Boston & Sandwich Glass Company in 1843, the first turn was on from 1 A.M to 6 A.M. with an interval of half an hour for lunch. At seven o'clock the second turn came on and worked until noon, with an interval at 8:30 for breakfast. At one in the afternoon the first turn came to work again and worked until six o'clock after which came the second turn. They worked until midnight, thus completing the 24 hours. The factory being worked night and day, it was not found necessary to keep it going more than four days a week, so that every Friday morning at six o'clock the men started on a holiday which lasted until the next Monday. The boys who were bound to an apprenticeship were obliged to work during the intervals between the turns, tending the glory holes and getting in a supply of wood for the boys who were to take their places. The fires were never allowed to go out. Mr. Kern added that the boys used to have pretty good times when the older men were away.

Schooling for these boys became something of a problem. Those who worked in the factory were employed either during the forenoon or the afternoon and as a half of the half-day remaining to them was needed for sleep, it followed that they had time for only a quarter of a day's school each day. To make up in some measure for this, they were obliged to attend school all day on Friday and Saturday when their elders were enjoying themselves.

Mr. Kern tells this story of a watchman: "It was the duty of the watchmen and sloarmen to go through the village at night and call the men who were to take the next turn. Those who did not respond on the first call were routed out by the boys. One night one of the sloarmen, who started on his rounds at midnight, after calling some of his men, met a friend who invited him into his house to have a social glass. One thing led to another and presently, under the cheering influence of sundry drinks, the sloarman forgot that there was such a thing as getting glassmakers out of bed. The men he had not called failed to show up and the manager, learning of it the next morning, called the luckless sloarman before him for a reprimand. 'To tell you the truth, gaffer,' was the explanation offered, 'I was drunk and I forgot there was anybody in Sandwich but myself.'

"There were no spare hands in those days and, if anyone failed to come to work, some man on the opposite turn would work over-time. Boys who worked overtime received tickets and were paid once in three months. Every Fourth of July the company remembered the boys with a present of 50 cents each, to spend on fireworks. No man was ever discharged for age or incapacity, so long as he could work at all. If he was unable to make good in the job he held, some other work was found more suitable to one of his age and physical condition. Men worked in the company's service from the time they were boys until they were able to work no longer. At Christmas time the company made presents of flour, or a ton of coal, or some other necessity of life, to the widows of men who had been in its employ. More than that, in times of panic, when work was slack and there might otherwise have been a good deal of suffering, the company gave away supplies, opening up a store and keeping a man in charge of it for that purpose.

"As was natural in a small town depending almost entirely on one big industry, the glass company showed many instances of what might be called paternalism. The heavier supplies, such as coal, flour, lumber, etc., were brought into town by the company and sold to the individuals. The company built houses for the workingmen, allowing them to pay for them on the installment plan. Gas was supplied the town through mains laid from the company's works—mains which still lie buried in the streets of Sandwich. The company also maintained the only fire apparatus the town possessed, with a crew of workingmen to man the hand engine.

"The out-of-the-way situation of Sandwich as regards transportation facilities made the problem of securing supplies an important one. There was no railroad in 1825 when the works were started and so all supplies, such as sand, pearlash, saltpetre, nitrate of soda, etc., had to be brought by water. The harbor of the town was choked with sand and it was some distance from the works to the water. One of the first things the company did was to construct a horse railway from the works to the water front. This was in 1827 and it is believed by old residents of Sandwich to have been the first horse railway in the United States. It was operated for many years to facilitate the transportation of lighter supplies. The heavier ones, which were brought in vessels, were transferred to scows in the harbor and these were poled through creeks or channels dug through the marsh, up to the factory wharf, a distance of about a mile.

"In the year 1848 the steam railroad was extended from Boston to Sandwich and the transportation problem promised to become simpler. It was not simplified at once, however, for the company had difficulty in making suitable terms with the railroad and was dissatisfied with the rates between Sandwich and Boston. Accordingly, in 1853, steps were taken to secure transportation facilities entirely independent of the railroad. The company built a steamer, the *Acorn,* and operated her between Sandwich and Boston. She brought all the light supplies and did something of a passenger business as well. The use of the steamer made necessary improvements in the harbor. In the old harbor, the depth of the water was constantly being lessened by shifting sands, so a new one was cut through in another direction, affording ample depth at all times. The *Acorn* did valiant service for a number of years, not only in the transportation of supplies but now and then as a pleasure craft. The workmen sometimes chartered her for a fishing excursion at the end of the week. There were no automobiles and no movies for diversions in those days.

"Before long, satisfactory terms were made with the railroad company so that during the Civil War the *Acorn* was sold to the United States Government. She was sunk somewhere near the Capes of Virginia during the Civil War.

"When the railroad came to terms, the glass company built a wharf at what was then called Cohasset Narrows, now Buzzards Bay, nine miles from Sandwich. Their coal was brought up the bay in vessels and from there by railroad to the works in Sandwich.

"When the works were started in 1825 there was one glasshouse. Later, in 1849, a second house was built, the two being known as the Upper and Lower houses. Each contained two ten-pot furnaces. In the beginning wood was burned both in the furnaces and in the glory holes and was continued in the former up to the time that its scarcity compelled the use of coal. About the year 1850 resin began to be used in the glory holes, continuing until the Civil War, when this commodity became too scarce and too valuable for any such use. When the war broke out the company had on hand around 700 barrels of resin which had cost something like 62c a barrel. The whole lot was sold to the government for $44.00 per barrel, a transaction that was obviously very profitable for the company. After gas was introduced for use in the factory, coke was burned in the lears for the first time, so far as I can ascertain, in the history of American glassmaking."

The "Upper house," or the original factory built in 1825 of which Mr. Kern speaks, was added to and connected with the 1849 building. The early house was a wooden structure, whereas the 1849 factory was built of brick. The old workmen referred to the two parts as the "Upper" and "Lower" house. Apparently during the ensuing years the wooden part was either torn down or built over into a brick structure. At any rate, it became so much a part of the Upper house that when a large new building was erected in 1871 (as shown on the map on Plate 14) the later edifice became known as the Lower house. No other explanation can be found for Mr. Kern's reference to the 1849 building as being the Lower house. The 1871 building was known by that name for many years.

Another writer has queried the date of the erection of the so-called "1849" building at Sandwich, since the photograph of the Manufactory in 1836 as illustrated on Plate 12 shows a second chimney. My documents indicate that between the years 1827 and 1840, the Boston & Sandwich Glass Company enjoyed tremendous growth and prosperity. From these records it is of importance to note, that on December 24, 1828, it was voted to erect a suitable building, for the manufacturing of glass. It is quite apparent that the original building put up in 1826 was wholly inadequate. In 1829 two new wooden dwellings were erected for the workmen.

In June, 1830, Mr. Jarves was authorized to purchase a new depot for the use of the Company. In April 1831, Mr. Jarves was voted the power to enlarge the furnace *"in the new glasshouse"* whenever he felt it should be desirable to do so. July 25, 1832, Mr. Jarves was authorized to enlarge the cutting shop, it being too limited for the business of the Company. In December of that year, Mr. Jarves was empowered to erect a new ten-pot furnace *"in the old glasshouse."* Apparently these buildings at that time were referred to as the "new" and the "old" glasshouses. In June, 1833, the directors voted that Mr. Jarves should erect a new brick packing house in addition to the improvements then being made on the glasshouse.

From these actual records it may be seen how rapidly the Boston & Sandwich Glass Company was expanding and they account for the buildings shown in the view dated 1836.

Under date of Nov. 23, 1825, Deming Jarves addressed a letter to William Stutson at Sandwich, now the property of Mr. James Gillinder of Port Jervis, N. Y., to whose courtesy I am indebted for permission to reproduce it in this volume. Mr. Gillinder himself comes from a famous glass family. He is a grandson of William Gillinder, who came to this country from England in 1854, and who eventually became a member of the firm of Gillinder & Sons of Greensburg, Pa. This letter is the earliest known of the Deming Jarves of the Sandwich period. It was written just after he moved to Sandwich. It is as follows:

Boston, Mass.   Nov. 23, 1825

I find the house we have taken is so large it will require a great deal of furniture. Am sorry we parted with so much. Wish to have the yellow chairs sent. Abby says Sally can use hers, she had a dozen. Send all the wash tubs, noggin,* piggin,† and those milk bowls. I cannot replace them easily, tried to get some today. We have worked hard and done but little. Furniture is higher than I expected. Should

---

* Noggin. A small mug or cup.
† Piggin. A small wooden pail or tub with an upright stave as handle. Often used as a dipper. Also produced in old glass.

be glad of some of my old furniture. I left some lamp wicks in the secretary side drawer. Give them to Mother. I suppose you were very glad to get rid of the folks at last. I long to see the children. Dear George, I hope he will not take cold. How soon does Mother mean to come up? Love to her and Sally. I want Sally to see you all. Our house is not half fixed yet and Abby will leave me Friday to go to ———— (sheet torn; undecipherable). She calculates to be with you next Tuesday.

Messrs. Waldron has white salts instead of blue sent him. They ordered blue. They are also charged for 2 ring. Dec. (decanters).

Send Messrs. Waldron 12 dozen pint taper tumblers, 7 oz.

I hope this winter has not yet set in and believe it will continue fair enough to send up goods till 20 next month. The weather here this day Tuesday commenced with light North wind and snow which has continued falling through the day. Wind varying from N. to N. W., snow two and three inches deep and cold. It now (the evening) clearing up and hope the weather be fair enough for my family to come up—if the *Polly* has not sailed wish you to send the yellow chairs as the present house is large and shall want them. Do not wish the *Polly* detained a moment for my account as it is more important to get the goods up for those who orders—as the business is now over, do not expect to get any more orders of consequence. Expect to be down shortly. Shall then bring down some patterns for best articles which will please the men—flint wines will be wanted in the Spring.

Have yours by S. Kerne and am glad to hear you have succeeded so well in getting forward. Please send me a memo of what articles the store will require for the fall and winter—also lumber, lime or any other articles.

Have Mr. Lapham add to all the batches about 10 lbs. lead to a pot.

Wish you would purchase several saddles of Venison. They are as cheap at 10¢ as beef is here.

The weather is warm. No wind. Snow melting. 12 o'clock noon.

On another sheet of the letter were notes and instructions. It is interesting to know that the orders show a great demand for "lamp glasses, all kinds." These were lamp globes and in the letter were sketches of types which we refer to today as Tulip.

PLATE 10

Early view of the Upper House, Sandwich, built in 1849.

PLATE 11

Early view of the Boston & Sandwich Glass Company, creek and dock.

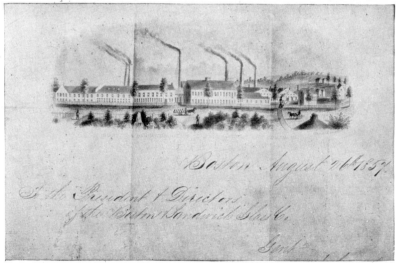

PLATE 12

Upper: "View of Sandwich Glass Works" Wood engraving, drawn from nature, under date of 1836.

Lower: "Boston & Sandwich Glass Company Manufactory. Sandwich, Mass." Dated August 26, 1857.

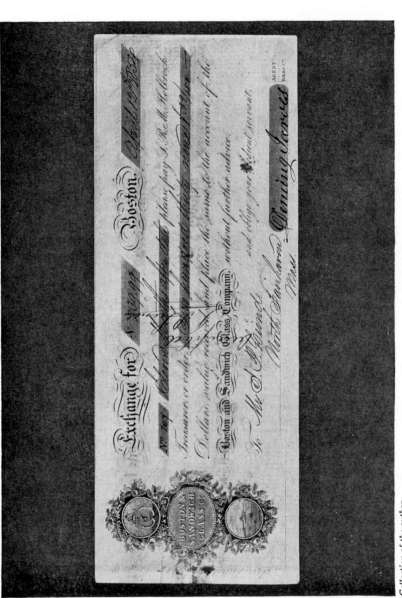

PLATE 13

Bank draft of the Boston & Sandwich Glass Company, signed by Deming Jarves, April 12, 1854.

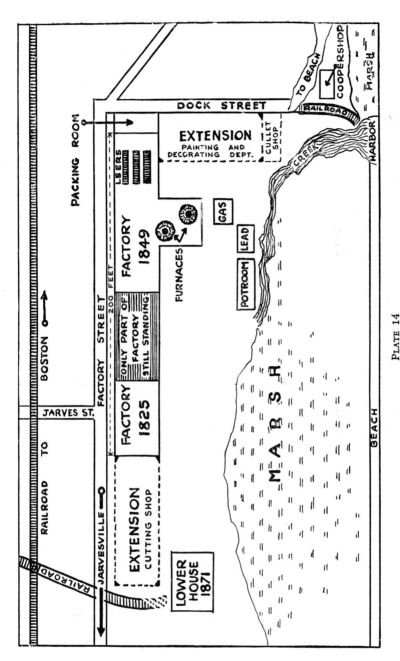

PLATE 14

A general outline showing the gradual development and growth of the Boston & Sandwich Glass Company. The original factory (1825) was absorbed into the main building in the process of expansion.

In the letter they are called "Liverpool lamp glasses, ½ Tulip." Jarves says: "The difference in the two last is only in the lip. Do not have the necks too long they do not appear well proportioned when long—let the bulb be in proportion to the lip. Have all made light as possible—and as many made each week as convenient. Michael Doyle can make two moves per week. Snowdon and Haynes for part of the large size and tell them to have thin lips. Cylinder Rose feet Lamps, common tubes and plated caps are much called for.

"A. T. Hall, Sumner and Hay and Atkins have had many of their rose feet lamps broke by bad packing. Hall had one-half of his broken—little or no straw being between them and laying a crost."

Such were some of the trials and tribulations that Deming Jarves had to meet in November 1825, at his little factory on Cape Cod, in the late fall before he organized it into what became known, the following spring, as "the Boston & Sandwich Glass Company."

The vast difference in the attitude of labor toward its grievances in 1845 and 1946 as well as the character of the complaints is interestingly shown by the protests of the Masters and crews of the schooner *Sarah* and the sloop *Osceola* who objected to Sunday sailings. A saintly crew of non-union sailors! The point may be made that the company's business was booming when it was necessary to break the Sabbath in order to keep the goods moving. But you will find no mention of pay for overtime or for Sunday work. The letters follow:

Sandwich, June 16, 1845

To the Directors of the Boston & Sandwich Glass
    Company

Gentlemen:

The undersigned citizens of Sandwich hereby respectfully represent, that the Packet Schooner *Sarah* is accustomed to leave Port not unfrequently on the Sabbath day. We feel thereby greatly aggrieved at what we conceive and apprehend to be a violation of a wise and irrevocable law of God and tending to undermine the foundation of morality and true religion and subversion of the prosperity of any people in proportion to the extent of such violations of heaven's established law. We hereby transmit a copy of the permanent Sabbath document No. 1 as expressing the sentiments we entertain respecting the observance of the Sabbath day; and we most respectfully and especially solicit your attention to the consideration of the resolutions contained in the first part of the pamphlet, pages 10, 11 and 12. Entertaining also the belief that it is in the power of the Directors of the Boston & Sandwich Glass Company to prevent and provide against the violation of the Sabbath by the sailing out of port of their vessels on the Lord's day as well as for their highest pecuniary interest to do so. We do most respectfully but earnestly request that you will promptly employ the means appropriate to secure the object of the undersigned.

Most respectfully yours,

And again:

Sandwich, June 16, 1845

To the Directors of the Boston & Sandwich Glass
    Company

Gentlemen:

The undersigned officers and crew of the schooner *Sarah* in your employ hereby respectfully represent that ofttimes we have been constrained to leave port on the Sabbath day from the consideration, lest we should not give satisfaction to our employers. We have feared that if the wind and tide were favourable and we did not improve them even though it were on the Sabbath we might be charged with negligence of duty. We have laboured some of us at least under the painful apprehension for years at the same time we have had the uncomfortable reflection that in our course, we were not giving satisfaction to our Creator. We have proportionably to our frequent violations of the law and rest of the Holy Sabbath been debard and shut out from the privileges of The Sanctuary and we are fully persuaded neither to our own or the pecuniary benefit of the Company whose servants we are.

> Your verrey obedient servants
> Capt.
> Mate
> Crew

> Sandwich, June 16, 1845

To the Directors of the Boston & Sandwich Glass Co.

Gentlemen:

The undersigned officers and crew of the Sloop *Osceola* hereby express their earnest desire that a mutual understanding shall exist that neither their own or the Company's Packet shall be expected to leave port on the Sabbath day.

Most respectfully your verrey obt. servants.

> Capt.
> Mate
> Crew

From the above, it may be seen that Deming Jarves was not seriously troubled with any autocratic demands by labor such as are heard today.

A series of excerpts of signal historical import taken from the minutes of the meetings covering the highlights of that period between 1828 and 1840 will provide a first hand delineation of the growth and development of the company:

"May 3, 1828—Mr. Jarves requested an augmentation in salary. At this meeting it was voted to erect a pier and shore on a piece of land near the Sandwich Works, which had been purchased from Mr. Jarves, for the more effectual security of the company's property.

Mr. Jarves was voted $50.00 per annum, as a compensation for his services in keeping the records of the company.

December 24, 1828—It was voted at a special meeting that Mr. Jarves be authorized and empowered to cause a suitable building to be erected at some convenient place on the company's estate in Sandwich, for the manufacturing of glass, agreeable to the plan and representation laid before the meeting.

January 23, 1829—It was voted that the company purchase 340 acres of woodland bought by Deming Jarves from William Fessenden and others, in the town of Sandwich.

December 6, 1829—Mr. Jarves was authorized from time to time, to make such shipments of glass on the company's Account to foreign and home markets for sale, provided said shipments were approbated in writing by one or more directors.

It was also voted at this meeting to build two new wooden dwelling houses on the company land near the factory for the accommodation of their workmen. The company store (which handled groceries and provisions of all sorts) was let to Mr. Joseph Pope.

Note: The directors took up the proposition of the company store by Mr. Cyrus Smith who ran into great financial difficulties and became indebted to the company.

February 23, 1828—Special meeting. Mr. Jarves laid before the board a proposition from the New England Glass Company to employ an Agent jointly, to proceed to South America and to examine into the situation of those markets for glass, and to obtain such other information as might be beneficial to both companys. It was agreed that the two companys should join in employing a suitable person to proceed to South America to ascertain the situation of those markets and pay one-third of the expense, provided that third did not exceed $300.00.

June 25, 1829—At a special meeting it was voted that the treasurer be authorized to borrow money from time to time, as may be necessary for the use of the company and sign notes in behalf of the corporation. A committee of three of the directors was appointed to approve the notes, these being Deming Jarves, Henry Rice and Andrew T. Hall.

At this meeting the directors approved of the purchase of the glass of the South Boston Flint Glass Company.

December 1, 1830—At a special meeting consideration was given to a notice from the South Boston Flint Glass Company that they were desirous of selling their property and closing up their business. They suggested that the New England Glass Company and the Boston & Sandwich Glass Company jointly become purchasers. Committees from both companys were appointed to consider purchase of the South Boston Flint Glass Company's property, tools, stock and material.

June 26, 1830—Mr. Jarves was authorized to purchase a new depot for the use of the company, the one at present being too small and not well calculated for their purpose.

Mr. Jarves and Benjamin Sewall were a committee fully authorized to sell the sloop *Sandwich* at public or private sale, as may best appear to the interest of the company. (The sloop *Sandwich* was sold to Mr. Jarves, who made the highest offer.)

(In 1830 the paid in capital stock of the Boston & Sandwich Glass Company was $178,927.77.)

October 16, 1830—Mr. Jarves was authorized to appoint a Mr. William A. Mayo, the company's agent at New Orleans, for the sale of glass manufactured by the company.

January 4, 1831—Mr. Jarves and Mr. A. S. Hall were appointed a committee to confer with a committee from the New England Glass Company upon the subject of regulating the prices of glass, packages and such other things as they deem necessary whereby the interest of the two companys may be promoted.

It was also voted, that the shipments made to foreign markets by Mr. Jarves under a vote of the directory made December 6, 1829, be approbated by the board.

January 4, 1831—It was voted to purchase the stock, tools and materials of the South Boston Flint Glass Company and a committee was appointed to confer with one from the New England Glass Company on the advisability of also purchasing their real estate.

April 21, 1831—It was voted that Mr. Jarves be permitted to

enlarge the furnace in the new glasshouse whenever he feels it expedient to do so.

June 21, 1831—Mr. Jarves and Mr. Andrew T. Hall were voted a committee to confer with the owner of a newly invented glass knob, upon the expediency of purchasing an interest in the patent.

January 7, 1832—Captain Stutson, resident agent at Sandwich made application for an increase in salary and it was voted that in consideration of his attention to company affairs that a grant of $200.00 be made him in addition to his salary for the past year.

July 25, 1832—Voted, that Mr. Jarves be authorized to enlarge the cutting shop, it being too limited for the business of the company. It was decided to build an addition to the cutting shop.

December 27, 1832—Mr. Jarves was authorized to erect a new ten-pot furnace in the old glasshouse and make such additions and alterations as he may deem necessary and proper, provided the expense of the same does not exceed $400.00.

June 11, 1833—Voted, Mr. Jarves is authorized to erect a new brick packing house in addition to the improvements now being made with the glasshouse, provided the expense does not exceed $3,000.

A report of the company's affairs under date of February 23, 1833, show a capital stock of $180,000 less $1,072.23 not paid in. Debts due, $67,360.52. Real estate value, $60,939. Personal property, materials, steam engine, packet sloop, etc., $126,046.77. Debts due and cash on hand, $90,376.69. This statement was prepared when the directors voted to adopt the Act of the Commonwealth "Defining the General Powers and Duties of Manufacturing Corporations," a law passed February 23, 1830.

November 22, 1833—Mr. Jarves lay before the meeting a proposition of Mr. George G. Channing to sell the Boston & Sandwich Glass Company one-quarter part of a patent owned by him for the burning of "Alcohol Mixture in Jennings Patent Lamp." This patent was purchased by Mr. Channing from Josiah Jennings. A four-part agreement was made among the Boston & Sandwich Glass Company, the New England Glass Company, Mr. George

Channing and Mr. William Carleton for the manufacture and sale of Jennings Patent Lamp and for the sale of the Alcohol Mixture. The Boston & Sandwich Glass Company paid $1,500 for their quarter interest.

The depression of 1834 had set in with the following results: On January 2, 1834, a meeting was called by Mr. Jarves because he wished the advice of the Directory as to how he should proceed as to selling and manufacturing goods, "under the present embarrassed state of the times." Mr. Jarves was advised to use his judgment and no vote was taken on the subject. Mr. Jarves and Mr. Hall were voted a committee to confer with the New England Glass Company on the subject of a reduction of wages in both factories. The workmen in the Boston & Sandwich Glass Company voted on March 26th a reduction of their wages! Mr. Jarves was authorized to suspend the Agency at Baltimore whenever he conceived it for the interest of the company and to dispose of the goods on hand as he thought proper.

July 17, 1834—Special meeting. "In consequence of the present embarrassed state of trade, the company deem it expedient to discontinue one of their furnaces, therefore: *"Voted,* that the company will stop manufacturing glass in their "X" House, so-called, for the present and that the agent, Mr. Jarves be directed to put the fire out as soon as circumstances will permit. *Voted,* that the agent, Mr. Jarves, have full power and authority to discharge such hands as are not required by the company and to cause such reduction in the wages of those who remain as will enable the company to continue on with the Manufactory.

Note: Once a year the company was required to insert in the Barnstable *Journal,* a statement of the company affairs as exhibited by the Agent, made in accordance to the Act of this Commonwealth, defining the duties of Manufacturing Corporations, adopted by the company and approved February 23, 1830, requiring among other things, an annual statement of their capital paid in and their existing debt.

September 23, 1834—Mr. Jarves was authorized to again start

the fires in "X" house and it was voted that he should confer with the New England Glass Company on prices of glass.

October 23, 1834—The clerk laid before the meeting a letter received by him from Mr. Jarves expressing his desire to resign the Agency and requesting another be appointed in his place. The letter was referred to a committee.

October 31, 1834—Special meeting, Mr. Jarves presided. The meeting was called to consider the expediency of increasing the dividends of the company. Some bad debts turned out more favorable than had been anticipated and the business was reported to be in a healthy, prosperous state, its reserve fund of profits being upward of $20,000. An extra dividend of $7.50 on each share, payable the next day, was declared. The company had customarily paid 5% semi-annually since the first year they were in business.

December 27, 1834—It was voted to accept Mr. Jarves' letter of resignation but it was placed on file and he continued in office. A Mr. Edwards was appointed the Company Agent in Baltimore. At this meeting a further dividend of 5% was declared.

June 8, 1835—Mr. Jarves was requested to look into the affairs of the Spirit Gas Company.

July 3, 1835—A dividend of 5% was declared as usual.

November 18, 1835—Mr. Jarves was authorized to purchase the two lots of marshland lying between the factory and the wharf of Harlowe & Company at $60.00 per acre.

It was reported at this meeting that the Agency in New Orleans had not been productive and had been a source of considerable expense, so it was concluded to close it up as soon as affairs could be put in order.

December 7, 1835—A meeting was called to consider the advisability of again increasing the capital stock.

January 1, 1836—Because of a fire in New York, in which the company would sustain a loss, it was decided not to declare the usual 5% dividend but to pay $25.00 per each share.

January 13, 1836—Deming Jarves was authorized to alter the furnace of the large glasshouse so as to burn coal.

July 5, 1836—A 5% dividend was declared. The capital stock was increased and that paid in on the new issue amounted to $48,475.

November 23, 1836—A special meeting of the directors voted to stop one of the glass houses when Mr. Jarves thought it expedient to do so.

January 4, 1837—*Voted,* to procure another new steam engine. After hearing Mr. Jarves' report of the condition of the Manufactory for the past seven months ending December 31st, 1836, it was voted in consequence of the high rate of interest paid in the negotiation of paper and the continued difficulty of getting their paper discounted, to be inexpedient to make any dividends until after the next account of stock was taken.

March 22, 1837—Affairs in the New Orleans office appeared to be in a muddled state.

April 15, 1837—Edmund Munroe resigned his office as treasurer after being with the company since their Act of Incorporation.

At this time the following was offered by Mr. Jarves: "Whereas it appears the pecuniary embarrassments of the treasurer of this corporation and the situation of its funds and liabilities are such that it is expedient that an assignment of the estate and effects of the company be made for the payment of its debts. Thereupon it was voted that Samuel Hunt, the present clerk of the Corporation be and is hereby authorized and directed to execute an assignment of all the real and personal estate of the corporation unto David Dudley, Deming Jarves and Richard Fay as assignees for the benefit of creditors according to the statutes in such case made and provided."

"Voted, that the clerk be directed to call a meeting of the stockholders to be held at this place on Wednesday next at 3 P.M."

June 8, 1837—Edmund Munroe paid the balance of his account, but it was voted that Deming Jarves be authorized to transfer back to Mr. Munroe four shares of the company stock which were transferred to him as Agent, to cover any balances Mr. Munroe might be owing the company as Treasurer of same.

June 12, 1837—Mr. John C. Henshaw was voted in as Treasurer to replace Mr. Munroe at a salary of $2,000 per year. Mr. Henshaw on his part, agreed to loan the company $20,000 at 6%.

June 21, 1837—300 circulars were printed and distributed to the stockholders, describing the state of affairs of the company. It was in a bad way financially. Mr. Jarves reported to the board that only about $18,000 of the proposed loan of $40,000 to the company from the stockholders had been subscribed and from appearances not over $30,000 could be depended on. The directors resolved to call on each stockholder individually and find out how much they could obtain as a loan to tide them over. $50,000 had to be paid in within the year or the letter of license from the company creditors would be void. It was voted to pay 2½% commission to any of the company members who would indorse papers to the bank.

August 18, 1837—A letter from Mr. Mayo, the Agent of the New Orleans office, stated he would come to the company office in Boston and adjust his accounts with the company provided no arrest be made of his person for a period of not to exceed six months while he was in the State.

Mr. Henshaw resigned his brief office as Treasurer, accepting no fee for his duties in office. Mr. Richard S. Fay was elected in his place.

September 4, 1837—*Voted,* to send a competent person to proceed to New Orleans and effect a compromise and settlement, if possible, of the company account with their agent Mr. William Mayo. It was agreed that the person selected should not receive or settle for less than $5,000.

October 31, 1837—At this time the company affairs appear to be in better condition. Assignees were requested to convey the property back to the company and it was voted that they be indemnified against any action or damage therefrom. Assignees were voted thanks for their faithful, judicious management of the company's concern and thanks were presented to the Traders Bank of Boston for the liberal and prompt advance to the company during the past April, by which the company was enabled to continue its operations and save itself from loss.

November 27, 1837—Mr. William Mayo of New Orleans objected to the power of attorney given the company representative and required that a further power of attorney be signed by Mr. Jarves.

December 7, 1837—At this time it was reported the capital stock of the company was $241,000. Debts, $223,908. The directors were now Samuel Fay, Deming Jarves, David Dudley, Joshua Crane, Richard S. Fay and Thomas C. Smith.

January 11, 1838—At this meeting it was voted to buy a new steam engine. Mr. Jarves obtained a lease from the company of some of their machinery for the purpose of manufacturing salt, for the sum of $200.00.

The Treasurer and Agent were authorized to sell company woodland at fair prices. (Coal was now being used.)

May, 1838—A letter from the resident agent at Sandwich, Capt. Stutson, was laid before the meeting which concerned charges preferred against him by William Fessenden. Capt. Stutson requested that these charges be investigated by the company.

July 9, 1838—Mr. Jarves requested to be relieved of making contracts for the company or to be held responsible for the errors or conduct of those serving under him.

August 1, 1838—An increase of wages to the men was voted by the directors.

September 26, 1838—Deming Jarves again resigned and it was voted that his letter be "laid on the table." A committee of three was selected to confer with Mr. Jarves.

In a letter of October 7, 1838, Jarves called the attention of the committee to the fact that the workmen had made application for increase of wages and in order to enable the Company to do this the workmen offered to make more pieces of glass during the same period of time. Jarves highly recommended that the committee study this situation and help the workmen out. Jarves included a list naming every single employee, the number of moves he made

in a day and how many he expected to increase it for the anticipated increase in wages. It is quite impressive 108 years later to
evaluate Jarves' method of attacking his problem of increased
wages. It resolved itself to increased productivity justifies increased
wages, and his analysis would do credit to a modern day industrial
engineer.

October 25, 1839, Mr. Munroe and Mr. Whitney were made a
committee to confer with the New England Glass Co. about con-
solidating agencies to sell glassware at Baltimore and Philadelphia.
Both companies agreed on Sept. 23, 1842 that there would be
no discount allowed on sales of glassware unless the amount exceeded $20.00. [Interesting as an example of the close working of
the two companies and their high degree of compatibility.

It is also of interest to know that an average of 5% dividends
on the profits were declared semi-annually during the first eight
years of the company's existence. It was not until March of 1834
(during the depression of those times) that at one meeting a dividend of $15.00 per share was declared instead of the usual 5%.]

Chapter IV

THE PRESSING MACHINE AND JARVES' PATENTS

Of the Deming Jarves patents, the most important were those connected with improvements in machines for pressing glass. The new manufacturing method was as revolutionary as the shift from the horse and buggy to the automobile. When the centuries-old practice of blowing all glass by lung-power was abandoned in favor of mechanical forms of pressure by means of molds and plungers, the industry was completely changed. Not only was volume production made possible, but labor costs were thereby so reduced that it meant lower prices for the consumer, which went hand in hand with greater profits for the producer. Glassware, both useful and attractive, was thenceforth available to all classes of buyers and purses.

There has been much speculation over how much credit should be awarded to Deming Jarves as an inventor of machinery for pressing glass. But he himself settled that point in the enlarged edition of his "Reminiscences of Glass Making," printed in 1865. He wrote: "Although it is commonly believed here that the invention originated in this country, the claim cannot be fully sustained. Fifty years back the writer imported from Holland salts made by being pressed in metallic moulds and from England glass candlesticks and table centre-bowls, plain, with pressed square feet, rudely made, somewhat after the present mode of moulding glass." That would put the "fifty years back" close to 1815. In the Boston Directory for 1815 and 1816, Jarves was listed as a member of the firm of Henshaw & Jarves, dealers in crockery ware. It must have been at that time that the salts referred to were imported by him. That he did not dwell at greater length upon such historically and industrially important points, is one of the many omissions that make his "Reminiscences" so disappointing. To be sure, he could not possibly have foreseen the Sandwich craze, or the craving for a more personal record of his own remarkable career, but the criticism of the book is fair. He did not "reminisce" as fully as he should have done.

According to Jarves, no improvement was made in this process in Europe from 1814 to 1838, where it was confined to common parts and square feet, but we cannot accept all his statements as wholly true. Of course, it is quite possible that he was not cognizant of improvements, though it is difficult to reconcile such ignorance with what we know of the alert interest manifested by him from his early days in everything that pertained to the industry. In 1865 he was seventy-four years of age. His memory might easily have played him false, which would account for so many other inexplicable lapses. Careful research has established the fact that the glass pressing machine was in active use in Europe within a year or two of the time when, according to trustworthy accounts, it was first employed at Sandwich. However, while it is true that so-called pressed glass was made in Europe before it was made here, the difference lies in the method employed. The Europeans used a "lemon-squeezer" type. Our contribution was the invention of the plunger and it was this, not just pressing, that revolutionized the glass industry.

Facilities for obtaining detailed information about what was being done industrially in distant lands were decidedly limited one hundred years ago. American manufacturers then were concerned chiefly with supplying local demands, rather than with seeking to excel European competitors. Dates are valuable only if or when they help to make the picture clearer. Nor is there much to commend in efforts to emphasize the need of a minute-by-minute chronology, particularly when there is reason to suspect such efforts to have been motivated by the desire to stress the inaccuracies of previous writers on the subject.

In a letter to a friend, the late Homer Eaton Keyes told of receiving photographs taken from an old catalogue of the "Cristalleries de St. Louis" and quotes the comments of the manager of the French factory who said that they began making those pieces at St. Louis in 1842–1843 and added, "Of course, at a time when in America no moulded style glass was made." Mr. Keyes commented: "This is fairly indicative of how little one country knows about the manufacturing enterprises of its neighbors," which makes it easier to excuse Jarves' statements. The popularity of the word *circa,* so often used in dating antiques, is easy to understand. Approximations in Latin are more apt to silence the stickler for accuracy than guessing in English.

A few years ago the authors of articles on American antiques which appeared in the newspapers and periodicals were chiefly concerned with supplying promptly the demand for information that grew more and more urgent as the number of collectors increased. They worked under serious disadvantage when they wrote about old American glass. Pressed for time they fell back on the printed work of still earlier writers, without checking their statements or, worse yet, accepted as facts the gossip of the trade and obviously apocryphal accounts of our early glasshouses and their products. The craving for stories, with young collectors, is apt to masquerade as a thirst for knowledge and ignorant or indifferent editors were as much to blame as the writers. Inexcusable errors were perpetuated. Collectors in those days accepted misinformation willingly and even gratefully, for "talking points" were needed and something—anything!—was better than nothing. To force a collector to be silent is a tragedy.

The vitality of many of the early errors is remarkable. Take, for example, the assertion that we made pressed glass before the Europeans did, notwithstanding the disclaimer of Deming Jarves who assuredly knew what he was talking about. In the book by Silliman & Goodrich, entitled "The World of Science, Art and Industry" are described the exhibits at the New York Crystal

Palace Exhibition, 1853–54. The information on pressed glass was obtained from J. N. Howe, agent of the New England Glass Company. We read: "The art of moulding or pressing glass in metallic moulds as a substitute for blowing and cutting, it is believed, is entirely of American origin, and although adopted to some extent in Europe, the products there are very inferior in beauty. Indeed, the process of moulding glass, so far as we can learn, is used in Europe only as a preparation for cutting, the labor of which process is thereby very much reduced."

There is evidence to the contrary in the products of Baccarat and other French and Belgian works, which are of a very high quality. It is true, of course, that pressed glass was not highly regarded abroad then or now. The fact remains that it has indisputably played perhaps the most important rôle of all time in the glass industry. While the fame of Yankee inventive genius is world-wide, particularly in originating new mechanical devices, we had much to learn from Europe, in the 1830's, not alone in artistic effects but in technical methods. Don't forget that we had to import our skilled workers.

Concerning the "invention" of pressed glass at the Sandwich works, the usually careful and thorough Joseph D. Weeks, in his "Report of Manufactures in the United States," prepared for the census of 1880, says:

"The invention of the American press [for glass] is ascribed to a Massachusetts carpenter in the town of Sandwich about 1827 who, wanting an article of glassware made for some purpose, went to Mr. Deming Jarves and asked him if he could make the article desired. Mr. Jarves told him it would be impossible to make such an article. The carpenter asked if a machine could not be made to press glass into any shape. The idea was scouted at first, but, on second thought, Mr. Jarves and the carpenter fashioned a rude press and made the experiment. This machine was intended to make tumblers and when the hot molten glass was placed in the mold which was to determine whether glass could be pressed, the experiment was witnessed by many glassmakers.* They were nearly all of the opinion that the experiment would come to naught and were greatly amazed when the result demonstrated that it was possible to press glass. The first tumbler that was manufactured in the rough, improvised press remained in Mr. Jarves' possession for many years and then passed into the hands of John A. Dobson & Company, a well-known dealer of Baltimore.† It was exhibited at the Centennial Exhibition by Mr. Hobbs, of Hobbs, Brocunier & Co., where it was accidentally broken by Mr. John H. Hobbs."

The experience of Deming Jarves differed little from that of other inventors of labor-saving devices. In one of the few letters of his which have been preserved, he wrote:

"The glass blowers on discovery that I had succeeded in pressing a piece of glass, were so enraged for fear their business would be ruined by the new discovery, that my life was threatened, and I was compelled to hide from them for six weeks before I dared venture in the street or in the glass house, and for more than six months there was danger of personal violence should I venture in the street after nightfall." (The magazine *Antiques,* October, 1931.)

It is important for Sandwich enthusiasts to read what Gustav Edmund Pazaurek, in his "Gläser der Empire—und Biedermeier-zeit," has to say in the chapter on "Blown and Pressed Drinking Glasses Made in Metal Molds":

"Probably the first drinking glass made not by blowing in a mold but by pressing with a stamp, was a cylindrical goblet with

---

* It is questionable whether glass in the earliest days was actually "poured." The average glass (or "metal") melts at 2500 degrees Fahrenheit. The Bureau of Standards says that with wood as fuel it is impossible to reach more than 2100 degrees Fahrenheit. This means that the gather would be like paste rather than a liquid that would pour. This fact answers many questions posed by the defects in numerous early pressed pieces. The threadlike marks on the surface of most all early pieces are indications that the thread of glass that dropped into the mold first (it was pressed upside down so that the design could be on the plunger, thus making a sharper, clearer impression) actually set before it hit the mold.

† Later information revealed that the famous tumbler was lent, through F. C. Sieman, who was associated with John A. Dobson & Company, to the Centennial Exhibition in Philadelphia.

a 'scaly cut' pattern.* This was made in 1827 by Deming Jarves at Sandwich, Mass., North America. But this piece surely must have been preceded by simpler objects, such as shallow sauce dishes or bowls. The English, who for a long time sought priority in this field, were first able to come out with an object so made in 1836, namely, a pressed high-stemmed tumbler by James Stevens of Bull's Head Court in Birmingham. This piece also must have been preceded by some that were easier to press. Other English manufacturers followed suit quickly in this field, without regard for the danger of ruining their own cut-glass industry. They include such men as John Ogden Bacchus, George Joseph Green and William Gammon of Birmingham, who, as early as 1834, had received a patent for the prevention of impurities on the surface of hollow, metal molds; Rice Harris, also of Birmingham, Apsley Pellatt of Blackfriars Bridge in Surrey, who back in 1831 received a patent, not only for his glassed-in pastes, but also for a new way of closing the metal molds. Later on, in 1845, Apsley Pellatt, together with Frederick Pellatt of Blackheath, Kent, extended his activities to figured flint glass.

"The flood of English pressed glass had already thrown their own market into confusion and disorder. It led to a drop of 200% in prices in other glass-producing countries, as for example, Northern Bohemia. Then, this was immediately followed by a deluge of pressed glass from France which made matters even worse, if such a thing were possible, because the French were not content with imitating diamond facet or cylinder cutting but added an abundance of relief ornamentation in all current styles. This in turn was possibly responsible for a change for the worse in the taste for glass decoration which was experienced previous to the middle of the nineteenth century. Gothic architectural motifs alternate with Renaissance and Rococo, all on a granulated background, but not well designed, except as it might appeal, as a novelty, to

---

* The literal translation does not convey the exact meaning in English. The tumbler was in a simple, pressed pattern, as illustrated on Plate 17.

the undiscriminating masses. The reason was the ridiculously low prices. A similar effect, produced by solid high-relief cutting, would have required a fortune. When one reads the catalogues of a leading firm in this particular field, namely by Launay, Hautin & Cie, of Paris, one is surprised by the more than abundant fullness of the most elaborate of the molds which towards the end of the '30's were already on the market, although the decorative elements can be traced back to a comparatively few types. Nor could one be less surprised to see how soon technical restraints and obstacles were overcome, when even bottles were produced with the patterns in sharp relief. Competition finally compelled Austria and Germany to engage in the general pressed glass madness. The factory of Johann Mayr of Adolph in the Bohemian Forest, noted for the excellent quality of its crystal glass, exhibited—in an incidental way, to be sure—at the Prague Exposition of 1836, some pressed glass 'with raised Arabesque ornamentation through the manufacture of which the French and Americans threatened our own cut glass works.' This quotation is from a report of the Exposition which went on to add that only 'in conjunction with fine glass cutting' could further prosperous development be expected. Josef Labmeyer (father of Ludwig) of Marienthal in Slavonia, also introduced the making of pressed glass. Fortunately, the production of pressed glass in Austria, particularly in Bohemia, did not become important enough to endanger art glass. At the Berlin Industrial Exhibition in 1844 the factory of C. W. Scheffler, from near Spremberg, was the only one to exhibit pressed glass. This was praised for its neat patterns. In the following decades, the expansion of the industrial export trade, together with the very great decline in good taste seen also in other lines, when people preferred to buy what was cheapest, provided it 'looked like something,' helped to increase the vogue of pressed glass, and with more and greater improvements in technical methods pressed glass began to resemble the cut glass more closely. A generation later, however, a reaction against it set in, which drove pressed glass, for the most part, into the hotel trade."

I do not think the translation of these passages in full is known to many collectors. An illustration of a French lacy goblet, as pictured in Pazaurek's book, may be found in the January, 1939, number of the magazine *Antiques*. A number of others are illustrated on Plate 173.

It is clear from the foregoing that Deming Jarves, writing in 1865, was not as well informed in regard to European technical methods and markets as his book would lead us to suppose. We have already noted his admission that pressing glass did not originate in this country, citing in corroboration his purchase of pieces from Europe fifty years before, but for some inexplicable reason he fails to tell when and where, or by whom, the first piece was made here. He must have been in possession of those facts. But he is assuredly entitled to all the credit he has received for his improvements in the methods and machinery for pressing glass in this country.

The first important record of an American patent for pressed glass that I have been able to trace is one issued to Henry Whitney and Enoch Robinson of Cambridge, Mass., under date of Nov. 4, 1826. It may well be that pressed glass was made first at the New England Glass Company, perhaps even possibly while Jarves was still associated with that company. Certainly pressed glass was made by Jarves prior to his patent of Dec. 1, 1828 for that patent covers an *improvement* in the method of pressing. It is to be hoped that further documentary evidence may come to light in the future. What we do know today is that to Jarves is due the credit for perfecting and putting into practical use the art of pressing glass.

The molds used were of brass which may account for the fact that none of the early ones in this metal survive today, for brass was too costly and it paid to remelt and use it for new molds. The iron molds when discarded were sold to junk dealers. Articles from brass molds have somewhat softer contours than those from iron molds. It has been said that molds of hard wood were tried out in the beginning but they charred too quickly and had to be discarded. Later on, iron molds were used everywhere, as they

Sandwich Glass

are to this day. The molds from which the mold makers worked were carved from wood.

As for the patents obtained by Deming Jarves, the first one of which I have found a record is dated February 2, 1821. It covered a machine for opening glass blowers' molds. It is interesting to recall that ten years later Apsley Pellatt of Blackfriars Bridge in Surrey, England, obtained a patent for a new way of *closing* metal molds. One writer asserts that in 1822 Jarves took out a patent for an improvement in the tubes for glass lamps. This is of relatively little importance. According to the *Journal* of the Franklin Institute, Jarves' next patent, under date of Dec. 1, 1828, is for "Pressing Melted Glass into Molds to D. Jarves, Boston, Mass."

"To make articles of pressed glass by the method in which they now are, and therefore have been manufactured, a mold, giving the *shape* and ornamental impression, has been required for *each* article manufactured; and the shape of the article or vessel intended to be made is preserved during the cooling of the metal, in a receiver of like shape as the mold, and thus the manufacturer is obliged to possess and use, a *mold* and *receiver* for *each* article, of different size and shape, which he makes.

"The improvement for which I ask an exclusive privilege, consists in pressing all the glass intended for the various articles and vessels to be manufactured, into sheets by a mold, which impresses upon the sheet of glass all the ornamental figures intended for the article or vessel to be made. I thus obtain, by the use of *one* mold, sheets of ornamented glass and out of these sheets the article to be manufactured, as to *size*, shape, and figure, is to be produced by receivers of the size, shape, and figure required. The sheets of glass (being impressed as aforesaid), are placed upon the receiver, and thus acquire its particular form and figure: And, should these sheets become too cool to settle readily into all of the shapes and angles and take the true shape and figure of the receiver, a *follower* of same shape with the receiver, is used to force the metal into all parts of the receiver in the usual manner."

This patent may have been a Yankee dodge to get around the

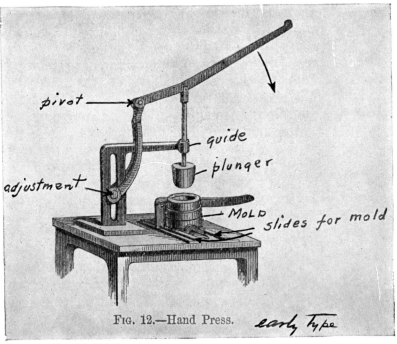

pivot
guide
plunger
adjustment
MOLD
slides for mold
early type
FIG. 12.—Hand Press.

Courtesy of Harry Hall White

PLATE 15

Early type of hand press for pressing glass.

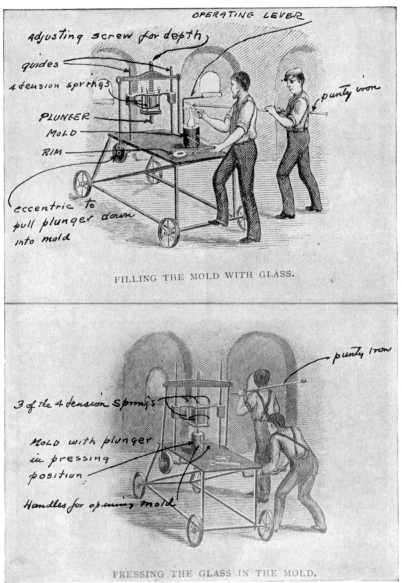

OPERATING LEVER

Adjusting screw for depth

guides

4 tension springs

PLUNGER

MOLD

RIM

punty iron

eccentric to pull plunger down into mold

FILLING THE MOLD WITH GLASS.

punty iron

3 of the 4 tension springs

MOLD with plunger in pressing position.

Handles for opening mold

PRESSING THE GLASS IN THE MOLD.

Courtesy of Harry Hall White

PLATE 16
Early method of pressing glass.

PLATE 17

Side and base view of the first pressed glass tumbler, made at Sandwich in 1827.

PLATE 18

Glass knobs were among the earliest articles made.

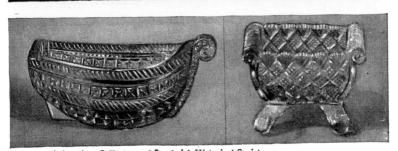

PLATE 19

Top row—Early curtain tie-backs with pewter stems.
Center row—Threaded glass.   *Lower row*—Two early salts.

patent of Henry Whitney and Enoch Robinson of Cambridge, Mass., dated Nov. 4, 1826. This patent reads: "Account of patent for manufacturing glass knobs for Doors, Drawers, etc., by making them in one operation without the aid of blowing." It contains a lengthy and rather involved description which would not be of interest to the readers of these pages beyond the fact that it gives the first account of the so-called "rim," an important part of the pressing machine over which there has been considerable controversy and also gives what I suspect is probably the first description of an early mold press. It is a matter of interest that pressed-glass door knobs were being turned out in quantity as early as 1826 and also glass bureau knobs with holes through them for the screw which held these knobs in place on the doors and drawers.

On June 11, 1829 another patent was granted to Deming Jarves of Boston "For an improvement in the manufacture of glass knobs for Drawers, Doors, Shutters, etc." This patent reads as follows:

"The glass knob, instead of being perforated, in the usual manner, for the reception of a metallic screw, is pressed into a mold, so made as to form the knob with a shank of solid glass furnished with a screw. On account of the brittleness of the material, the shank is made large. The claim is to the making of glass knobs 'having a glass shank, with a screw upon the shank.' " (One such knob is shown on plate 18.)

This patent is of particular interest because the belief was long held that glass knobs with a threaded glass shank to screw into the wooden drawer were the earliest type of glass knobs made in this country. Certainly they were crude and not so practical as those having the removable metal screws. However, the patent to Henry Whitney and Enoch Robinson of Cambridge, Mass., under date of Nov. 4, 1826, dispels all doubt as to which of the two was the earlier.

Following Jarves' patent for pressing glass into molds, the next one in importance is probably that issued on May 28, 1830, "For an improvement in glassmakers' molds: Deming Jarves." It is given under "American Patents" in the "Repertory of Patent Inventories," London, 1831, as follows:

"The improvement claimed is for the joining of a handle, or handles, or other similar projections, on glass cups, by pressure, at one operation, instead of attaching them to the cup after it has been blown, in the way heretofore practiced.

"The mould is to be made in the usual manner, of brass, or other suitable metal, excavations being provided for the formation of the handles. The plug or piston, which is to form the inside of the cup, is made to fit exactly into a *rim* which forms the top of the mould, so that when it is pressed down none of the fluid glass which has been put into the mould can escape at the top, but will, by the pressure, be forced into the cavities described.

"The claim is to the forming the mould in the manner above indicated."

This is the patent containing the word "rim" that was later, possibly, to become known as the "ring." The term "rim" was first used, so far as I have been able to learn by Henry Whitney and Enoch Robinson of Cambridge, Mass., in their patent for glass knobs. It would appear that infringements on these early patents did not entail the expensive long-drawn-out litigation of today for in 1830, just four years later than their patent, Jarves was using the word "rim" in describing a part of his patent for forming handles on cups.

The interest in the rim or ring has come about because of the crudeness of the edges of the earliest pressed glass plates, giving the impression that there was no ring or rim to control the thickness. Plates and various dishes are found with the edge a quarter-inch thick on one side and a half-inch thick on the other side of the same article. There were always three parts * to the early mold press, but the relative thickness depended on how straight the plunger descended. If it went down straight and accurately the thickness of the article was the same throughout but if it

---

* This must be qualified to the extent of limiting it to the use of the cap ring, which seems to have been quite general by 1830.

shifted, even slightly, as it struck the disk, the result was an uneven thickness. Such pieces are encountered frequently in early Sandwich dishes which were made before the methods of pressing were perfected.

Almost all the early pressed Sandwich pieces, so eagerly sought today, show imperfections which to my mind are interesting historically. They are the defects of their period and collectors should prize these specimens precisely for the marks that reveal how quickly the industry developed with us. The following characteristic indications of age in the early pressed glass made at Sandwich during a period when molds and machinery for making such ware were in their infancy are as follows:

1. Thick, heavy pieces, ¼ inch to ½ inch thick, caused by over-filling of molds.
2. Dishes or cup plates, uneven in thickness from plunger not descending evenly.
3. Cup plates or dishes in which the mold did not fill, leaving smooth, round edge or also in handles, a space which did not fill.
4. Surface ruptures or hairlines, often noted on cup plates.
5. Fins, resulting from molds not meeting snugly.
6. Blurred surfaces, caused by excess heat. This would occur in pieces made after 1836.

All of the above indicate inadequate skill in working methods or crudeness of operation before the art of pressing glassware was perfected.

In the minutes of a meeting held on September 20, 1855, we find reference to a patent dispute, covering the processing of hollow glass knobs, silvered on the inside, sealed or unsealed, used for drawers or doors. This patent was originally taken out by the New England Glass Company but the Boston & Sandwich Glass Company, despite the close relationship of the two, infringed upon this patent and, finally, through devious technicalities continued the manufacture of the knobs. This item, however, was of relatively small moment in the over-all picture.

A letter from the Company files outlining an accepted proposal for the manufacture of iridescent glass and the necessary patent is given below:

Philadelphia, March 12, 1878, addressed to Mr. Fessenden:

Dear Sir: Not having heard from you in reply to my last, I suppose your Board of Directors has not met yet to consider my proposition in reference to the irridescent glass. I would suggest the following: The Company to pay me $1000 in cash, $250 at once on receipt of agreement and balance in one, two and three months, after having learned the mode of producing the glass and 5% to be paid for royalty on all sales and shipments of this kind of glass made by you. Messrs Caldwell & Co. on Chestnut Street have lately received a lot from England which looks very beautiful and sells fast at high figures. Wine glass and decanters and all bar goods look well and colored wines and liquors add to the brilliancy of the irridescent colors. I hope you will be able to arrange matters satisfactory for me. The chemist who arranged with me for the right for this country, also sold the right for England to Webb & Sons, Salviati in Venice and two or three parties in Bohemia and Germany. Shall be pleased to hear from you at an early day and remain,

Yours truly,

W. A. H. Schreiber.

It is of great interest to find that George Fessenden gained access to various glass houses in Europe. A letter from Mr. Rogers, written in Brussels under date of May 12, 1869, indicates the importance of Mr. Fessenden's search. To quote: "Mr. Fessenden is more astonished than I am at what he sees and finds. There are many new articles that the company can get up at the cheap rate with the improvements he is finding out and with which other companies cannot compete. He will also get new styles, patterns, etc."

Only a few months later George Fessenden assigned a patent

to the Boston & Sandwich Glass Co. for improvement in molds for glass from gas carbon for which the company paid him $4,500.

In the confusion which followed in the wake of the Civil War business was, of course, greatly affected. Taxation had increased tremendously and the Eastern factories were beginning to feel even more grievously the threats of Midwestern competition. Accordingly, the pressing need for improvement in methods and reduction of operating costs.

Chapter V

FIRST TYPES OF GLASS PRODUCED

Among the earliest records of the types of glassware Jarves was making at Sandwich is that contained in his letter reproduced in the preceding chapter, under date of November, 1825, some four months after the factory started operation. In this letter he mentions tulip-shaped lamp globes and illustrates different shapes, including a modified tulip and a round one. Also cylinder "Rose feet" lamps, salts in crystal and blue, "pint taper tumbers" and "two-ring decanters." He went into specific detail on the lamp globes as to shape and dimensions and accompanied his instructions with pen line sketches. He further added that there would be a demand for "flint wines" in the Spring.

Also under date of November, 1825, an advertisement by Deming Jarves appeared in the Boston *Columbian Centennial,* as follows:

The inscriber informs his friends and the public that his Flint Glass Manufactory in Sandwich is now in full operation and is ready to receive and execute orders for any article in that line—particularly Apothecaries, Chemical and Table Wares, also Chandeliers for Churches and Halls, Vase and Mantel Lamps, Lamp Glasses, and all other articles usually made in similar establishments, and on as favorable terms.

Orders directed to Sandwich, Mass. will receive prompt attention.

DEMING JARVES

Since he was sole owner of this enterprise, Jarves simply signed his name to the advertisement. At the New England Glass Company he signed it "Agent," as he did later at Sandwich when the company was reorganized and incorporated the following Spring.

The first account book of the factory, now in the possession of

Henry Ford, deals with expenses, but a few items of glassware are mentioned incidentally. Dated April 1, 1826, is a bill for "decanters" and "inks" and in July 1826 are mentioned "Ship Tumblers." In November 1827 are listed "Essence Vials" and "English Tumblers" and in May 1829 appears a bill to Jarves for "bottles." It would appear that the earliest articles produced were those which were most in demand for everyday purposes, such as various types of lamps, globes ("Liverpool lamp glasses"), salts, inks, decanters, pharmaceutical supplies in the way of blown medicine bottles and tumblers of all sorts for use in bar rooms, ships, hotels, etc. Pedestals were manufactured extensively, both blown and pressed, as standards for lamps. According to William E. Kern's account book, the following items were made on July 30, 1825, which would bear out the items mentioned in Deming Jarves' letter:

"Chamber and high blown stem lamps, lamps on foot, peg lamps." During the next few months were produced "Six-inch round dishes, heavy plain inks, button-stem short lamps, moulded salts for cutting, moulded mustards, Liverpool lamp glasses, small and large rose foot lamps, oval moulded 9-inch dishes, tulip lamp glasses, cylinder lamp glasses, flint licquieurs, cologne bottles, flint champagnes, 5-inch moulded patty pans, center dishes, 38-pound bowls, 21½-pound bowls and bird boxes."

The "moulded" glass referred to above plays such an important part in present-day collecting that it is treated at length in the chapter entitled "Blown Molded" ("three mold") glass.

In the same account book, dated Nov. 4, 1826 are listed "Lafayette chamber cylinder lamps" and "Lafayette lamps" and on March 9, 1827 are listed "7 Lafayette salts, $1.16" (Illustrated in the chapter on Salts). The trade name of Lafayette being used on several items is either indicative of Lafayette's popularity in this country as a result of his visit in 1825 or else Jarves may have found it a profitable name for a popular export item.

Cup plates are first mentioned in this record on April 20, 1827, and were listed as Number 1, Number 2 and Number 3—which leaves us without a clue as to the pattern. They are priced at 4c., 5c. and 6c. each which strengthens the feeling so often expressed that pressed glass was cheap glass.

Apparently some of the earliest glass for cutting was made by Sandwich as early as 1825, for it may be noted by the reference to the "moulded salts for cutting." Among my fragments are flint diamond cut pieces, similar to contemporaneous English and Irish types. It was a surprise to find fragments of pressed diamond-shaped pedestal feet for salts, exactly like many Continental styles. Apparently these types were soon discontinued in favor of simpler pressed paneled, footed salts, so often found in brilliant sapphire blue, deep amethyst, emerald greens and the hues of which Jarves was particularly fond. These salts undoubtedly preceded the first stippled or "lacy" types. The periods of the manufacture of the different styles of the early wares so overlap that fixing exact dates is an extremely hazardous venture. It is possible to approximate the time with some accuracy by studying not only the piece but also the exact spot where the corroborative fragments were found. Haphazard excavations afford too slight a basis for dogmatic assertions. For really valuable information we are indebted to Mr. Francis Wynn of Sandwich. Because of his painstaking, systematic excavations it is possible today to learn much of the history of glassmaking at Sandwich and to correct some of the many errors incurred by the earlier writers as well as dealers and collectors who, to be fair, could not tell at the time what secrets had lain buried in the earth for decades.

Chapter VI

THE MIDDLE YEARS
1840–1858

The middle years at the Boston & Sandwich Glass Company, or from 1840 to 1858, when Deming Jarves severed his connection with the concern, were fruitful years, marked by action and progress. It was a well-knit and cohesive organization with Jarves at the helm. Jarves' own letter of review approximating this period is quite valuable to the historian, so the substance of it is related herewith. It was in December of 1852 that Jarves submitted this letter for the information of the stockholders, who, he said, deserved to be acquainted with the condition of the factory.

Mr. Jarves related that in 1836 an attempt was made to increase the capital of the Company to $100,000 but the mode adopted failed. The storm of adversity the following year prostrated the concern and the capital of the Company was reduced by various losses to leave little over $100,000. From that period to 1847 the Company labored under many adverse circumstances but were enabled to replace all the lost capital. They reduced the cost of real estate and machinery, and added a new pot and clay building. From 1845 to 1848 the demand for their glass increased beyond their ability to supply the wants of their customers. It was also believed a more convenient and better method could be adopted to enable the Company, by labor-saving machinery and improvements in the real estate, to manufacture glass at less cost. A course of improvement was then adopted. From year to year various improvements were introduced, costly machinery erected so as to completely renovate and rebuild part of the factory and place it in complete working order. In 1840 the real estate of the Company stood on the books at a cost of $95,000, tools at $32,000. Since that period there has been added to the machinery alone not less than $50,000 and the real estate more than doubled, which was paid for by the profits and the original cost more than annihilated. Notes receivable were $195,104. On the same day their notes receivable on hand amounted to $105,380; bills receivable, $116,907; glass in agents' hands, sold or unsold, $190,000; reserve fund $60,000.

Now that perspective has been gained through Deming Jarves' eyes the significant events of each year are worthy of examination.

In the year 1840, prosperous times were rapidly approaching. The paid in capital stock of the Company was $220,400. The factory was undergoing improvements. A year later, despite moneys spent for items such as a new furnace, the paid in capital stock by May 1841 had increased to $293,850.

Building and improving, the Company was anxious to produce glass that would attract and meet popular demand, at the same time showing a good net profit at the end of the year. Dividends would prove to the stockholders that their trust had not been misplaced. Through good times and adversity their average was more than good, even though an occasional dividend was necessarily passed.

Excerpts from records of the company at this particular period in the history of the Boston & Sandwich Glass Company will assist in conveying a more realistic picture of the times, the Company's affairs and working conditions.

June 7, 1841—Joshua Crane was elected President of the Boston & Sandwich Glass Company for the ensuing year.

October 13, 1841—At a special meeting, it was voted "That the vote which prohibited the selling of goods to the trade at Mobile and Augusta be rescinded." Also, "Voted, that the Treasurer be requested to pay Mr. Jarves for the brick used at Sandwich for the Pot House, furnished by Mr. Jarves at Boston prices." Note the widespread sales of glass even reaching into the South— we know of New Orleans as an outlet, too.

January 3, 1842—A new Board of Directors was chosen with Joshua Crane, President; Samuel Hunt, Clerk; Richard Fay,

Treasurer; Deming Jarves, Andrew T. Hall, Samuel Quincy, Directors.

September 26, 1842—Voted, "In concurrence with the New England Glass Company, that from and after January 1 next, no discount on any one sale of glass made by the Company or any of its Agents, shall be made unless the sale and delivery at one time shall amount to twenty dollars." The Agent was instructed to send a printed circular in regard to the above vote to each one of the trade in the city. Also, at this time it was voted that the company would sell Mr. Deming Jarves, unless otherwise ordered, the following articles: Lamp glasses, shades and lantern glasses at twenty cents for the carton; bottles, being of two gatherings, twenty-five cents per carton. The cutting to be charged at the rate of fifty per cent on the amount, subject to usual discount of credit.—Jarves apparently had a profitable side line in his merchandising activities.

At this same date, it was voted that the Agent be directed to put the Furnace into full operation, provided the reduction in wages submitted at this meeting, could be carried into effect.

January 24, 1843—Salaries of some of the officers of the Company, were reduced. A committee on retrenchment was appointed to ascertain if any further reduction or saving could be made in the compensation the company was paying for labour and services, or for lead, ash or fuel or saving in any department of the manufactory.—Here we have a cycle of depression in the company affairs.

The Agent, in concurrence with the Agent of the New England Glass Company, was authorized to have a public sale of 1,000 to 1,500 packages of glass, to be held the following March. This procedure afforded a means of disposing of surplus—though hardly a profitable one.

May, 1843—A three percent dividend was declared.

June, 1843—In a report of company affairs, the paid-in capital stock was $300,000 and the amount of all debts due, totalled $90,535.19.

September, 1843—Deming Jarves suggested the workmen at the factory be allowed some portion of their salary during a time when the furnace was stopped for repair. It was voted to allow them a quarter of their usual pay, amounting to $643.90, for which the workmen in turn would endeavor by greater diligence and attention in increasing the quantity and quality of their work, to thereby reimburse the company. [Interesting as an example of benevolence—Jarves undoubtedly had inspired a high degree of cooperation among the workers. Today such a gesture on the part of management might well go unrewarded.]

January 11, 1844—It was voted to lease a new company store, the rental not to exceed $1,500 per year. After some discussion by the Directors, it was agreed that Mr. Jarves erect two stores on Federal Street, Boston, to be rented to the Company at $1,600 per year, the Company to pay the taxes. [Jarves was an entrepreneur of no mean ability—his interests were far beyond our usual concept of a general manager.]

February 27, 1844—Mr. Jarves was authorized to erect a furnace at the Factory for the manufacture of lead, for the use of the Company. Mr. Jarves was further authorized to erect a small furnace at the factory for the manufacture of colored glass. **Mr.** Jarves was also authorized to regulate the rate of wages to the cutters.

A letter was read by the President from Mr. Jarves, notifying him of his intention to resign the Agency of the Company at an early day.

It was voted once more than Mr. Jarves' letter be referred to the next Board of Directors. Apparently the affairs of the Company were not being run in accordance with his ideas. Certainly there must have been considerable friction, as he had signified his intention of resigning several times before.

June 3, 1844—It was decided to have monthly meetings of the Board of Directors, instead of the usual annual meeting, plus the special meetings.

The annual statement of the Boston & Sandwich Glass Company

as of May 1844 declared a capital stock paid-in of $300,000 and all debts amounted to $95,090.

June 17, 1844—A letter from the stockholders to the Directors was read at a monthly meeting, on the subject of the affairs of the Company, relating to the present price of glass and inquiring if changes could not be made to promote the general interest of the concern and if this could not be effected, whether it would not be for the interest of all concerned to stop the works and wind up the business.

The communication was referred to a committee of three, to confer with other companies upon the subject of an advance on the prices of glass and to report thereon. Even as in our day stockholders laid down the law to the Directors. Apparently the business depression was still a serious matter.

July 1, 1844—A very important meeting was held, which was attended by a special committee of three from the New England Glass Company to consider steps to be taken in order to satisfy the stockholders of both companies in reply to letters addressed to each on June 17th, asking for some kind of action.

The committee from the New England Glass Company was composed of J. N. Howe, Jr., James Langley and James Ellison. The Sandwich factory committee included Deming Jarves, William Carleton and Joseph Hay.

The subject of the two communications signed by a number of the stockholders of each Company and addressed to the Directors of the New England Glass Company and to the Directors of the Boston & Sandwich Glass Company, calling the attention of each Board of Directors to the present reduced price of their manufactured goods, and inquiring, if by concert of action between the two companies, prices could not be advanced, etc., was laid before the committee and they unanimously recommended to the Directors of the two Companies that they adopt the following regulations to govern their Agents in the sale of their manufactured goods:

Article First

From and after July 1, 1844, all sales of glassware shall be made at net prices and no discount or commission allowed on sale made by either Company on any pretense, or for any consideration whatever, excepting to the present acknowledged Agents of the Companies, viz: T. D. Moore & Company, William M. Muzzy, T. D. Hastings, A. Edwards, Sheffield & Company, Field & Company, or any other established by the vote of the Directors of either company.

Article Second

No longer credit than six months is to be allowed to any purchaser, and all purchases are to be settled for on the same time; or, five percent discount for the cash in lieu of the six months credit, if paid within 15 days can be allowed and, when any purchaser declines or neglects so to settle, no further credit is to be given till he or they comply with the above.

Article Third

No sales to be made at prices less than heretofore and the Agents of the two Companies shall, from time to time, consult together for the purpose of advancing the prices of such articles as they may deem expedient, and prices so agreed upon and mutually signed shall be subject to all the pains and penalties of the *Fifth Article.*

Article Fourth

To protect the Companies from misrepresentations of purchasers if a charge is made of underselling, or if any violation of these *Articles* is made known to either Agent, it is his duty to inform the other of the charge and the name of the person who makes it, so that a free investigation may be had either by the Agents or by the committee, as provided in the *Fifth Article.* And it shall be no justification for the infringement in any way of this agreement, or any part thereof, that the Act complained of was committed from ignorance, or by clerks, or persons in the employ of the company.

Article Fifth

That the Agents of the two Companies each give a bond to conform to this agreement, and carry the same fully into effect, and for any violation of the same, to forfeit not less than Fifty, nor more than Five hundred dollars to be determined by a committee of two or more, one-half to be chosen by each Company.

Article Sixth

When either Company wishes to dispose of glass at auction, due notice shall be given the other, that they may join in the same.

Article Seventh

As it is desirable that the Agents shall do all in their power to promote the interest of the Companies, it shall be fully understood and agreed by them, that, if either Agent or any one in their employment buys or sells glassware on his own account or for others, he is to be bound by this agreement and subject to the same forfeitures as are provided for between the two Companies.

Article Eighth

It is agreed that this agreement shall continue in force, until notice in writing, of one month shall be given by one Board of Directors to the other of its desire to withdraw from it, which notice shall be signed by the Clerk of the Company, and at the expiration of one month, from the date of said notice, this agreement to be considered annulled.

The monthly meetings were to be held between the 15th and 20th day of each month.

An interesting example of price fixing and a practice of collusion which is frowned upon today!

This agreement was duly drawn up and signed by all members

of the two committees. From the nature of the statements in the articles, it must be deduced that certain objectionable practices had gone on, which may have been the cause, at least in part, of Mr. Jarves' decision to resign. He finally drew up his own set of rules and regulations.

In October, 1844, it was voted to restore in full those salaries which were reduced 20 percent during less favorable times. At this meeting, the subject of Mr. Jarves' letter dated May 28, 1844, resigning his Agency was taken up, and it was voted that the same be referred to a committee of three, to confer with him on the subject of his letter and to request him to continue the Agency for the present and to report thereupon. Mr. Crane, Mr. Hay and Mr. Carleton were chosen. It was also voted, that the same committee of three be instructed to inquire into the expediency of changing the location of the factory, at some future time.

October 18, 1844—Mr. Jarves was authorized to make such alterations in the ash furnace as he may deem necessary or to erect another furnace. Mr. Jarves was also authorized to engage the services of Mr. Palgemyer (spelling impossible to decipher accurately) to manufacture colored glass at a salary of $1,200 per annum, on such terms and time as he may think expedient.

January 21, 1845—Letters were received from several of the Southern agents pertaining to regulation of the prices on the glassware. Improvements continued to be made in the factory property such as woodwork painted in the buildings and Company owned houses—a new fireproof brick building was erected for the storage of glassware and materials.

June 2, 1845—A fishing expedition was planned for June or July in Boston Bay, and the stockholders were invited as well as anyone else deemed proper by the committee.

In 1845, the capital stock paid-in was $300,000.

January 30, 1846—A letter was laid before the meeting, from persons engaged in the glass trade in Boston, requesting the Company to take into consideration the expediency of discontinuing the retail part of the business from their store in Federal Street.

The Agent was authorized to install a ten pot furnace, to replace an eight pot one.

It was also voted that the Treasurer procure for John Lebuce a letter of credit on London for two thousand pounds sterling, to be used by him for the benefit of the company, if necessary, during his intended tour of Europe.

The Company affairs were in a slightly improved condition, as a 5 per cent dividend was declared.

November 2, 1847—The Agent was ordered to have a ground plan of the land in the vicinity of the Manufactory made, showing the buildings thereon, for the use of the Directors.

December 14, 1847—It was decided to erect a new building for a mixing house, machine shop, etc., to be erected in the Spring.

January 26, 1848—It was voted to sell land owned by the Company in St. Louis, Mo., at $1400.00.

April 17, 1848—Capt. Stutson resigned his position, to take place in July. Resignation was accepted. Later he reconsidered and retained his position.

May 25, 1848—Voted to erect a new building for the manufacture of glass.

June 27, 1848—Mr. Jarves was authorized to take appropriate measures, at the joint expense of the company and others interested, in the patent of stoppers purchased of Mr. Dillaway, and to secure the Company's right under the same and engage counsel to prosecute it.

The Company purchased land, and built a wharf at Cohasset Narrows in order to facilitate freight shipments by the newly-built Cape Cod Branch Railroad. Several meetings were held to discuss terms. Mr. David Greenough, Esq., and Deming Jarves represented the Boston & Sandwich Glass Company.

October 27, 1848—A quantity of glass was sent to New Orleans to be sold.

November 29, 1848—The Directors proceeded to Sandwich to inspect the new Laboratory building, which was nearly completed.

Meetings were held to inspect and discuss some lead purchased from Sturbridge, which proved to be bad.

February 14, 1849—Mr. Jarves was authorized to purchase a suitable vessel for the use of the Company to run between Cohasset Narrows and Southern ports.

January 2, 1849—Trouble developed over some patents, priority on which was claimed by Mr. Jarves.

March 16, 1849—The death of the President, Mr. Joshua Crane, was announced. Mr. Joseph Hay was appointed to his place—*pro tem.*

March 1849—At a meeting, Mr. Jarves was authorized to make such arrangements as would be necessary to carry freight from the wharf at Cohasset Narrows to New York and elsewhere.

July 10, 1849—*Voted,* not to subscribe to stock of the Cape Cod Branch Railroad.

The Boston & Sandwich Glass Company decided to sell their land at Cohasset Narrows to the Cape Cod Branch Railroad.

January 1, 1850—It was brought to the attention of the Directors of the Company that their small furnace was so burned out that it consumed an extra quantity of fuel, and it was recommended a new eight pot furnace be put in, as large as the cone would admit, without delay. Also, that measures be taken to enlarge the X furnace as, when the present one was put in, in 1845, the cone was not of a capacity to receive a furnace as large as required and from motives of economy, the furnace was reduced to fit the cone, but this proved to be a bad mistake. The cone should have been taken down and a larger one erected. It was recommended that it be done as soon as circumstances admit and, as it was very desirable to reduce the height of the furnace to save fuel, it was proposed to have the pillows of the cone braced by iron standards. It was voted to proceed with these recommendations.

Of more than passing interest is a letter Jarves wrote to the executive committee, describing in minute detail his experiments with every form of coal in order to determine which would be most economical for the factory use. His thoroughness and careful attention to every detail were outstanding and served to establish him firmly as a man who was meticulous to the nth degree.

February 19, 1850—A regular monthly meeting of the Board of Directors was held. Principal discussion concerned the sales of Company goods by Agents in other cities. New York Agent's sales totalled $74,477.48; Philadelphia Agent, $36,103.04, and Baltimore, $30,019.36. It was figured that the loss in goods sold in New York was 22%; in Philadelphia, 25⅓%, and Baltimore sales broke even.

Regular Meeting, March 20, 1850.

Trouble with the Cape Cod Branch Railroad appeared imminent, though the directors voted to attempt to make them come to terms by friendly means, if possible. It was voted to refer all matters relating to the freight on the railroad to Mr. Jarves, with full authority to manage and regulate the same.

At this meeting, mention was made that the new eight pot furnace had been installed and recommendations were made for alterations in the annealing kilns and that the walls be extended to give more room.

April 30, 1850—At a meeting of the Directors Mr. Jarves presented a letter received by him from the President of the New England Glass Company, regarding certain patents used by the respective companies. This matter was referred to a committee of three, consisting of Greenough, Fenno and Carleton, to report a course of action on the above communication.

May 17, 1850—It was voted that $18,000 be appropriated for dividends and that a 3 percent dividend be declared payable on the following Monday, the 8th day of July.

May 22, 1850—At a special meeting held at the house of Mr. Sewall Fessenden in Sandwich, Greenough and Carleton were chosen a committee with full powers, to negotiate and purchase a piece of land adjoining the factory belonging to Mr. Jarves, if they could agree to terms. Also, the committee was to proceed to Cohasset Narrows and examine the wharf property there, with reference to extending the same.

June 1, 1850—A revised set of By-Laws for the Company were adopted.

June 4, 1850—A notice was published in the Sandwich *Observer,* that the paid-in capital stock of the Company was $300,000 and all debts due it amounted to $44,716.49.

July 2, 1850—It was voted to purchase an additional piece of land adjoining the Company land at Sandwich, from Mr. Jarves at $2,000.00.

July 9, 1850—The Agent and Treasurer were authorized to continue the present arrangement with the Barnstable Bank for the loan of $6,000.00 and $3,000.00 from the Falmouth Bank, and to reduce such loans from time to time, as the same become due.

It was voted at this same meeting that the Treasurer be authorized to borrow from time to time, until the next annual meeting, upon the Company's note, in addition to the sum borrowed of the Barnstable and Falmouth banks, such sums not to exceed $20,000.

September 25, 1850—Mr. Jarves informed the Directors that it would be inexpedient to let their X furnace run out, for the purpose of erecting a larger one, on account of his inability to supply the orders of the customers, but he would recommend that a new cone furnace be built, south of the present X furnace, and the glass house be enlarged for that purpose. It was voted that the Agent be requested to take measures at once to carry these recommendations into effect. The Agent was authorized to further extend the west wall of the X glass house, to give sufficient room for a lear for the furnace now being erected.

January 10, 1851—At a regular meeting, the Directors decided to have their annual dinner on Wednesday the 15th, and that the President and Clerk be a committee to carry the same into effect, and to invite the company usually asked on that occasion.

May 22, 1851—A meeting of the Directors was held this evening at the house of Mr. Fessenden in Sandwich at 8 P.M. Mr. Greenough stated to the meeting that there was a piece of ground now in the market that bounded the southern part of the Company land which was very desirable to have, if it could be purchased at a reasonable price, as it would hereafter prevent others building too near the Company's premises. It was voted to purchase this land at not more than $1,000.00. Greenough and Carleton were chosen a committee to make the above purchase.

It appears that accounts on the Company books against Church and Munroe were next taken up and it was voted that the account of Mr. Church should be made out on the terms agreed upon by the committee with him. If he does not cooperate, his account is to be placed in the hands of the Company's attorney for collection. It was also voted that a demand be made on Mr. Munroe to refund the amount charged to him on the books of the Company and, if he does not agree to an adjustment, he also will be sued.

February 13, 1852—Apparently more trouble was brewing between the Cape Cod Branch Railroad and the Company. The railroad's freight rates were so high that Mr. Jarves was authorized to pay one dollar per ton for Company freight, as well as other merchandise, to be transported by water on condition that the Company's freight in all cases was to have preference.

March 20, 1852—At a special meeting, Mr. Jarves was authorized to take such measures as he might think proper, to protect the rights of the Company and to prevent a Mr. Shivereck * from taking out a patent for the Company's method of supplying rosin to the furnace. It was also voted that Mr. Jarves be authorized to discharge Mr. Shivereck when he deemed it expedient.

April 3, 1852—Mr. Jarves was authorized to continue his credits to certain customers in California and to appoint R. Swain & Company, Agent in San Francisco.

May 19, 1852—Mr. Jarves was authorized to sell the stock of the Cape Cod Branch Railroad owned by the Company at such price as he may deem proper, and that $500.00 reduction be made in this stock and the same carried to the debit of Profit and Loss.†

* Mr. Shivereck had sent a communication to the Boston & Sandwich Glass Company, saying he intended to take out this patent.

† At a previous meeting (July 10, 1849), it was voted not to purchase stock in this railroad, but the company did so later.

Excerpts from the Company letters, which were held intact by the Treasurer, as well as those taken from the Minutes of the meetings, have been chosen as being most representative of the growth and progress of the company. Extracts cited deal largely with the first hints of trouble in the ranks of labor, as well as the difficulties presented by a suit brought against the Company regarding a patent infringement by the New England Glass Company. Among the excerpts from the records of Trustees' meetings are the following:

June 7, 1853—The Treasurer was authorized to borrow, as needed, a sum not to exceed $25,000.00 over the period of the ensuing year for the use of the Company's obligations. It was also voted, that in the future, no bills be paid, either at the Company store or at the factory in Sandwich, unless first approved by Mr. Jarves and that the Clerk furnish a copy of this vote to the Bookkeeper of the Company store in Boston and to the Manufactory in Sandwich.

October 11, 1852—An invitation was extended from the Board of Directors of the Boston & Sandwich Glass Company to the President and Directors of the New England Glass Company, to visit the Company's works at Sandwich on the 27th and dine with them on that day.

November 13, 1852—A very important meeting was held by the Directors at the office of the Treasurer at 75 State Street, Boston. The President, Joseph Hay, presided. The following preamble and votes were offered by the President and unanimously adopted:

"The Directory of the Boston & Sandwich Glass Company have been proud of the high reputation which the men in the Company's employ have, as a Body, heretofore sustained.

"The reputation and prosperity of the Company are dependent, in no small degree, upon the reputation and prosperity of the workmen. The misconduct and evil example of a few individuals bring reproach upon the whole body of operatives. One Black Sheep spoils the flock!

"The Directors are bound to protect the reputation of the Company and the workmen from the injury occasioned by the bad character and conduct of the individual in their employ. They have no wish to attempt the exercise of any unnecessary control over the personal habits of the men—to say what they shall eat or drink, but they are determined to protect the interests of the Stockholders and not to retain in their employment any whose habits are bringing disgrace upon the Establishment, unfitting them for the skillful performance of labor or obstructing the labor of others.

"Therefore, it is unanimously Voted:—That the Agent of the Boston & Sandwich Glass Company be, and he is hereby instructed and directed, to discharge from the Company's employment unconditionally, any person or persons, whatever position they may occupy, who, after due notice given, and reasonable time for amendment allowed, by the habitual or occasional use of intoxicating drinks, unfit themselves for the proper discharge of their duty, or interfere in any way with the discharge of the duty of others.

"Voted:—That this vote be printed and a copy placed in the hands of every workman in the Company employ.

"Voted:—That the Agent be authorized to take immediate measures to introduce gas into the Factory, by procuring the necessary apparatus for that purpose.

"Voted:—That the Agent be authorized to enclose the open ground in front of the Factory with an iron fence.

"Voted—That the Agent be instructed to fill up the vacant land on the South side of the Factory and prepare the same for the location of another furnace, as soon as it can be conveniently effected."

At a special meeting on October 21, 1851, the Directors of the Boston & Sandwich Glass Company decided that it had become difficult to comply with the agreements they signed with the New England Glass Company, June 29, 1844, and it was voted that the Boston & Sandwich Glass Company serve notice on the New

England Glass Company that they desired to withdraw from the agreements. These were entered into after a petition, signed by the stockholders in both Companies, was sent to Directors of both Companies that the prices on their glasswares were too low. Eight articles of agreement were thereupon entered into, governing the manufacture, sales and prices of both Companies' wares, and placing restrictions on the activities of the Agents of each company. The Eighth Article included a stipulation that the agreements could be terminated at any time on a thirty-day notice.

February 26, 1853—Capital stock of the Boston & Sandwich Glass Company was increased $100,000.00.

May 14, 1853—Mr. Hay and Mr. Carleton were chosen as a committee to arrange for the rental of the new Boston store between the Company and the firm of Jarves & Cormerais. (The Jarves referred to was George Jarves, another son of Deming Jarves.)

May 18, 1853—A special meeting was held at the home of Sewall Fessenden in Sandwich and the subject of putting up a gas works to light the factory was fully discussed.

June 6, 1853—Deming Jarves served notice on the Company that, in the future, he must charge a commission of one percent for personally endorsing Company notes, which covered the provision of the money for their pay roll. For many years he had performed this service free of charge.

November 9, 1853—A meeting was held at which Mr. Holbrook was elected new Clerk *pro tem.* (Samuel Hunt, the faithful clerk who had recorded all the meetings of the Company from the date of its formation, had passed away.)

Nov. 26, 1853 the Clerk of the Company wrote the Cape Cod Railroad that notice be given to the Cape Cod Railroad Company of the intention of the Boston & Sandwich Company to terminate any and all contracts with said Railroad Co. for the conveyance of merchandise of the corporation on the first day of July, 1853. [This is significant since it portends the decline of the Company's dependence on the Cape Cod Railway.]

November 26, 1853—Mr. Greenough was duly voted in as Clerk of the Company. A committee of two was also appointed to make arrangements for securing the services of John Jarves, as head of the laboratory department.

December 17, 1853—At a meeting of the Board of Directors, it was decided that the Boston & Sandwich Glass Company and the firm of Jarves and Cormerais, should each pay one-half the rent and taxes of the new store in Boston, and that they would share equally the expense of fitting the place up. (In view of later developments, this decision had an important bearing.) It was likewise voted that John Jarves be paid a salary of $44.00 per year.

It was also voted that Mr. Deming Jarves be authorized and requested to take measure for the erection of a new glass house and furnace, to be in readiness for use in season, or to take the place of any one which may be required to "let out."

February 25, 1854—It was ordered, "that all Officers and Agents at the factory be notified that no person is authorized to employ or dismiss another, or to make any purchases or contracts on behalf of the Corporation, or in any way to bind the Corporation, without instructions from the Agent; and that the Directors will insist upon the strict observance of this regulation."

May 1, 1854—At a meeting of the Board of Directors, it was voted that "whereas this Corporation is at all times ready to pay its operatives a just compensation for their labor and equal to other similar corporations, it is therefore, voted—that any combined attempt on their part to force the Corporation to increase their pay, be met by a prompt and decided refusal on the part of the Agent, and that he be authorized to allow the fires in the furnaces to be discontinued, in case of the refusal of the men to work at reasonable prices."

Labor troubles had begun.

At the same time an important change in the by-laws was made to read as follows: "Meetings of the Board of Directors shall be called at the request of any member thereof, by personal or written notice from the Clerk, and any three of the Directors shall constitute a quorum for the transactions of business at any meeting of the Directors duly notified."

July 20, 1854, Deming Jarves wrote the Directors that they were all well acquainted with the great advance of price in labor and materials used in the factory equal to $65,000 to $70,000 per year over the cost of 18 years ago, since to produce the same weight of glass was equal to a 15% advance over regular selling prices. To overcome this by advancing prices had given him undue anxiety and solicitude. He had made every effort in his power to obtain prices corresponding to the advance in his raw materials but little as yet had been done. He asked that a committee be appointed to examine the subject. The salesmen could give them all the information they needed. He said it is an evil surrounded with difficulty for, if we reduce our factory to three furnaces, we add much to the expense of the remaining three, although the stock at the time was large enough to handle all sales. He said, in all probability they would have to sell at a loss the production of nearly one furnace, which might not yield the cost of the articles and it was not desirable to leave the field to their competitors. He said by reducing the Manufactory to three furnaces, no doubt the product could be disposed of at private sale and auction sales avoided. Jarves then solicited advice and directions.

July 22, 1854—It was resolved, that, in the opinion of the Board, it was for the interest of the corporation that the Agent should meet the market in regard to prices. This decision was not a helpful one for Jarves.

November 21, 1854—The Agent, Mr. Jarves, suggested that the factory produce more small articles and fewer large ones!

February 24, 1855—The Treasurer stated that the Company had $5,995 in bills of the Shipbuilders Bank of Rockland, Maine, which had failed. It was voted that Mr. Greenough proceed to Rockland, investigate the affairs of the bank and sell the bills, if a satisfactory price could be obtained.

March 12, 1855—Mr. Greenough reported he had been to Rockland, had seen the receivers of the Shipbuilders Bank and that they

declined to give any opinion of the value ~~of the bills or any infor-~~
mation as to the assets of the bank. One of the receivers was
willing to pay 25 percent of the value, which Mr. Greenough
declined. So he returned to Sandwich with all the bills intact!

April 20, 1855—A committee was ordered appointed to inquire
and report whether the Company be under any obligation in regard
to the education of persons in its employ.

At the same meeting, a communication from Causten Browne,
attorney for the New England Glass Company, was presented
alleging an infraction of their patent by the Boston & Sandwich
Glass Company in the manufacture and sale of hollow glass,
silver-lined knobs, and threatening a suit if this continued. Mr.
Greenough was instructed to investigate and report whether the
Company was liable for any such infringement.

May 3, 1855—At a Directors' meeting, Mr. Greenough reported
that the Company was under no obligation in regard to the education of any persons in its employ, except such as might be contained in any indentures of apprenticeship. He also reported that
the New England Glass Company had brought suits against the
Boston & Sandwich Glass Company, as threatened in the letter,
from Causten Browne. It was voted that Mr. Greenough be
authorized to retain such counsel as should be necessary to defend
this suit.

May 7, 1855—Deming Jarves sent in a written resignation from
the Company, giving as his reason, ill health. He asked to be
released from the care and responsibility attending his situation,
for he did not wish to receive compensation for services he could
not perform to the fullest extent and satisfaction of the stockholders. (See Plate 5.)

May 31, 1855—The full Board of Directors assembled at Sandwich. It was voted that the eight pot furnace be taken down and
a new ten pot furnace and cone be erected in its place. The Agent
stated that the mold room of the X house required to be enlarged,
and that the roof needed to be reshingled.

June 4, 1855—Joseph Hay was re-elected President of the company. At this time the capital stock actually assessed and paid in was $475,207.00 and all existing debts totalled $120,404.00.

July 7, 1855—It was voted that the Agent be authorized to make a consignment of glass, not exceeding $4,000.00 in value, to Callao, Peru. Also, that the Agent be authorized "to execute any and all orders for hollow silver-lined glass knobs."

Mr. Jarves once more offered his resignation, and on motion of Mr. Fessenden, it was laid upon the table. (This particular resignation may have had to do in part, with the patent litigation with the New England Glass Co.)

October 1, 1855—At a meeting of the Board of Directors, the President laid before the Board the correspondence with Mr. Cartwright, President of the New England Glass Co., in relation to their suit against the company. It was ordered that the same be entered at large upon the records, and the originals placed on file.

The question of the violation of the New England Glass Company patent rights on silver-lined knobs by the Boston & Sandwich Glass Company was apparently a tempest in a teapot so far as actual action was concerned.

The President of the New England Glass Co. wrote to Joseph Hay, of the Boston & Sandwich Glass Company on September 18, 1855, stating that the suit of his company "was brought solely to vindicate their rights to their patent, but that inasmuch as their Directors have been informed in answer to their bill, that the Boston & Sandwich Glass Company since the date of the patent, have neither made nor sold—and do not mean to make or sell any such knobs as the patent covers, the New England Glass Company Directors have full faith in this declaration and have therefore ordered their suit to be discontinued."

The above letter was handed to Mr. Greenough, who had charge of the suit, and the President of the Boston & Sandwich Glass Company asked him for a full report. It may be noted here that the Agent, Mr. Jarves, was authorized to continue producing the knobs, whereupon his resignation previously mentioned was handed in.

Mr. Greenough reported at length on the case to Mr. Hay, denying that the Boston & Sandwich Glass Company had ever stated they would discontinue making the knobs. The New England Glass Company made a court motion for an interlocutory injunction against the Boston & Sandwich Glass Company—that is, a temporary prohibition until the case should be decided.

The Boston & Sandwich Glass Company opposed the injunction for reasons contained in ten specifications which were filed with the Court. The first six denied in various forms the complainant's right to the patent, and the eighth, ninth and tenth were technical objections. The seventh objection stated, "The defendant Corporation has not manufactured or sold, since the issuing of the said letters patent, any hollow glass knobs for doors or drawers, silvered on the inside, sealed or unsealed, such as are described in said letters patent."

The Court refused the interlocutory injunction, and the action was discontinued before the time for making an answer to it arrived.

Mr. Hay replied briefly to the President of the New England Glass Company denying that the Boston & Sandwich Glass Company had made any declaration that they would not produce the knobs and that he hoped the suit would be withdrawn, but certainly not without a clear understanding of the facts of the case. Thus it appears that the Boston & Sandwich Glass Company won, on a technicality.

The circumstances surrounding Deming Jarves' resignation from the Company have been treated in the earlier chapter dealing with his life. However, to preserve the continuity of thought brief mention will be made here at the risk of repetition.

A Director of the company, one R. S. Fay, asserted that the association between the Company and the partnership of G. S. Jarves and Cormerais had, from 1854 on, cost the former "upwards of $50,000 per year." George S. Jarves was a son of Deming's. He and his partner, Henry Cormerais, acted as sales representatives, sharing a store on Federal Street in Boston. Resentment of this seemingly unjust accusation, plus failure to reconcile their opposing views, culminated in their joint severance from the company.

There were other factors which contributed to this situation. Earlier dissatisfaction on Jarves' part curtailed production, and reduced salaries—these played a part in bringing about the sad condition. The symptoms of labor trouble and dissension were becoming increasingly apparent.

The following entries taken from Minutes of the Directors' meetings make clear the difficulties under which the Company was being conducted and contribute a background out of which grew the charges of Mr. Fay.

A school was about to be opened at Sandwich and some of the apprentices wished to attend it, so it was voted that "if the plan of schooling the apprentices met the approbation of the Board, the Agent would be authorized to make the necessary arrangements for their attendance at the Corporation's expense if, upon inquiry, the School should be found to be a satisfactory one."

March 19, 1856—Application was made for a contribution to assist certain parties who had expended fifty thousand dollars to bring about a reciprocity treaty with the Canadas. It was voted that in the present depressed condition of glass manufacture, the Directors did not feel warranted in donating any money.

At this time, the Corporation did contribute two hundred and fifty dollars towards the establishment, in the town of Sandwich, of an Office of Communication with Brewer and Baldwin's "line of magnetic telegraph."

June 4, 1856—It was voted that the Agent be requested to put out the fire in furnace number 4 as soon as consistent with safety. The Agent stated that, by the extinction of furnace 4 and by the decrease in the number of moves worked at the other furnaces, the production of the factory might be reduced one-third part, without extinguishing another furnace. It was the expressed opinion of the Members of the Board, without dissent, that this should be done, but no instructions were given to the Agent.

June 30, 1856—At a meeting held this day, Mr. Jarves laid before the Board a written communication addressed to him and signed by Joseph Marsh and Charles Lapham, as a committee on behalf of the operatives employed in the larger or Upper factory. This letter was read and ordered placed on file and it was resolved —that the Board had received the communication with surprise and regret, and could not believe that it expressed, as it purported to do, the unanimous sentiment of those whom it undertook to represent. A compliance with its requisitions would take the management of the factory from those to whom the owners had committed it, and would place it in the hands of others employed and paid by the owners for a wholly different service. "The authors of a letter so extraordinary cannot fail to perceive that it must meet but one reception from the Board."

It was decided to reduce the factory to two furnaces, so that arrangements could be made for the manufacture of glass at such reduced cost as to enable the Company to sell at market prices. On June 30, 1856, the Directors of the Boston & Sandwich Glass Company were: Joseph Hay (President), Prentiss Hobbs, Deming Jarves, David Greenough, and S. R. M. Holbrook.

A considerable amount of general business was under discussion, which finally ended with the following conclusions:

"That, in view of the present depressed state of their business and the discouraging prospect for the future, [the directors] deem it their duty to reduce as much as possible the expenses of the factory, believing it to be but just that, when the stockholders are receiving no dividend, those who are attached to the factory should either produce more or receive less compensation and thus share the misfortunes of the business: Therefore, *Voted,* that all nonproducers in the employ of the Corporation who receive eight hundred dollars or more, annually, such as the Agent, the Treasurer, the Salesman, the Bookkeeper, the Superintendent at the factory, the Paymaster, the two Foremen of the glass houses and the Foreman of the cutting shop, be paid from and after this date, at a rate of ten percent discount from their present compensation, until the stockholders shall receive a dividend. Passed unanimously."

September 8, 1856—It was decided that a committee of three be appointed to meet and confer with a committee to be appointed by the New England Glass Company on the subject of auction sales by the two Corporations.

It was suggested that Mr. Jarves "work up the cave metal and coloured cullet, if he shall think it profitable to do so."

On April 2, 1857, among other resolutions, it was voted that no person in the employ of the Corporation be allowed to purchase goods of the Corporation without the knowledge and consent of the Agent.

May 3, 1857—At a meeting of the Board of Directors, the Agent (Mr. Jarves) submitted to the Board the accounts of the past year's business at the factory, showing its earnings to be $38,587.28, subject to deduction for bad debts, and about $3,200 earnings of the steamer *Acorn.*

On Monday, June 29, 1857 a long and busy meeting was held by the Board of Directors. It began by Mr. Jarves submitting a report in writing relating to the business for the past month and concluding by placing in the hands of the Directors his resignation to take effect at a future day. Before adjournment, however, he withdrew his resignation. It was *Voted,* that the subject of the Agencies in New York and Baltimore be referred to a committee of two, to consider and report at the next meeting, some improved mode of accomplishing the business.

Also *Voted* that hereafter no invoice be permitted to leave the counting room of the factory without the examination and certificate of either LaFayette Fessenden, or in his absence, Mr. Waterman.

Voted, that a trial be made of the manufacture of green glass, and that the Agent report from time to time.

It was also decided, in accordance with the recommendation of the stockholders at the last annual meeting, that Mr. Jarves be requested to transfer to the Treasurer the insurance policies held by him in favor of the Company, and that thereafter the Treasurer make out the Insurance under the advice and direction of the Board.

July 27, 1857—The most important decision at this meeting was that Mr. Jarves be instructed to close the agencies at New York and Baltimore as soon as could be done without prejudice to the interests of the Company. A letter from Jarves & Cormerais was read and decision postponed until later.

It was *Voted,* that henceforth no goods be sent to California except upon satisfactory acceptance payable in Boston or New York.

August 31, 1857, the letter from Jarves & Cormerais was taken from the table and it was *Voted,* that the same be referred to a committee of two to consider and report thereon at the next meeting. Mr. R. S. Fay and Mr. Joseph Hay were chosen for the committee.

The subject of terminating the engagement of Mr. Sewall Fessenden with the Company, as Salesman, was referred to a committee.

September 28, 1857—At this meeting Mr. Fay reported that it would not be expedient to disturb the existing arrangement with Jarves & Cormerais. He suggested that the Company dispense with the services of Mr. Sewall Fessenden.

October 26, 1857—Business at this time was apparently at a low ebb, as it was voted that the two furnaces then running be reduced to one as speedily as the Agent thought advisable and a letter was submitted from the President of the Company, recommending a reduction of salaries.

November 9, 1857—The following persons connected with the Company had their salaries reduced as follows:

S. R. M. Holbrook, Treasurer	$1,200 per year	
Deming Jarves, Agent	2,800 " "	
S. H. Fessenden, Salesman	1,200 " "	
Henry Spurr, Salesman	800 " "	

William Stutson, Factory Agent.........	800	"	"
C. C. P. Waterman, Paymaster	800	"	"
Charles Southack, Clerk (Factory).......	600	"	"

Voted, that the Company does not require the services of Mr. LaFayette Fessenden in the counting room, but have decided to pay him $400 per annum, rather than discharge him.

Voted, that F. F. Hamblin's bill for cutting, amounting to $33.22 be paid and that the Agent be instructed to inform Mr. Francis Kern that his conduct in the employment of said Hambling is regarded by the Board as unauthorized, partial and highly prejudicial to the harmony of the workshop and the interests of the Company.

Voted, that from and after December 1st, next, the salary of Mr. Francis Kern be at the rate of $500 per annum.

November 30, 1857—The Agent was authorized to contract for running the *Acorn* from Provincetown during the winter.

The solicitor reported that so much of the tax assessed by the town of Sandwich as appears to be upon "machinery, molds, patterns and stock" is illegal, and thereupon *Voted,* that the tax be paid under protest and that a suit be brought to recover all taxes illegally assessed during the past six years by the town.

April 26, 1858—Sewall H. Fessenden resigned his position as Salesman.

April 26, 1858, George Jarves and his partner wrote, "Several months since we addressed a communication to your Board in regard to a separation of the Company and ourselves, which we believe has never been acted upon. The object of this is to call your attention to the matter with a view to bring about that result at as early a date as possible." In the attempt to reconstruct the various events which took place and led up to Jarves' resignation, some notice should be made of the communications of George Jarves with the Company. Apparently they (Jarves and Cormerais) had been in the position of attempting to sever the association with the Company a considerable time previous to the charges brought by Mr. Fay. It is difficult to believe that they would have been so anxious to break off a connection which was considered by Mr. Fay to be so highly lucrative At least this point, together with various other happenings would bring one to the conclusion that a considerable element of doubt must rest in the mind of the impartial historian concerning Fay's accusations.

A communication was received from G. D. Jarves & Cormerais which was read and referred to the committee on the same subject, appointed last August 31st.

May 31, 1858—At a meeting of the Board of Directors, the usual business matters were examined and discussed. When the meeting was adjourned, it was directed that a further discussion take place at Mr. Jarves' rooms in Sandwich on Wednesday, June 2, 1858, at 8 P.M. The notice in the book of Minutes of the meetings merely read as follows:

"The Board met pursuant to adjournment, at Sandwich. Present Messrs. Hay, Jarves, Carleton, Hobbs and Greenough and continued in deliberation and discussion and examination of the affairs of the Company till midnight, when it was adjourned." (Signed) D. Greenough, Clerk.

Please note that Mr. Fay, who was instrumental in all the trouble-making, was *not* among those present.

On June 9, 1858, one week later, a meeting of the Board of Directors was held. After balloting for President, Mr. Joseph Hay was again elected. A letter from Deming Jarves containing his resignation as Agent was then read and on motion it was voted to accept it. The following letter from Jarves & Cormerais was also read:

Boston, June 9, 1858.

TO THE PRESIDENT AND DIRECTORS OF THE BOSTON & SANDWICH GLASS CO.

Gentn.

It is but justice to Mr. Jarves who has been your Agent so long—

and to myself who have been in your service so many years that some further notice should be taken of the statement of Mr. Fay— that since the year 1854 the Company had lost by their connexion with us upwards of fifty Thousand Dollars pr year. Causing it to be infer'd by the stockholders that Mr. Jarves handed over to me the best part of the orders—while I, equally dishonest appropriated the same.

If at some time when it will suit the convenience of the Directors I would like to meet the Directors at the store with a view of Examining the letters and the general way of doing business that they may understand the matter (with all deference) better than I think they now do.

I have no doubt that Mr. Fay believes such to be the fact—and— Believing it I am very glad to hear it express'd.

I wish you to believe also—that notwithstanding the Connexion is so lucrative to us in your view—I am not only satisfied but quite happy at the prospect of its severance and only look forward to its consummation amicably.

With a majority of your Board, I have but a passing acquaintance —but one recently added has known me from infancy (Mr. Francis). I am unwilling that he should believe that I have lived by fraud rather than by the sweat of my brow.

It is due to Mr. Jarves, for whatever sins of omission or commission by the firm I alone am responsible—and I alone should bear the blame from which I shall not shrink.

Very respectfly

Henry Cormerais for self and
G. S. Jarvis & Cormerais

On motion of Mr. Fay this was laid on the table until the next meeting along with a letter from the same firm, dated April 26, 1858 and produced by Mr. Hay. It was also voted that all present employees of the Company be notified to continue their present duties under the direction of the President and Treasurer and that all letters addressed to the Agent be opened by Mr. Fessenden or the Bookkeeper and disposed of as might be required.

In another ledger devoted to the Minutes of the meetings, a different picture is presented. This notice is under date of June 7th instead of June 9th, and may have been a special meeting. It states in part: "Mr. Jarves then asked permission to address the meeting as probably the last opportunity he should have and he proceeded to give a brief history of his connection with the business of the Company for thirty-two years and ended by declining the further Agency of the Company. Mr. Fay made a few remarks in reply to a portion of Mr. Jarves' address. Mr. Hay, the President, addressed a few remarks to the meeting, in further explanation of their position and of the conduct of the Directors. A long discussion of the accounts ensued, in which Mr. Cartwright, Mr. Jarves and the President took part."

July 21, 1858—A letter to Deming Jarves asked how much he wanted for the ship *Acorn*. Jarves was then out of the Sandwich Company. The writer asked the lowest cash price, time of delivery, and condition of the boiler. This ship may have been the personal property of Jarves.

Capital stock of the Company was increased $200,000, of which $192,600 was actually paid-in between the first day of March in the year 1853 and the first of July, 1855.

In the latter part of 1858, the Cape Cod Railroad agreed to transport all glass and other light freight of the Boston & Sandwich Glass Company from said Company's works in Sandwich to Boston for $1.85 per ton and all their heavy freight from Sandwich to Boston for $1.65 per ton. Packages of glass of the usual weight, 200 pounds each, or ten packages to the ton, would be transported at $1.55 per ton. The cost of transporting the Company's glass from their Wharf at Cohasset Narrows to Boston and from Sandwich to the Wharf was at 42c per ton.

The following September there was an exchange of letters between the partners Jarves and Cormerais and the Company which emphasize sharply the strange attitude taken by the latter. They read:

Reported Sept. 25, 1858.
Correspondence between Committee on separation and
Jarves & Cormerais

Copy   Boston, Sept. 7, 1858

Gent.

The Com. appointed by the Directors of the B & S Glass Co. "to
arrange terms of separation as occupiers of the store with Mess. Jarves
& Cormerais, make these propositions.

The Glass Co. will vacate the premises in the course of three mths
on condition that Mess. Jarves & Cormerais assume the whole rent &
pay to the Glass Co. one half of the value of the fixtures belonging
to both parties. Or:

The Glass Co. will assume the lease of the premises & pay to
Mess. Jarves & Cormerais one half of the value of the fixtures belonging to them jointly; the same term of three months being allowed
to obtain accomodation elsewhere.

Please reply to this note immediately & send the same to the
Firemans Insur Office.

Vy respectfully
NAT. FRANCIS
For the Committee

Mess. Jarves & Cormerais

To the Committee apointed by the Directors of the Boston and Sandwich Glass Company to arrange terms of separation with Mess.
Jarves & Cormerais.

Gentlemen:

Your note of the 7th is at hand and has received from us a thought-
ful consideration.

For you—the dissatisfied parties—who joind us after we had hired
the store—whose acts alone have rendered a separation necessary or
to be desired—to gravely present us with the option of doubling our
present expenses—or moving out of our own store at a large outlay
of time and money—and, at least double what we now pay for the
same accomodations—is to use the mildest form of expression *Very
un reasonable.*

Your propositions are therefore decidedly but most respectfully declin'd.

If the Company desire to move we shall assent on the following conditions—they to leave the fixtures until the expiration of the lease —or, until such time as we may vacate the store when you can come into the possession of your proportion.

The matter of damages to us by the non performance of your compact to be submitted to three impartial business men who shall decide whether we receive something or nothing—If the former, *how much.*

We have had and still do entertain a sincere desire to accommodate and bring the matter to a satisfactory settlement—and, will do all in our power to aid it. But, *we* have *rights* which, we think, thus far, the Company have manifested no disposition to recognize or respect.

This offer to remain open until the Eighteenth day of September— and no longer. After that date my time will be employed in my own business to such an extent as to preclude my attentions to this for several months.

Very Respectfly Your

G. S. JARVES & CORMERAIS

Nat. Francis Esq.
  Firemens Ins. Office
    Boston

Thus ended any connection with the Boston & Sandwich Glass Company by members of the Jarves family, which included Deming, père, and John and George, his sons. The most interesting glass produced at the factory was made for the most part, while Deming Jarves was the guiding genius. The most revolutionary changes in the art of glassmaking occurred while his hand was at the helm. While the Company prospered for a time after he resigned, nothing of importance happened to add to the history of the Boston & Sandwich Glass Company.

Chapter VII

LATER YEARS

1860–1888

Upon Jarves' departure from the Boston & Sandwich Glass Company, there ensued a flood of requests for increases in salary. The period was heralded by Capt. Stutson's request in 1860, with an appropriate reference to the prosperous fate of the business.

In April of 1863 Mr. Henry Spurr asked for a raise, saying that he had been with the Company since 1849 and had made only three such requests. Henry was a patient soul.

George Fessenden, in 1866, sought increment to his daily wage. He relates ingenuously that Mr. Kern left the works on the first of May without even coming near to say that he was going. Mr. Kern was very careful that he should have no information from him as to the batch he was using or where the smaller materials for coloring could be found. On the contrary he remarked to a person as he left the factory that "he had left and there is no one left behind that can keep the works going, not one that can even make a pot of 'take metal.' " In the face of all this, he, Fessenden, went into the factory, picked up the loose ends and made the glass. He says the glass was better than they had been accustomed to. The quality of the metal continued to improve, but for two or three weeks the glass "came poor and the color cordy."

In the same year, a committee was appointed to ascertain if the Boston & Sandwich Glass Company could not compete with the New England Glass Company in the manufacture of glass. The committee had several interviews with Mr. Kern on the subject who claimed that as good glass could be made at Sandwich as at East Cambridge. He accounts for the failure heretofore in the matter to the use of purchased cullet of inferior quality. The committee visited Sandwich and made a thorough examination, staying overnight in the town in order to do so. Particular attention was paid to the quality of the glass then being completed and it was their opinion that it was very nearly, if not quite, equal to the best glass made by the New England Glass Co. They reported more care had been taken in composing and mixing the batches than before and, if success continued in this respect, they would not fall much behind their competitors in quality.

On September 15, 1866, Edward Haines wrote the Directors of the Boston & Sandwich Glass Company, stating that with their permission, he would present for their consideration a picture of the difficulties going on in the factory. He related that a little more than a year ago, in the summer of 1865, there was formed a club called the Glassmakers' Protective Union. He was persuaded later to join. Subsequently the Union passed a vote to request a higher rate of pay and chose a committee to confer with Mr. Fessenden. Mr. Fessenden gave them to understand that he would do what was right. A list of every man's wages was made out and what the Company was willing to give. Haines thought it was honest and just. A meeting was called of all the men, who thereupon rejected Fessenden's offer and passed a vote demanding 15% increase, or not fill any more glass on Friday. Haines went on to say: "Gentlemen, I acknowledge that after being called up several times, I did vote. I also told them that it was a very rash act for there was not one-third of them that could live one month without work. I also regretted that act. In a short time the South Boston strike came and I and others were called upon to sustain them in their outrageous act. I told them, No, I would never sanction such acts as those and I never will. 'Sink or swim, live or die!' Gentlemen, they say the reason I don't go with them is because I don't get paid enough. It is false. The Boston & Sandwich Glass Co. have always treated me honestly and just, both in prosperity and adversity. Gentlemen, last week they chose a committee to see me and others to pay our dues and if we did not they would not work. If this is not threatening to strike, pray tell what is.

Gentlemen, I can talk but write very little. I have been in the Sandwich Glass Co. more than 38 years. I came to Sandwich when a mere boy and I have always been considered an honest man and by the help of the Almighty I mean to die one."

This situation marks the beginning of serious labor difficulties which were to beset the Boston & Sandwich Glass Company, and which were later to prove more troublesome.

The committee's report indicates that the profits for the year were very small; something like $10,000. Not a very propitious time for the workers to have sought an advance in wages.

A few items of interest are listed for the year, 1869. George Fessenden asked again for an increase in salary, saying that: "You will find upon inquiring that making cheap glass requires constant care and supervision, to say nothing of the anxiety attending it." He also mentioned Midwestern competition and the intensity of that competition. The minutes refer to the great weight of taxation which followed the Civil War, falling very heavily on industry.

This year is also notable for the visits Fessenden made to various European glass houses. He purchased various molds, copyrighted improvements and, in general, seems to have brought back a great deal of useful information. Apprehension was expressed in official quarters lest Fessenden leave for other companies with the valuable data he had secured. He was subsequently paid $4500 in cash for the assignment of a patent pertaining to the improvement in molds for glass from carbon gas.

The Company was ostensibly in urgent need of devising ways and means of reducing operating costs in order to meet competition. George Fessenden's trip was a step in the right direction.

The dearth of available material in the 1870's as in the preceding ten years, has compelled the author to detail intermittent items which contribute somewhat irregularly to the general picture. The material presented has been gleaned from correspondence, excerpts from company records and other reliable sources.

Committees reported the net earnings for 1869 were $48,140.11.

Bad debts amounted to $4,823.98. A superior steam engine was added, of 60 H.P., and three new boilers besides a quantity of valuable tools and machinery to the plant at Sandwich, the value of which stood at $40,000.

Henry Spurr on March 25, 1871, asks again for increase of salary to $3500 per year. Henry was a persevering soul!

March 29, 1871, an accountant went over all of the Company's books and found them in good order. It was a prosperous year, but bad debts persistently were out of proportion to the earnings of the Company. The earnings were $46,180.19. The bad and doubtful debts amounted to $7,853.18.

On November 9, 1872, the Company's warehouse, located at 26 Federal St., was destroyed by fire, with its "elegant and attractive stock" reduced to almost nothing. A large portion of the Company's insurance was with the Manufacturers, the City and Firemen's Companies to the amount of $35,000. It appears that the insurance companies were insolvent and could not pay the $35,000 for which the Company was insured. A net profit of $30,000 appeared in spite of the considerable loss otherwise occasioned by the fire, variously estimated from $15,000 to $25,000 on the stock. In view of all circumstances, including the state of trade, and its prospects, the committee recommended that the April dividend be passed and that the charges to the insurance companies be carried to Suspense Account and the collection thereof be referred to the expectation of a moderate dividend in October. Again, in regard to the fire, another statement says that all their valuable stock was destroyed but owing to the energy of the Agents, their books were fortunately saved, with the exception of one stock book. The amount of stock in the warehouse on the 9th of November was not exactly known but was estimated to have been from $60,000 to $70,000. Upon this stock, there were insurances to the amount of $45,000. Apparently only one of these policies paid up because the Company received of the $45,000 only $10,000. The fire naturally hindered the exhibition and sale of their glass. There was a short strike in the Company.

A March 25, 1874 report speaks of the New York panic of Sept. 1873 and its result upon general trade. The panic found the Company with a large and desirable stock of recently manufactured glass for which there was no demand. The result was that they had to carry forward a 25% larger stock than they had anticipated. A committee was appointed to find a suitable warehouse for the Boston & Sandwich Glass Company goods. Profit for the year 1874 was $17,783.54. Glassware on hand, subject to 25% discount was $105,580.44.

Dec. 31, 1874, the same committee made up the books for the year and found that their profit had been $17,749.00; their bad debts amounted to $8,783. [Notice that bad debts were about 50% of the net profit!] The Company did not occupy their new store until the first of June, 1874 when they left their close quarters, occupied from necessity, after the great fire, so the Company felt they just had six months of the year 1874 to consider for sales value.

Mr. Pickering, the then President, reported in 1875 that the works at Sandwich appeared in better condition than ever to meet the demands of business. Stocks on hand were all in good shape and not of unsuitable or onerous amount and the opportunity for display in sale of goods, so far, better than ever before.

Capital stock had grown to $400,000 in 1876. Glass on hand amounted to $195,327 less the usual discount of 25% allowed the trade. Nevertheless they still could not pay a dividend due to the unprecedented depression of all trade. Besides the amount of the Company's bad debts was inexplicably too high.

In April 1877 all the employee's salaries were reduced. Also a good many of the officials' salaries were reduced. At that time Mr. Fessenden, as Agent, was getting $4500 a year. Henry F. Spurr, who had devoted so many years to the Company received $2500 per annum.

The faithful Henry Spurr was poorly rewarded. Under date of Boston, April 15, 1878, the President, Mr. Pickering, wrote him as follows:

"Dear Sir: The Directors of the Boston & Sandwich Glass Company have directed me to reply to your letter of Jan. 1, 1878, that neither the business nor the interest of their stockholders seem to them to warrant any increase on the salaries paid but rather the reverse. If, therefore, you can as your letter at its close seems to intimate, place yourself in some other business on favorable terms, the Directors would not wish on their part to interpose any obstacle. Long faithful services ought to be always acknowledged but they do not give the Directors any warranty to go out of the plain paths of duty which by instruction of the stockholders is to reduce all expenses to the lowest minimum. Very truly."

In March of 1878, Company officials considered closing the plant. They were in the unenviable position of having a large stock of glass to unload on the market right after the New England Glass Co. had dumped theirs heavily with considerable sacrifice. It was suggested that the capital be reduced from $400,000 to $200,000. Glassware consigned totaled $27,000; that on hand approximated $168,000, less a 35% discount. The Company had managed to keep out of debt, yet the experience of the past year had tended to convince the Directors of the desirability of a reduction in capital. Tremendous losses would result in forcing nearly $200,000 worth of wares upon a disorganized market. The conclusions of a meeting held in July of 1878 revealed some highly significant facts. The committee reported that: "We have held a number of meetings and have had before us separately all the principal persons connected with the several departments of the business. We have questioned them for the purpose of obtaining all the information possible and heard their suggestions as to the difficulties which have led the Company to its present condition. We have also interviewed the leading persons connected with the crockery and glass ware trade in this city and, after a thorough examination, were satisfied that the main difficulty was the general stagnation of business throughout the country. We are also of the opinion that there has not been the energy and deep interest in the success of the Company there should have been on the part of all the employees which is so essential for success at all times, especially at the present. From the information obtained, we believe it to be for the interest of the Company to chiefly confine itself to the manufactory of the highest grade of glass. Our ware has a good reputation. The only fault mentioned to us was a water brilliancy and a slight change in color. This, our superintendent was aware of and had already taken measures to remedy and from an experiment made since, we believe he has accomplished it and our glass will hereafter stand equal, if not superior, to any in the market. Our superintendent at Sandwich has suggested several changes in the management of the works so as to reduce expenses which we recommend should be carried out, and we also advise that the accounts of the factory be so kept as to enable us to obtain the actual cost of the product of each pot of glass. The committee, after a full consideration, recommend that the works be continued for six months longer and if at the expiration of that time no better result is shown, we are of the opinion that the works should be closed. If the employees are impressed with the fact that the life of the Company depends upon the result of the business for the next six months, we can not but feel a different result will be shown."—This was signed by four Directors of the Company.

August 12, 1878, Arthur Pickering the President, resigned. His letter reads as follows:

"Gentlemen: For some time past I have endeavored to find out why we have been unable to make a dividend. Certain facts were patent. We have had ample capital and skill in manufacture and our employees have been spurred up to make all the sales they could, and yet the result has been a large annual loss and a rapidly decreasing capital. It would seem as if to go on much longer must result in zero. Besides one reason for heavy losses is the large rent and salaries that we have to pay but I can not accept this as a solution of the difficulty. From the western market and cheap glass, we are on all hands shut out. There remains to us the seaboard and under what conditions do we contend for the seaboard trade? For the tariff, we have a protection of 40% but this is only an apparent protection because all the articles we need in our manufacture, with the exception only of sand, are heavily taxed, in some instances, more than 40%. We all know that foreign capital is satisfied with a smaller profit and foreign labor is cheaper than our own. We have to contend with foreign capital, foreign labor and a tariff so arranged to nullify any protection which we might claim for an American manufacturer. Under such conditions, I believe that every pound of glass that we turn out is made at a loss and, as so believing, I cannot conscientiously go on adding to our stock and it is better that you should have a harmonious Board, so I now resign my position as a Director of the B & S Glass Co." * [It is important to note here the reversal of thinking which means that the Company would now confine itself to the manufacture of fine glass and abandon the attempt to meet what was apparently ruinous competition in the cheaper wares.]

In 1879 at one meeting the Company officials decided to continue operations for another six months. Actually, the Company went on for another ten years.

* By a liberal use of expressions, capitalization, and spelling common to the days of Jarves and his contemporaries, it is felt that the reader will recapture more nearly the flavor of the original documents from which these excerpts were taken.

Chapter VIII

INTERESTING EARLY BLOWN GLASS

So numerous were the interesting "off-hand" pieces made after hours by the men at Sandwich that to try to tell the story of all of them would be to undertake an impossibility. Collectors whose first questions are always where, when and why, may as well be content with the particular specimen *sans* the talking points.

It is difficult, after so many years have passed, to be sure whether or not certain of the pieces we find today were company products, that is to say, part of the normal commercial output, even when the discovery of several proves them not to be over-valued "uniques." For example, there is the rare blown glass bank with a rooster ornamenting the top, which may be considered the most superb of that class of articles blown at Sandwich. The stem is bulbous and hollow and has an American coin of 1831 enclosed within it. Only a few perfect specimens of this bank are known to exist today but doubtless others were made which have suffered the fate of most fragile things. The bank may be seen on Plate 20. One came to light only lately but it was damaged, the bird having been broken from the top.

It was a common practice for glass blowers the world over, especially after the seventeenth century, to place coins in the hollow stems of various articles that they produced. It was the most practical way of "dating" the piece. Lately I saw a loving cup with a mint coin of 1831 in the stem and a drinking glass, similar to a rummer, also with a coin, dated 1833. Such coin-dated pieces were also blown by workmen at the New England Glass Company of Cambridge, Mass., during the same period. Another curiosity made at Sandwich was a blown flint glass goblet of the plainest type but with a hollow stem enclosing a miniature doll, standing in all her naked glory, not over an inch high.

The rooster was for years a favorite ornament at Sandwich. We find him proudly perched atop sugar bowls and on other pieces. A tiny font, automatically replenished from the attached glass reservoir, sports a gay looking bird, pictured on Plate 21. This is among the treasures owned by the Sandwich Historical Society. Apparently this attractive device for thirsty birds was quite popular since enough fragments have been found to justify the belief that they were produced on a commercial scale. A similar one is in my collection. The main body is sapphire blue, the round knob on the top is crystal. The odd little oblong font is crystal with an applied blue rim.

One of the most interesting of the "made to order" historically authenticated blown pieces, is illustrated on Plate 22. But for the indisputable evidence of its origin, experts would probably pronounce it foreign. It would be another instance of how difficult and hazardous it is to venture on attributions. The chalice was made to order at the Sandwich factory for John Jarves, as his gift to his fiancée, Mary Waterman. The handsome engraving, believed to be the work of Frank Lapham, depicts a knight in armor on horseback. He carries a shield on which in small lettering are the initials "J. W. J." On the reverse side is inscribed "Mary Waterman." They were engaged in 1854 but her parents thought she was too young to be married, so they sent her away to a girls' school on the Hudson. She later married John Jarves, at the age of eighteen. The exact date of the wedding is not known but it was not later than 1855. This would date the vase as blown in 1854. It is an exquisite bit of work, not only in the engraving, but also in the gold decoration of the lower part. It is now owned by the grand-daughter of Mary Waterman Jarves, who has lent it to the Sandwich Historical Society where it may be seen every summer during the Society's annual exhibition.

To judge from the number of pieces of scent bottles found among the fragments, they also must have been made in volume quantities. Most collectors are familiar with those very small bottles with flattened sides and chamfered corners found in a

PLATE 20

The rarest example of blown Sandwich glass. A bank, with rooster ornament
and enclosed coin dated 1831.

PLATE 21

Early bird drinking font, with rooster decoration.

variety of colors, fitted with small pewter screw caps. They make a fascinating specialized collection, for they vary in shape, while the range of colors is amazing—bright hued opals, purples, blues, canary yellow, violet, jasper and even in marbleized effects. The latter are often in opaque shades with white streaks running through them. The earlier varieties of scent bottles are usually ribbed or swirled. They come in brilliant emerald greens, sapphire blues and deep amethysts. These lacked the pewter caps, being originally fitted with cork stoppers. Another fascinating variety of scent bottles is that which collectors call the "sea horse," considered by many the most appealing of all. It is very seldom that two are found alike. Being individual pieces, they vary in size and coloring. Some are of striated crystal marked with milk white, recalling old Nailsea glass. They are really tiny bottles with one tightly curled up end, suggesting the little *Hippocampus,* whence their nickname. These bottles may be found in all sorts of colors and also with applied decoration of contrasting hues. Many other factories made nearly all of the types of scent bottles described, for the early glass blowers were an itinerant tribe. Nevertheless, Sandwich did more than its full share, to the joy of collectors a century later.

Among the fragments, a great many pieces similar in style to the so-called "Jacony" baskets have been found. These were made both in crystal and in solid color, as well as in crystal flashed with such hues as contrasted effectively. I found one piece in crystal flashed with red, that looked for all the world like painted glass. As a matter of fact, Sandwich did much color flashing, as evidenced by innumerable fragments. The Sandwich Historical Society owns a fragment in clear, frosted and amber which may have come from a goblet. It is a beautifully engraved medallion showing a house, trees, etc., and serves to emphasize again the dazzling variety of work done at Sandwich.

Elaborate epergnes with delicately wrought leaves were another Sandwich product, highly prized by their owners today.

For many years it has been my belief, shared by careful students of American glass, that Sandwich made at least some of the greatly sought after, so-called "Stiegel paneled vases." For one thing, some of these are more delicately blown and are much lighter in weight than others. While I scout the "touch" system as a guide to glass lore—a method some people use so effectively on lecture platforms, or the "feel," of glass, I do not think anyone will question the fact that there is a difference in texture to be found on these vases. Moreover, they were produced in the colors Deming Jarves loved best; brilliant sapphire blue, brilliant emerald green and a deep, fine amethyst. He may well have been the maker of the heavier types, granting to Stiegel and others the honor of having produced those which were much lighter. Among my fragments is a piece in amethyst of the same pattern noted on the bases of some of the paneled vases. Other rarities include fragments of the miniature paneled vase.

Among the Sandwich fragments of considerable importance which have been unearthed during the late 1930's were pieces of amethyst "expanded diamond" toilet bottles of the type attributed to Stiegel. A base was found in a brilliant amethyst but other fragments bordered on a plum shade. These interesting pieces were excavated from a depth of five feet below the surface. Amethyst pattern molded toilet bottles have sold at staggering sums and collectors rate them in the top rank of desirability. It is, therefore, of tremendous interest to learn that both the paneled vases and diamond quilted bottles of erstwhile Stiegel fame were also produced by the Boston & Sandwich Glass Company.

Attributed to Nicholas Lutz, a skilled Sandwich workman, are the articles in Venetian style which not even the most ardent Sandwich devotee would suspect of being a Cape product. On Plate 23 are shown two small tumblers, a very beautiful pair of vases and a finger bowl and plate. The finger bowl is turned to show one of two glass medallions which adorn the sides. A child's face is imprinted in the center of it. The top is finished with a crimp of glass which has a small opening, as though it had been designed for a locket. Several of these have been found among the fragments excavated at Sandwich. The bowls are in blue, gold and white and in rose, gold and white, swirled or striped, as may be seen in the picture. The vases are tall, one being in amethyst and white and the other in blue and white. The little tumblers may be found in several sizes and shapes, as well as in innumerable color combinations.

This type of blown ware, so reminiscent of early Venetian glass, was made in Europe over a long period of years. It never lost its popularity. Gustav Pazaurek illustrates it in his book, "Gläser der Empire, und Biedermeierzeit," as "Striped glass," period 1845.

Many collectors have entertained a vague notion that Nicholas Lutz began work at Sandwich almost from the beginning of its operations. Since the Striped glass was popular in this country at the time of the Centennial in Philadelphia in 1876, it seemed as though he must have worked at Sandwich later than has been suspected. A letter from his son, Mr. V. E. Lutz, gave a most interesting account of his life. The letter follows:

"My father, Nicholas Lutz, was born in St. Louis, Lorraine, France, and started his apprenticeship at the local glass factory (Cristalleries de St. Louis, founded 1767) at the age of ten and continued until he became of age to serve his four years of service in the French army.

"He later came to this country and located at Whitemills, Pa. He was then called to the Boston & Sandwich Glass Company and worked there from 1869 to the closing of the factory in 1888. Father then went to New Bedford and worked for the Mt. Washington Glass Works and from there to the Union Glass Works at Somerville, Mass.

"Although he was a master workman in all lines of glass making, he specialized in fancy colored glass, nappies and bowls for cutting, chandelier arms and thin glass and stem work.

"Also he did considerable work at the old home here. He had a work shop set up with tallow lamp and made different kinds of fruit and flowers, etc., for paperweights for the Boston & Sandwich Glass Company. For his friends he made threaded pens, flasks, paperweights, cigarette holders and many fancy articles of different designs." Additional information about Mr. Lutz's work will be found in Chapter XXVIII.

The cutting and engraving departments of the Boston & Sandwich Glass Company were important adjuncts of the factory. Frederick T. Irwin has recorded that in the late 60's and early 70's as many as fifty of the best glass cutters in the country worked in the cutting shop as well as a number of engravers. "When work was slack in the cutting room, the cutters bought blanks from the Company and cut patterns of their own design which were submitted to the superintendent. If these met with his approval, they were sent to the salesroom, and the filling of any orders from these designs was given to the designer of the pattern. Sometimes, if officials of the Company were pleased with a pattern, or it became popular, the Company bought it from the originator. This indicates that fine cut glass filled a very important place in the Company's output."

Many special orders were executed besides their regular commercial output. The finest of flint glass stem-ware blown at Sandwich, often engraved with the initials of the original owner, may still be seen in many New England homes. Charles W. Lapham, who gathered the first piece of glass on July 4, 1825, is quoted as having said: "If it's glass we make it!"

Presentation pieces are always of particular interest. On Plate 24 is an interesting example of a cut and engraved flower holder which was ordered by a Mr. Sherman, a stockholder in the company, as a wedding present for his sister-in-law, Sarah Fuller. The heavy flint glass panels are engraved with the vintage pattern. One panel has a wreath with the name "Sarah Fuller." Both the stem and the base are cut. It is now owned by a grand-daughter who resides in California.

Ornamental as well as useful glass of the type of the Sarah Fuller piece were made over a long period of years, so it is hazardous to attempt to date them, lacking specific evidence.

Another type of blown glass which is seen more frequently in

New England than elsewhere is the "threaded" glass. Sandwich workmen are responsible for many of the most beautiful pieces, which were produced in a wide variety of forms and colors. It required a high degree of skill to apply the threads. The earlier specimens often show an expanded diamond pattern, when held to the light. On Plate 25 is a window of threaded ware, taken in the Sandwich Historical Society building. There are baskets, hats, toilet bottles, fingerbowls and plates, besides many ornamental objects. Sometimes part of the article was threaded and the balance engraved or etched. It was made over a period of years and it is possible to distinguish the earlier ware from the later by the workmanship. The earlier was heavier in weight except on some of the ornamental vases, and the threads were much thicker than on the later pieces. On Plate 19 may be seen three threaded articles belonging to the Sandwich Historical Society.

It is quite likely that this particular type of threaded ware, which was purely a commercial product, was inspired by the still earlier blown "off-hand" pieces, many of which were decorated with threads. Those pictured in this chapter do not properly belong with early blown glass, since they were not produced before the late 60's or possibly the 70's, but there was no other heading in this book that would cover such types of glassware.

It was not my intention to attempt to describe in this chapter more than a small portion of the early blown pieces made in Sandwich. No mortal could live long enough to authenticate and list all of them. All that it appeared feasible to do was to point out some of the more interesting types, and to stress the wide scope of work done in the famous factory at the Cape. The praise we hear on all sides is not always competently expressed but the reader may rest assured that it is amply deserved.

Chapter IX

BLOWN MOLDED GLASS

It is both curious and irritating that one of the lines of early American glass most popular with discriminating collectors should give rise to so many conjectures and provoke so many unanswered questions. It has not even been properly christened. For years no one knew which factories produced it, therefore it was attributed to Stoddard, N. H. Later it was definitely established beyond all question that it was never made at Stoddard but at nearby Keene. But it was never known as Keene glass. To this day, old time dealers still call it "Stoddard" and every collector still knows what they mean.

The "Stoddard" designation—always intended to include a line and not a factory—in time was superseded by the far more stupid, "Three Mold." Thousands of persons to whom the unfortunately widely accepted trade name of "Three mold" meant any piece of glass that showed three mold marks found on the majority of the utterly different pressed glass, have made life miserable for collectors of the erstwhile "Stoddard." They read of the high prices paid for unusual pieces of "Three Mold glass" and instantly believe themselves to be the possessors of priceless treasures—in the shape of late pressed ware that shows the precious trinity of mold marks. There is a crying need for an acceptable designation of the blown molded glass that once was "Stoddard" but has since been designated as "insufflated," "molded," "blown molded" and "three mold." Not one of these generic denominations is adequate. Considering them all there can be no question that going back to the old "Stoddard" designation would be the simplest way out, for it must be frankly admitted that what is really wanted and needed is a generic name by which this particular line of early American glass, in its entirety, should be known. It is of relatively little importance except to carping pedants, that it never was made at Stoddard. No one claims that all Pitkin flasks were made at Pitkin but when a collector says or hears "Pitkin flask" he knows what is meant, irrespective of markings, pattern, variety, size or provenance. Such qualifications would serve only to differentiate one style cf "Pitkin flask" from another. It is far more inconvenient and confusing to have no satisfactory generic name than to accept one which was used for years before sticklers for 100% accuracy condemned it because it misrepresented the geographical provenance of the article. Its origin was a misattribution but usage gave it life. Russian leather need not be Russian and suède gloves do not come from Sweden. We buy chamois skins that were never worn in life by any *Rupicapra rupicapra* as it blithely skipped from Alpine crag to crag. And Ohio Stiegel is not Stiegel. "Stoddard" has been abandoned, never to be taken back, so it is futile to plead for its return.

I have always felt that there must have been a time when this "Stoddard-three-mold-insufflated-blown-molded glass" must have been designated by its various makers by both generic and specific names. When it was being produced by factories East and West, there must have been an accepted recognizable trade name. Those who call attention to the advertisements of "Molded glass" to describe "Three-Mold-Stoddard"-etc. glass, should remember that the same word "Molded" was used by much earlier makers to designate glassware that certainly was not what we mean today when we speak of "Three Mold." "Blown Molded" is not specific enough. It would include pieces that also are blown molded but that nobody would dream of designating as "Three Mold" or "Stoddard" or "Insufflated" or any other of the labels that we are now more or less illogically asked to use. "Three Mold" is as much a misnomer as "Stoddard," for some "Three Mold" is really two-mold or four-mold and nobody goes about differentiating them by calling them as "insufflated two-mold" or "insufflated four-mold." That is the objection to "Blown Three Mold." Mrs.

Knittle made a brave effort to popularize the word "insufflated" to describe "three-section contact blown-molded" glass but it failed, probably because "insufflated" conveyed no exact meaning or picture to the average collector who had taken a short cut from "three-section-contact-blown-mold" to "Three Mold." A trip to the dictionary in search of "insufflated" left them no better off, although it enabled them to realize that, as Mrs. Knittle herself admits, "the process employed in giving this glass its pattern apparently defies exact description for their seems to be an exception to nearly every rule concerning it."

In my own thinking, the matter was resolved by the discovery of a reference in one of Deming Jarves' letters. He speaks in one paragraph of "blown molded glass or that which was blown into hinged iron molds." Undoubtedly these remarks are relevant to this subject of controversy or what I have termed "blown molded glass." The preponderance of factual data, and certainly ordinary common sense point to the use of this term. I shall term it "Blown Molded," differentiating the various patterns by simple descriptive names, several of which are already in use. The classification into divisions favored by some writers are too vague and general, like "geometrical," for instance or "Baroque," etc. They are really sub-divisions. It is as absurd as classifying humanity in terms of skin pigmentation when what is desired is to differentiate *Homonide* from *Mammalia*. Individual differences could be specifically described by using sub-titles. A nomenclature that would enable us to tell at once exactly to which sort of glass an item belongs is, I fear, beyond the power of any but a genius. Indeed, it may be that the only solution lies in a carefully illustrated check list and numbers. The Marble system for cup plates, of course, could not be followed with entire success, for many blown molded pieces were finished by hand and therefore all are not exactly alike whereas cup plates, being pressed glass, consist really of a series of replicas which can be numbered and catalogued easily. It was hoped that collecting "Stoddard" or "Three Mold" or "Insufflated" or "Blown Molded" glass might have been made easier by a not over-elaborate or a not too general or too technical classification of types and individual specimens. A tendency toward an attempt to attain a scientific meticulosity of descriptive verbiage has been observed of late in some of our most gifted writers. Haphazard collecting is to be deprecated and full information should always be welcomed. But the owner of an automobile does not have to be a world-famous expert on explosive engines or automotive vehicles to be a first class driver or to understand his machine or to enjoy his car. It might be well to remember the case of the old German scholar who, after working his entire life on a book about the Greek particle, regretted, on his death bed, that he had not confined himself to the dative case.

More than a hundred years have passed since this type of blown molded glass was first made and sold on a commercial scale. Careful research has brought to light much that is both interesting and instructive but much still remains to be learned. Through the epochal excavations of the late Harry Hall White at factory sites, it is known that it was made at various glassworks from Massachusetts to Ohio.

For years, our collectors have regretted that so little was known of the rôle they felt sure Sandwich must have played and now at last, chiefly through the efforts of Francis Wynn in excavating at the Sandwich factory site, we are able to know and name the large number of patterns that were made there, not alone in clear but in several colors. In fact, it can be said that for a long time the Sandwich works were the most prolific producers of this type of glass. This had long been suspected but writers on the subject could only suggest that some "three mold" undoubtedly was made at the Cape, until an article was printed in the New York *Evening Sun,* making public evidence unearthed by Mr. Wynn.

The types of Blown Molded glass made at Sandwich vary, in most cases, from types made at the other factories named. Collectors in general have assumed that Yankee ingenuity, as usual, saw profitable possibilities in manufacturing and selling at low prices something resembling English and Irish cut glass of the period.

Jarves not only was a highly resourceful manufacturer but he was of English descent.

There are several distinct types of Blown Molded glass. A simple explanation of the differences between the various types of blown glass is given below, for the benefit of the beginner. With the thought in mind that the average reader is not interested in highly technical details of manufacturing methods, a few lines will suffice to explain those terms which the novice may find confusing in reading what are really technical treatises on glass which have recently appeared in trade periodicals.

"Off-hand" pieces are those made after hours by the workmen, often as gifts for friends. They gave the men an opportunity to test their own skill and ingenuity. Such pieces do not always represent the actual commercial output of the factory.

The earliest blown glass may be divided into the following classes:

1. "Off-hand," which would include any sort or type of piece blown by individual workmen, after regular working hours.
2. Blown Glass: That is, blown by the human breath and shaped and finished by hand with glassmakers' tools.
3. Blown Molded: This heading should be sub-divided to include:

    1*a*. Pillar molding, probably the earliest form of molded glass. According to Apsley Pellatt, writing nearly 100 years ago, this method was used by the ancient Romans though only in making small articles. The metal mold was one-third the size of the object to be produced. The blower, upon removing the piece from the mold when it was half formed, finished it by flashing, shaping, etc. It was reheated for fire polish. Pellatt mentions the use of "pillar moulding" for salt cellars, toilet bottles, and chandelier work.

    2*b*. Pattern molding. A development of pillar molding. A large class of articles may come under this heading. As the term implies, it covers those pieces blown into a part-sized mold, having a distinct pattern. The object was finished after being removed from the mold by further blowing and expanding of the design. Thus there are ribbed, fluted, diamond-patterned, swirled, etc., pattern-molded pieces.

3c. Molded: Forerunner of the "Blown Molded" style described below. It is termed "Molded" merely to differentiate it from the patterns produced from the full-sized two, three or four-part hinged molds. While it is heavier and appears to be of a later period than the thinner "insufflated" or "blown molded" (three mold) it is really earlier. It was produced by blowing the glass into one-part molds, which, at least on the smaller objects, were full-sized. After being removed from the mold the top edges were finished by hand. It is apparently a further outgrowth of pillar molding. The difference between Molded and Blown Molded (even though both are "blown") is that the Molded was made thicker and heavier, so that the inside surface of the glass is smooth. On the Blown Molded, which was an easier process, and therefore merely an off-shoot of the Molded, the glass is lighter in weight and usually, though not always, depending on the thickness of the glass, the indentations of the design may be felt on the inside surface. Molded glass is usually found in a diamond quilted or ribbed pattern, or a combination of both, in oval, oblong or round shapes, often with beveled corners on the oblong dishes. It was produced to a small extent at Sandwich in the early days, as fragments of it have been found, but was apparently discontinued in favor of the lighter and more easily made Blown Molded. See Plate 26.

4d. Blown Molded. A distinct class, as descrbed in this chapter, produced by blowing into a hinged two, three or four-part mold, giving to the object its pattern and also its finished form, except for the neck and lip of decanters, and the applied handles. The types of patterns are classified as: Baroque, Geometric, Arched, etc.

Deming Jarves was fully acquainted with the method of pillar molding while he was connected with the New England Glass Company. In his book, "Reminiscences of Glass Making," he writes: "English glassmakers considered the patent pillar glass a modern invention until a Roman vase was found being a complete specimen of pillar moulding. Pellatt states in his work that he had seen an ancient drinking vessel of Medrecan form, on a foot of considerable substance, nearly entire, and procured from Rome, which had the appearance of having been blown in an open-and-shut mould, the rim being afterwards cut off and polished. This is high authority and with other evidences that might be cited, goes far to prove that the ancients used moulds for pressing, and also for blowing moulded articles, similar to those now in use."

In any case we know now that Blown Molded glass was made in large quantities at Sandwich prior to 1849, for all the clear and colored fragments, with the exception of the so-called "dark glass" (dark amber and deep olive-amber) were found under a building which was not built until 1849. It is more than probable that molded glass was produced at Sandwich from approximately 1826 until the vogue died down, sometime in the 40's, when the pressed glass began to crowd it from the market.

Lacking adequate evidence to the contrary I do not today believe that Sandwich ever made the dark colored inkwells of which so many fragments were found. These did not come from beneath the building erected in 1849 but were scattered all over the yard and in particular near a building that was erected in 1871. Further, on examining these fragments closely, every piece bore undoubted evidence of having seen considerable service, for they all had wear marks on the base, except one or two pieces. They could not have been purchased for cullet for there is no evidence that Sandwich was ever, at any time, a producer of much dark glass. Another reason is seen in the fact that Deming Jarves loved color too much and bright shades of blue in particular. Some day the reason why so many fragments of the inkwells were found there may be learned as further excavations are carried on. Mr. Harry Hall White, whose invaluable work extended to excavations of the Kent, and Mantua, Ohio, Coventry and Keene, N. H., and Vernon, N. Y., factory sites, went over the inkwell fragments with me and found that three types of the dark inkwells were from Coventry and two from Keene. Clear Blown Molded inkwells were made at Sandwich but not in the patterns made at Keene or Coventry. Two of them are illustrated on Plates 32 and 54.

Among the early fragments, most of the colored pieces were in dark brilliant blue, a few in amethyst and opalescent and others in light green.

In a memo book under date of 1859 loaned to me by Mr. Clarence Haines (presented to Mr. G. L. Fessenden by William Stutson, 1865) are a large number of the most important formulas used at Sandwich, with directions for making up the batches. In studying the colors I find very little mention of dark colors. They run in the book, as follows: "Mixture for silvering glass; how to prepare the glass for silvering; ruby glass (preparation of the gold, used in ruby); flint glass for coating; best flint; Moorland Flint, Blue for coating; Canary; Opal; dark blue; light blue; white agate; amber; amethyst; purple; light purple; dark purple; Red Jasper; Olive green No. 3; green; light green; Turquoise, Black; Flint crystal."

Prof. Alexander Silverman, of the University of Pittsburgh has borne testimony to the remarkable range of color of Sandwich glass. He is quoted at length in the chapter on Deming Jarves.

In a Dictionary of Arts and Sciences, published in London in 1754, an interesting note is found about opaque white. It states: "Glass porcelain, the name given by many to a modern invention of imitating the chinaware with glass." It further mentions Mr. Reaumur, the famous scientist and also inventor of the thermometer that bears his name, (1683–1757) "who was the first that carried the attempt to any degree of perfection." Apparently milk white glass was first made in an attempt to copy porcelain at a lesser cost. The process was taught at Sandwich by one Rice Harris, expert from England, who was paid $5,000 and his expenses, for his services.

The Sandwich Blown Molded patterns have certain characteristics which set them apart, as for instance, the different types of bases, that through the exhumed fragments are now safely established as Sandwich products. One designer or moldmaker there made a point of using some form of concentric rings on the base, ranging from a few to a number sufficient to cover that area. I do not mean that a piece is *not* Sandwich unless it has a concentric ring base, because they were used on dark glass inkwells, but that a great many of the various articles made there do show it. On the contrary, I have a small creamer in a plaid pattern with concentric ring base (pontil mark in center), which carries a British registry mark on the inside. Who copied from whom is a problem that may never be solved.

Another favorite type of Sandwich base is the rayed, and these are found in five forms. They run as follows:

Number 1. Rayed to center.
Number 2. Rayed to dot in center. (Later type, used on some vinegar bottles.)
Number 3. Rayed to pontil in center.
Number 4. Rayed to a large circular disc in center.
Number 5. Rayed to concentric ring center.

There are more rayed and concentric ring bases than any other types in their blown glass. Of course, they made the plain clear bases which every factory used, as well as an interesting type with large indentations in a ring around the base which looks very like a sunflower. Number 3 and the concentric ring types of bases are shown on Plate 28. A foot fragment and other small pieces are illustrated on Plate 29.

Collection of the author

PLATE 26

MOLDED SALT DISHES OF THE EARLY 1820's

These were all produced from full-size molds and the rims ground smooth.

PLATE 27

Rare miniature pieces, all of Sandwich origin, with the possible exception of the creamer at the right, which is an unique specimen.

PLATE 28

Miniature decanters and cordial glasses, with corresponding Sandwich fragments.

PLATE 29

Footed salt with Diamond Sunburst and Chevron pattern together with Blown Molded fragments excavated at Sandwich.

PLATE 30

Upper—Quarter-pint decanters.
Lower—Footed salts and hat in familiar patterns.

PLATE 31
Blown Molded caster bottles and salts.

It was not until 1920 that the "Upper house," built in 1849, was torn down. The foundation was left intact until 1933 when the bricks in the flooring were removed. Underneath this foundation the bulk of the earliest pieces made at Sandwich was found, by Francis Wynn. All of the "three mold" fragments, with the exception of the dark glass inkwells, were discovered there and also all of the very early pressed glass Heart patterns and about two-thirds of all the lacy fragments. They were located under the part of the building where the leers and furnaces stood.

Among the "three mold" fragments are pieces which so far I have been unable to identify with any specimens known to us. Unlisted patterns are still dug up from time to time, which add to the record of Sandwich triumphs.

Blown Molded pieces were made at Sandwich in a wide variety of forms, from the "toy" or miniature pieces to large celery vases (originally termed celery glasses) sugar bowls and punch bowls. Colored pieces are particularly coveted by collectors today.

On Plate 27 may be seen a number of the toy or miniature pieces. I have never heard of any of these particular pieces in color except the little decanters, which have been found in yellow. Experience has taught me that anything can happen in the way of colored Sandwich pieces so it would not surprise me if some day one of my correspondents wrote me that she had any pattern of the Blown Molded decanters or creamers in color.

Illustrated on Plate 28 are other miniature pieces together with corresponding fragments found at the Sandwich factory site. The fragment of the cordial appears to be white, but the discoloration comes from having been buried so many years. Footed salts made at Sandwich are found in at least six well-known forms. These include:

1. Diamond Sunburst with dot center alternating with diamond quilting. A wavy chevron pattern on foot. Large, with plain belled top. Crystal and in blue. Plates 29 and 30. In dark blue, Plate 34. Concentric ring base.

2. Sunburst and diamond quilting, alternating. Diagonal ribbing. Ribbed rounded foot. Plate 30. Base rayed to a large circular disc in center.
3. Diamond quilted, ribbed foot. Top belled and plain. Few were made in amethyst. Plate 31.
4. Diamond Sunburst alternating with diamond quilting. Design on foot is herringbone but appears to be small pointed leaves pointing upward. Usually found in a small size and in a brilliant sapphire blue. A number of blue corresponding fragments have been found at Sandwich. Plate 31.
5. Sunburst with bull's eye center, alternating with diamond quilting. Ribbed rounded foot. This pattern may be seen in a number of pieces but is rare. A hat and tumbler are illustrated on Plate 32. Salt on Plate 31.
6. Diamond Quilted Sunburst alternating with diamond quilting. Ribbed foot.

A few rare examples are found in which the bull's eye in the center of a sunburst has become distorted in the making and is oval, instead of round. Plate 31.

Most of the salts come in crystal but they are not particularly uncommon in a brilliant sapphire blue. Amethyst is the rarest color. Light green (bottle glass) also is rare but not so highly prized by collectors as the varying shades of purple. Among the Sandwich fragments is an amethyst piece, of the herringbone pattern. Many shades of blue were used in the early days, a rare one being a gray-blue.

Caster bottles were in demand quite early, and Sandwich turned out a number of different forms. Most beautiful is the nonagonal one shown in the center of Plate 31 which has a concentric ring base. The design consists of sunbursts with dot center alternating with panels of diamond quilting. Around the lower part is a wide band of herringbone. A variation of the same bottle is shown in the upper left-hand corner of the same plate. Another desirable form, shown on Plate 31, has a band of diamond sunbursts running around it. Not very many examples of the bottle with the Tam o'Shanter stopper are known. An interesting mustard bottle is shown on Plate 40. It is swirled in the lower part, instead of having the vertical ribbing that is most frequently encountered. Common types, produced in large quantities, were paneled and are found in different shapes. The salt and pepper shakers are shown on Plate 33.

Vinegar bottles, sometimes erroneously referred to as toilet bottles, must have been a great favorite with Deming Jarves or with his customers for they were produced in a number of forms and a wide variety of colors. Four are illustrated on Plate 35. A large quantity of the fragments and various types of stoppers have been recovered in excavating. Three types of bases were used: the smooth or plain, the concentric ring and the rayed. As for colors, I have seen them in all shades of blue, from a light blue to a deep sapphire and from a gray-blue to a violet. In amethyst the shades also vary. One specimen was found in purple with splashes of white. These were made in crystal, both ribbed and swirled. Those seen most frequently are sapphire blue, so any other shades, with the exception of crystal, are rarer. Early stoppers for use in vinegar bottles, toy decanters and other small decanters are shown on Plate 36. All of these were excavated at Sandwich. One other early type, not illustrated, has a round flat top with diagonal ribs. The ribs on both sides slant toward the right and therefore, when the stopper is in place in a container, the light showing through it gives a prismatic effect. The rarest stopper is a Blown Molded one, in the shape of an acorn, in the quilted pattern. Since one of these was found in an old decanter which had always been in the possession of one family in Sandwich, I lean strongly to the belief that it is of Sandwich origin. In later pressed patterns, some of the knobs were also shaped like an acorn.

Not a great many clear glass inkwells are found but three forms were made at Sandwich which can be authenticated by fragments. Probably the most attractive is the one shown on Plate 32. Another specimen exactly like it is in the collection of Mr. Albert E. Shaw of Webster, Mass., the chief difference being that Mr. Shaw purchased his many years ago for fifty cents and I paid $27.50 for mine at a New York auction and was congratulated on my bargain. At that rate, Mr. Shaw could buy fifty-four more inkwells—if he could use H. G. Wells' Time Machine and ride back to the halcyon days when glass collecting was merely a hobby and not a luxury.

The second known crystal inkwell is in the collection of Mr. Albert C. Marble of Worcester, Mass. It has the plain sunburst, as may be seen on Plate 54. A third type in crystal sold at the Alfred B. Maclay auction (1939). It is taller than the others I have seen, and slopes in at the top. The base has a wide band of vertical ribbing, with sunbursts alternating with diamond quilting above. It may be that many others will be found in collections but if they are of Sandwich origin they will undoubtedly follow one of the many designs used in the hats.

Collecting hats is an interesting hobby and no set is complete without a few of the Blown Molded styles. On Plate 38 are shown six varieties, all but one of which are unquestionably of Sandwich origin. The doubtful one is in the upper right-hand corner. It seemed safe to include it, since a mustard bottle has been found in the same pattern.

These Sandwich hats may be found in crystal or in sapphire blue. The dark blue ones are scarcer and much more valuable. The shapes and sizes of the hats vary considerably because they were made from tumblers or from inkwells and the reshaping into head-gear while still plastic was done by hand. The very small hats are much scarcer than the usual toothpick holder size. It has been more or less of a tradition that all these hats were made as containers for toothpicks but whether they were exclusively used for that purpose so early is debatable. The later pressed glass ones certainly were, for they are so listed in many of my old trade catalogues of pressed ware. Precisely when the American toothpick habit started is for historians to study.

The largest hat known in this series is that shown on Plate 32. It was made from a tumbler mold. After counting the ribs to be

PLATE 32

Tumbler and hat, made from the same mold in the rare Bull's Eye Sunburst. Clear glass inkwell, with Diamond Sunburst.

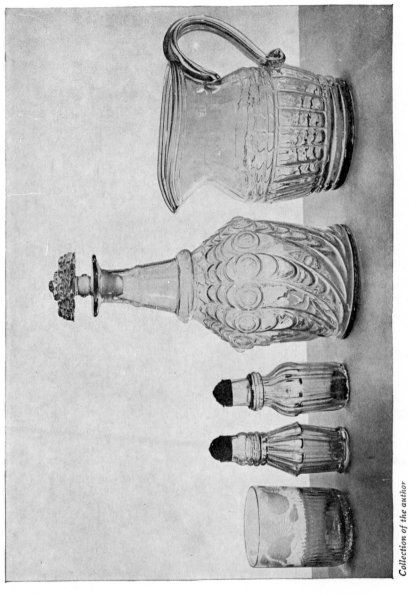

PLATE 33. BLOWN MOLDED GLASS

PLATE 34—BLOWN MOLDED GLASS IN COLOR

Examples of pitchers, salts and a hat, all rare in sapphire blue.

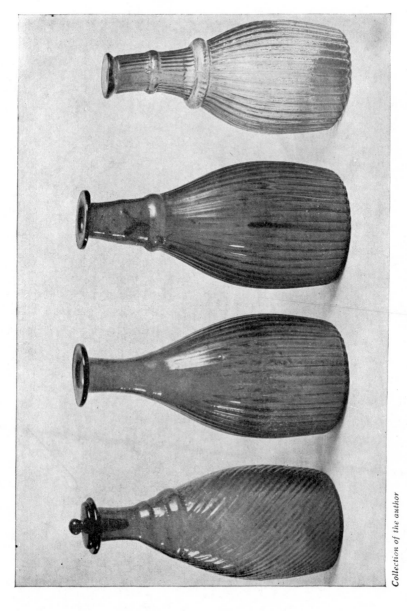

PLATE 35

Group of Blown Molded Vinegar bottles in varying shades of blue.

PLATE 36

Examples of early types of stoppers, found in excavations at Sandwich.

PLATE 37

Diamond quilted sugar bowls, the lower with band of diagonal ribbing.

PLATE 38

Blown Molded hats were made in many, though not in all, of the patterns used on other objects.
Period 1828-1840.

sure they were the same, I was gratified to find I had a fragment which corresponded exactly. The large plain bull's eye in a Sunburst is the rarest of any of the Sunburst patterns. The tumbler illustrated alongside the hat is a large water tumbler size.

A hat having the Herringbone pattern around the lower part and Diamond Sunburst above, is shown on Plate 30. This covers all the hat patterns made at Sandwich, so far as is known at present.

To illustrate how two hats in the same pattern may vary in size, a sapphire blue one is shown on Plate 34 exactly like the middle one in the top row of Plate 38. Collectors would do well to be content with one in each pattern, for to attempt to collect the variations in brims and height would make theirs an endless task, without the true collecting thrill.

The collecting of Blown Molded wines and cordials is a rare luxury for they are scarcer than the hats and therefore more expensive. A representative group of all the forms to be found is shown on Plate 39. The one in the center with the crude, rounded bowl I believe may be one of the earliest, if not the earliest produced. I found two of them, some years ago, in Rhode Island. As may be noted from the photographs, the foot is uneven, with every indication of having been finished by hand and not too carefully. The base has a rough pontil mark. The bowl on both glasses is uneven; in fact quite crooked. I class them as among the rarest items obtainable today, in this type of glass.

The first one in the row is found more frequently than any of the others. It is not unlike some of the Irish glasses though the one illustrated is of American origin, and I believe it to be Sandwich. Numerous small fragments of this pattern have been found, too small to be possible to tell from which object they have come.

It took a long time to assemble a set of eight of these glasses, which one well-known collector insists are Irish. I do not agree with him but I have not found it possible to accumulate that many of any of the other shapes. The barrel-shaped wine is quite rare.

The two cordials on the ends are also extremely rare. Prior to

1929 they sold at exorbitant prices. A fragment of one, having the concentric ring base, is shown on Plate 28.

Sandwich made tumblers in many sizes, from the toy whiskey tasters two inches high, shown on Plate 27 to flip glasses as large as wine coolers! Several examples are shown on Plates 32, 33, 40, 41, 42, 43 and 44.

Taking the smallest sizes first, the toy tumblers or whiskey tasters have already been discussed. Many fragments of them were found at Sandwich, having either a concentric ring base or a clear base. The pair of tumblers next to them on Plate 27 are only slightly taller but are shaped like the large flip glasses. In fact, I have heard these referred to as miniature flips but I believe they probably also served their purpose as whiskey tasters.

On Plate 40 in the lower row may be seen a tall glass, shaped like the tapering whiskey tasters. This was doubtless intended for a wine glass of some kind. The other glass in the lower row may not be of Sandwich origin but since swirls were used on some of the Cape articles, it seemed well to include it. The pattern is not particularly interesting and I have never seen it except on these glasses—all of the same shape and approximate height.

The first tumbler in the upper row is crude and may very likely be counted among the first produced. It will be noted that it has a simple band of diamond quilting and one row of vertical ribbing. More elaborate forms would naturally follow. The second water tumbler (in the center, top row) is a fairly common pattern, found in numerous pieces such as the hats, decanters, flip glasses, etc. The barred-shaped tumbler on the end, with Diamond Quilted Sunburst is much rarer. A collector would do well to pick up any of these glasses, if he can buy them at a reasonable price.

The whiskey tumbler shown on Plate 43 is also exceedingly scarce. The pattern is a typical Sandwich design, having bands of diagonal ribbing and the plain Sunbursts alternating with diamond quilting. Next to it will be noted a mug which is the same tumbler with an applied handle. Mugs are rare as well as a desirable item in any collection.

The water tumbler on Plate 33 was blown in a three-part mold and has a wide band of vertical ribbing, further enhanced by an engraved design of leaves above it.

All collectors are familiar with tumblers, wines and mugs enameled with bright colored flowers, the mugs often bearing inscriptions so that they are usually referred to as "Friendship" mugs. It is interesting to note that no fragments of these have ever been found at Sandwich, so far as I can learn. Since Deming Jarves was so extremely fond of color, it seems odd that he did not go into producing them on a large scale. Both England and Germany exported them to this country in enormous quantities and that may be the reason.

The water tumbler with the rare "Bull's Eye Sunburst" on Plate 32 has already been commented on.

The plainest of the Blown Molded flip glasses are those having a band of diamond quilting flanked on each side by vertical ribbing. It is the most common of all the designs. One is shown on Plate 44. A rather large flip is illustrated on Plate 42 at the beginning of the row. It is probably the second most common pattern encountered. Next to the pint decanter is shown another flip glass with straight sides. These are less usual than those which taper toward the base. The rarest on that Plate is the barrel-shaped flip in the same pattern. All barrel-shaped flip glasses are eagerly sought after.

Among the handsomest flip glasses to be found are the two shown on Plate 41. Their particular beauty lies in the increased elaboration of the design. The larger glass on the end having the Diamond Quilted Sunburst is choice and scarce. The double band of diagonal ribbing below the principal motif is always an added attraction. Next to it, on the same Plate, is another rare flip having a double-ringed Bull's Eye Sunburst, alternating with diamond quilting. This is also a rare and highly desirable piece for collectors.

The group of Blown Molded syrup jugs on Plate 45 are unidentified as to source. Strangely enough they were all sent in to me from Texas and I have never encountered any others like them.

PLATE 39

Rare wines and cordial glasses. The misshapen one in the center may well be among the earliest produced.

PLATE 40

Early tumblers, tall wines and a covered bowl

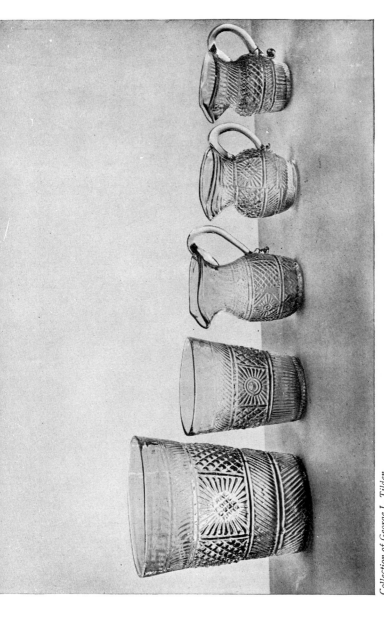

PLATE 41—BLOWN MOLDED FLIP GLASSES AND CREAMERS

Left to right: Patterns 1, Diamond Quilted Sunburst; 2, Double-ringed Bull's Eye Sunburst; 3, Diamond Sunburst 4, Diamond Quilted Sunburst, 5, Diamond quilting with diagonal ribbing.

PLATE 42

Two Blown Molded flip glasses, half-pint decanter and tumbler, all in the same pattern.

PLATE 43—SUNBURST MOTIF IN BLOWN MOLDED GLASS

Left to right—Pint pitcher, half-pint decanter, creamer, whiskey tumbler, handled mug.

Collection of the author

PLATE 44

Diamond quilted pint decanters, flip glass and half-pint pitcher.

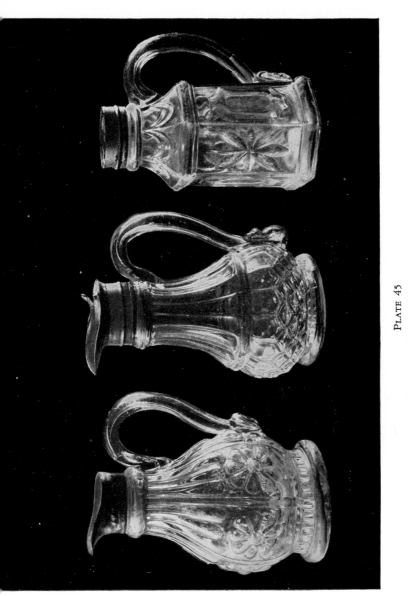

PLATE 45

Unidentified Blown Molded syrup jugs.

Blown Molded pitchers were made in a wide variety of sizes and patterns at Sandwich. Colored ones are highly prized by collectors.

From the toy pitchers shown on Plate 27 the next in size would be the small creamers, in which three different patterns are illustrated on Plate 41. The largest follows the design already noted on several pieces such as the footed salts, inkwells, hats, etc., so it is obvious that the same designs were carried out, ranging from little pieces to large ones. The Diamond Sunburst alternating with panels of diamond quilting is a favorite pattern among collectors. The next pitcher is equally rare. The Diamond Quilted Sunburst is seldom seen on creamers. Of interest in this particular piece is the unevenness apparent in one section. Apparently the blower must have let one hinged section of the mold slip, for the piece does not join evenly. This is merely indicative of the primitive methods in use at an early day. The smallest pitcher on the end is the most interesting of all, for it was made in a two-part mold and has three little table rests on the base. The design of the pitcher (diamond quilting with diagonal ribbing) is a common one at Sandwich but the three table rests is an uncommon departure from the usual types made in New England.

The commonest type of pitcher is that one illustrated on Plate 44. These are found in all sizes, from very small creamers to a quart size.

Deming Jarves was so artistic that one wonders why he made so many of the plain paneled pieces. They have little to recommend them from a standpoint of aesthetics but they may have been "best sellers" in those days, and business was business then as now. On Plate 33 is shown a quart-sized pitcher in a particularly brilliant impression. Caster bottles, vinegar bottles, decanters and pitchers were made in this design. Pitchers and decanters were produced in numerous sizes, from small to large. I have found both the creamers and small decanters in a brilliant sapphire blue but the largest pieces in color are rarer.

A particularly fine impression of a large pitcher in the Sunburst pattern is shown on Plate 43. Footed creamers are more scarce than those without the addition of a foot but may be found from time to time. Illustrated on the same Plate (43) is an excellent example of such a creamer, in the Sunburst pattern, with a ribbed foot. Other footed types carry the pointed leaf effect (an exaggerated herringbone) noted on the small blue salt. It is encountered most frequently (when found at all!) in bright sapphire blue, like the salt.

Another very rare pitcher sometimes found in dark blue is pictured in the lower right-hand corner of Plate 34. There again the Diamond Sunburst is seen alternating with a diamond quilted panel. It has a chevron design about the foot. In addition there is a row of Diamond Sunbursts above the main motif around the bowl. One will note a row of a similar style of Diamond Sunbursts on the hat in the same picture. I have large fragments of such a pitcher in crystal, taken from the Sandwich excavations.

A quart pitcher in the baroque "Shell" pattern is seen in the center on Plate 34. Since the decanters in this design were made in quarter-pint, half-pint and quart sizes, I believe the pitchers were also, in sapphire blue as well as in crystal.

A design seldom encountered is one that bears a close relationship to other Sandwich Blown Molded patterns and that is the larger pitcher shown on Plate 46. The only other piece I have seen to match is the quart decanter. Both were in clear glass. The chain design as seen around the bowl of the pitcher may also be seen on numerous objects in blown glass, when the only embellishment is a chain. It may be noted on the quart decanters on Plates 46 and 47. To identify the pitcher I am calling it Baroque—Chain with Heart.

One more unusual pattern in a pitcher is that illustrated on Plate 46, also influenced by the baroque style. Specimens of these pitchers are rare and I have never seen any other items to match. Numerous fragments would establish it as of Sandwich manufacture. For purposes of identification, I am calling it Beaded Arch.

Other pitchers than those illustrated were produced, following most of the familiar patterns seen in the decanters. I have learned that almost anything made at Sandwich in clear glass may turn up in color, for Deming Jarves probably took more interest in color work than any other man in the glass industry—in his day or in ours.

For a collector who likes to specialize, the field of blown glass decanters is a wide one. Sandwich made them in crystal and a bright dark blue, with a very limited number of yellow ones for good measure. The amber, olive-amber and olive-green were produced at Keene, N. H., and at Vernon, N. Y. An aquamarine decanter with an order of vertical ribbing, the reverse of the Sandwich type was made at Kent, Ohio. By a reverse order, I mean that the typical Sandwich design has the diamond quilting in the center band around the object with vertical ribbing on each side of the band. As noted elsewhere, this is the commonest of the Blown Molded patterns. The Kent decanter has a coarse broad band of vertical ribbing around the center of the decanter, with a broad band of diamond quilting on each side of it.

There are other patterns in dark glass decanters but none that can be attributed to Sandwich. The favored color at this factory was the familiar brilliant sapphire blue.

Probably the size of decanter that attracts most collectors, excluding the toys, is the quarter-pint. A group of these is shown on Plate 30. Certainly it is the scarcest size and there is something quaint and very appealing about their diminutiveness. Moreover, they don't take up so much room on the shelves! Those illustrated are all of the same patterns noted in other articles already treated. In my travels I have come across fewer quarter-pints than any other size but I presume others than those pictured were made. Half-pints come next. One is pictured in the Sunburst pattern on Plate 43. I have seen the Shell (baroque) pattern in clear glass and in sapphire blue. Other half-pints in Sandwich patterns include the one shown on Plate 42, as well as plain paneled types; the common diamond quilted with vertical ribbing; and the Diamond Sunburst with herringbone like the quarter-pint in the center illustrated on Plate 30. Another interesting piece, not illustrated, has the Sun-

PLATE 46

Upper—Baroque quart pitcher, Chain with Heart.
Lower—Quart decanter, Chain pattern. Pint pitcher, Beaded Arch.

PLATE 47—BLOWN MOLDED QUART DECANTERS
Star pattern.   Chain with Heart.

PLATE 48

Fragments of decanters and stoppers excavated at Sandwich.   Period 1830-1840.

PLATE 49

Complete decanters corresponding to fragments shown in preceding illustration.

PLATE 50

Unidentified Blown Molded decanters, which may be of Sandwich origin.

Collection of the author

PLATE 51—QUART DECANTERS

Left to right—1. Waffle Sunburst; 2. Diamond Sunburst; 3. Concentric ring Sunburst; 4. Diamond quilted Band

Collection of the author

PLATE 52

Quart Blown Molded decanter in a rare ribbed pattern.

burst showing a concentric ring with dot in the center alternating with a diamond quilted panel. The lower part of this decanter has a band of vertical ribbing. Over the Sunburst band about the center is a row of diagonal ribbing.

There are quite a number of quart decanters in authenticated Sandwich patterns, judging by the fragments that came from beneath the 1849 building. Two are illustrated on Plate 49 and fragments of the two decanters, as well as the stoppers, are shown on Plate 48. The decanter on the left is a baroque pattern and might be considered the most elaborate of the Blown Molded patterns. Pitchers were made to match in clear as well as in dark blue. The Arched decanter on the right I have never seen except in a quart size. Pitchers were also made. I have never seen one in color but they may exist. The Horn of Plenty (blown, not pressed) decanter on Plate 33 has not yet been authenticated as Sandwich but may some day, if more fragments throw additional light on the point.

Three rare decanters which have not yet been identified are shown on Plate 50. They are all quarts, the one in the center being unusually large. These are being shown for the benefit of collectors, in the hope that it may lead to more information about them. It is doubtless wishful thinking that makes me feel that they may be identified as Sandwich later on. As this is written, I have found a perfect specimen of the quart on the left, with an exquisite lacy stopper in a mushroom shape.

On Plate 51 are four decanters in such pleasing designs that they are all favorites of the collector. Number 1, reading from the left, is called Waffle Sunburst to differentiate it from other Sunburst designs. As there is no other variation of this same pattern, this name will serve the purpose. Other pieces were made to match, a rarity being the covered sugar bowl. There were also bowls and sauce dishes (shallow saucers) flip glasses, tumblers, mugs, etc. The same pattern was used for decanters in dark glass at Keene, N. H., but in a different shape. The Keene type of bottle slopes, without any shoulders, to a tapering neck. I know of no reason why Sandwich should have used the identical design in different forms, unless the Keene molds were purchased when the factory closed down or the pattern was copied by the moldmaker.

Number 2 on the same Plate (51) is the Diamond Sunburst pattern, with concentric ring center, which has been discussed in creamers, large pitchers, etc. It would appear that on the very small pieces, such as the hat and small creamers, there is a dot in the center of the sunburst, with one concentric ring around it, but as the piece increases in size, such as in the quart decanter, we encounter a double concentric ring around the dot.

Number 3 on Plate 51 is the Concentric Ring Sunburst, which is not encountered very frequently in clear glass. This is another pattern which Keene made in dark glass decanters without the flange. I cannot solve the mystery at this writing as to why Sandwich happened to make these in clear glass with the addition of the flange. The concentric ring with dot in center is one of the very earliest of Sandwich designs, carried out on numerous bases as well as on various objects so we could expect it to be used in the decanter design as well.

The quart decanter on the end of Plate 51 cannot definitely be attributed to Sandwich at this time, as the fragments have been too small to be absolutely certain, but it may be proved before long. For identification purposes it might be named Diamond Quilted Band.

The large globular baroque decanter with chain running about the center of the bowl, shown on Plate 46, is quite scarce. It will be noted that, so far, it is the only decanter with a foot, which is a departure from the usual form. I have never seen any other pieces than the decanter in this pattern though they may exist. So far the decanters have only been found in clear glass. The base has concentric rings. Corresponding fragments were found at Sandwich.

Another unusual decanter which is not seen frequently is the one bearing a medallion encompassing a twelve-pointed star, as pictured on Plate 47. Stoppers bearing the star were made to match. To date I have not seen this pattern except in clear glass quart and pint decanters. A collector is said to own a blue one but for some inexplicable reason he refuses to let anyone see it. On the same Plate (47) is another decanter which has been filled with a colored liquid in order to make the design, which is rather thin, show more clearly. This design was discussed under pitchers and called Chain with Heart. I have not seen it in any other forms than pitchers and decanters, and they are scarce at that. The quart ribbed decanter on Plate 52 is rare in that size.

To cover minutely every sauce dish and bowl in every size and pattern made at Sandwich is well nigh an impossibility. The smallest preserve or honey dish I ever saw measured 3½ inches in diameter and had the simple diamond quilting and vertical ribbing. Plates and bowls were made in nearly all the more familiar Blown Molded patterns. Shallow sauce dishes or sauce plates are fairly common. Deep dishes are scarcer and large bowls are rare. Any such pieces, from sauce dishes to bowls are extremely rare in color.

It is difficult to photograph bowls to show the pattern in a satisfactory manner so only one group is shown on Plate 53.

Sugar bowls, celery vases and large objects such as punch bowls, come under the heading of the superlative in Blown Molded glass. The sugar bowls vary greatly, as may be seen in the three examples illustrated on Plates 37 and 54. They may be found also with Sunburst motifs as well as with an open foot, instead of the solid glass styles as illustrated. Perfect examples in color are extremely rare.

There are different patterns to be encountered in celery vases, but the most familiar is shown on Plate 54.

The unique celery vase on Plate 55 came from a well-known collection and sold at a fairly modest sum at auction in the Parke-Bernet Galleries in New York City. The reason for the bargain was not due to any imperfection but because a dealer whispered around that it was "Irish" glass! Nevertheless an experienced collector bought it.

In "Irish Glass" by M. S. Dudley Westropp, a somewhat similar celery glass made at Cork, is illustrated but the diamond pattern is

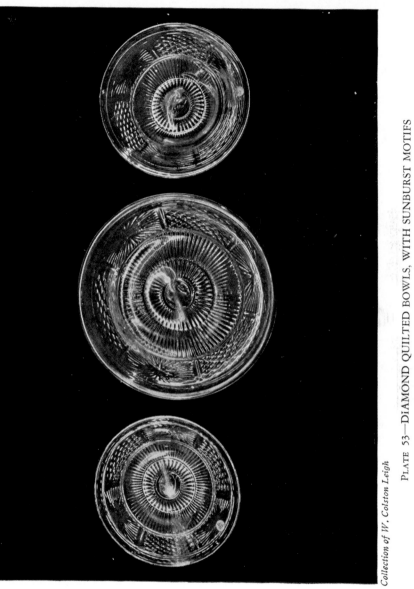

PLATE 53—DIAMOND QUILTED BOWLS, WITH SUNBURST MOTIFS

Sizes: 7⅜ inches   10 inches   8⅜ inches

PLATE 54

Rare examples of a Blown Molded celery vase, sugar bowl and an
inkwell with Sunburst motif.

PLATE 55

Rare diamond quilted celery vase of a type made at Sandwich; period 1828-1840.
Design possibly copied from Irish (Cork) "Diamond Cutting and Flutes Celery Glass."

larger and there are more "flutes" on the side. It is shorter and the clear top is bent downward to such an extent that the piece has more the appearance of a vase than a celery holder or celery glass. I have found enough examples of panelled, diamond quilted pieces at Sandwich to feel reasonably safe in attributing this piece to that factory. More forms of the diamond pattern, both in blown and pressed glass, were made at Sandwich than in any other factory. I still have in my possession unidentified Blown Molded pieces with panels which so far have not fitted into any known whole specimens. In fact, there are still many unidentified fragments which must some day be found to be counterparts of some rare pieces. The celery is similar to some of the larger, heavy decanters which carry a large diamond pattern. The foot bears a rough pontil mark. It is a unique piece, fit for any museum.

Probably the greatest rarity in "three-mold" Blown Molded glass is the punch bowl. A few are known and are in the possession of collectors and museums.

Chapter X

CUP PLATES

In discussing cup plates, I always assume collectors are aware that the little plates were used over a century ago to hold the tea cups after pouring the very hot tea into saucers to cool. The earliest were of china and they antedated the glass plates. It should be kept in mind that tea drinking originated with the Chinese, who took theirs quite hot and that early cups were often handleless. Our forefathers, one hundred and fifty years ago did not consider it bad table manners to drink their tea from saucers. The great Dr. Samuel Johnson absorbed his scaldingly hot, and the sound of his cautious intake was audible in the neighborhood. And students of our Colonial period will tell you how before the Boston Tea Party, people asked for a *dish* of tea.

The cup plates saved soiling the linen or marking the mahogany tables and therefore they were in general use over a long period of thrifty years. They are divided by American collectors into two groups: "Historical" and "Conventional." The Historicals, as the title suggests, deal with famous persons or events. Some of the Conventionals are simple in design, while many others have lacy motifs woven into intricate ornamental patterns. They were made in quantity by the Boston & Sandwich Glass Company as well as by several Midwestern manufacturers. There is also evidence that some may have come from the Philadelphia district and others from an early glasshouse in or near Baltimore. They date approximately from 1827 to 1850, though some were carried on well beyond the latter date.

Illustrated on Plate 56 is a group of the cup plates which I believe to be among the earliest produced, if not actually the earliest. Development of designs may be worked out in the chronological order in which I thoroughly believe they grew. It is reasonable to suppose that the finely stippled lacy glass was an outgrowth of simple patterns used at the beginning, when the molds and appliances were still undergoing mechanical improvements.

Figure 1 at the top of Plate 56, is a thick, heavy, clumsy plate which is simplicity itself. The border has heavy vertical lines and the center is rather crudely rayed. Examples of this plate have been found more than a half-inch in thickness. I have seen one that weighed a half-pound!

Next to it, in the upper row on the right, is the same plate with a very slight elaboration. The chief difference is in the center where you will note a dot in the middle of the three concentric circles. About the sides of the base is ribbing—or rings. The left-hand plate in the middle row has a slightly narrower border and five concentric rings in the center, still with the dot in the middle. The next step in the evolution of design is seen in the right-hand plate in the middle row. Fan-shaped ornaments are used in the border instead of the severe, heavy vertical lines. The center of the plate remains much the same, except that the concentric circles have increased slightly in size but the dot is still there. This plate is a quarter-inch thick as compared with the other three, most of which are at least a half-inch thick.

The fan border used on so many of the early Sandwich pieces, though undoubtedly continued for a time, lost its vogue after the more ornate plates appeared with the heavily stippled background, popularly referred to as lacy Sandwich. On the plate in the lower left-hand corner, it will be noted that the border is scalloped, the fan tapers into a circle, and each fan alternates with a tiny ornament. The five-pointed star in the center is just the beginning of a great number of variations of stars ornamenting the centers of cup plates, though they vary in size and style. It will be noted that the plate in the lower right-hand corner with a waffle center has the same border as that with the star center. Following are other cup plates, all with the thick edge and conventional designs but still not the stippled background.

The earlier heart designs originated in this period, probably about 1828. I do not refer to those thinner plates with the stippled background shown on Plate 63 but to the thick, heavy pieces having a heart in the border alternating with a sheaf of wheat, and four interlaced hearts in the center. Among Mr. Marble's group of cup plate pictures, the identifying numbers would be: 176, 177, 178, 179, and 564. One is pictured in a 5-inch size on Plate 105. Many nappies, large plates and bowls were produced in the same patterns and there were other variations not to be found in the cup plates, such as a heart alternating with a lyre, or a heart alternating with a flower, illustrated in Plates 65 and 66.

Our Pilgrim furniture was rather crude. The designs of the earliest silver also were simple and so it was natural that the earliest cup plates should be plainer than a later generation demanded. Pressing machinery for making glassware was in its infancy, both at home and abroad. While there is no one alive today to tell us of these first presses and no records of particular value, we do know that the one for pressing cup plates was a three-part affair. The earliest molds at Sandwich were usually made of brass.* The figures were cut on the plunger and pressed upside down. The surface die was at the bottom and a cap ring controlled the rim. If the plunger went down unevenly, or the mold slipped, then the piece would be thicker on one side than on the other. It is not uncommon to find dishes of this period (1827–1830) with one side a half-inch and the other a quarter-inch in thickness. Changes in methods and technique must have been rapid at this stage of experimentation. For instance, the earliest plates with the vertical lines in the border and rayed centers have been studied and all showed a definite seam straight across the center of the plate and yet, in Marble's Number 160, which has five concentric rings and is obviously of a later period than his 389, which has no rings,

---

* After the first few years of pressing, brass molds were largely discontinued. Brass was too soft to be practical and its melting point was too low.

this line is not seen, nor is it apparent on any later plates. Surface scratches and other seams, sometimes erroneously referred to as "straw marks," are found on virtually all cup plates as well as on most of the larger bowls, plates, etc. They are accounted for by one writer as being due to the fact that at Sandwich, the reheating or annealing process to render the glass less liable to breakage, was carried to a point at which the object was almost at the melting stage. The result was little seam-like marks which the uninformed like to assure dealers are either cracks or imperfections that greatly lessen the desirability of the piece.* It is well to warn new collectors that cup plates were never meant to be used for ash trays! They are affected by extreme heat or cold and will usually crack if a lighted cigarette is left on one.

The late Mr. Harry Hall White was of the opinion that the seams or "fissures" were opened as the face of the glass cooled. It shrank more rapidly than the still viscous interior, until, like a too tight garment, it had to yield somewhere to the strain. He wrote: "Such strains might have been avoided if mold and plunger could have been kept at a uniform temperature so as to prevent the occurrence of prematurely cooling areas." (From the magazine *Antiques*.)

Whoever collects early Sandwich glass is bound to hear all manner of stories purporting to furnish explanations of the reason for these characteristic features or marks. Their number is legion and they reach incredible heights of absurdity. In the Boston *Transcript* appeared the following, apparently printed in all seriousness:

"Mr. Wilfred Wheeler of Hatchville, down on the elbow of Cape Cod, has a very interesting explanation of the famous Sandwich line which is found in many specimens of that type of glass.

---

* This firepolishing apparently began at Sandwich along about 1840 and reached its peak by 1860. In the early days at Sandwich imperfections occurred when the annealing, or the reheating process which renders glass less liable to breakage, was too cool. The outside cooled more rapidly than the inside, thereby producing stresses that caused these cracklings. Another cause was a too cool mold. Lacy dishes having an elaborate over-all pattern did not show so many imperfections because the design covered them.

The line is a fault evidently caused by a horsehair or other imperfection in the mould, and the probability is that the fault is intentional, rather than the result of carelessness or inefficient workmanship. Mr. Wheeler, who is not only well versed in local Cape history, but was also a former Commissioner of Agriculture for Massachusetts, ventures the belief that the Sandwich line was a deliberate fault, weakening the structure of the dish and causing it to break easily, thereby necessitating the replacing of the total sale of the factory's product. The reasoning is ingenious, and possibly with a great deal of foundation, but the Prowler will wait to hear from the defenders of Sandwich integrity before taking any stand on the question."

The "foundation" of the horsehair iniquitously used in a red-hot mold at the bottom of a mass of molten glass to provide for the easy fracture of the plate showed great commercial sagacity! The easier a flawed dish is broken the more readily it sells!

Several of the earliest types of cup plates were used as feet for small whale oil lamps. One such lamp is illustrated on Plate 188. I have a fragment of one of the earliest, like Mr. Marble's Number 158, converted into a three-step lamp base. It is a crude, heavy affair, a half-inch thick on the edges. The following cup plate patterns are among those used as bases for lamps and accordingly were made thicker when intended for that purpose: Marble's Numbers 281, 282, 315, 337, 417, and 506. The known varieties of cup plates number in the neighborhood of 1,000, but, of course, not all were produced at Sandwich There is no need to list here other than such cup plates which so far as is known at this time may be attributed to Sandwich, based on the corroborative fragments found at the factory site. However, it is safe to assume that of many Sandwich plates no fragments have been unearthed. A list is given of the localities to which Mr. Marble ascribes certain other cup plates.

It has seemed to me that it would be helpful to give to collectors a shining mark at which to aim. With this in mind, I requested two well-known specialists, Mr. James H. Rose and Mr. George L.

Tilden, to submit a list of the ten Historical and the ten Conventional cup plates which each considered rarest, whether or not the plates were of Sandwich origin, since the end sought was merely the determination of relative rarity. It was interesting and important to find that both experts, without consulting each other, agreed on the selection. Mr. Marble went over the list and it was concluded to omit one Conventional, Number 570, since there is some doubt as to whether it was originally intended for a cup plate and we substituted Number 767, a rare heart pattern of which very few specimens are known. I could not resist adding an additional Conventional plate which is so rare that Mr. Marble has only recently added it to his collection. The ten rarest Historicals are illustrated on Plates 57 and 58 and the eleven Conventionals on Plates 59 and 60. They are not listed in the order of their local rarity, since many collectors might question the arrangement.

Since this volume first appeared in December 1939, the relative rarity of several of the plates has changed. As sometimes happens, a few of a rare number come to light, thereby causing another rare plate to make its way to the top of the list. From the original "first ten" Historicals, an Eagle plate supplants the Steamboat with hairpin border (834) and another rare Eagle (824) supplants the Maid of the Mist, with stars (288). It has also been found that the Log Cabin (Number 339) now upsets the one formerly pictured, Number 333.

Among the Conventional plates, there are even more changes. From the first eleven, five have dropped from top places. Curiously, nearly all the rarest plates are attributed to the Midwest. From this fact, it may be deduced that nearly all New England cup plates were made in larger quantities. Relative rarity varies in different sections of the country. The matter of their respective desirability obviously depends on the individual collector. According to Mr. Marble's numbers of identification, they are as follows:

HISTORICAL PLATES

(Illustrated on Plates 57 and 58)

1. Washington, round 753
2. Major Ringgold 387
3. Constitution, round 407
4. Fulton, round 527
5. Eagle 834
6. Plow, octagonal 568
7. "Union Glass Works" boat, octagonal 556
8. Eagle 824
9. Log Cabin 339
10. Concentric Eagle 504

CONVENTIONALS

(Illustrated on Plates 59 and 60)

1. Basket of flowers 785
2. Six-pointed star, similar type to above........ 462
3. Lacy Conventional....................... 607
4. Lacy Conventional....................... 832
5. Eight circles in center, 4 large, 4 small 575
6. Lacy, with considerable detail 644
7. Nectarine 826
8. Conventional Scroll 751
9. Rare heart pattern, nine hearts 767
10. Gothic arch, octagonal 594
11. Lacy Conventional 534

Color has not been taken into account as it would make the list too confusing.

A few observations in regard to these plates may be of interest, particularly to new collectors.

The round Washington which heads the list came to light for the first time in 1938. Two specimens were found, both in Ohio. They are like the same plate which comes in octagonal form with a rayed design around Washington's head, so it may be assumed that the plain one is earlier, the latter having the addition of the more decorative rays. (Plate 57.)

There is one cup plate, bearing the bust of Jenny Lind, which is not included in this book because of the doubts surrounding it. There are many cup plates which are exceedingly rare but it is hazardous to assert that there is only one example in existence. The chances are all against the "uniqueness" of any object which was made in quantities. Molds were too expensive for a glass-house to make one specimen only and then destroy the mold. Of course, the Jenny Lind plate may be foreign, for the Swedish Nightingale was a European favorite. If the plate is of trans-Atlantic origin, it may not have been exported to America on a commercial scale. More data concerning it may be forthcoming some day but the cup plate was refused a place in my list by the unanimous vote of those most competent to pass on the subject.

Returning to the ten most popular Historicals, Number two on the list is a Major Ringgold. All the Ringgold plates are rare but this one in particular was selected because this type with the center faintly stippled is less frequently found. (Plate 57.)

Number three in the Historical group is the round Constitution. It is so referred to because it also comes in an octagonal form, as does Number four on the list, the round Fulton. Number five is an Eagle plate so rare that most collectors are not familiar with it. It was found in the Philadelphia area and so far, only one is known.

Number six on the list (Plate 58), the octagonal Plow, is particularly scarce, especially in perfect condition. It is a Midwestern plate, as are many of those which are octagonal in form. At first glance, not quite so much historical significance attaches to it as to the others in this group, but it is almost certain that the Plow, emblematic of agriculture, came out during William Henry Harrison's campaign in 1840 when he was hailed not only as "The Hero of Tippecanoe" but also as "The Farmer of North Bend." The border on many of his campaign handkerchiefs consists of a succession of plows. Sandwich produced a bowl at that time hav-

PLATE 56
Evolution of design at Sandwich. Period 1827-1830.

PLATE 57
Five of the ten rarest Historical cup plates, largely Midwestern,

PLATE 58

Five of the ten rarest Historical cup plates from New England and the Midwest.

PLATE 59

Five of the eleven rarest Conventional cup plates from New England and the Midwest.

PLATE 60
Six of the eleven rarest Conventional cup plates, largely Midwestern.

ing a log cabin in the center and around the border a factory, a ship, and a man plowing, all equally typical emblems of the Hard Cider Campaign. These bowls were made elsewhere than at Sandwich, as I have found four varieties of them. Two are shown on Plate 89. Number seven, the octagonal plate picturing a boat, is marked "Union Glass Works Pittsburgh 1836". This was made by Parke, Campbell and Hanna of Pittsburgh. Number eight on this list was formerly awarded to the Maid of the Mist, with stars. This has been replaced by an octagonal Eagle, Number 824. It is so rare that few collectors have seen it. Six specimens are known, all imperfect. They were discovered in Hickory, Pa., just south of Pittsburgh. In considering Number nine, the Log Cabin, the selection was difficult. It was finally concluded to show Number 339 instead of 333. There are a number of Log Cabin variations, some of which are common. The log cabin and cider barrel was a popular subject during the 1840 Harrison campaign. Not more than seven or eight of Number 339 have been found and all of them were discovered in the Philadelphia area. Number ten is a concentric Eagle plate to date found only in opal and a cloudy blue-opalescent. It was difficult to photograph clearly enough to show the detail of the eagle in the center of the plate, which is very small and often rather blurred. This may very well have been the first Eagle design made. (Plate 58.)

About the selection of the ten rarest Conventional plates there may be room for a mild controversy. The matter is of no great importance, but you may be sure collectors will find it difficult to procure any one of the listed plates in a hurry. Two of them are so scarce that it was only lately that Mr. Marble added them to his famous collection. On this list, Number one plate shown on Plate 59 has a large basket of flowers in the center and a border of eighteen sheaves of wheat. For reasons that I find difficult to express clearly, I am inclined to think that it may have been made by the New England Glass Company. Perhaps it is a form of instinct developed by long familiarity with glass. In any event, the plate does not look to me like Sandwich and it most certainly does not have a Midwestern appearance. It is thick, early and heavy. Two are known at present. Number two looks enough like it, in a general way, to be considered a companion piece. It also is thick and heavy and has eighteen sheaves of wheat in the border. The metal is of a peculiar cloudy-clear unlike any other plates I have seen. Only one specimen has been found. There are a few others quite similar but not so rare which belong in the same group. Number three is a replacement. This time Number 607 was chosen. It is a lacy conventional in which eight or ten specimens are known and they were all found in the Pittsburgh area. Number four is another replacement, this time being Mr. Marble's 832. Two of these rare plates have been found to date, one in Pittsburgh and the other in Ravenna, Ohio. (Plate 59.) Number five is a truly conventional pattern, having four large bubble-like circles in the center together with four others, smaller in size. Seven specimens are known at present, which were mostly found in the Midwest. Number six is brilliant and lacy with a more elaborate design than any of the others. Judging by the frequency of the findings in one locality, it is probably a Pittsburgh product. (Plate 60.) Number seven is reminiscent of the Nectarine pattern made at Sandwich in plates, sauce dishes and bowls. Even so, one would be justified in questioning its "Sandwichicity," because of the border serrations, which are unlike those seen on authenticated specimens. Number 826 replaces the former 661, though the only difference is in the style of border serrations. This flower design, which I christened "Nectarine" in 1939 when "Sandwich Glass" first appeared, is usually found in the Philadelphia area. More of these are known in green than in clear glass. Number eight is a Midwestern plate. Only about nine of these are known at present. Probably the rarest of the Heart series is Number nine (Marble's 767) of which only six or seven are known. It is the one plate carrying so few hearts: There are but nine. Number ten is an octagonal plate with a Gothic Arch design almost certainly of Pittsburgh origin. It is difficult to find in good condition. Number eleven was added for good measure. It is a typical lacy conventional design but it is very rare. Three specimens are known and they were all found in New England. (Plate 60.)

While the above list of chosen rarities represents the ultimate for even experienced collectors, it must be said that forthcoming years will inevitably bring about changes.

Another question which perplexes collectors involves a plain Conventional plate (Marble's 120), which has a waffle center and simple Conventional border. The question is: Why is this type of plate found in a much heavier metal with a silver bust of some well-known person encased in it, such as Lafayette, Napoleon, or a bewhiskered gentleman who may be the French King, Louis Philippe? Not many of them turned up in this country but all of them have a little hole bored in the top in which an ornamental brass fixture can be fitted for hanging on the wall. These plates do not all have borders of the same pattern as may be seen in the illustrations on Plates 61 and 62.

In the English "Dictionary of National Biography" the sketch of Apsley Pellatt says: "In 1819 he (Pellatt) took out a patent for 'Crystallo-ceramie or glass incrustation which consisted in enclosing medallions and ornaments of pottery ware, metal, or refractory material in glass.' He is said to have received the idea from a foreigner who resided abroad." This would indicate that the idea was not original with Pellatt and that the process might have been already in use on the Continent. The name of the man who gave him the idea is not mentioned. In later decades, the "glassed-in pastes" enjoyed periods of popularity in Europe. Pazaurek, who did not like the inroads of mechanical production into the field of "art glass," commented that the "least objectionable were those of the late 50's and they were touched up a bit by cutting, even though the cutting sometimes merely removed the mold marks. The busts of Franz Joseph, Emperor of Austria, and his Empress Elizabeth (seen in the museum of Industrial Arts in

Courtesy of James H. Rose

PLATE 61—"GLASSED-IN PASTES"

Not cup plates but made in various European countries for use as ornaments, suspended from the wall.

PLATE 62

Bust of Napoleon. Plate probably made in France by "glassed-in paste" process patented by Apsley Pellatt in England.

PLATE 63

Authenticated Sandwich cup plates with corresponding fragments and additional pieces taken from the site of the old factory. Period 1827-1835.

Prague and in the collection of C. Baer, Mannheim) of King Friedrich Wilhelm IV of Prussia in the Berlin Hohenzollern Museum and in the collection of G. W. Schultz of Leipzig, were soon followed by other royal heads as well as by heads and figures of Saints and Madonnas, such as were still made in Baccarat in the 70's."

In my opinion, very little of this type of work was done in our country. There is no evidence of it at Sandwich. We may have copied the pattern of Marble's 120 plate from the English or French or they may have copied it from us. The Waffle pattern was a favorite abroad. I do believe most of the silver bust work was done early by Apsley Pellatt and later by the workers in Baccarat. A very beautiful flower vase of lacy glass was brought to me from France. In one side is encased a silver bust of Ste. Catherine. There is very little doubt of this being a product of Baccarat.

On Plate 63 may be seen entire specimens of cup plates and fragments taken from the site of the Sandwich factory, showing how the identification of patterns was arrived at. The list of those identified to date does not give the color variations. These were so numerous and varied in tints as to make the list too confusing to compile. I may say that the following colors are the most frequently seen: Opal; many shades of blue; several shades of green, including peacock and emerald; yellow; violet and amethyst. Curiously enough, ruby or pink cup plates have never been found. Following the plates identified as Sandwich are those attributed to other factories by Mr. Albert Marble.

SANDWICH

Identified fragments of Sandwich cup plates listed according to Marble Numbers.

Fragments			Variants		
2	131	288	10	400	663
3	136	309	28	418	664
4	148	384	29	426	675

Fragments				Variants		
5	149	402		31	460	680
6	164	404		32	492	685
7	170	485		41	523	712
8	176	555		57	541	716
9	178	600		68	563	717
24	180	601		109	564	722
25	181	603		117	572	723
26	186	608		137	578	734
27	193	617		143	581	737
33	194	620		177	583	738
34	195	633		179	595	
35	203	677		182	596	
39	204			219	597	
40	205			294	598	
42	212			301	599	
45	213			302	609	
90	216			305	619	
107	220			334	621	
108	222			366	633	
118	223			393	644	
128	262			394	650	

New England Glass	Fort Pitt	Pittsburgh	Midwestern
82	15	54	269
83	16	55	278
98	50	185	352
99	245	255	429
120	266	271	436
137	279	279	503
146	658	332	527
182	38	369	540
290	278	428	568
405	329	429	575
490	527	556	594
643		613	644
716			658

Sandwich Glass

English	Ohio	Dyottville	Pittsburgh & Sandwich
696	258	260	289
704	451	387	369
721	467	403	442
	351	412	
	456	413	
	606	634	

Chapter XI

THE CONNECTING LINK

Collectors should realize that the beautifully stippled so-called "lace" glass was the outgrowth of the simpler designs that preceded it. The sophisticated, more elaborate types came later. In the chapter on cup plates is an illustration of the development in design. Something of the sort happened also with the larger pieces.

On Plate 64 are shown three of the early seven-inch plates, all having a waffle pattern center but different borders. On one is a very simple fan border. The second has a fan border, with a little flower alternating with the fan. The third plate has the fan border with the addition of round and square ornaments. The surface edge around the scallops is beaded. These three plates are good examples of the early development in design. The plainest of the three is said to have been made at the Vernon, N. Y., factory but I cannot vouch for it.

On Plate 104 is still another example of a plate which may be numbered among the earliest. It will be noted that the border is quite lacy but the center is still in the waffle pattern. The upper edge is beaded, as are many pieces produced during this period. All these plates have thick edges and are exceptionally heavy for their size. In the same illustration are two plates in a still more elaborate pattern, called Shield and Pine Tree. The centers are similar but one border is considerably more elaborate than the other. The surface edge of the scallop on both these pieces is also beaded, but the vogue for that particular phase of ornamentation went out almost entirely when the Heart series came in, even though it was retained on a few dishes and cup plates.

On Plates 65 and 66 are two of the largest bowls made in the Heart pattern. The one on Plate 65 is the simpler, with its border of alternating hearts and lyres. This border combination is not found on small pieces, on which a small sheaf of wheat replaces the lyre. The bowl on Plate 65 measures 10¾ inches in diameter and is extremely heavy. The edge is fully a half-inch thick on one side and a little over a quarter-inch on the other side. The border has a heart and a small eight-petaled flower, alternating. The upper edge has three tiny flowers embossed on it, above the larger flower in the border. The desire to embellish the top edge had not been abandoned entirely. It is seen on Heart cup plates and other small pieces of the same series. The diamond-shaped pattern that fills the bowl of this large dish was a change from the square waffle and was in vogue for a short time. The conventional design in the base of the bowl combines eight hearts, with a diamond motif and scroll above them. Fragments of the various Heart patterns were found buried four feet beneath the surface, when the excavating was done beneath the foundation of the building which was erected in 1849. A few lacy fragments taken from this site are shown on Plate 68.

On Plate 67 is another huge bowl which has not been particularly popular with collectors, perhaps because of its too massive appearance. Diamonds in four different sizes make up the design. I have never seen this bowl in a small size nor the same pattern in any other pieces.

There are so many variations of the Heart design that to treat them all at length would nearly fill another book! All manner of pieces were made, such as cup plates, small plates in several sizes, sauce dishes and small bowls besides large bowls and deep dishes, the last-named shaped much like our modern soup plates. On Plates 105, 106 and 107 are several of the variations. The one on Plate 107 with the heart border alternating with the sheaf of wheat with a stippled background in the edge is the connecting ling leading to the higher types of lacy glass with their more elaborate designs, all of them with stippled backgrounds. It is these lacy, silvery-toned pieces in unique patterns originated by the famous glass factory, that have made the name of the little

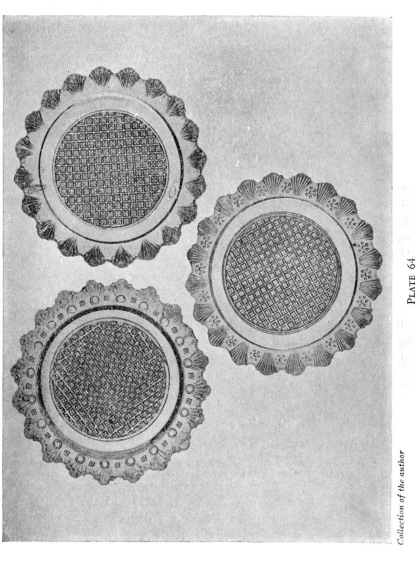

PLATE 64

Early pressed plates (7 inch) which preceded those with stippled backgrounds, circa 1828.

PLATE 65

Large bowl (10¾ inches) of the Heart series, circa 1830.

PLATE 66
Large bowl (9½ inches) of the Heart series, circa 1830.

PLATE 67
Unusually large, heavy bowl, circa 1830.

PLATE 68

Fragments of lacy Sandwich glass, found in excavations under building erected in 1849.

town of Sandwich on Cape Cod, Mass., known the world over. Moreover, the highly decorative lacy pieces that followed the simple ones started the intensive period of lacy production, which was from approximately 1830 to 1840.

A few collectors have expressed the opinion that they do not care to add the Heart pieces to their collection because they are not "lacy" glass. It is not, but it is earlier and therefore no collection of this line of Americana can be called complete or truly representative without it. The forerunners of the "lacy" glass have not been properly valued. It is to be hoped that in the future, collectors will overlook their less artistic merit and properly esteem their historical associations. Pilgrim furniture cannot compare with Chippendale for grace and beauty of design but it has been eagerly collected notwithstanding or perhaps chiefly because of its crudeness and the stories it tells. Early Sandwich glass has more to recommend it, in point of appearance, than most of the early pine furniture over which so many faddists ran wild.

Chapter XII

LACY SALTS

As in the case of cup plates, Sandwich undoubtedly produced many more of the lacy variety than have been identified from fragment findings. Comparing the small pieces excavated from the factory site with whole specimens is an almost endless task, but it has been possible so far positively to attribute over fifty patterns to this Cape Cod glasshouse. What has impressed all those who have spent much time studying these fragments has been not so much the wide variety of design as the amazing color range. There are undoubtedly more colored salts in proportion to the total number produced than there are colored cup plates. In fact, there is more color to be found among the salts than any other single lacy collectible item, which would include cup plates, sauce dishes, plates, bowls, sugar bowls, creamers, et cetera.

Among the earliest of the Sandwich salts are those extremely heavy, clumsy affairs which were big enough to meet the requirements of an entire family. Families were larger in the brave old days and salts were made to accommodate the customers.

Two are shown on Plate 69 as a matter of interest and comparison, even though they do not properly belong in the category of "lacy" salts. One is in crystal and the other in fiery opal. Others were made in canary, sapphire blue and amethyst. There is quite a wide variety of patterns in these plain styles, since every factory making tableware in the early days produced salt dishes, either in original designs or copied from other makers.

Before mentioning those salts which possess historical interest, attention should be called to those with covers. They are among the rarities in which a collector delights. Three are illustrated on Plate 69. The one in the center is in opal. They also are found in milk white, opaque powder blue and in crystal. Covers must have been intended originally to keep out the flies and the dampness or else it was deemed desirable to enhance the decorative appeal of the piece as a table ornament. The covers were so often broken or lost, that to acquire complete specimens today has become quite a problem.

Another pattern in the covered salt is that at the end of the line in the same picture. The beaded double scrolls are very effective and the basket of fruit, which may be seen on the side, was a favorite design at Sandwich in the early period. These are rare, but collectors may still successfully pursue them in opal, dark blue, light opaque blue, green and crystal. Curiously enough, the lacy design is printed on the *inside* of the covers, which does very well on the crystal salts because it shows through. On the opaque, because of the density of the color, it does not show at all.

There are a few salts having historical associations and these are always of particular interest, even though all are not of Sandwich origin. Probably the earliest is that bearing the portrait busts of Washington and Lafayette, shown on Plate 70. It has been ascribed by some collectors to the New England Glass Company. In any event, no fragments of it have so far been found at Sandwich but, in the absence of proof one way or another, it seems proper to include it here for the benefit of collectors. Most historical pieces were inspired by some special occasion, but it was never necessary to await a special event for a Washington-Lafayette piece.

Among other marked salts of special interest is the "Lafayet" boat salt. Several varieties of these exist, each of which is described in detail at the end of this chapter. No adequate explanation of why a boat-shaped salt should have been marked "Lafayet" has ever been offered. Fragments were found among the earliest lacy pieces at Sandwich, but even these would not have been early enough for Lafayette's visit in 1825. Nor is there any explanation of the curious spelling of "Lafayet." One of the most popular men connected with the Sandwich Company was George Lafayette Fessenden, affectionately referred to as "Lafe." He succeeded Deming

Jarves on his retirement in 1858 but the marked salts were too early to have been named for him. In an old account book, under date of March 9, 1827, are listed "7 Lafayette salts, $1.16." These might have referred to the boat salt or to the marked Washington-Lafayette oblong salt. It is interesting to note that, whichever style was meant, they were 16½ cents each! Today the "boats" are worth many times that figure in clear glass and still more in good colors. The "Lafayet" boat series must have been a popular line, for they were made in three variations and in numerous colors besides clear glass. They are fairly common today though always in great demand because of the historical association, despite the fact that little history of the salt itself can be told.

An attractive salt, widely sought by collectors because of its rarity, is that marked "H. Clay" which has a small locomotive in the base. (Plate 72.) It has been suggested that it was inspired, or even made up on a special order, to commemorate the running of the Lexington (Kentucky) Railway. No more plausible explanation has been offered to account for the engine, since Henry Clay was the principal stockholder in the railroad. His name on any object was a good Whig selling point for decades. He was a favorite son—the same old "Coon" at the Whig convention until after his defeat by Polk for the Presidency in 1844.

No steam engine was ever named after Henry Clay, so far as I can learn, but an amusing account of the first train to run on the Lexington road is given in a book entitled "Wonders and Curiosities of the Railway" by W. S. Kennedy, written in 1884. It will be of interest to any collector who is fortunate enough to find one of the rare marked "H. Clay" salts. The story runs as follows:

"In 1831 there was no railroad west of the Alleghanies and south of the Ohio River. In that year the wealthy inhabitants of Lexington, Kentucky, wishing to be thought no whit less enterprising than Cincinnati and Louisville and even aspiring to surpass those cities in glory—having doubtless heard with wonder of the doings of the locomotive in South Carolina and New York—began to take measures to build a railroad of their own. Frankfort was the nearest available town on the Kentucky River. Accordingly it was resolved to build the railroad to that town. Henry Clay was an influential stockholder in the road. It was finished in 1838 or 1839. The road was laid out in a very crooked manner, the engineers affirming that it was an advantage to have it so, since the conductor could look back along the curves and see his train more conveniently! The cars were at first for passengers only. They were drawn by two horses or mules, and were made to hold four persons, like the old stagecoaches.

"The cars of the Lexington railroad were two-story structures, the lower story being for ladies and children, and the upper one for men—though in warm weather many ladies preferred the top, at least before the locomotive was put on the road. This first locomotive was a ridiculous little affair made by a Lexington mechanic. It had no cab, and the tender was an open box-car with room for a small supply of wood, and for a hogshead of water which was filled by pumping from a well at the side of the road. In place of a 'cow-catcher,' or pilot, two large beams projected in front and had hickory brooms attached to them for sweeping the track. The blacks regarded the engine with awe and fear, considering it to be the work of the 'debbil,' and its disuse was hailed by them with joy. They thought horses good enough for them. When the locomotive was first put on the road, the directors celebrated the event by inviting guests to make an excursion to Frankfort in a 'brigade' of little platform cars. When the excursionists were drawing near to that town it began to snow, and lo, and behold, the engineer took shelter with his locomotive under a shed, and refused to budge an inch further, declaring that the 'slick' track would be so dangerous that the train might be derailed! Accordingly, many of the passengers had to foot it home."

In examining the engine on the marked H. Clay salt, it will be noted that it lacks a cab and that the tender appears to be loaded with wood, thereby seeming to confirm the description in the foregoing quotation.

The marked "Providence" salt is shrouded in mystery but at this

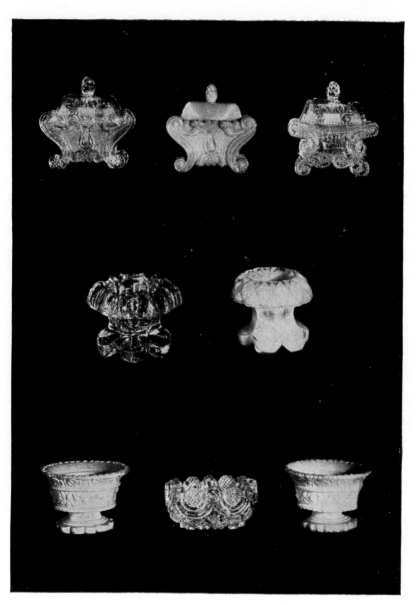

PLATE 69
Group of salts, including three rare types with covers.

PLATE 70
Early salts, including the rare Washington-Lafayette.

PLATE 71
Group of early salts.

PLATE 72—FIVE MARKED SALTS

Upper—"Sandwich, Lafayet."   Side view and marked interior.
Center—"Jersey Glass Co."; Locomotive "H. Clay."
Lower—"Providence"; "N. E. Glass Company, Boston."

time the easiest solution is that it probably was also made up on a special order.

The early salts marked "N. E. Glass Company Boston" were obviously produced by that company and in quantity, for they are the commonest of the marked pieces today.

The "Jersey Glass Co. Nr. N. Y." salt offers another interesting problem. It closely resembles the N. E. Glass Company marked specimen, though there are slight variations in the design. There was a Jersey Glass Company in Jersey City, and it is possible this concern may have been responsible for the piece that bears the name of a factory that specialized in blown glass. Another possibility is that the mold might have been purchased from a mold maker at the New England Glass Company or from Sandwich. The latter explanation is easier to accept because the marked Jersey pieces are extremely scarce and are most often found in a light green color in which not many of the oblong salts of this particular shape and design were made. Pittsburgh produced its own boat salts, similar to the marked Sandwich-Lafayet types. An example is not illustrated here but collectors will find them with a seven-pointed star on the paddlewheel and marked "Pittsburgh" on the stern. There is an anchor in the base and a cable cord around it, which forms the rim the salt rests on. This is the last of the marked pieces.

Another unmarked boat salt illustrated on Plate 19 may be of Sandwich origin, though there is no proof of it at this writing.

The Eagle-Cadmus salts are rare and interesting. Two variations are pictured on Plate 75. Sailing vessels have always been popular as decorative motifs. In the early days they were more often displayed in commemoration of an event than they are today, when the market is flooded with lithographs of ships, paintings, ships models, etc., of no particular historical interest or significance. When sailing vessels or early side-wheel passenger steamers are impressed in old glass, the lack of evidence corroborative of their identity makes any attempt to name the particular vessel it is supposed to represent rather hazardous. One ship, said to be the *Cadmus,* is displayed on a cup plate and also is found in a round salt where it alternates with an eagle, both of which are enclosed in medallions. The *Cadmus* was a sailing-vessel built in 1816 by Thatcher Magound of Medford, Massachusetts, and was selected, so the story goes, to bring Lafayette to this country in 1824. The voyage took thirty-one days. On its arrival at New York, the first of innumerable celebrations in honor of the Nation's guest, greeted Lafayette. For years the people of the United States were determined to prove to the world that republics are not ungrateful, and Lafayette was commemorated in all manner of articles. Next to Washington he was the most popular of the Revolutionary soldiers —hence the *Cadmus* on both cup plates and salts. The Cadmus-Eagle salt is rare today, especially in one variation.

Among the most beautiful of the salts are those in light opaque powder blue, the color which, I have been assured by one of his descendants, was Deming Jarves' favorite. Two round ones are illustrated on Plate 69. The shades of blue vary, often appearing to have a silvery hue. The top rim carries a flower and leaf pattern, while around the bowl are small, dainty flowers and leaves in relief. They obviously bear some relationship to the flower pot in the frontispiece, both undoubtedly being of the same early period. The two salts are almost alike, except for slight variations in the design and the wider scallops in the foot of one. To date they have been found only in a light opaque blue but all specimens of these salts are exceedingly rare. The same salt pattern may be found flat, minus the foot. One has been found in clear glass and another in sapphire blue so possibly other colors may exist. The rarest color in any salt is ruby. Two ruby lacy ones are known to date, one of which has been on exhibition in the Metropolitan Museum. An example is shown on Plate 73.

Descriptions of nearly one hundred salts are not apt to prove interesting reading but in order to make their identification simpler for collectors, I am appending at the end of this chapter a brief description of each salt to correspond with the Plate numbers.

PLATE 73
Lacy salts in color.

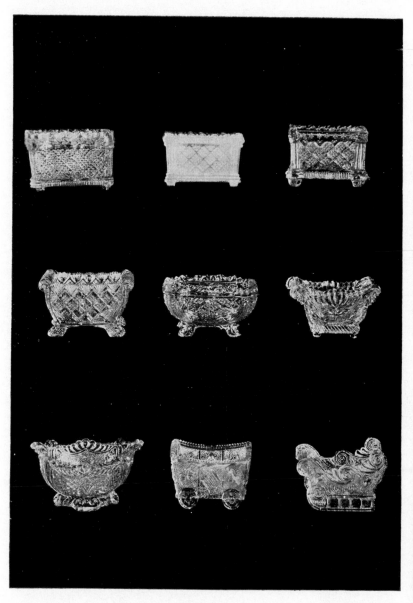

PLATE 74
Group of choice lacy salts.

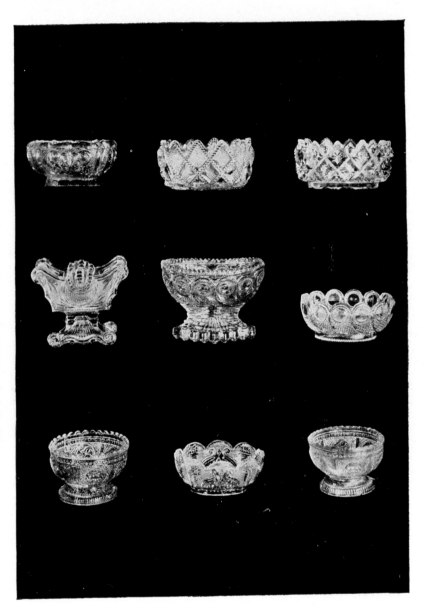

PLATE 75

Group of choice salts, including the two variants of the rare Cadmus-Eagle.

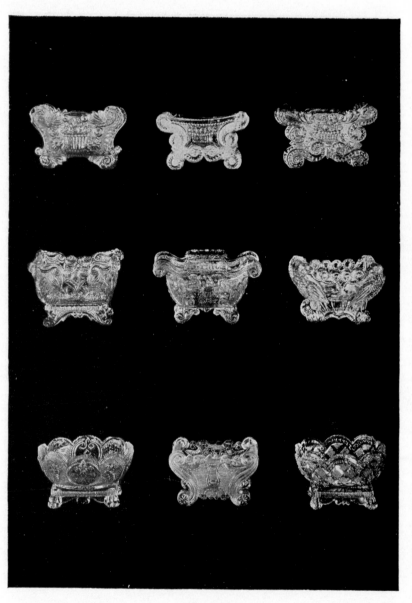

PLATE 76
Rare lacy salts.

PLATE 77
Lacy salts.

PLATE 78
Lacy salts.

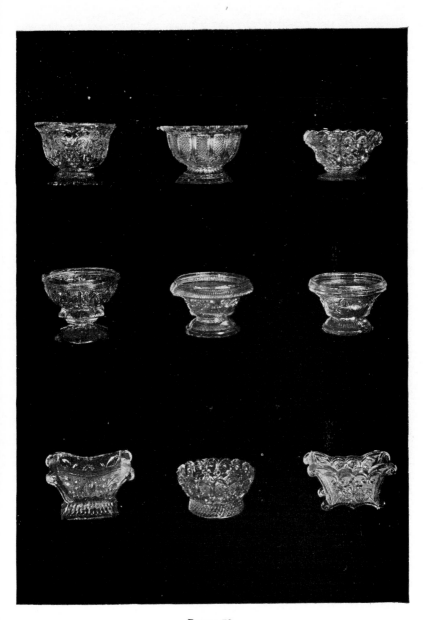

PLATE 79
Lacy salts.

KEY TO SALTS

PLATE 69

Top row, from left to right:

1. Covered salt in crystal. Scroll forms side and feet. Lyre on each side, small cornucopia decoration on top edge and also inverted, beneath lyre. Design on inside of cover; pineapple knob. Colors: Milk white; opaque powder blue; crystal. Extremely rare.

2. Same as above, in opal. Extremely rare.

3. Covered salt in crystal. Heavy design with double-beaded scroll forming ends and feet. Basket of flowers on each side against stippled background. Design on inside of cover which does not show through on opaque ones. Colors: Opal; dark blue; light or deep opaque blue; green; crystal. Rare.

4. Heavy crystal salt, scalloped foot.

5. Heavy opal salt, scalloped foot. Wide diamond pattern on top edge.

6. Opaque light blue round salt with scalloped foot. Shading of color varies, showing a silvery tint. Top rim has flower and leaf pattern. Bowl has dainty flowers in relief with row of leaves above it. Colors: Opaque blue. Exceedingly rare.

7. Oval flat salt, exceptionally heavy design. Scalloped top, with circles forming edge, one with fine diamond pattern alternating with a smaller plain one. Heavy diamond pattern printed with waffle design around lower part. Petalled pattern on base. Sapphire blue; clear.

8. Opaque light blue round salt, with small scallops on foot. Similar to Number 6 except flower and leaf design around bowl varies. Coloring is deeper blue, showing some streaks of white. Two known, one which did not show any white.

9. Not illustrated. Same as above without foot. Sapphire blue; clear. Very rare.

PLATE 70

Top row:

1. Washington-Lafayette. Oblong with scallop and point top edge. Heavy, round columns with small, round feet. Early

bust of Washington on one side, lettered "Washington." Reverse bust of Lafayette in oval medallion marked "Lafayette." Lettering is so faint on some specimens a magnifying glass is needed. Bust of Washington is not enclosed in a medallion. Large acorn on one end and flower in other. Leaf and berries in the base. Color: Clear. Rarest of salts. Has been ascribed to N. E. Glass Company.

2. American Eagle with 13 stars. Oblong salt on small rounded feet. Four fluted columns. Scallop and point top edge with border of leaves around top band. Sheaf of wheat on each end, star in base. Color: Clear glass. Scarce. Not positively identified as Sandwich.

Lower row:

3. Oblong salt with basket of fruit on each side. Four plain round columns and small round feet. Scallop and point top edge. Flower on each end. Oval space on base marked "N. E. Glass Company Boston." Wreath around oval. Crystal and in colors. Fairly common.

4. Oblong salt, undoubtedly made by same company that produced Washington-Lafayette salt. Scallop and point top edge. Urn of flowers on each side. Bee Hive on one end and large Scotch thistle on the other. Conventional ornament on the base. Not so valuable as Washington-Lafayette salt because it has no historical interest but it is early and rare. Possibly N. E. Glass Company. Color: Clear.

PLATE 71

Top row, from left to right:

1. Oblong salt having four stippled hearts on each side with Gothic arches below against stippled background. Large arch with two stars on each end. Four small rounded feet and rayed base. Colors: Opaque blue; emerald green; crystal.

1A. Not illustrated. Somewhat similar rectangular flat salt. Four hearts on sides, two on ends. Fine cut pattern on sides and ends, beneath hearts. Corners mitred. Heavy glass. Opalescent. Exceedingly rare.

2. Oblong salt, chariot race on each side, medallion with dolphin on each end. Two types.

   1*a*. Base has double fleurs-de-lys and six stars. Star on base of each foot. Have seen this style in clear glass only.

   1*b*. Opaque shades, such as blue or white, have conventional, circular impression on base and larger pointed star on foot. Rare.

3. Oblong salt, with urn of flowers on each side. Same as Number 4 on Plate 70.

4. Oblong salt, basket of flowers on each side, marked "N. E. Glass Company Boston" on base. Same as Number 3 on Plate 70.

5. Oblong salt, with basket of flowers on each side, similar to others in this series. Base is marked "Jersey Glass Co. Nr. N. York," outlined with row of small dew drops. Same salt may be found with no mark in base except heavy twelve-pointed star impressed in it. Colors: Light green; clear. Rare. Base pictured on Plate 72.

6. Washington-Lafayette salt, same as Number 1 on Plate 70. This picture shows bust of Washington, which is not enclosed in medallion, while the one on Plate 70 shows Lafayette in medallion. Leaf and berries in the base. Color: Clear. Rare.

7. Large oblong salt, probably made by same company as above. Four rounded columns and scallop and point top edge. Basket of fruit and festoon of leaves on each side. Flower on each end. Sixteen-pointed ornament on the base. Small round feet like others in this series. This is only specimen known though others must exist. Undoubtedly early. Very heavy clear glass.

8. Smaller oblong salt, unquestionably made by same company as above. Rounded columns and scallop and point top edge. Two birds perched on urn, two cornucopias and border of same leaves as larger salt above, on one side. Reverse has heavy basket of flowers and border of leaves. Flower on each end. Eight-pointed star impressed in base. Four small rounded feet. Heavy, early salt. Color: Clear.

PLATE 72

Top row, from left to right:

1. Boat-shaped salt, marked "Lafayet" on side paddle wheel, "B. and S. Glass Co." on end, "Sandwich" on inside of base and also marked "Sandwich" on outside base, with scrolls on either side. Please note there are four varieties of the marked "Lafayet" salts.

2. Not illustrated. Boat salt, marked "Lafayet" on paddle wheel, "B. and S. Glass Co." on end and "Sandwich" inside base. On this variety the outside base is not marked but has in its place, a beaded ornament.

3. Not illustrated. Boat salt marked "Lafayet" on paddle wheel, "B. and S. Glass Co." on end and no mark on inside base. Outer base has a scroll pattern, instead of beaded ornament or "Sandwich." Colors: Sapphire blue; opal; opaque blue; canary yellow; clear and possibly other colors.

3A. Boat salt marked "Lafayet" with star on side, two windows on stern, conventional ornament on base. Only one known at present. Clear glass. Exceedingly rare.

4. Illustrated on Plate 19, boat-shaped salt, unmarked. Heavy glass, apparently quite early. Clear glass; opal; sapphire blue.

5. Not illustrated. A somewhat similar boat salt was produced by a Pittsburgh concern at the same period and is marked "Pittsburgh" on the stern. In the base is an anchor. Clear glass; sapphire blue.

5A. Same as above, with anchor on base. Marked "Robinson & Son Pittsburgh" on stern. Clear glass. Scarce.

6. Oblong salt, corner columns and small knob feet. Sides decorated with basket of fruit in relief and ends with a spray of roses, consisting of one flower, a bud and three leaves. Base lettered in three lines, "Jersey Glass Co. Nr. N. York." Colors: Light green; clear glass. Scarce.

7. Oblong salt, basket of flowers on each side and Hairpin pattern at the ends. In the base is an early locomotive drawing one car. Beneath the rails and cross ties is letter in italics, "H. Clay." Exceedingly rare. Clear; peacock-blue; opalescent.

8. Large deep, oblong salt. Conventional design on sides with

diamond-shaped ornament in wreath against rather coarsely stippled background. Acanthus leaf corners, scrolled top edge and splayed feet, scrolled at ends. End panels have shield with double-headed eagle. Double-leaf and diamond ornament in base, marked "Providence." Colors: Clam bisque; clear glass. Very rare. Side view shown on Plate 76.

9. Oblong salt, basket of fruit on each side in relief, ends decorated with spray of roses. Same as Number 6 except slightly different arrangement of spray of flowers. Base marked "N. E. Glass Company Boston" in raised letters, not very clearly cut. Three slight variations of this salt. Colors: Opal; clear glass. Common in crystal. Side view shown on Plate 71.

PLATE 73

Top row, from left to right:

1. Sapphire blue round salt, 2¾ inches diameter, on collared base. Row of beads around plain top edge. Bowl has heavy scroll against stippled background. Collared foot also carries heavy scroll design. Eight-pointed star with circle in base. Have only seen this in dark blue but other colors may exist. Rare. Origin uncertain.

2. Brilliant sapphire blue lacy salt, with partition in center dividing it in two parts. Finely stippled background having three large conventionalized leaves on each side. One leaf on each end. Heavy design in base with six-petaled flower in the center. Scrolled feet and apron. Have only seen this in sapphire blue but other colors may exist. Rare. Origin uncertain.

3. Round emerald green salt, with scalloped top edge. Diamond-shaped ornaments and scrolls against rather coarse stippling. Round collared foot, stippled, with vine running through it. Have only seen this salt in green. Origin uncertain.

4. Amethyst round salt, shallow, with scalloped top. Exceptionally fine stippling. Four-petaled flowerlike ornaments around the bowl. Collared base, also stippled like above, with scroll design running around it. Fine waffle all over base. Have only seen this salt in amethyst. Rare. Origin uncertain.

Lower row:

5. Oblong salt, double-beaded scroll forming sides and feet. Heavy beading on scrolls. Beaded ornament on sides in place of usual basket, with five petals against stippled background which is outlined with beads. Rayed base and ends ribbed with heavy half-circle ornaments. Color: Brilliant ruby red. Only two are known to date in this color.

6. Oblong salt in green. Basket of flowers on each side. Dainty vine running across the top band. Twelve-pointed star impressed in base. Four round columns and small round feet. Colors: Green; clear. Scarce.

7. Unusual salt with scrolled ends and feet, deeply cut out top edge. Medallion on each side, with shell ornament in center, against stippled background. Three variations of this salt. This has plain top edge across the ends. Base has fine diamond printing all over and ends carry a petaled ornament against a stippled background. Only specimen of this salt found to date in sapphire blue. Rare.

7A. Not illustrated. Most common variation of above has scrolled ends and feet with cable or rope edge on top of ends. Stippled with conventional ornament on ends similar to one on cup plates and lacy dishes. Base has squares with a flower in the center. Colors: Opal; clear.

8. Early, heavy salt with six large scallops on foot. Rare in peacock blue, as illustrated. Also found in clear and other colors.

PLATE 74

Top row, from left to right:

1. Diamond waffle pattern. (There are a number of variations of this salt, the chief difference being in the band across the top and the base design.) Serpentine sides and ends. Scalloped top edge. Band of small leaves above the diamond waffle. Fluted columns. Ribbed band around the base. Small round feet. Eight-pointed star imprinted in the base. Clear glass. Rare.

2. Smaller and lighter in weight than other varieties. Band of

small hobnails around the top. Scallop and point top edge. Wider ribbed band across base. Small ball feet. Fluted columns, straight sides. Heavy twelve-pointed star in base. Brilliant opal with bluish tint.

3. Diamond waffle, with band of small stars across the top. Scallop and point top edge. Wider ribbed band across base. Heavy ball feet. Fluted columns. Heavy sixteen-pointed star impressed in base. Colors: Sapphire blue; clear.

3A. Not illustrated. Diamond waffle, similar to others except for a band of diamond waffle pattern across the top. Scallop and point top edge. Ribbed band around base, round pointed feet. Heavy star impressed in base, having twenty points. Colors: Brilliant sapphire blue; lighter violet blue.

3B. Not illustrated. Diamond waffle, similar to others except for a band of festoons across the top. Fluted columns, small scallop and point top edge. Ribbed band around base. Round feet, blunt, not pointed. Sixteen-pointed ornament imprinted in the base. Sapphire blue.

4. Oblong diamond patterned salt with rounded ends having heavy roll at the top. Diamond pattern on sides, ends and base. Paw feet. Clear glass. Scarce.

4A. Closely similar to above except for large bear's paw feet clasping round ball. Illustrated on Plate 19. Clear glass. Scarce.

5. Unusual salt having elaborate conventional design in relief. Oblong with rounded corners and belled ends. Diamond-shaped ornament on sides, splayed feet. Rounded corners have horizontal ribbing. Colors: Opal; dense milk white; clear. Rare.

6. Lacy salt of unusual design. Top has scrolled ends and corners are decorated with acanthus leaves. Sides have small dainty design against stippled background. Ornamented heart on one end and three-leaf clover on the other. It has an oblong base having a heavy cable cord around it and rests on four small feet. Base has star in center. Clear only. Rare.

7. Large oval deep salt with eight scalloped points to top edge which is ornamented with deep ribbing and bent over on ends. Background has dainty diamond pattern, with scroll design on sides and ends in heavy relief. Also four cornucopias with

fruit and flowers. Star base. Brilliant and lacy. Rare in colors. Colors: Opal; amethyst; clear.

8. Carriage salt. Oblong, on wheels. Sides have three panels, diamond-shaped ornament in center, stars in two end panels. Coarsely stippled. Conventional ornaments on ends, rayed base with circle in center. Clear glass. Scarce.

9. Sleigh salt, on sled. Dainty scrolled design on sides, against stippled background. Base rayed with clear circle. Clear glass. Scarce.

PLATE 75

Top row, from left to right:

1. Oblong salt with chamfered corners on small clear oblong collared base. Scroll and conventional ornament on each side against rather coarsely stippled background. Same design, smaller, on ends. Three clear heavy flutes, pointed at top in each chamfered corner. Heavy scroll design in base. Clear glass. Scarce.

2. Oval flat salt in extra large diamond pattern. Diamonds outlined by heavy beading. Top edge has one large point alternating with small point. Colors: Opal; opaque white; sapphire blue; opaque light blue; clear.

3. Oval flat salt similar to above. Large diamond pattern, each diamond being cut with a star-shaped ornament in the center. Coarse saw-toothed edge. Colors: Amethyst; clear glass.

4. Unusual salt with scrolled ends on high pedestal foot. Shell-shaped ornament on sides with crescent moon of ribbing underneath it. Foot is oblong and has four scrolled feet. Rayed underneath base. Clear glass. Rare.

5. Oval peacock eye (or peacock feather) salt on diamond-shaped four-stem base. Bowl decorated with peacock eyes, top edge finely scalloped. Foot scalloped, with hobnail type table rests underneath. Rayed under base. A large salt, with clear ring to glass. Clear glass. Rare.

6. Peacock eye large oval, flat salt. Twelve large scallops on top edge. Star base. (Base designs vary.) Rare in color. Colors: Sapphire blue; light opaque blue; dark opaque blue; clear.

7. Cadmus-Eagle. Early round salt with collared base, having six medallions with eagles and ship Cadmus alternating. Plain scalloped top edge. Large eagle imprinted in base. Colors: light green; clear glass. Rare.

8. Oval salt on low collared base. Top edge has eight deep scallops. Conventional ornament on sides against stippled background. Four cornucopias. Star base. Well established Sandwich design. Colors: Opal; varying shades of green; amethyst; clear.

8A. Not illustrated. Variant of above in brilliant sapphire blue. Very similar, except base has two rows of beading, a cable cord and conventional ornament in the center instead of Star base. Sapphire blue. Rare.

8B. Not illustrated. Same style as above, eight scallops, ribbed on edge. Same size except medallions on the sides have heart-shaped ornament containing four diamond-shaped figures. Cornucopias have more flowers. Base has twelve-pointed ornament impressed in it. Deep steel blue. Very rare.

9. Cadmus-Eagle. Variation of Number 7. The same, except it has a vine around top edge, instead of the scalloped edge. More rare than Number 7.

PLATE 76

Top row, from left to right:

1. Oblong salt with scrolled ends. Feet are scrolled with leaves forming short apron. End scrolls outlined with beading. Sides have basket of flowers and two rosettes against stippled background. Base carries cross bars. Colors: Sapphire blue; light opaque blue; green; opal; clear. Fairly common.

2. Double beaded scroll forming ends and feet. Basket of flowers on each side against stippled background. Same as Number 3, Plate 69, except without cover and in opal.

3. Variation of above, larger. Double beaded scroll forming ends and feet. Sides have basket of flowers and rosettes against stippled background. Basket of flowers rests against lower scrolls, which are larger in this variation. Top edge has wide scroll over basket of flowers, instead of straight top edge.

Scrolls under basket are separated, with pointed ornament between. Twelve-pointed star in base. Clear glass. Rare.

3A. Not illustrated. Covered salt in crystal. Heavy design with
double beaded scroll forming ends and feet. Basket of flowers
on each side against stippled background. Design on inside
of cover. Pineapple knob. Ends have six vertical stippled lines.
Concentric circles on base with star in center. Colors: Clear
glass. Exceedingly rare.

3B. Not illustrated. Same as above except ends have row of half-
circles and base has six-pointed star in center, with rays running
from star in center to sides and ends, making a complete rayed
effect. Colors in this variation, covered: Crystal. Open, in
following colors: Emerald green; opal; amethyst. Rare.

3C. Same as above (*b*) except the base has an added *stippled line*
between each line of the rays running from the star. Colors in
this variation, covered: Crystal. Open: Opaque blue; opal;
sapphire blue. Rare.

Middle row:

4. "Providence" salt. Large deep, oblong salt. Conventional design on sides with diamond-shaped ornament in wreath against
rather coarsely stippled background. Acanthus leaf corners,
scrolled top edge and graceful splayed feet, scrolled at ends.
Each end of salt has shield with double-headed eagle. Two
types exactly alike except for base.

   a. Large oak leaf in base with plain band on each side. Colors:
   Light green; sapphire blue; crystal. Rare.

   b. Same, with double leaf and diamond ornament in base,
   marked "Providence." Colors: "Clam bisque," clear glass.
   Rare.

   According to tradition, these were presentation salts, made by a
   special order at Sandwich. Their being presentation pieces is
   doubtful as there are two forms and quite a number have been
   found.

5. Eagle "Sofa" salt. Large outspread eagle with shield and 13
stars on each side. Sofa shape with heavy rolled top ends.
Acanthus leaf decoration on corners. Ends have pattern similar

to Princess Feather. Scrolled feet. Eight-pointed ornament on base. Clear glass. Very rare.

6. Eagle salt. Four large eagles perched on balls which form feet of salt. Body of eagles shape the sides. Each bird (two on each side) has coiled rope in beak, forming top edge. United States shield is suspended from rope. Ends have diamond-shaped ornaments made up of small stars. Base has large twelve-pointed star. Colors: Opaque white; opal; brilliant sapphire blue; crystal. Rare.

Bottom row:

7. Oval, stippled salt with eight wide scallops on top edge. Design consists of a medallion enclosing conventional ornament with four diamond-shaped pieces. Four cornucopias filled with flowers. Oval on oblong base, which has a fluted band around it. Paw feet and scalloped apron. Clear glass. Rare.

8. Oblong stippled salt with scrolled ends. Lyre on each side with two cornucopias above and two inverted below lyre. Same as Number 1, Plate 69, except open. Clear; amethyst.

9. Diamond all-over pattern oval salt with wide scallops at top, edged by a heavy row of dots. Oblong base with a fluted band around it, paw feet and scalloped apron. Colors: Emerald green; sapphire blue; crystal. Rare in colors.

PLATE 77

Top row, from left to right:

1. Oblong salt on four feet. Oval and diamond chain around the top. Conventional scroll on sides against stippled background. Two types were made, fragments of one having been found at old factory site at Mt. Vernon, N. Y. Alike except for following differences:

   a. Heavy fourteen-pointed star in base. Colors: Light amber; brilliant sapphire blue.

   b. Lacy design in base consisting of a double fleur-de-lys banded by a row of dots. Colors: Light green; dense olive green; light blue; gray-blue; yellow; crystal. Latter is probably Sandwich.

2. Early, heavy oblong salt with ornament having seven petals on each side, against lightly stippled background. Scrolled or "wavy" top edge. Leaf scrolls on corners. Collared base. Colors: Amber; sapphire blue; emerald green; crystal. Scarce.

3. Small, sleigh-shaped salt, of somewhat later period. Sides have spray of leaves against stippled background. Collared base with fine ribbing. Base rayed. Colors: Sapphire blue; amber; opaque white; crystal. Fairly common.

4. Oblong salt with rounded ends on very shallow fluted base. Five-pointed star in waffle pattern on rather coarsely stippled background, with small star above it, on each side. Star on each end and scroll design in base. Heavy shield-like ornament on each rounded corner with spray of leaves below it like a pendant. Colors: Amethyst; clear. Rare.

5. Same as above, except shorter, deeper and corner design varies. Leaf design on corners follows all the way down. Scrolled design on the base is against stippled background, instead of clear. Clear glass. Rare.

6. Octagonal salt with flaring sides. Conventional designs in panels and in base. Plain serrated top edge. Colors: Amethyst; crystal. Rare.

6A. Not illustrated. Same as above in an earlier salt, or at least it appears to be earlier, for it is slightly larger and heavier. Octagonal, with flowers in panels, such as fleur-de-lys and rose, with eagle in base. Eagle appears to be in flight and is shown with olive branch and three arrows, with shield on breast. Clear glass. Extremely rare.

7. Unusual oblong salt with clear double scrolls forming ends and feet. Double clear hearts and scrolls on each side against stippled background. Clear tulip on each end on stippled ground. Six-pointed star and four circles on base. Clear glass. Rare.

8. Small, shallow oblong salt with chamfered corners. Ribbed top edge. Vine-like pattern around bowl, on stippled background. Double-step oblong collared base with fine ribbing on sides. Small diamonds in base. Colors: Opal; crystal. Light in weight, probably fairly late.

PLATE 78

Top row, from left to right:

1. Two-part oblong salt (partition in center) with fairly heavy scrolled design in each panel, forming medallion enclosing conventional ornament. Lightly stippled background. Ornamental design around foot. All-over diamond pattern on base. No proof of origin, but appears to be American.

2. Two-part oblong lacy salt with heavy paw feet. Rather elaborate design against stippled background. Chain border along base. Clear glass. Appears to be American, but no proof of origin.

3. Two-part salt with ribbed top band and base. Cable cords form corners and divide center panels. Lightly stippled background with ornament in each panel and in ends. Rayed base. Clear glass. No proof of origin.

Center row:

4. Hexagonal lacy salt in light amber. Leaf and small shell ornaments against very finely stippled background. Top rim plain. Base has small diamond pattern. Origin doubtful.

5. Round 3 inch salt, on collared base. Beads around top edge. Attractive design of leaves and stars around bowl. Foot has fine ribbing. Very small diamond points all over base. Clear glass. Origin doubtful.

6. Hexagonal salt, very similar to Number 3 on this Plate. Smaller, but with acanthus leaf and small shell ornaments in panels. Clear glass.

7. Shallow, small round salt. Stippled all over, including collared base, which has scrolled design around it. Four medallions around bowl with large clear jewel having scroll attached to each side of it. Clear glass.

8. Hexagonal salt, acanthus leaf at corner of each panel. Top edge smooth but band underneath has ribbing. Hexagonal foot with diamond point decoration. Clear glass. Origin doubtful.

9. Small round salt, somewhat similar to Number 6. More elab-

orate design around bowl against stippled background. Collared base has panels of vertical lines and rows of small beads or dewdrops forming panels. Top edge plain. Beaded around top edge of stippling. Clear glass.

PLATE 79

Top row, from left to right:

1. Early round salt with heavy design of grapes and leaves. Round footed base. Rim in top, as if it might have had cover. Clear glass.

2. Round salt like paneled diamond point. Stippled panels with fans at top terminating in row of stippled hearts around base of bowl. Foot has conventional design. Cross in center of base. Cable cord on edge of foot base. Clear glass. Rare.

3. Round salt with scallop and dot top edge. Eight panels, each with hourglass against stippled ground. Octagonal foot with diamond and dot all-over design in base. Fairly early. 2¾ inches in diameter. Clear glass. Rare.

4. Round salt on clear hexagonal base. 2¾ inches in diameter. Background lightly stippled. Design of double scroll with circle consisting of seven dots. Plain top edge. Double, clear foot. Very unusual. Clear glass. Rare.

5. Round footed salt with finely ribbed band around top. Exceptionally fine stippled background. Clear scroll around bowl. Round foot, with finely ribbed band.

6. Same as above, except top rim plain and entire design is faint and stippled background lighter. Rather crude. Clear glass.

7. Sleigh-shaped salt with oblong base. Large jewel in center of sides, outlined by smaller beads. Scroll of leaves on each side of jewel, against stippled background. Jewel on each end. Ribbed oblong collared base. Rather crude salt, of poor quality. Clear glass.

8. Round clear salt, 2¾ inches in diameter. Scalloped top edge, having one dot in each scallop. Conventional design around bowl, against stippled ground. Collared base has tiny diamond

hobnails in all-over design. Base has flower in center and concentric circles of dots covering balance of space. Clear glass.

9. Sleigh-shaped oblong salt. Nicely scrolled top edge and feet. Sides have spray of three-petaled flowers against stippled ground. Same on ends. Base has very small flowers in mesh in an all-over design. Clear glass. Rare.

Chapter XIII

MINIATURE LACY PIECES

Among the rarities of the lacy Sandwich period are the miniature pieces. These are very popular with collectors. There is the sentimental appeal of their tiny size and their inevitable association with entranced children. Moreover they nearly all appear to be of Sandwich origin. So few of them are to be found compared with adult pieces that it is doubtful whether any other factory ventured actively in this field. They must have been popular at the time they were produced, for many of them were made in colors, as well as in clear glass.

According to an old tradition which is still current, these pieces were really salesmen's samples. The drummers found it possible to sell the larger dishes by showing the toy pieces, which were so much easier to carry about than full-size samples which not only would break too easily but were bulky. By story-hungry collectors the legend was accepted as the *raison d'être* of the toy dishes. The plausible "explanation" duly became "history." Unfortunately, it is a matter of record that the Boston & Sandwich Glass Company employed no drummers at that time and, moreover, none of the toy pieces is of a design that corresponds with the designs of any of the larger dishes.

Among the most frequently found of the miniatures are the tureen and tray. These come in two sizes, both of which are pictured on Plate 80. They are very brilliant and lacy in clear glass and the colored pieces are quite lovely. A great many fragments of the toy pieces, both in clear and colors, were found in the filled land, in a place where they must have been dumped during the 40's. Numerous fragments, many of them in color, are in my collection. Whatever their price might have been at the time they were made, today the colored pieces are more highly esteemed and command considerably higher figures than those in crystal.

The design is the same in the small and large tureen but the larger is made to appear more brilliant because the pattern is outlined by dewdrops. A fan-like ornament decorates the sides and cover. The tray has a border of flowers similar to those in the plates and washbowl. The tray of the smaller set measures 2⅝ inches. The larger tureens are rarer than the smaller and apparently were not produced in such a wide variety of colors. I have seen the smaller sets in amethyst, yellow, opal and in various shades of blue, besides clear glass.

The toy creamers are still fairly plentiful in New England and nearly all collections of lacy Sandwich contain a few specimens. They measure 1½ inches high and were made in three styles. The usual type is illustrated on Plate 80. One variation has a scalloped instead of a plain round foot. Another has a tiny rosette handle, as may be seen on the cup and saucer in the same row. The rosette of solid glass consists of five little loops. It was not a very practical handle for, being so tiny, it is difficult to grasp securely. They probably were something of an artistic novelty and, of course, childish fingers could grasp them far more easily than the grown-up's could. After all, these toys *were* intended for children to play with in the 1830's and not for collectors to hoard in the 1940's— and onward.

Three styles of cups and saucers may be noted in the middle row on Plate 80. As with the creamers, two styles of handles were used, one of the usual type and the other with the rosette. The two on the end are the most frequently seen. They have a dainty flower pattern against a stippled background and may be had in clear glass and in opal, sapphire blue and clam bisque. The term "clam bisque," comes straight from New England, for I have never heard it used anywhere else to describe a color. The shade, for the benefit of inlanders, may be described as the color of clam water—a cloudy, grayish white, without opaline tints.

An exceedingly rare cup is that in the middle of the center line on Plate 80. It is 1¼ inches high and has three conventional shell ornaments around the bowl, each one alternating with a diamond-shaped ornament. A cable cord runs about the base as well as around the brim. The cup is handleless. Very few of this variety exist but of the known specimens, one is in sapphire blue, another in opaque blue and the others in clear glass. This is a Midwestern design.

Of the oval vegetable dishes, three different sizes and patterns are known to collectors, with three variations of the medium size. These are all shown on Plate 81, with the exception of the variants.

The oval dish in the upper left-hand corner of Plate 81 is medium sized. It measures 2⅞ inches long and has a finely scalloped edge. It is a brilliant, lacy piece. The same dish may be found with a wider scalloped edge. A second variation is somewhat deeper, with a heavier scalloped edge and coarser stippling.

The largest of the miniature oval dishes is shown in the upper right-hand corner of Plate 81. It has a conventional shell ornament, similar to that in the rare cup and saucer. This dish is shallower than the others and measures three inches long. So far as I know, it has been seen only in clear glass. It has been definitely established as being of Midwestern origin.

The smallest of the toy oval dishes is illustrated just below the two larger. Though any of the miniature lacy pieces are scarce enough, this one is most often found in New England, which is natural enough, since the factories of that section catered to the local trade. It is quite small, only 1¾ inches long, and has eight scallops on the top edge, which is beaded. The bowl carries a scroll design against a stippled ground. These may be found in clear, opal, opaque white, and possibly other colors.

Among the tiniest of the toys is a round bowl of the same design as the cups and saucers, with the addition of a finely scalloped rim and collared foot. It measures 1½ inches in diameter and has been found in opal as well as in clear glass. These are quite rare. One is pictured in the same line as the creamer on Plate 80.

Next to it, on the same line, is another very rare, footed hexagonal bowl. It has a conventional design against a brilliantly stippled background. The foot is also hexagonal and has a finely ribbed edge. So few are the known specimens of this bowl that it must be listed among the extremely rare.

Another similar footed bowl, not illustrated, has a Gothic Arch pattern around the bowl. The foot has a small, diamond point pattern all over the base. It is rather crude in workmanship. A variant of the same footed bowl is 1⅝ inches high, with a fine honeycomb pattern on the base.

A larger footed bowl, not illustrated, is 1⅞ inches high. It has a plain top edge with a row of dots around the outside, forming a band. There are six sprays of flowers around the bowl against a finely stippled background. The plain collared foot is covered with stippling underneath the base.

Collectors are always intrigued by the little miniature plates, four of which are illustrated on Plate 81 and others on Plates 82 and 83. These are considerably smaller than cup plates, the largest measuring 2½ inches in diameter. The most frequently found are the upper two shown in Plate 81. They are alike except that one is heavier and the stippling coarser. The border of the plate has dainty flowers and leaves. In the center is a rather large conventional design. Both are usually found in clear glass and rarely in colors. I know of one in dark blue, in the style of that with the finer stippling. A little soup plate may be found to match but these are exceedingly scarce.

In the lower left-hand corner of the same illustration, the plate appears at first glance to be like the others but on close examination, a slight difference may be detected in the border. A row of tiny vertical lines above the flowers in the edge makes this piece quite uncommon.

The plate in the lower right-hand corner, next to the preceding, has the same center as all the others but the border is entirely different, consisting entirely of concentric circles. These are fairly common.

The plates in the lower row of Plate 83 are similar in design to those in the center of Plate 81. Avid collectors will find minor differences, such as the width of the scalloped edge, number of serrations and quality of stippling. In a field as limited as lacy miniatures, these trifling details offer an allure to those interested in the spirit of the chase for the elusive. The plate at the left is 2¼ inches in diameter, and rests on a plain rim. The similar plate next to it measures 2⅛ inches, and it rests on a tiny beaded edge. The flower and leaf border varies.

The plate at the left above those described, in the center of Plate 83, has ten small thumbprints on the shoulder, or border, dividing this section into 10 small panels. Beads surround the edge, underneath the surface. The edge the plate rests on is 10-sided, with a star-like ornament in the center. It is not stippled so lacks much of the appeal of the others in this series. It is 2½ inches in diameter.

At the right of the plate with thumbprint border is a scarce one, seldom seen, also 2½ inches in width. The border carries concentric rings. The center design has a familiar appearance, because it is the same found in the center of so many of the well-known Heart cup plates. The outer rim is perfectly plain. This plate has been seen in few collections.

The two plates in the middle row of Plate 82 are the rarest in this group. Of the two, the opaque blue at the left is rarest of all. It is very small—2 inches in diameter. The rim carries a conventional border of leaves and the center is covered with delicate concentric rings, so fine as not to be apparent in the photograph. It is a fairly light opaque blue, with the silvery sheen noted on the rare salts and cup plates known in this color.

Next to the blue plate, is an interesting one having two hearts pierced by crossed arrows in the center, enclosed in a wreath of leaves. The border has four hearts and scrolls interwoven in the design. It has a scallop and point edge. Any collector should be happy to find either one of these two rare plates.

Below the opaque blue plate on Plate 82, is an early heavy one, seldom seen, in a Waffle pattern. This one measures 2⅛ inches and the edge is plain.

Next to the Waffle pattern plate, is a deep one, which appears to be of Midwestern origin. It is not usually found in New England, but does appear in Ohio and Pennsylvania. It has a cable edge and cable tablerest. The design is a conventionalized shell and scrolls. It measures 2¼ inches.

Among the rarest of the lacy miniatures may be counted the tiny rectangular-shaped footed dishes, seen in the top row of Plate 82. They are 1⅝ inches long by 1⅜ inches wide. The design is conventional, with little tulips showing against the finely stippled background, in the mitred corners. The foot is scalloped. In the illustration may be seen a side view and the interior of the bowl. Three of these dishes are known to date.

In the upper row of Plate 83 are two views of miniature Sandwich candlesticks. These are slightly over 1½ inches high, with an hexagonal base and round socket. These may be found in clear glass and in color. In my collection is one in amethyst that was found discarded and buried in the Sandwich dump because it was slightly crooked. The pontil on the base is so heavy that it will not stand up, but this will not be found in perfect specimens.

Not illustrated, is another miniature in the form of a flat iron. Apparently these were made in quantities, in clear glass as well as a full range of Sandwich colors. They are scarce today, but offer a challenge to collectors, who could very well specialize in seeking a shelf full of them, in their jewel-like colors. They measure approximately 1¼ inches long by 1 inch wide.

Particularly dear to the hearts of the children, when they played at keeping house a century ago, must have been the miniature washbowls and pitchers. The two styles made at Sandwich are illustrated on Plate 80. The prettier of the sets is stippled. The pitcher has a basket of flowers on each side with a six-pointed star above it. The washbowl has a finely scalloped rim and festoons of flowers running around the bowl. There is a star in the base and a cable cord on which the rim rests. These were made in clear as well as in

PLATE 83
Two views of Miniature candlesticks and four plates.

PLATE 82

Upper: Miniature rectangular footed dishes, side view and center of bowl.
Lower: Opaque blue miniature plate and three others in clear glass, the one in lower right being Midwestern.

PLATE 81

Miniature lacy pieces. Oval dish at upper right is Midwestern.

PLATE 80
Miniature lacy pieces.

opal and in various shades of blue, including a dark sapphire which is rare.

The other set made at Sandwich is in a perfectly plain pattern, in clear and in colors.

Probably the rarest of the miniature pieces are the compotes. Four are illustrated on Plate 80. The smallest one measures 1⅝ inches in diameter by 1½ inches high. It has a conventional design around the bowl which is lightly stippled in the center. The foot is simply clear and round, with the base rather heavily rayed.

The largest of the compotes is 2⅞ inches high by 2⅞ inches in diameter. The bowl, fairly deep, with a scalloped top edge, is lightly stippled and panelled, with two different flowers in the panels, alternating all the way around. The foot is clear, with a rayed base.

The type of compote most frequently encountered by collectors, when they find any at all, is on an average 1⅞ inches in diameter and 2 inches high. The bowl is shallow with a lacy design of flowers against a lightly stippled background. The pedestal has a small knob in the center and the base has two steps, rayed underneath. I have never seen any of the compotes in color and all of them show a cruder workmanship than the other pieces described in this chapter.

Among the oddities of miniature articles are two tumblers, one 1½ inches high and the other 1⅜ inches high. The taller is in sapphire blue, of a conventional design, that seems disproportionately heavy. The background is stippled. Below the pattern is a band of small diamond points. The smaller tumbler is in a very small diamond point pattern, with a plain marginal band above it. There is a star in the base. These are the only two specimens of toy tumblers that I have seen so far. One is in dark blue and the other in crystal.

One odd early cup, minus the saucer, came to light in a bright sapphire blue. It is of the handleless variety, with an arched pattern bowl and a star in the base.

Another curious piece may be described as a covered salt. It is in an opaque light blue, with a small handle on each side. The background is stippled with a beaded, scroll design. The cover is plain on top with a lacy design underneath, which, of course, does not show through. The base carries an eight-pointed star in a circle of beads or dewdrops, rayed to each side and the corners, from the circle. This is an exceedingly rare piece. Other rarities may appear from time to time, though with all the years of intensive collecting in this country, it would seem that most of the patterns must be known by now.

Chapter XIV

SAUCE DISHES

During the many years that the Boston & Sandwich Glass Company were in operation, they probably produced a greater variety of sauce or preserve dishes than of any other single item. From the earliest days to the very last, they were still making sauce dishes, many of them in odd patterns, not important enough to identify. This chapter deals exclusively with those produced during the lacy period. Most of them were in a $4\frac{1}{2}$ inch size, though a few ran $4\frac{1}{4}$ inches, which are the usual sizes for sauce dishes.

The commonest design to be found in New England is one known as Roman Rosette. An example may be seen in opal, on Plate 84. They were made in a little $3\frac{1}{2}$ inch size, known today as "honey" dishes, in 4 inch sauce dishes and in no end of other sizes, which were originally termed nappies. These were mostly in clear glass, though they are not uncommon in opal. Now and then a colored piece may be seen, usually in sapphire blue, yellow, amber, or amethyst.

Below the Roman Rosette sauce dish is another known as "Plume." This design was made early at Sandwich in flint glass. Many years later it was copied by one of the Pittsburgh factories in lime glass. Some of the earlier Plume dishes are seen in opal as well as crystal, and in a variety of forms. Sauce dishes, nappies and compotes were produced, with and without a stippled background. I have never seen any of the opal pieces stippled but they may exist. Examples in amethyst are rare.

Next to the Roman Rosette sauce dish is a small bowl in a pattern typical of the early period at Sandwich. It is not so well known as the others, though it is fairly common. The pattern is called Stippled Bull's Eye, and may be found in sauce dishes and bowls, in opal and clear glass. Possibly compotes also were made, though I have never seen any.

Below the Stippled Bull's Eye is a Diamond Rosette bowl, which is quite similar to the Roman Rosette. It lacks the diamond-shaped ornaments around the rosette in the base, which seem to have been moved above the chain design in the border. The edge has a plain serration, instead of the wide scallop and point used on the Roman Rosette. This dish is seen less frequently than any of the others, yet it may be found in clear and in opal.

Of all the sauce dishes produced during the lacy era, the two designs best known to collectors today are the "Crossed Swords," and the "Peacock Eye." Although there are a number of variations of the Peacock Eye, all of them come under that general classification. A third dish is common enough and should be as well known as the others but it never was christened with a name that clung to it. Among at least a few collectors this pattern has been known as the Oak Leaf, so it may as well remain under that title. All three sauce dishes are shown on Plate 85. The two other sauces illustrated on that page are quite scarce.

The collecting of lacy Sandwich glass has become so popular the country over that the need of a suitable nomenclature, such as was established for pattern glass, has become more urgent. Giving adequate names to the various types and patterns of this glass would help collectors in so many ways that it is not necessary to dwell at length on this point. One of the purposes of this book is to attempt to establish such a nomenclature.

To return to Plate 85: The Crossed Sword pattern is found in at least two sizes of sauce dishes and occasionally a piece comes to light in color. I have seen it in sapphire blue.

To differentiate two such well-known types of Peacock Eye, it would seem well to call the one next to the Crossed Swords (top row), the Rayed Peacock Eye, since the dishes in this more elaborate form usually have a rayed base. A wide number of pieces were made, from $4\frac{1}{2}$ inch sauce dishes to large bowls of varying sizes, compotes as well as pickle dishes. I have seen an oval relish dish in this pattern in a most peculiar shade of dense greenish-black, though when held to the light it appeared to be purple. Odd colors of almost any dish made at Sandwich may be found by collectors, for color was a specialty of that factory and surprises of this character never cease.

Below the Crossed Swords dish, in the center of Plate 85, is one of the rarest of all the sauce dishes. It has a border of flowers and leaves and a conventional ornament with leaves in the base. The flower is one of the most attractive to be found on any of the lacy dishes. Since it was never known by any name at all, it has been christened Nectarine. It is exactly the same flower as seen on one of the chosen ten rarest of the Conventional cup plates, Mr. Marble's Number 826. It occurs on two other sauce dishes and bowls in larger sizes than the one just described, though in a variation, the border and bases of the others being entirely different.

The Oak Leaf sauce dish, next to the Nectarine, may be found in clear glass and in colors. The pattern was widely used also on large bowls, which would be very rare, in color, for the smaller dishes are generally, though not always, the colored pieces.

The Peacock Eye sauce dish in the lower row is usually found in the $4\frac{1}{4}$ inch size, with the scrolled eye base. Probably no other lacy design is better known to collectors at large than this pattern. It appears on everything, from salts to compotes. The salts as well as the small sauce dishes are frequently seen in color.

The sixth sauce dish on the page is also rare. Aptly named Double Leaf, it is a brilliant, lacy design, with the leaf motif predominant. The edge is similar to that on many of the large Oak Leaf bowls and the border design resembles it closely, though it is more elaborate.

At the top of Plate 86 is an interesting 5 inch plate with a crown and "V. R." in the center. In the floral border is "W. R." in very small lettering, which makes one wonder if the initials were intended for Victoria's predecessor, King William IV, and also whether the same border design might not be found in some piece made during the "sailor King's" reign and the letters kept through a mold maker's oversight. While it might possibly be Sandwich, enthusiastic or perhaps excessively patriotic collectors have advanced the theory that this plate might have been made at the Cape for export to England but, if it was turned out at Sandwich it would have been intended also for domestic consumption. The coronation in 1837 of Victoria, the first English queen since Anne, surely would have made the front page in America, to use a phrase of one hundred years later. On the other hand it is to be borne in mind that by the time we had reached the period of intensive manufacture, both English and Continental works were also busy producing pressed glass. "V. R." stood for Victoria Regina. Being in Latin, the initials would be understood everywhere. The "W. R." might stand for William Rex.

Next to it is a 5¼ inch octagonal deep dish in which a Thistle motif predominates. It is a scarce piece, brilliant and lacy.

In the middle line is another variation of the Nectarine pattern, with the flower in the center and a scroll border in which the flower is incidental to the design. Any of these plates are rare. This one measures 5¼ inches.

The other sauce dish in the center, in an attractive design, is found in a wide variety of bowls and deep dishes, some with the same center but different borders. The eleven-petaled rosette in the base is similar to a favorite motif used in Europe on lacy dishes of the period. The border has an arch alternating with a conventionalized flower so this pattern has been named Gothic Arch. The one illustrated is in a 5 inch size.

The Peacock Eye bowl with rayed center is another variation in size, measuring 5½ inches in diameter.

The last sauce dish on this page is the 6 inch octagonal deep dish with a five-pointed star in the center. The border has shell-shaped stippled medallions, each one with a different flower or ornament. It is called Shell Medallion. There is a fleur-de-lys above each medallion, at the intersection of the panels. These dishes are rather scarce. They also are found in a 5⅛ inch size as well as in compote form.

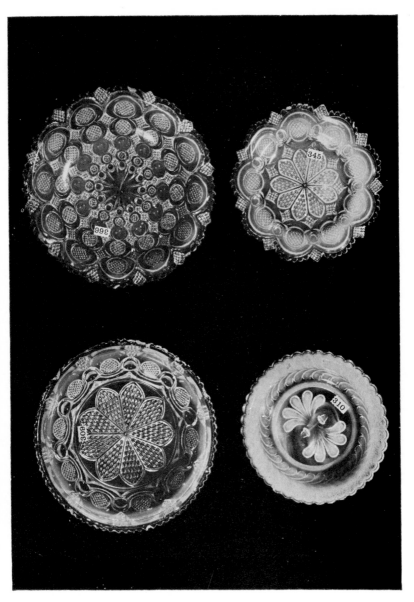

PLATE 84
Early sauce dishes and small bowls.
Upper—Stippled Bull's Eye; Roman Rosette.
Lower—Diamond Rosette; Plume.

PLATE 85—SAUCE DISHES

Left to right. Upper—Crossed Swords. Rayed Peacock Eye.
Center—Nectarine. Oak Leaf.
Lower—Peacock Eye. Double leaf.

PLATE 86—LARGE SAUCE DISHES

Left to right. *Upper*—5 inch plate, Crown in center. 5¼ inch, Thistle.
Center—5¼ inch, Nectarine. 5 inch, Gothic Arch.
Lower—5½ inch, Rayed Peacock Eye. 6 inch, Shell Medallion.

PLATE 87—LARGE SAUCE DISHES

Upper—Crossed Swords, 5⅜ inches. Shell pattern, 5½ inches.
Lower—Star Medallion, 6 inches. Nectarine, 5½ inches.

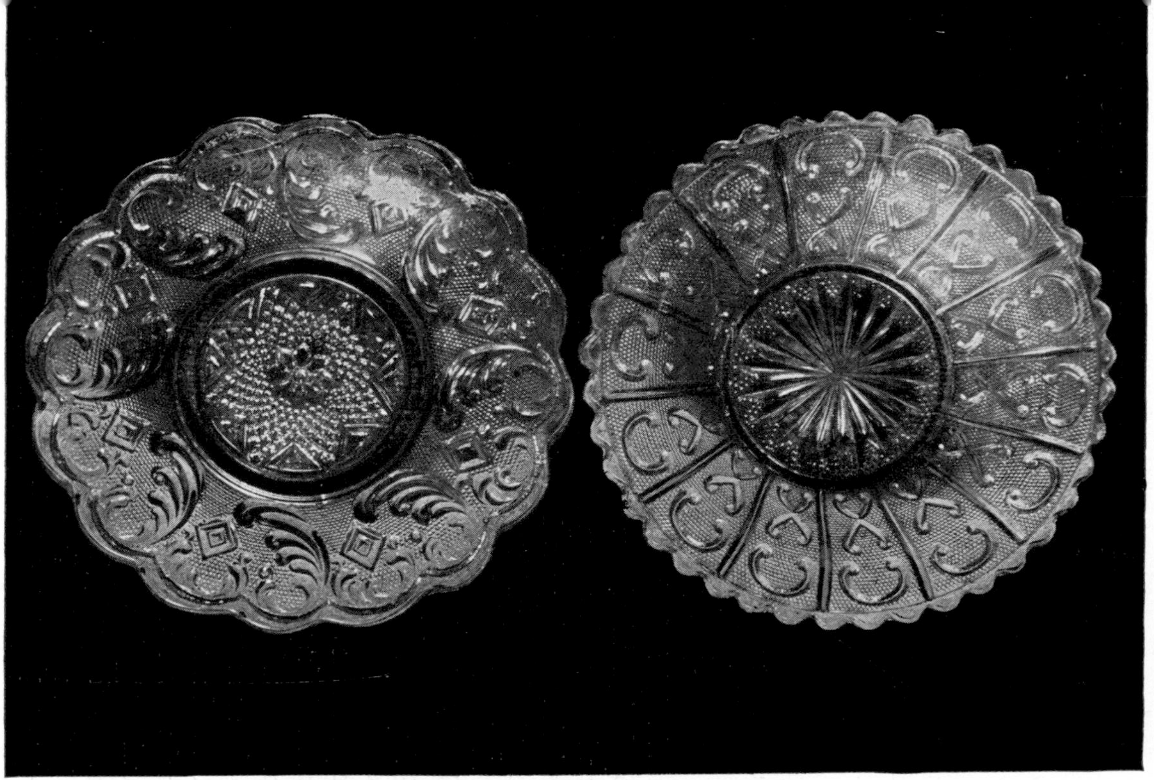

Courtesy of the Sandwich Historical Society

PLATE 88

Small sauce dishes, found frequently in color.

Plume and Diamond. Panelled Scroll.

The four dishes on Plate 87 should really come under the heading of "Nappies" rather than sauce dishes, since they are in a larger size.

The larger Crossed Swords nappy in the upper row is similar to the sauce dish except for the size and slight variations. The ornament in the border, commonly known as "Princess Feather," is filled in with diamond points as usual, but the ornament next to it, formed by two feathery leaves that meet overhead, has the background covered with wavy lines, instead of being stippled. Both varieties have a star in the center. There is a star over the heart in the next medallion of the larger dish which is lacking in the small. Also, all of the background of the border in the larger dish is of heavy lines instead of stippling. These are seen in 5⅜ inch and in 6⅜ inch sizes. Another point of difference is in the scalloped edge. The larger dish has plain serrations while the smaller one has a wide scallop alternating with two small ones. Other variations having the Princess Feather motifs are described in chapters dealing with compotes, plates and bowls.

A favorite Sandwich pattern is shown in the upper row of Plate 87 with the shell border. Quite a number of different dishes may be found in this design, from cup plates to compotes. The deep dish illustrated is in a 5½ inch size. Most of these pieces are very brilliant and lacy, though the one illustrated contains a number of black specks in the metal, indicating either a poor batch or careless workmanship. The dish has twelve scallops or points and a plain serrated edge. The base has two Princess Feather medallions and two urn-shaped ornaments against a stippled background. In the center of the base will be noticed a smooth spot, not filled in with stippling. Often bases were stuck on, being attached where the smooth spot is, thus making a compote. In many of the dishes this clear space is taken up with a star and beads or dewdrops. A 6¾ inch deep dish and also a 6¾ inch plate may be found in the Shell pattern, besides compotes.

A rather rare dish is the 6 inch hexagonal-shaped bowl, in the lower row on Plate 87. There are three different ornaments alternating in the border and a small six-pointed star in the center of the base, together with a larger six-pointed broken star. The edge has a scallop and point, completely stippled.

The last dish in the group is another of the Nectarine series in a 5½ inch size. An unusual feature is the border, near the edge. It will be noted that the stippling, instead of meeting the rim evenly, has a row of points all the way around. The bowl has flowers and leaves alternating with a conventional leaf ornament. There are three stars under each floral motif. The base has four small stars in the center around the diamond-shaped ornament. The outside base has a double cable cord running around it. This is another choice and unusual piece that any collector might take pride in owning, but they are not easily found in the perfect condition we should like to have them. These sauce dishes, bowls and nappies received hard usage and the glass, which is brittle due to the high lead-flint content, was not capable of withstanding careless handling or extremes of heat and cold.

On Plate 111 are two more sauce dishes which are found quite frequently. The Daisy with Peacock Eye border was made in clear and colors at Sandwich, though it is one of those patterns that an expert would hesitate to ascribe to any one factory without unusually adequate proof. It is something like furniture of a transitional period, showing the influence of two eras. The base is stippled but the border is not, yet the design in the border has some coarse stippling in it. Many fragments of this dish were found among the heaps of lacy pieces. Bowls were also made in clear and in colors, with the border swirled, instead of having straight panels.

In the small bowl next to it, closely related to the Crossed Swords design, the border has four Princess Feather motifs, each filled with diamond points, alternating with a large star and two small ones, all against a stippled background. The center has a pin-wheel effect bordered by a scroll with a star in each intersection. The whole dish has the brilliancy and silver sheen which is associated with the best of the lacy glass.

On Plate 88 are two small sauce dishes which were probably produced shortly before the popularity of the lacy glass began to wane. The dish on the left is a familiar pattern. It was made in a wide range of colors, as among fragments excavated at Sandwich are pieces in blue, amber, yellow, amethyst and green, besides clear glass.

The dish on the right is probably slightly later than the preceding. It is not as thick and is lighter in weight. Fewer of the latter are seen but they were also produced in several shades of color.

A hexagonal $5\frac{1}{2}$ inch dish of unusual beauty in the Hairpin pattern is shown on Plate 96. Large round deep bowls were made as well as round plates but I have never seen round sauce dishes in this design.

Chapter XV

SMALL LACY BOWLS
(6½ to 8 inch)

The most interesting of the smaller bowls happens to be the only one of historical interest and accordingly has become known as the "Industry" bowl. It was made in four variations, two of which are shown on Plate 89. The crudity of at least two of the variants is so marked as to considerably lessen the likelihood of a Sandwich origin.

Most attractive of the four is that which has the scalloped edge and fine stippling in the background. It is assumed that this bowl was produced during the William Henry Harrison campaign in 1840, for the historic log cabin and cider barrel are plainly apparent in the base of the dish. Around the bowl is a factory, ship and a man plowing. These are emblematic of industry and commerce. Harrison was also known as "The Farmer of North Bend," hence the man at the plow.

The plate with the nicely stippled background is found with a plain and also with a scalloped rim. Another Industry bowl with a stippling so coarse as to resemble a mesh is shown in the same illustration. A similar example is found without any stippling at all, giving it an exceedingly crude appearance.

The Pineapple motif is said to be one of the earliest designs utilized by Sandwich. Examples of it are rare but not beautiful. On Plate 90 is shown one of the early Pineapple bowls, measuring 6¾ inches in diameter. There are four medallions in the border, each containing a pineapple. Against a very lightly stippled background are flowers and many small stars. The dish rests upon a cable cord and there are two stars in the center of the ornament in the base. The edge of the bowl illustrated is at least a half-inch thick on one side and a quarter-inch on the other, thus dating it among the earliest pieces produced, that is, before the pressing machinery was perfected.

The three other bowls on Plate 90 all employ the Princess Feather medallion, which must have been immensely popular during the period in which it was produced, since so many variations were made.

The bowl at the top of the page, next to the Pineapple dish, belongs to the Crossed Swords series combined with the Princess Feather medallion. It measures 6½ inches in diameter and has the herringbone background, like some of the oblong trays, instead of the stippled groundwork. In the border are two medallions each enclosing a large stippled heart with a star over it, and two others, each filled with small diamond points. There are still more stars in the border, making it altogether a rather elaborate design.

In the lower row, the bowl on the left has four of the so-called Princess Feather medallions in the border, each filled with diamond points. Also, there are four small rosettes of leaves. The dish rests on a cable cord rim and has a small four-pointed ornament in the center, as well as scrolls and leaves. It is the plainest of this series, and measures 6½ inches in diameter. The scalloped rim on the edge is stippled, which effect may be noted from time to time on Sandwich pieces.

Next to it is a bowl of the same size which also has a stippled scalloped rim. This dish has four Princess Feather medallions, each with a star and four other large stars, all against a finely stippled background. The base has a star in the center, enclosed in scrolls. There is a cable cord on the base on which the dish rests.

On Plate 91 is another of the Princess Feather bowls in a 6½ inch size. It is like one described above except that the scalloped edge is not stippled but plain and the base rests on a double cable cord.

In this same picture is shown the crudest of all the Princess Feather dishes, which is in a 6½ inch size. The metal is poor to begin with and the stippling so coarse as to be barely discernible. There are four crude Princess Feather medallions enclosing an unusually large stippling, and small leaf rosettes around the bowl. The dish rests on an extra large cable cord. It is difficult to account for the production of such a crude, dull specimen.

Next to this piece is the crudest dish, with the poorest impression, illustrated in this book. I have heard it referred to as "Pittsburgh," but there is not enough evidence as to its origin to determine who deserves the blame. The base has a lyre surrounded by a wreath and this design is against a lightly stippled ground. The border has a conventionalized hour-glass in a combination with a Three-Feather motif. It is not the fault of the photographer that the pattern shows so poorly, for there was almost nothing to picture. This piece may be dismissed as an early and unsuccessful attempt to produce a lacy effect.

A fragment from a similar bowl, excavated at Sandwich, is pictured on Plate 68. It will be noted that the edge on the authenticated Sandwich piece has an even scallop, whereas the serrations on the bowl in Plate 91 have a wide scallop alternating with three small ones.

The remaining bowl illustrated on that page is in an unusual pattern and is also found in compote form but only rarely. The bowl has a border of five-petaled rosettes with a chain pattern below it made up of lozenges and round discs. The base has a four-pointed star in the center, surrounded by more of the five-petaled ornaments and scrolls. There is a cable cord on the rim of the base.

The two 7½ inch Tulip and Rosette pattern bowls on Plate 92 appear to be alike at first glance but they differ in the edge. One has plain serrations or even scallops and the other has a scallop-and-point edge. These rather common dishes are in a striking pattern. Around the bowl is a scrolled design suggestive of tulips, with an ornament alternating with each flower. The base is brilliant with a six-petaled rosette in the center of which is a double concentric ring with a central bull's eye. These dishes are more lightly stippled than many others but they are brilliant and lacy. Both are of late Midwestern origin.

Three of the plates illustrated on Plate 93 are related. They all carry the same flower in what has been named the Nectarine pattern. The one in the top row with the flower in the center is exactly like the sauce dish described in the chapter dealing with those dishes. There are always a few variations in the larger pieces. This dish is 7⅜ inches in diameter, with a plain scalloped edge. The border around the bowl is of the same design as the sauce dish with the scroll, flowers and leaves. In the center of the base is a spray of flowers, with a double cable rim on which the bowl rests. It is a particularly heavy dish, brilliantly stippled, as are most of those in the Nectarine series.

The Nectarine bowl next to it in the upper row (Plate 93) is 7¼ inches in diameter and 1¾ inches deep, which is deeper than usual. A flower with leaves forms a decoration which alternates with a conventional ornament around the bowl. There are four of these flower motifs and four rather large bull's eyes, one under each of the flower motifs. There is a double row of dewdrops in the base, which shows a conventional ornament with a flower in the center.

The third in this series is in the lower right-hand corner of the same Plate. It is a 7¼ inch deep dish with a double-step in the bowl. The edge has twelve large scallops which in turn are made up of smaller scallops. The border design is popular with collectors. It has flowers, shell-like ornaments and double circles, alternating about the rim. The dish itself rests on three heavy scrolls which make up part of the design. All of these plates would date from the intensive period of lacy manufacture, that is, from 1830 to 1840.

The last bowl on Plate 93 is one of a wide series, which can be differentiated by their rims. The one illustrated, 7¼ inches in size, is in the Oak Leaf pattern with a plain serrated edge bordered by a fairly heavy row of dewdrops or beading. It is a shallow bowl, only 1½ inches deep.

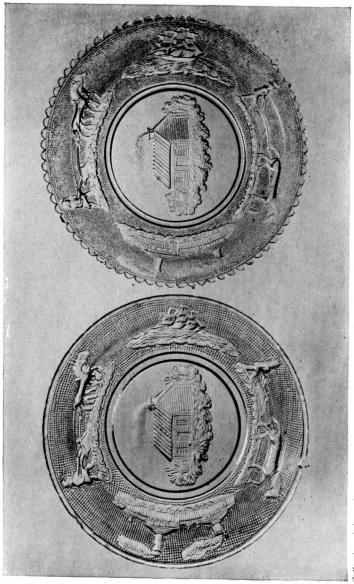

PLATE 89

Two examples of the log cabin, "Industry" bowls.

PLATE 90
Three bowls with variations of the Princess Feather medallion.
Upper left, early Pineapple design.

PLATE 91
Four early small bowls. Two employ Princess Feather medallions.

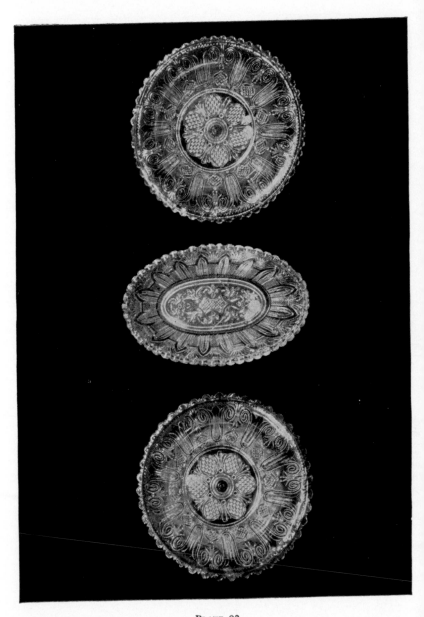

PLATE 92

Two 7½ inch bowls with different edge serrations. Oval deep dish. Top bowl and lower one are of late Midwestern origin.

PLATE 93

Four lacy 7½ inch bowls. Three are in the Nectarine pattern and the fourth is Oak Leaf.

PLATE 94
Four choice 8 inch lacy bowls.

In the top row on Plate 94 is pictured the rarest variation of the Princess Feather pattern. It cannot be called the most beautiful but it is by far the most difficult to find. It is in a 7¾ inch size and has four medallions around the bowl, each enclosing a basket of fruit against a stippled background. Between the medallions and leaves are scattered stars. The base design has four conventional ornaments and four stars. The dish rests on a fairly heavy row of dewdrops instead of on the cable cord so often used at Sandwich.

Next to this dish in the top row is a Thistle bowl in an 8 inch size. This is a favorite among collectors of Sandwich glass and may also be found in plates. The border design consists of a scroll with thistles and the base is unusually attractive. It has two thistles and a rose in the center, within a circle of coiled cable cord. In each coil is a tiny six-petaled flower. It is typically Sandwich although admittedly the rose and thistle suggest England and Scotland.

In the lower row on Plate 94 is another Princess Feather bowl. This variation has been described in the chapter on sauce dishes. It is a brilliant lacy piece with the silvery sheen in which collectors delight. A rather large smooth circle in the center indicates that these bowls were often used for compotes, the pedestal being fused on the clear space. Now and then a piece appears which for one reason or another did not have the pedestal added. This does not constitute a defect and in no way lessens the value of the dish.

The remaining bowl on Plate 94 in the Anchor and Shield design is an uncommon pattern which I have seen only in shallow bowls. It is 8 inches in diameter. Around the bowl alternately are a large leaf and large shield. On each side is a scrolled ornament enclosing an anchor. While the dish itself is stippled, the edge has a narrow border of vertical lines, running down toward the figures about the bowl. The base has a vine of flowers enclosed in a double scallop around the edge, and the entire center is stippled. This is one of those unusual pieces that any collector would be glad to add to his treasures.

An 8 inch bowl was produced in the Hairpin pattern (Plate 96) and I have never seen any larger size in this design. The Hairpin may be numbered among the most beautiful patterns known to be of Sandwich origin, though some Midwestern pieces carry the same design, probably plagiarized.

Chapter XVI

OBLONG TRAYS AND OVAL DISHES

Just where the term "lace" glass as a designation for the type of Sandwich glass which does suggest early laces originated, no one has as yet been able to say. Considering the possibility of such a derivation I studied carefully many books on laces, old and modern, and failed to find any facts which might justify the generic name given to that style of glass, except for the single instance of a butterfly motif (in lace), which was not after all distinctively or exclusively applicable to lacework. On Plate 95 are shown two of the only lacy dishes with butterflies on them. These Butterfly pieces are found in three sizes. A variation, without the butterflies is illustrated on the same page. Still another variation, without any stippling and bearing quite an unattractive design, was produced somewhere but is not worthy of illustrating. The largest of the Butterfly trays measures 10 inches by 7 inches and is quite rare.

There are two small pin trays which were made at Sandwich that are not illustrated in this book, though they should be mentioned. They are oblong, with curved sides and rounded corners. The design is delicate and lacy and they are found with a plain rim or with a scalloped edge. In New England they are still quite plentiful today.

Probably the most beautiful dishes which surely should be classed among the most desirable of the oval trays are those in the popular Hairpin pattern. A group is shown on Plate 96. It must have been enormously successful at the time it was produced, for a great variety of pieces in unusual shapes were made. The rarest dish is the largest illustrated in the group. Its great beauty cannot be adequately conveyed by a photograph. It is oval, pointed at each end, and the ends tilted over. The border on this largest piece is slightly more elaborate than the others in the panels which make up the Hairpin design, since the space to be filled is larger. It measures 10 inches long and 7½ inches wide. The next smaller size is 8⅝ inches long by 6¾ inches wide.

The only oval dish possessing historical interest is shown on Plate 97. It has round medallions all around the border, one with an eagle alternating with another showing the ship *Cadmus*. This same pattern is found in salts but in no other pieces. The oval dishes were made in two or possibly three sizes.

The heavy, brilliant dish below the Cadmus has Princess Feather medallions with stars in the center, a motif often seen in sauce dishes and bowls. Alternating with the medallions are leaves and stars. Any of the oval dishes are scarce but this one is quite rare.

The largest of the three oval dishes on that page is in a Gothic Arch design with a double fleur-de-lys in the base. It measures a bit over 9 inches long by 6 inches wide.

Two pairs of oval dishes are illustrated on Plate 98. The style of those at the top has always been considered rare because of the shape. Certainly it must have been a difficult mold to make, for the three panels at the ends are all flaring. At any rate, this brilliant dish is a desirable one to own. They were made only in the 8 inch size, so far as I know.

Below, on the same page, is a pair shallower than the majority of the oval dishes. They have a double horn of plenty in the border and Princess Feather medallions in the base. The rim of the base rests on a cable cord, a device frequently used at Sandwich. These dishes are also 8 inches long and are rare.

On Plate 99 at the top of the page is another of the particularly lovely, large brilliant oval dishes. It may be found in more than one size but the design numbers among the rarest. The detail shows so plainly in the picture that it need not be described here.

Below it, in the same illustration, is another scarce dish, in an attractive heavy design, though not so lacy or brilliant as the one above. It is an excellent example of a piece made in a mold which

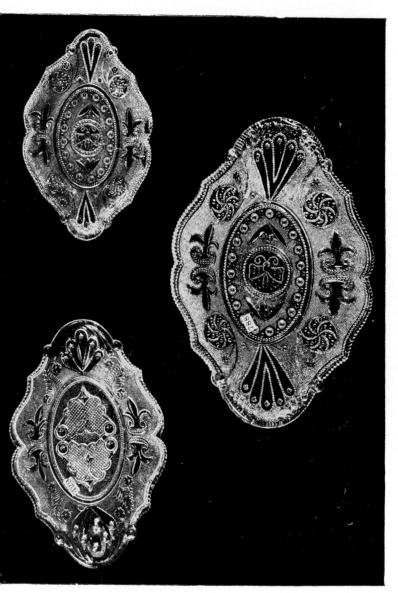

PLATE 95

Butterfly trays and a variant.

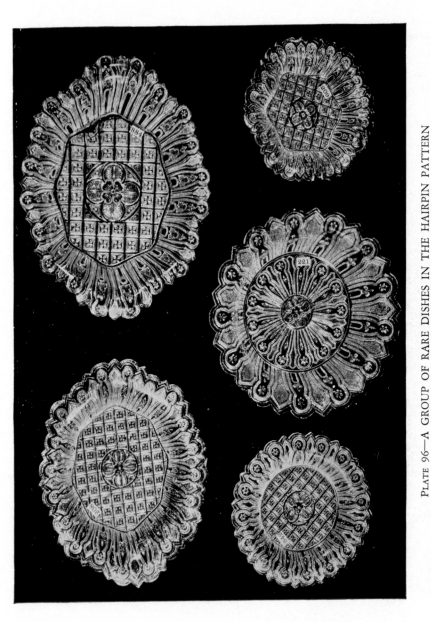

PLATE 96—A GROUP OF RARE DISHES IN THE HAIRPIN PATTERN

Upper—Oval deep dish, 8⅝ x 6¾ inches. Large oval, 10 x 7½ inches.

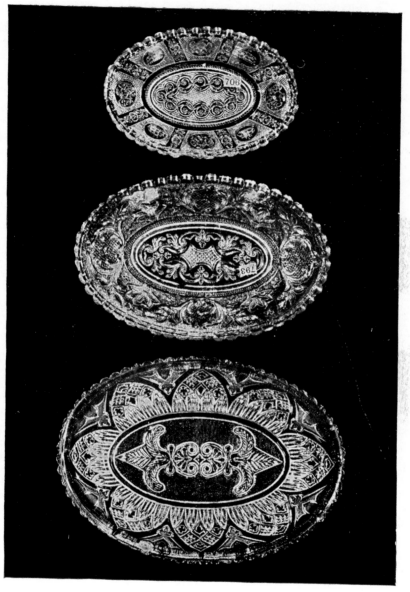

PLATE 97
Oval deep dishes, including the Cadmus-Eagle.

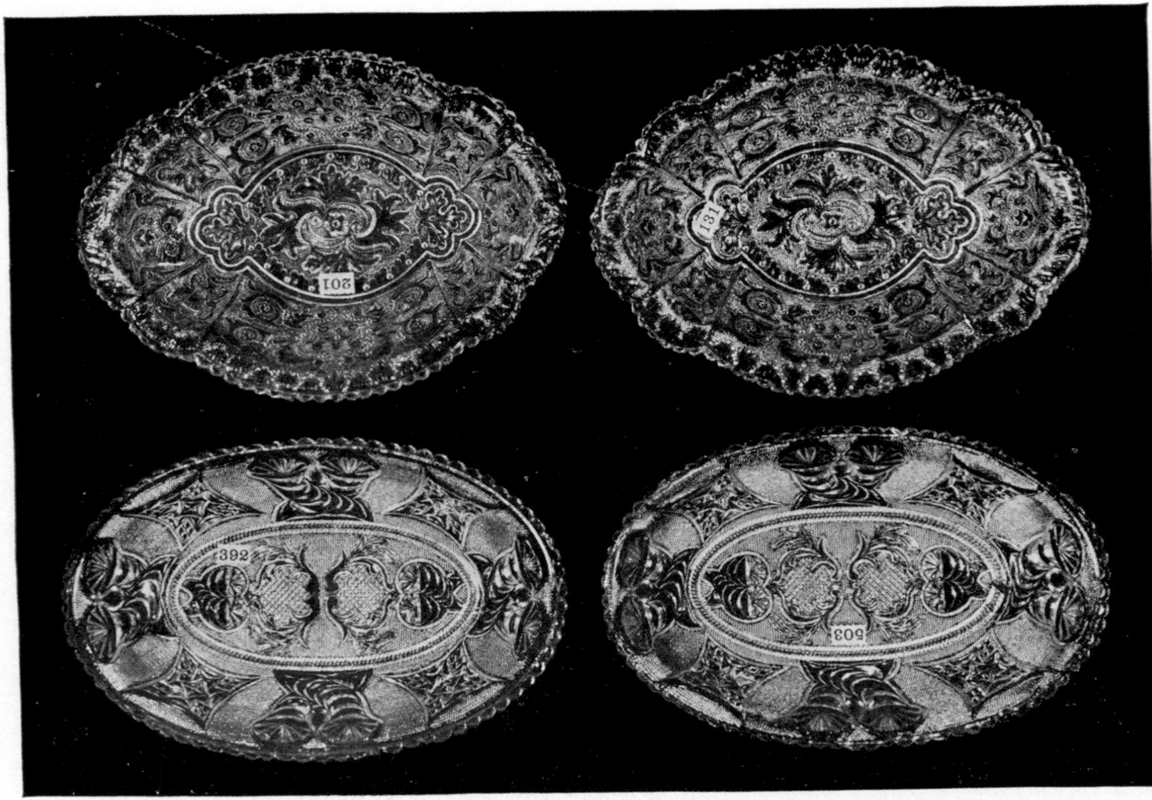

PLATE 98

Two pairs of rare oval dishes.

did not completely fill, for it will be noted that one end does not have the full scallop-and-point edges. Such pieces should be deemed interesting specimens of early workmanship, when the industry was still in the experimentation stage, instead of being regarded as defective items not worthy of a place in a collection. A true collector will share this view.

One more handsome example of a large oval lacy dish on Plate 92 is heavy and brilliant, with a border of pointed arches alternating with a torch-like ornament. The edge of the dish is thick with a plain scalloped rim. Not many examples of this rare pattern are known.

It is difficult to say what the designer had in mind when he planned the long, narrow tray on Plate 100. The center is not stippled. It has two shield-shaped figures with a fan-like ornament in each corner. The border is stippled, having a curious design composed of a diamond alternating with a round disc which has a diamond-shaped tail hanging from it. The tray is scarce but cannot be listed among the really beautiful pieces that Sandwich produced. Certainly it is not a companion piece to the rare Constitution tray illustrated in this book as being among the rarities, even though it is the same shape and approximate size. It measures 8¼ inches by 4½ inches, and is sometimes found in color, though it is rare in any shade except clear glass.

Among the oblong relish dishes, the most common motif employed by the designers were Gothic arches, leaves and thistles, suggesting European influence. The three trays on Plate 101 vary in size but as they increase in size there is space for a slightly more elaborate pattern. It will be noted that the small one at the top is the simplest, lacking the small flower on each side of the corner leaf. The largest, at the bottom of the page, has two flowers on each side of the corner leaf, and the base and the arches are more elaborate. Also, the pointed figure connecting the arches varies from that in the two smaller trays. These three oblong trays will be encountered by collectors more frequently than any of the other designs in these dishes. Almost any of the commoner trays may be

found with the bases stippled or *sans* stippling. The three sizes
are 6⅛ inches by 4⅝ inches, 7 inches by 5⅛ inches, 8¼ inches
by 6⅛ inches.

The next most common of these oblong trays on Plate 102 in
the center, on the right, is of the well-known Thistle pattern. It
has a scallop and point top edge, with or without a cable cord
running along it. They were made in a number of sizes. The one
illustrated is 9 inches by 6½ inches.

Less frequently found, is the tray shown next to the Thistle, with
a star in the center, and wide scrolls around it. This was made in
three variations, as may be seen by comparing it with the two on
Plate 103. The bases of all are closely similar, having a star in
the center with a flower at each end, enclosed in heavy scrolls. The
chief differences are in the borders. The one on Plate 102 has a
flower in each corner and on the sides, with a leaf in the end panels.
The upper one on Plate 103 also has a flower in each corner but
the sides have scrolls with a heart-shaped ornament in the center
and in the ends, simple scrolls. The one beneath it on the same
Plate shows very slight variations in the base, a flower in each
of the corners and a conventional ornament on each side. The ends
also have conventional ornaments.

The unusual feature of these last three dishes is that the designer, possibly seeking another background than the usual stippled
one, ventured something new. The first one described, with the
flowers in each corner and the sides and a leaf in the ends, has for
a background a very small herringbone pattern. Even the base has
faint wavy lines in it. The effect, on the whole, is rather brilliant.
The second one at the top of Plate 103 also has a sort of a herringbone background in fine stippling, with the same sort of work in
the base but it is not quite so brilliant or interesting. The third,
below it on the same page, is the smallest in this series, measuring
6¼ inches by 4¼ inches. The background of the sides and ends
is made up of wavy lines, which produces a still different effect.
The base is stippled. The workmanship does not seem characteristic of Sandwich, so that had I not seen fragments of these dishes

PLATE 99
Rare large oval deep dishes.

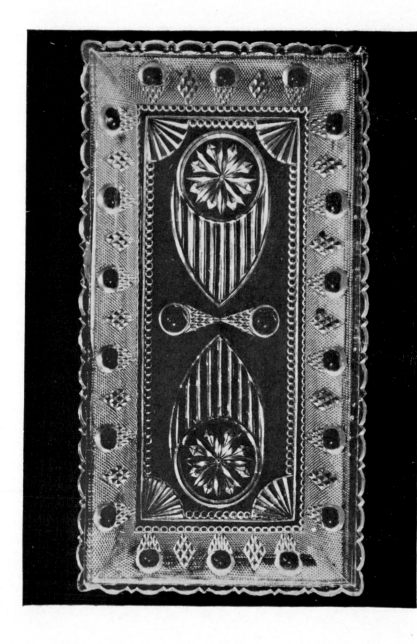

PLATE 100

Oblong shallow tray

PLATE 101
Gothic oblong dishes in three sizes.

PLATE 102

Small and large oblong deep dishes. All except center row are of Midwestern origin.

PLATE 103
Large oblong deep dishes. The largest is Midwestern.

which were excavated at the factory site, I should have doubted their Sandwichicity.

The two oblong dishes in the top row of Plate 102 and the two in the bottom row, all have the scalloped edge with bull's eyes, which smack of Midwestern tendencies of design. Other distinguishing factors must be taken into consideration. The quality of the glass, the differences in the appearance of the stippling together with the style of the serrated edge lack the Sandwich look. I hope more light may be thrown on Midwestern production, as well as that of other localities in regard to lacy glass, for we know that much was produced outside of New England.

The dish in the top row at the left on Plate 102 has an interesting design of pointed arches surmounted by fleur-de-lys on the sides, a thistle in each corner and an arch with two stars above it on the ends. The base is the most elaborate of any of the trays, having a star with fourteen points in the center, numerous circles that look like so many bubbles and also thistles. Another smaller dish like it is illustrated in the bottom row. It has a few minor differences, small elements of the pattern being omitted because of the reduced space available in the smaller size.

The other large dish at the top of Plate 102, known as the Lyre pattern, also has the same dull quality of glass and same general characteristics as the Thistle patterns in this group. Lacking a positive birthplace there is, however, the fact that no bull's eye pattern border edge fragments have as yet been found on Cape Cod, so far as I know.

The Lyre dish is large, with a lyre in each corner and conventional ornaments and stars on the sides and ends, against a stippled background. The base has a large diamond-shaped ornament in the center, with scrolls around it and a flower in each corner.

A smaller example of the same dish is illustrated in the lower row on the same page. The flowers in the corners of the base were omitted, for lack of space.

The large tray at the bottom of Plate 103 has coarse stippling and a curious mixture of design. It appears to be of fairly late Midwestern origin.

Chapter XVII

TEA PLATES

(6 and 7 inch)

Today we do not know what use was made of the small plates, mostly in a 6 inch size, that were so much in vogue over a hundred years ago. It was believed by one writer that they were "tea plates," but in an old catalogue I found them listed merely as 6 inch plates. The size would indeed seem a trifle small for the writer's explanation. In any event, they were in use for a great many years, not only in the early pressed glass era, but later on when complete sets of tableware were made to match. In fact, the only pressed glass plates prior to the Civil War period, when such patterns as Bellflower, Horn of Plenty, Cable, etc., were popular, were the 6 inch size. To be sure, Sandwich made large lacy plates, but these were for cake.

Among the earliest of the small plates were those plain specimens described in a previous chapter and shown on Plate 64. Others of the same period, which preceded those with the stippled background, are shown on Plate 104. In the upper row the Trefoil design with hearts in the center, and a Daisy border, is in a $5\frac{3}{4}$ inch size. The early piece below it, with the lacy border and waffle center, is of the same dimension. The other two plates in Shield and Pine Tree, are both 6 inches. Although the centers of these two are similar, slight differences are apparent, for the border of the upper is considerably more elaborate than the lower, which is not stippled. The leaf design beneath the Pine trees and shields adds considerably to the lacy appearance of the upper plate.

On Plate 105 are four variations of the Heart series. Two of these are 5 and 6 inch plates having the Heart with Sheaf of Wheat border and interlaced hearts in the base. The only difference between them is omissions in the detail, due to one being smaller.

The larger, for instance, has two stars at the base of each heart which are lacking in the smaller and, in addition, the larger plate has more beads or dewdrops above the sheaf of wheat. There are more of the pieces necessary for a table service to be had today in this pattern than in any other of the period. It is even possible to get together a small table service. Unfortunately for "complete set" collectors, the goblets and tumblers were not made.

On this same Plate (105) is a 5 inch sauce dish with a heart border unusual in that it has eleven large hearts and small sheaves of wheat alternating. A cable cord runs along the edge of the rim. This variation is less common than the others. The bowl has a diamond waffle, diamond points and a conventional ornament in the center.

The last plate in the same illustration is a 5 inch size and fairly scarce. There are fourteen stippled hearts in the border and a clear background. The base has an eight-pointed star in the center against a light stippling.

On Plate 106 are three more plates having hearts as a chief motif. The large 8 inch plate with heart and lyre border is rare. The background of the border is stippled, which is a variation almost never found in this particular pattern.

Another unusual dish illustrated on the same Plate is a 7 inch plate with the border of large hearts alternating with a conventional ornament, instead of the usual sheaf of wheat. The center border about the base has shields and sheaves of wheat in lieu of the usual combination of shields and pine trees. The rim has a cable cord edge. Though this is called a "plate," it is deep in the center. Specimens of this variety are rare.

The last of the Heart plates in the series on Plate 106 is the 6¼ inch, with the large hearts and small sheaves of wheat, alternating. It is similar to the smaller one shown on Plate 105 except that the border of the larger carries thirteen hearts instead of eleven. There are so many variations in forms, sizes and patterns of the heart plates and dishes that one may well wonder if a collector could ever be sure of having them all.

And still more variations of heart motifs, on Plate 107! Another plate with a deep center is that one having the cable cord rim and border of large hearts and sheaves of wheat. It is a different border from that of the similar piece on Plate 106. The latter carries a conventional ornament between the hearts, instead of a sheaf of wheat. The centers also vary, as the one on Plate 107 shows fewer details.

Next to it in the lower row is a variation of the heart-bordered piece on Plate 106, being more elaborate, with small sheaves of wheat between the hearts in a stippled background.

The last of the heart variations, shown in the upper row, has five hearts about the base and a vine running around the rim. It is not as thick as the others and the design is thin, making it difficult to photograph satisfactorily. A small cable cord encircles the edge.

The last plate on Plate 107 is Midwestern. I have never seen any pieces with this edge among fragments dug up at Sandwich. Everything about it differs from the types that a careful student of Sandwich glass would recognize. The character of the stippling, the quality of the glass, all give it a different feel and appearance. Moreover, this type is usually found in Pennsylvania or the Midwest and not in the East. There is a series of them which is quite as typical of another factory as the series of Peacock Eye, Princess Feather and Heart motifs are typical of Eastern works. They have not been so widely collected because the West has not been combed for glass so thoroughly as the East, which for many years has been the heart of the glass collecting territory. On another illustration in this chapter will be seen a typical Sandwich dish beside a Midwestern and a French plate, which show clearly the stylistic differences.

Four early plates in opal are shown on Plate 108. It is extremely difficult to bring out clearly in a photograph the design on this white glass, but there is enough detail to enable the collector to make a satisfactory identification.

The one in the upper left-hand corner has the pattern on the back, being so turned in order to show it to better advantage. The border has shields and pine trees and the base a band of shields and ornaments about a conventional ornament.

The plate next to it was the most difficult to picture distinctly because of the very light relief of the design. It has a cable cord edge and the border consists of eight medallions having two feather-like ornaments emerging from a basket.

The Acorn and Oak Leaf design on the plate in the lower row, being in much heavier relief, photographed somewhat better. It is a beautiful plate and rarely found, which holds true of many of these in opal. The center of the Acorn plate has a few beaded, concentric circles.

The rim of the last of the white plates has a cable cord edge and border of eight cornucopias, two on each side facing one an other, with a flower between them somewhat closer to the edge of the border. The cornucopias are filled with fruit and flowers, which was a favorite motif of the Sandwich designers.

On Plate 109 are two 6 inch plates well known to collectors. Both have a wreath of acorns and leaves surrounding a medallion above which is a star. One medallion has a bust apparently intended to be of Washington because, though it bears no resemblance to anyone in particular, it is inscribed "Washington George." Naturally they are known as the "Washington George" plates.

It has been suggested that the moldmaker when he did the lettering, carelessly forgot to allow for the reversal of position in stamping and placed the cart before the horse, but it is easier to believe that such an error would have led to the junking of the mold. Moreover the letters themselves were properly cut. The bust in the center could be taken for Washington only by accepting the label. It is well to remember that in many European countries it was quite customary to give surnames first, and the moldmaker may have been a foreigner or the plate intended for export. At any rate, a large number of these plates were made, since almost every collection of lacy glass boasts of at least one. In 1832

PLATE 104
Early 5¾ and 6 inch plates.

PLATE 105
Heart variants, in 5 and 6 inch sizes.

was celebrated the hundredth anniversary of the birth of Washington and makers of prints, statuettes, chintzes, plates, etc., took advantage of the public's interest to produce and sell all manner of commemorative articles. The plate may date from that year.

The companion piece has a different edge. Instead of the scallop and point rim, it has a wide scallop with two small ones between. The center is much the same except for a conventional ornament in lieu of the bust. Being strictly a conventional plate, it has not the commercial value of the marked Washington.

On the same Plate (109) are two 6 inch Peacock Eye plates, the Peacock Eye being perhaps the most frequently used motif at Sandwich. It is found on salts, plates, bowls, compotes, mustard jars, as well as in several different forms.

The plate in the upper row has convex eyes in the border and a scroll design in the center which is more widely employed in bases than any other. The lower plate has concave eyes and a more elaborate base. It is possible to accumulate enough of these plates for a table setting within a reasonable time, particularly the one with the "Scrolled Eye" center.

How much four 6 inch plates may vary and still be popularly listed under "lacy," may be learned from a glance at Plate 110. The most beautiful and "laciest" of them is in the upper right-hand corner. The border has alternating flowers and bull's eyes against a background of very fine wavy lines, such as are seen on some of the oblong trays. The attractive leaf pattern around the bowl is helped by a finely stippled groundwork and by a contrasting band which is not stippled. The ornament in the base also adds to the charm of the plate. There are other plates of this general character. One is illustrated on Plate 113. They may be classed among the choicest in lacy Sandwich of this size.

The plate beside it in the upper row is scarce. It is quite similar to one of the sauce dish patterns listed as Double Leaf. Since it will be a difficult one for collectors to identify, I am naming it Leaf and Scroll. It will be noted that it has the double border design on the edge, frequently found on large plates and bowls.

PLATE 108
Four early opaque white plates. Period 1830-1840.

PLATE 107

Three Heart variants. Odd plate, upper left, attributed to the Midwest.

PLATE 106

Early plates. Period 1828–1840. Three belong to the Heart Series.
The fourth is the Plaid pattern.

The border has leaves, flowers and a fern-shaped ornament in a scroll. The elaborate center design has a six-pointed star.

In the lower row of Plate 110 is a plate I call "Sunflower" because of the impression the pattern gives of that flower. It is a heavy plate, having fine diamond points between the clear petals. It cannot be said that this plate is positively Sandwich. It is usually found in the Philadelphia area.

Next to it is a coarsely stippled plate that is of Midwestern origin. To date, no fragments of it have been found, and it lacks the silvery sheen that one looks for in the best Sandwich pieces. The center has a Peacock Eye effect, with beading forming the tails of the feather-like motif. The border has shell-like ornaments, flowers and double circles, alternating. I should suspect this plate of being later than the others, perhaps produced when the zest for lacy glass was abating.

On Plate 111 the two top plates, in a $4\frac{1}{2}$ inch size, are generally referred to as "toddies," probably because a large toddy glass would naturally require a larger plate to hold it than a cup plate. The one on the left is well-known among collectors as the Grape Vine and Harp. It is found in clear glass and not infrequently in color. At one time it was considered rather rare but so many have turned up that today it is deemed fairly common.

Next to it is a less common toddy. It has a border of large clusters of grapes on a clear ground. Below the grapes is a narrow border of roses with a conventional ornament in the center, all against a stippled ground. It is an attractive little plate.

Below the Grape Vine and Harp toddy is a rare 5 inch plate in the Rose and Thistle pattern. It is very lacy and has the silvery tone of the glass that collectors so admire. The edge has a border of leaves and bull's eyes. In the bowl are two roses and two thistles, with a large conventional ornament containing four bull's eyes.

Beside it is another rare 5 inch plate. In general appearance it is much like the Shield and Pine Tree series. It has a cable edge on the rim and a rather thin design. The border has a modified acorn motif and the base two star-like ornaments woven into a conventional pattern. These plates are scarce. The two sauce dishes also illustrated on this plate are treated in Chapter XIV.

Busts of famous persons were rarely ever used to adorn Sandwich glass, though it was a common practice abroad. One exception is that of Queen Victoria, illustrated on Plate 112 in a 6½ inch size. For some time these plates were thought to be foreign, but since Sandwich was such a large producer it would seem likely that it must have done a considerable export business and studied other markets than ours. It is well established that the Victoria cup plate, having the same border as the Henry Clay (Marble's Number 502), is of Sandwich origin. The workmanship of the 6½ inch plate is much finer. It depicts Victoria as a young woman wearing a large crown. The lettering "Victoria" is above her head. Below the bust is a wreath of shamrocks, roses and thistles. Since Victoria was crowned Queen of England in 1837, this plate may well have been produced to take advantage of the interest aroused the world over by her ascension to the throne, which would date it at that year. After her marriage plates appeared with the profiles of both Victoria and Albert.

Next to the Victoria plate in the upper row on Plate 112 is a twelve-sided one in a brilliant lacy pattern. It may be found in 6¾ and 6 inch sizes. The conventional design consists of leaves and a shell-shaped motif. The base has four large leaf ornaments alternating with four shell-shaped ones. The little flowers seen in the border of the larger plate are omitted on the smaller.

Next to the Victoria plate, the rarest in the illustration is the Eagle, in the lower row. It is a 6 inch size with scallop and point edge and border of acanthus leaves and smaller fleur-de-lys. The large eagle in the center is circled by thirteen stars. The plate rests on a double cable cord, one on each side of the rim of the base. This is the rarest of the larger Eagle plates. It is of Midwestern origin. Another type is the octagonal shape, made in several sizes. It is illustrated in the chapter treating of larger pieces.

The last and largest plate on Plate 112 is in the popular Shell pattern, which was produced in a number of forms, starting with the little cup plates. The one illustrated is 6¾ inches, and is rather deep in the center. The edge is twelve-sided, with a plain scalloped rim which is completely stippled. The border has Shell motifs alternating with diamond ornaments. The base has two Princess Feather medallions and two conventional ornaments, each with a star. In the smaller pieces, the stars have been omitted. The glass is heavy, brilliant and silvery, being one of the favorite lacy patterns.

The 7 inch plate at the top of Plate 113 with the large eight-pointed star in the center is the only example of this particular type I have ever seen. It is lacy and of a good quality of flint glass but it is one of those exasperating pieces which would make one reluctant to attribute it to any particular factory without adequate proof of its origin. The plate next to it in the upper row has Sandwich characteristics but apparently it was not made in quantity, for examples of it are exceedingly scarce today.

Below are two plates which one may, with a fair degree of certainty, ascribe to Sandwich. The lacy in the 6 inch size is related to similar types, one of which is shown on Plate 93 and another on Plate 110. They differ somewhat but they clearly are all the work of the same designer. Each employs flowers, leaves and bull's eyes with a striking similarity, and all have the same style of scalloped edge. That is, there is a wide scallop which is in turn made up of smaller ones. The border has a scroll of leaves and flowers alternating with bull's eyes. In the bowl are two thistles, two roses and four large double circles. The base has a wreath of leaves, like those on the bowl of the plate illustrated on Plate 110. It would be interesting to know more of the life and work of the moldmaker capable of such fine designing.

The 5 inch plate shown on Plate 113 has the scalloped, cable edge, often found on cup plates. It is a heavy piece considering its size and is of a fairly early period.

On Plate 114 is an attractive variation of the Peacock Eye, not illustrated elsewhere in this book. It is a 7 inch plate with the Peacock Eye border and thistles in the center, which make a pleasing combination. One specimen of this plate has been found in yellow.

Of all the known Sandwich designs, none will ever excel in popularity that of the Hairpin pattern. Plates were made in 6 and 7 inch sizes. As a rule they are thick and heavy. A group in this pattern is shown on Plate 96.

On Plate 115 are illustrated three plates, each of which is an example of the difference in technique during approximately the same period.

The plate at the top is typically Sandwich. The glass is heavy, brilliant and soft, with the silvery tone. It is brilliant without suggesting brittleness or newness. The stippling is fine and even. The plate below it on the left is European, probably Baccarat. In the French work the detail of the design is in higher and sharper relief than ours and the metal itself has a different depth of clarity than Sandwich glass. Furthermore, a diamond pattern in the base with a rosette in the center is typical of French glass. The plate itself is heavier in proportion to size than the Sandwich pieces. This holds true of most early foreign glass of a corresponding period.

Apparently the lacy glass, as we term it, was known abroad as "granulated" or "pebbled" and not as "lacy" glass. It was designated according to the pattern against the pebbled background, such as Oriental, Rococo, Gothic, et cetera. The Gothic was the most popular.

In the lower right-hand corner is a Midwestern plate. Research workers have not done as much in the Midwestern and other areas as they have in New England. Compare what has been written about New England factories with what has been published about the products of the Midwestern, the Philadelphia or the Baltimore glasshouses.

Mr. John Ramsay, of Canton, Ohio, has been doing valuable research work in the Pittsburgh area. It is sadly needed. There

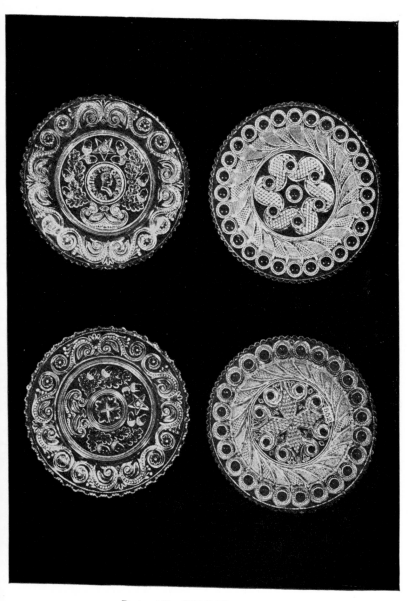

PLATE 109—SIX INCH PLATES

Upper—"Washington George" plate. Peacock Eye plate.
Lower—Variant of above. Peacock Eye plate.

PLATE 110

Six inch plates. The one at lower left is usually found in Philadelphia area. The lower right is Midwestern.

PLATE 111
Four small plates and two sauce dishes.

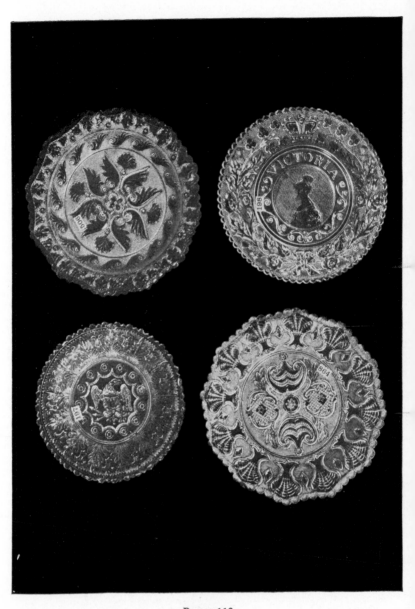

PLATE 112

Four lacy plates, including a rare "Victoria" and an "Eagle." The Eagle plate is
Midwestern.

PLATE 113
Four early lacy plates.

PLATE 114

Upper—Peacock Eye mustard cup with cover. Sauce plate of same pattern but not designed to use with cup.
Lower—Peacock Eye and Thistle plate.

PLATE 115—EACH FROM A DIFFERENT FACTORY

Top—Sandwich, Rayed Peacock Eye.
Left—French, probably Baccarat.
Right—Midwestern.

were about twenty factories in the old Pittsburgh glass district to three in New England and collectors would be interested to know more about them. Mr. Ramsay has a record of the purchases by a "store boat" from Mulvaney Ledlie & Company of Birmingham (Pittsburgh). Among these purchases were a number of items including 3 inch cup plates. There are also records of cup plates made by Bakewell, to say nothing of the marked "Fort Pitt" pieces or of the Union Glass Company's wares. The needed evidence will in time come in driblets as it has with the authenticated Sandwich pieces. There was little proof positive of the lacy and blown molded pieces until Mr. Wynn uncovered the evidential fragments in his excavations on the site of the old Sandwich factory. Certain types of cup plates and of 6 and 7 inch plates similar to the example illustrated are typical of some as yet unnamed Midwestern factory. It may be confidently expected that more light will be thrown on the origin of such pieces before long.

Chapter XVIII

LARGE LACY BOWLS AND PLATES

One of the most interesting of the Sandwich plates is octagonal shaped, with an eagle and thirteen stars in the center, illustrated on Plate 116. Since it was made in at least three sizes, the demand for it must have been considerable at the time it was produced. The one pictured is in the 7 inch size. The ornament above and below the eagle in the border does not appear elsewhere in the design. There are four stars, also in the border, one under each of the smallest motifs. Although a great many of these Eagle plates must have been made, they are scarce today. Anything typically American or with historical associations logically appeals to true collectors, hence the plate's popularity.

A printed description cannot convey adequately the beauty of some of the huge lacy bowls turned out during what may be termed the "intensive" period of manufacture of this style of glass. The largest size known in a bowl with a stippled background is 12 inches. An example is illustrated on Plate 117. The design is typically Sandwich, being a combination of the Peacock Eye with Princess Feather medallions. Such perfect examples merit a place in any museum. Few specimens are known of these 12 inch bowls. They appear so very large when placed beside any of the numerous smaller pieces that one wonders how such big bowls could have survived the myriad mishaps that can so easily befall fragile flint glass.

The next size in a bowl is the 11 inch, another museum piece, shown on Plate 118. It is the only one known to me, though, of course, there must be others in collections I have not seen. However, I doubt if there can be many, for the quality of the glass makes it highly susceptible to heat and cold and many were broken in the days when heating plants in homes were not as efficient as they are today. The larger pieces would naturally be more apt to crack than the smaller ones in the cold pantries of early days. Some later-day families who had inherited these choice pieces kept them wrapped in flannel, for they had heard from their elders how easily such pieces cracked or snapped during New England winters. One woman even kept her treasures in the folds of a feather bed.

The bowl on Plate 118 is one I have never seen in smaller pieces, though there may be some extant. It is a particularly rare pattern, combining a trefoil with a circular medallion enclosing a bull's eye. Nearly all of the larger pieces have several counterparts in smaller ones, sometimes in different forms.

Another example of a truly beautiful lacy bowl is the 10 inch size on Plate 119. Once again the Princess Feather motif predominates, this time with a clear diamond-shaped ornament in the center, instead of the usual star or bull's eye. There are four in the border that alternate with four curious conventional ornaments. All 10 inch bowls or larger are extremely rare.

A favorite with collectors is the handsome, though rather ornate, 9 inch bowl shown on Plate 120. It is one of the showiest designs of all. The four large fleurs-de-lys in the border stand out boldly, in contrast with the delicate wreath of roses in the center of the base. Over each fleur-de-lys is a thistle, as the rose and thistle are usually combined. The four large Princess Feather motifs have a clear "thumb spot" in the center, which is still another variation from the star or bull's eye. There is a border of stars below the larger motifs and the scalloped rim of the bowl is stippled. This dish is among the most desirable of the group.

The next smaller bowl after the 10 inch size is the 9½ inch so-called "Dahlia," illustrated on Plate 121. It is a brilliant, unusually heavy piece with a six-pointed ornament that has a large center of fine diamond point, and looks more like a large star than it does a flower. The stemless "Dahlia" has large leaves on each side which alternate with another conventional ornament.

PLATE 116
Rare octagonal plate with eagle and thirteen stars.

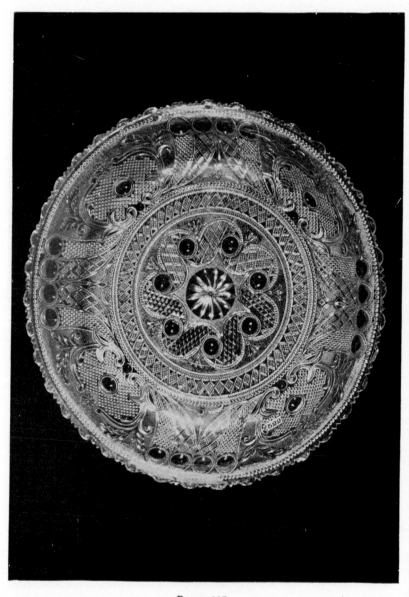

PLATE 117

Extremely rare 12 inch bowl.
Princess Feather medallions alternate with Peacock Eye motif. Period 1830–1840.

PLATE 118
Rare 11 inch lacy bowl. Trefoil with circular medallion.

PLATE 119

Rare 10 inch bowl. Princess Feather medallion with diamond motif.

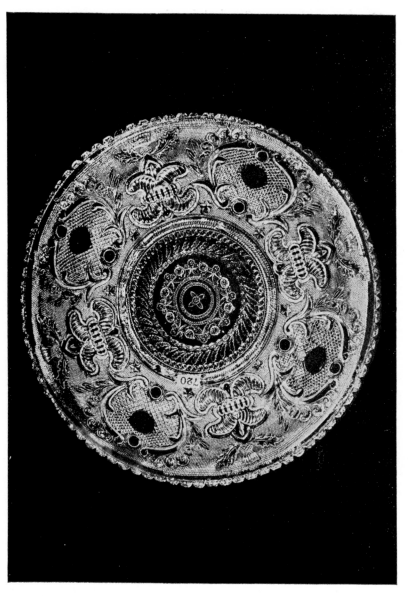

PLATE 120
Rare 9 inch bowl. Fleur-de-lys and Thistle pattern.

The base has a double cable cord and an unusually heavy rim on which the dish rests. Other forms are found in this beautiful pattern, including a compote, illustrated in the chapter on footed dishes.

A slightly smaller bowl, measuring 9¼ inches in diameter, in the Acanthus Leaf pattern is illustrated on Plate 122. It is an early heavy glass, brilliantly stippled. In the border design, leaves are prominent, and of the six conventional ornaments, two have a star beneath them. In the center of the base is a six-petaled rayed flower with the border design carried out around it. There is a double cable cord, encircling the base, which is clearly shown in the picture.

A very beautiful and rare deep dish with a wide flat rim, in the Feather pattern is shown on Plate 123. This is another of the exceptionally large dishes measuring 10 inches in diameter. There are some variations of this plate that are not so elaborate and somewhat less attractive. The five-pointed ornament in the base has a background of a small diamond mesh, with a little flower in the center of each diamond.

One variation is illustrated in Plate 124. It is 9½ inches and has a wide rim but is fairly deep in the center, somewhat like a modern soup dish. The borders of the two plates are almost identical, but the centers are entirely different. The 9½ inch piece has a large quatrefoil in the center against a plain stippled ground.

The unusually large bowls and plates are seldom found in color but, to illustrate how surprises never cease in the way of color work at Sandwich, an example of this same plate was found in crystal with the narrow border between the tips of the feathers and the outside rim banded in a beautiful, clear amber! The skill with which that band of color had been applied troubled collectors, to whom no explanation of the technical process was given. Several refused to buy this plate suspecting that the color had been painted on and would doubtless wash off with lye. It was finally learned that the amber band had been "flashed" on and thereby made a permanent part of the piece on the second heating or annealing. Expert glass blowers say, moreover, that there are other ways of applying color on such pieces.

This type of work was often done at Sandwich, even in very small pieces, such as cup plates. Last year a Benjamin Franklin (ship) cup plate came to light which had been flashed with amber, so that the plate looked to be wholly of amber glass. Only in the edge of the rim was it apparent that the core, as it were, was of crystal.

On Plate 125 are two more of the Feather with quatrefoil pieces. One is a 9½ inch plate and the other a deep bowl. The depths of the dishes cannot show in photographs in which the aim is to show the details of the design. A side view would be needed but after all, it is the design which is the most important feature.

Three variations of the Oak Leaf pattern are illustrated. The many varieties and sizes of plates and bowls attest its contemporary popularity.

On Plate 126 is illustrated the largest in the group. It is 9¼ inches in diameter. Since it was photographed a larger bowl, 10½ inches in diameter, has been found. The differences between the several varieties lie chiefly in the edge of the borders and in the design in the bases. As a rule, bowls in the Oak Leaf are shallower than in other patterns and are more flaring. The one in Plate 126 has a narrow border of three petaled leaves which runs along the scalloped edge. The one on Plate 127 has the same edge also, the only difference being in the center design in the base, which is necessarily less elaborate because it is smaller. It would be virtually the same but for the much deeper scallops in both of the center ornaments.

Some of the Oak Leaf bowls are found in a much more brilliant glass than others. In the styles shown on Plates 126 and 127 I have seen the 7⅛ inches; 7¼ inches (both 1¼ inches deep) ; 8¼ inches, 1½ inches deep; 7¾ inches, 1⅛ inches deep (shallow; almost a plate) ; 9 inches, 1¼ inches deep. This style has a double step or slight rim in the middle of the bowl.

Another variation of the Oak Leaf bowl, with a beaded border next to the edge instead of the band of leaves, is shown on Plate 128. The design of the base also is much less intricate, as the four-pointed beaded portion of the pattern is omitted. Fewer specimens of this type are encountered than those with the leaf edge. I have seen it in the following sizes: 10⅜ inches, 1¼ inches deep; 9¼ inches, 1½ inches deep; 6½ inches, 1¼ inches deep. It may very well be that other sizes were made but I have listed here for the benefit of collectors only those that I have actually seen.

In Europe, by reason of its imposing Cathedrals, the Gothic arch was the favorite pattern in lacy glass. At Sandwich it was used much less frequently. Deming Jarves had his own ideas of designing and, for all his artistic temperament, was merchant enough to realize that Gothic architecture and decoration did not have the same connotations in America that they did in Europe.

On Plates 129 and 130 are two large bowls which show a foreign influence more than any others produced at Sandwich. The 9½ inch heavy bowl on Plate 129 does not have any stippling. The border has arches, with a pointed conventional ornament between them. The large base design is known on other Sandwich pieces. The glass is brilliant and on the whole it is an attractive piece. These Gothic Arch bowls were also made in a 9 inch size, shallower, with flaring sides as well as in 7¼ inch, 5⅛ inch, and 4⅛ inch sizes with scallop and point edge.

On Plate 130 is a 9 inch bowl in a pattern very like one of European manufacture. It has been widely copied, even by today's makers. The latter copies are in more modern forms and the design varies somewhat, particularly in the stippling, which is much coarser. The pattern of the base is exactly like that used in the Gothic Arch bowl. This dish is especially brilliant and lacy. A number of sizes were made, some with slight variations. For instance, a bowl may be found in the 7 inch size, exactly like the 9 inch but the 6 inch size has coarser stippling and has a cable edge on which the dish rests. The 5 inch size rests on concentric rings instead of on the cable. The 4⅛ inch size is like the 9 inch.

One of the most beautiful and popular patterns produced at

PLATE 121
Rare 10 inch bowl, Dahlia pattern.

PLATE 122
Acanthus Leaf 9¼ inch bowl.

PLATE 123
Rare 10 inch deep dish, Feather pattern.

PLATE 124
Feather 9½ inch deep dish with quatrefoil center.

PLATE 125
Deep bowl and a 9½ inch plate, in Feather with quatrefoil center.

Sandwich is today called the Tulip. Since the same name is firmly established as identifying a pattern of the later pressed glass era, it might be well hereafter to designate the lacy as "Tulip and Acanthus Leaf," to avoid confusion.

On Plate 131 are shown two large Tulip and Acanthus Leaf bowls. The one above is another in the very rare exceptionally large size, measuring 10½ inches in diameter and 2 inches in depth. The bowl has four large tulips with leaves on either side of the flowers. The base also has tulips. Near the rim, on which the dish rests, is a heavy row of large beading. The edge of the border is decorated with bull's eyes but they are of a different style than those on the Midwestern pieces. Instead of a plain serrated or evenly scalloped edge, it has one scallop with two small ones in between. Also, there is a small hobnail between each of the large hobnails, making a more ornamental edge and one of a different character than is usually found on Sandwich pieces.

Below it, on Plate 131, is another Tulip bowl, in the 9¼ inch, which varies slightly. The edge is quite different, having a dainty design in lieu of the bull's eyes. The dish rests on a cable cord and does not have the row of heavy beading in the center, seen in the larger piece. In other details, they are almost alike. Other bowls were made in the 8½ inch size, and in 7½ inch, too. The latter size have a rim around the upper edge, as though they might some time have had covers.

The Peacock Eye pattern has been described fully in the chapters on sauce dishes and plates. On Plate 132 are two large bowls of types familiar to collectors. The larger is a brilliant lacy piece, 9 inches in diameter. This style in compotes also comes with a pedestal. Everything was made in the Peacock Eye, from little cup plates and salts up to large bowls and compotes.

The smaller bowl is of the 7½ inch size, which is comparatively common.

A very unusual Peacock Eye piece is the large oblong vegetable dish pictured on Plate 133. There are very few specimens known. It is found only in this size and in compote form, on a standard. An

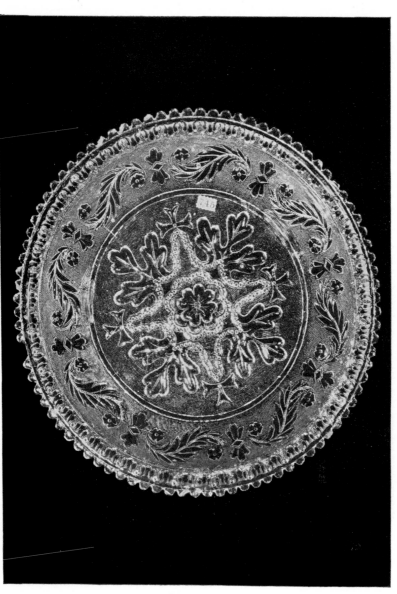

PLATE 126

Oak Leaf 9¼ inch shallow bowl.

PLATE 127
Oak Leaf shallow bowl.

PLATE 128
Oak Leaf bowl with beaded border.

PLATE 129
Gothic Arch 9½ inch bowl.

PLATE 130
Daisy 9 inch bowl.

illustration will be found in the chapter on compotes. The oblong dish is 12 by 9 inches, with beveled corners each having two Peacock Eyes. The sides and base also carry out the Peacock Eye scheme of decoration. There is very little stippling on this piece, which is not quite so lacy and glittering as others of that group.

The lower bowl on Plate 134 was not discovered until within the last two years, so it must be listed as extremely rare. Lately another was found in the Philadelphia area. It has a large eight-pointed ornament in the base, surrounded by a row of heavy beading. The border has shields enclosed in medallions, alternating with sizeable fleurs-de-lys. The 7 inch cobalt blue bowl above it was made in clear and in colors. A sauce dish is illustrated on Plate 111 with the Peacock Eye border paneled, instead of swirled.

The $8\frac{1}{2}$ inch Princess Feather bowl on Plate 135 is the last in the series. It has four Princess Feather medallions, each with a star against a fine diamond point background that alternates with four large leaves and stars. This base has a four-pointed star and leaves. There is a double cable cord around the rim upon which the dish rests. The same style of bowl is found in a $6\frac{1}{2}$ inch size without the cable round the base and in a $5\frac{1}{4}$ inch size, with the double cable cord but with a very coarse stippling that lends a rather crude appearance.

The commonest cake plate produced at Sandwich was the octagonal Bee Hive, made only in a $9\frac{1}{4}$ inch size. Some of these plates are brilliant, while others are exceedingly dull. The border has shields, scrolls, grapes, acanthus leaves, etc. In the center of the base is a small hive with bees. Thistles and five-pointed stars alternate about the beehive. The usual edge is a clear scallop, though I know of one collector who owns an example having a stippled scallop. In addition, I have heard of an authentic specimen of this plate in blue and another in yellow. It is exceedingly rare in color. A Beehive plate is pictured on Plate 136.

For some reason, reproductions of the Beehive plate have been made. I cannot conceive that they have enjoyed a wide sale, for they would not deceive even the most inexperienced collector. The

PLATE 131
Two large Tulip and Acanthus Leaf bowls, with edge variations.

PLATE 132
Two large Peacock Eye bowls.

PLATE 133
Large oblong vegetable dish, in Peacock Eye.

PLATE 134

Upper—Cobalt Blue Daisy with Peacock Eye border.
Lower—Large Shield with Fleur-de-lys bowl.

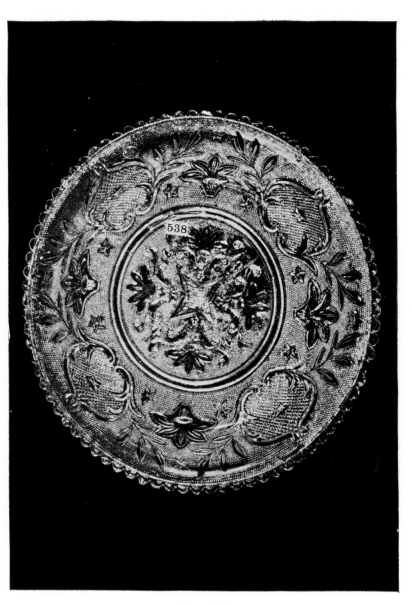

PLATE 135
Princess Feather 8½ inch bowl.

PLATE 136—OCTAGONAL CAKE PLATES

Upper—Beehive 9¼ inch plate.
Lower—Rose and Thistle 8¾ inch plate.

first copies came out several years ago, one in the usual size and the other much larger, measuring about 13 inches. During the last few years they have been on the market in several sizes, both clear and in colors. Since the originals were of heavy lead-flint glass and only in a 9¼ inch size, all the fakes in green, amber and crystal, from a bread-and-butter size up to a large tray, obviously proclaim their lack of authenticity. There is no ring to the glass, they are not so heavy and they have a bright and shining surface. So far, this has been the only attempt to reproduce lacy Sandwich glass.

In the old memorandum book of William Stutson, dated 1859, I find 9 inch Beehive plates listed. It is not easy to believe that these plates continued to be made and sold by Sandwich so long after the great popularity of lacy ware was a thing of the past in a commercial sense. Of course, it is not beyond the range of possibilities that the demand for this particular plate may have persisted on a scale sufficient to make it profitable for manufacture, either on general or special order, at a time when what is now known as "pattern glass" had gone into mass production with consequent lower prices. The fact that Beehive plates are found today in much greater numbers than other handsomer styles strengthens the belief that Beehives might well have been produced for years after the demand for lacy glass had practically ceased.

On Plate 136 is shown another large octagonal plate in the Rose and Thistle design. It is 8¾ inches or a half-inch smaller in diameter than the Beehive. The base has a large flower which looks more like a sunflower than anything else. The border has a flower in each panel. A smaller sunflower than that in the base alternates with a thistle and a rose. It is a beautiful plate, seldom found today outside of private collections.

Chapter XIX

LACY COMPOTES AND COVERED DISHES

Collectors will find that compotes were made in patterns which they will usually recognize, since for the most part they are really familiar plates or bowls on a standard or pedestal. Naturally there are always exceptions. The octagonal compote on Plate 137 is in a pattern which I have never seen duplicated in any other form, though such may well exist. The designer apparently had in mind utilizing everything that had been executed in the way of backgrounds at Sandwich, for we find that there is a different flower in each of the eight panels, all against differing grounds. For instance, there is a wild rose against a background of vertical lines; a rose against a stippled herringbone ground; another flower against stippling, etc., all of which makes for quite unusual effects. The compote is large, being 9¾ inches in diameter and 6½ inches high. The bowl is deep and the pedestal rather short. The knob stem of the standard is fluted inside and the heavy round foot with a scalloped edge has a stippled lacy design of acanthus leaves on the outside surface instead of underneath. It is an exceptionally rare compote, as indeed all compotes are, particularly the large ones or those in unusual patterns.

The covered vegetable dish shown above the compote on Plate 137 is among the handsomest pieces produced at Sandwich. They are rare, although more of them have come to light than specimens of many other dishes. It is not unusual to find the bases without covers but to obtain them complete, in perfect condition, is an event. By "perfect" I do not mean absolutely free of blemishes of any kind because finding proof specimens in early lacy glass is practically an impossibility.

There are two styles in the covered vegetable dishes, as may be seen on Plate 151. The two covered pieces at the top were photographed to illustrate the chief difference, which is in the brim. It will be noticed immediately that one piece has a grape border and the other a simple stippled border. The covers are alike. In the lower part of the picture is shown a base with the cover beside it, so that the reader may have a clear view of the design in the base. On each end is a large conventionalized Princess Feather. The sides have a Princess Feather medallion, flanked by decorative baskets of fruit. Collectors will find a dozen of the vegetable dishes with the plain stippled brim, to one with the grape border, but both deserve a place in any collection.

An important discovery was made when the porcelain dish, bearing a Meissen mark of the 1820's, was discovered. This rare dish is illustrated on Plate 152. It is *exactly* like the base of the lacy vegetable dish in the rarer form, having a border of grapes on the surface edge. The porcelain dish is hand-decorated in a vivid blue and gold. From letters in my possession, it is known that the Boston & Sandwich Glass Company sent men from their organization to Europe to gain information concerning manufacturing and design. While Sandwich designs show little foreign influence, in this case the lacy dish appears to be a direct copy.

An exceptionally large compote in the Peacock Eye pattern is illustrated on Plate 138. It is 10½ inches in diameter and 6 inches in height. Bowls of this size are all exceedingly rare but in compotes they are still more difficult to find. The base has the "scrolled eye" seen in the centers of various dishes in this pattern. The hollow pedestal shows four closely set heavy ribs and the round foot has scrolls underneath. The design may be seen through the glass. The covered bowl or butter dish on Plate 138 is a form seldom found in Peacock Eye or in any other pattern of early lacy glass. It measures 7½ inches in diameter and is shallow, with an attractive petal knob which is open at the top. Covered compotes on a standard are also found in this design, though any covered lacy dishes are rare. This little butter dish is a particularly desirable piece.

On Plate 139 is still another of the extremely rare compotes in a 10½ inch size. It is in the Tulip and Acanthus Leaf pattern. The rim of the dish has a clear scalloped edge with large and small hobnail, as noted in the chapter on large bowls. The pedestal is short and the foot carries the Plume pattern.

The Tulip and Acanthus Leaf compote may be found in a 7½ inch size. It also has the Plume design on the inside of the foot, while the edge of the latter has an unusual scalloped rim.

The Plume pattern was also used for a compote. One is pictured above the Tulip, on Plate 139. Apparently this design originated at Sandwich, or at least in this country. It is of an excellent quality of flint glass, stippled above and below the design. The pedestal has a knob stem with a scalloped edge on the rim of the foot, just as on the smaller Tulip compote, which is not illustrated.

Probably the most artistic pedestal found on any compote is shown on the Dahlia, pictured in Plate 140. It is triangular in shape, with the graceful scrolls in the standard outlined with beading. There are three paw feet, that recall those used by our famous American cabinet maker, Duncan Phyfe.

The bowl of the Dahlia compote is shallow. It is 9½ inches in diameter and stands 5⅝ inches high. The pattern is clearly illustrated in the chapter on large bowls.

Collectors would do well to remember that almost any of the various style of pedestals pictured may be found attached to any of the different patterns of bowls. Apparently the workman either took the nearest at hand or suited his own fancy in this regard. I have actually seen the 9¼ inch Bee Hive cake plate, which was never made in bowl form, with the same pedestal shown in this illustration of the Dahlia compote.

One of the rarest compotes in this series is that one in the Heart and Leaf pattern shown on Plate 141. Only two are known at this writing, although doubtless there may be others in private collections which have not come to my attention. The Heart motif alternating with a leaf also occurs in a bowl minus the pedestal. The compote has a pointed arch design and an ornamental round pedestal and foot.

Next to the Heart compote is another unusually large one in the Peacock Eye pattern with the Scrolled Eye design in the center. It is seldom one finds a large lacy compote on a perfectly plain clear glass hexagonal foot but this is merely another proof that anything may be expected by the student of Sandwich glass.

Like Tennyson's brook, the stream of rare compotes seems to go on forever, toward delighted collectors. On Plate 142 is shown the only one known of this particular oblong type. The vegetable dish to match is illustrated in the chapter on large bowls. This compote is simply that same vegetable dish set on a graceful standard. It will be noticed that the pedestal's top is closely similar to the triangular-shaped one with paw feet, save that the base is round. It is a large, rather showy piece, not quite as brilliant as others because of the scanty stippling in the bowl.

The rayed Peacock Eye bowls also were made up into their quota of compotes. On Plate 143 are shown a very shallow compote on a low foot, and also a deeper bowl on a higher foot. Among other pictures of compotes (Plate 148) may be seen the plain, swirled Peacock Eye bowl on exactly the same pedestal as the shallow rayed compote on Plate 143. The large Peacock Eye piece on that Plate is an 8½ inch size. The pedestal has a heavy round knob in the stem and the round foot is rather coarsely stippled underneath with a scroll design and stars.

The shallow rayed Peacock Eye compote is really a 7 inch plate on a standard.

Four compotes are pictured on Plate 144. In the upper left hand corner is a 6½ inch Oak Leaf pattern bowl on a pedestal of the same style used on two of the Peacock Eye compotes. The compote next to it in the upper row is rather more unusual and has been called the "Arrowhead" pattern. The bowl is decorated with pointed, stippled loops. The base has an unusually attractive design, consisting of a cord so coiled as to make a border of loops. In the center of each loop is a flower. The foot is particularly

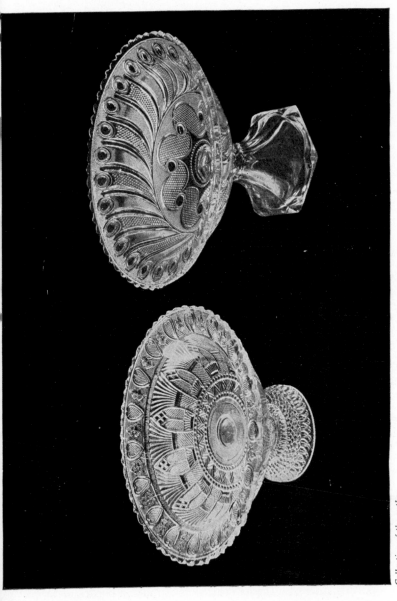

PLATE 141

Rare large Heart with Leaf compote.   The Peacock Eye in an unusual combination with a clear, hexagonal foot.

PLATE 140
Rare Dahlia compote. Scrolled pedestal with triangular base and paw feet.

PLATE 139—RARE LACY COMPOTES

Upper—Plume pattern.
Lower—Tulip bowl, Plume pedestal, all original.

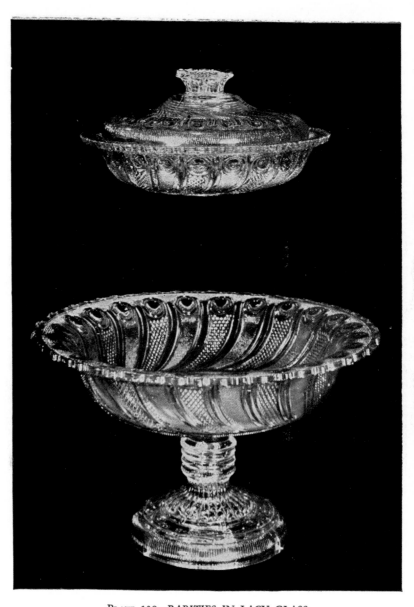

PLATE 138—RARITIES IN LACY GLASS

Upper—Peacock Eye butter dish.
Lower—Exceptionally large Peacock Eye compote, 10½ inch.

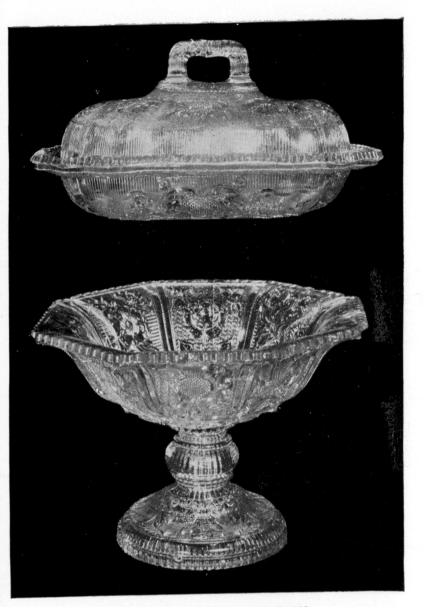

PLATE 137—RARITIES IN LACY GLASS

Upper—Large covered vegetable dish.
Lower—Octagonal compote with flowered panels.

attractive, being lacy and stippled. The compote comes in a 7 inch size. It is of Midwestern origin.

The larger compote in the lower row is in the Thistle and Lily pattern. The bowl has a scroll with lilies above and thistles below the vine-like pattern. The foot differs from others in the wide brim, which is fluted or ribbed. The flat part of the base carries a stippled design underneath, with four stars and scrolls. The dish is 8 inches in diameter.

The last compote on this page is small, but it has the tallest pedestal of any. The top of the shallow 6 inch bowl has a border of curious five-pointed leaves. Below it there is a chain effect of diamonds and double circles. In the bottom of the bowl is a four-pointed star. The pedestal has a heavy knob stem and the round foot is elaborately decorated with a heavy design.

All of the compotes described from Plate 144 are extremely scarce, with the possible exception of the Oak Leaf.

Of the six compotes on Plate 145, four are in patterns that are alike.

The center piece at the top of the page is in the Daisy pattern, so familiar to us because a similar pattern was made at Baccarat and exported to this country until relatively recent times. The one illustrated is unquestionably of Sandwich origin. The spreading, hollow type of foot with acanthus leaf decoration is typical. This compote is in a 7 inch size. One like it in a 5 inch is pictured beside it, with the difference that the shape of the knob in the stem is not the same.

At the right of the larger Daisy compote is a very rare octagonal Eagle compote with a design of thirteen stars, as on the plates described in Chapter XVIII. The bowl is deep and the heavy hollow pedestal is ribbed on the inside, producing a pleasing decorative effect. The foot also carries the acanthus leaf in relief on the outside, which is scalloped on the edge. Finely stippled concentric circles adorn the inside of the foot, which is a trifle over-elaborate, as the concentric circles show through the glass, giving it a blurred appearance.

In the center below, on Plate 145, is a compote in the scarce Nectarine pattern. The pedestal is similar to that of the Eagle dish. Flowers, leaves and bull's eyes, alternate on the border of the bowl. Below this design is a band of clusters of grapes and in the base a wreath of leaves. It is a small compote, only 6 inches in diameter. All dishes in the Nectarine pattern are both scarce and desirable.

The Nectarine dish is shown between a pair of small 5 inch octagonal compotes with pedestals exactly like those of the Eagle and Nectarine compotes. The base has a design with eight leaves and there is a different flower or ornament in each panel of the bowl. They are exceedingly rare, as lacy compotes are seldom found in pairs.

Two particularly beautiful compotes, both of them in a variation of the Nectarine pattern, are shown on Plate 146. Each has an elaborate pedestal; one, triangular-shaped with paw feet and the other, a hollow stem fluted type, with acanthus leaf decoration in relief on top of the foot and concentric circles underneath. The bowls have a scroll of leaves and flowers around the border. The dish with the triangular-shaped foot is somewhat out of proportion as the pedestal appears too large for the shallow bowl. They are both heavy, brilliant lacy glass.

Most collectors are familiar with the compote shown on Plate 147, which has a bowl like the base of the oblong covered vegetable dishes. It may be found in clear and in colors, though, of course, the colored specimens are very rare. The pedestals vary in the clear, though colored examples are usually of the simple fluted type shown in the illustration. The variant has plain panels without the feather-like decoration. These dishes are not found covered. It would seem that in the process of attaching the base to the foot the top, while still plastic, was bent out of shape. In any event, the shape is distorted enough so that covers do not fit. The Princess Feather motif and baskets of flowers predominate in the design on the bowl. This compote may be found in the following colors, besides clear glass: Yellow, light (smoky) blue, sapphire blue, "Peacock" (bluish green), and amethyst.

PLATE 142

Rare large oblong Peacock Eye compote with interesting scrolled pedestal
and round foot.

PLATE 143
Rayed Peacock Eye compotes with differing pedestals.

PLATE 144

Four interesting types of lacy compotes. The one at the upper right is Midwestern.

PLATE 145

A group of nine lacy pieces in lead glass, including some of the early Sandwich productions.

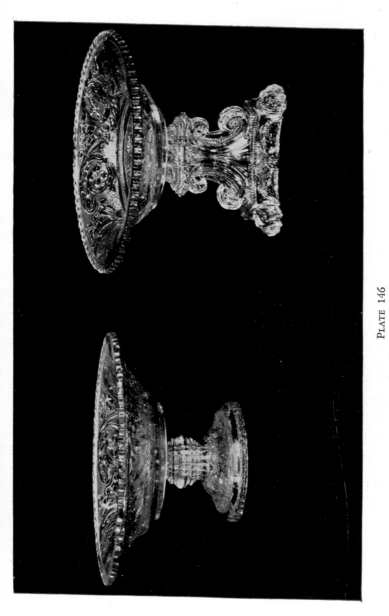

PLATE 146

Compotes in the Nectarine pattern.

Two attractive compotes in the Paneled Diamond pattern are seen on Plate 148 and also two in the Peacock Eye pattern. The two in Paneled Diamond vary, both in the pattern on the bowls and in the pedestals. The upper is in a 6½ inch size. It has a clear panel alternating with another in a diamond design, sometimes referred to by old glassmakers as "Strawberry cut." Each panel is finished at the top with a fan-like ornament. The pedestal has a large knob and the foot fine ribbing, with a row of dewdrops above and below.

The lower compote is in a 6¾ inch size. The bowl varies from the one above it chiefly in the ornament which finishes the panel. Instead of the fan-like motif, the clear panel has three loops of small dewdrops and the diamond panel, two half-diamonds which are left clear. Above the panels a single row of dewdrops encircles the bowl. The pedestal is exactly like those on the two Peacock Eye compotes.

The two Peacock Eye compotes on Plate 148 are alike except in size. Each has a row of dewdrops above the "eyes" on the upper edge and the bases have the Scrolled Eye seen in so many of the Peacock Eye pieces. The pedestals are alike.

Two Princess Feather compotes are pictured on Plate 149. The larger, on the low foot, is in the 7¼ inch size. There is a variation in its design which I have not seen in any other form, though such may exist. The Princess Feather medallions, from which this pattern takes its name, have a solid diamond point in the center. At the top and bottom of this medallion is a curious little ornament resembling a wheel. There are four medallions around the bowl, as well as leaves and stars. The foot is heavy, solid glass with a border of leaves against a stippled ground, which shows dimly through the thick glass.

The second compote on Plate 149 also has the Princess Feather medallions, each of which encloses a star. There also are other stars in the border. Around the base of the bowl is a wreath of leaves and scrolls. It is in a 6¼ inch size. The pedestal is the rather elaborate type which seems to have been most used, with a

PLATE 147
Rare compote found in blue, amethyst or yellow, as well as clear glass.

PLATE 148
Two Peacock Eye and two Paneled Diamond compotes.

PLATE 149
Two lacy Princess Feather compotes.

PLATE 150—GROUP OF LACY DISHES

Upper—Pair of lacy cups and saucers.   Peacock Eye footed bowl.
Lower—Pair of lacy egg glasses.   Heart with Sheaf of Wheat comboe.   Pair of whiskey tasters.

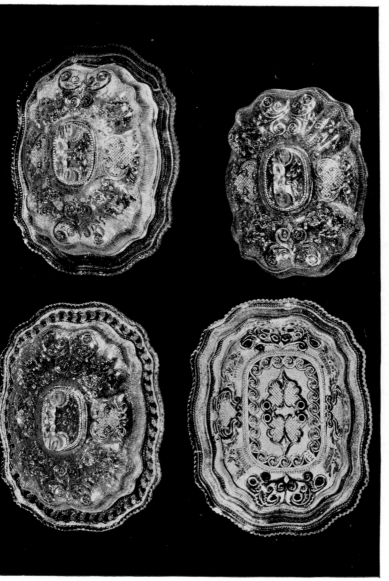

PLATE 151—COVERED VEGETABLE DISHES

Upper—Pair of dishes, covered, showing differing brims.
Lower—Base to dish, with cover at one side.

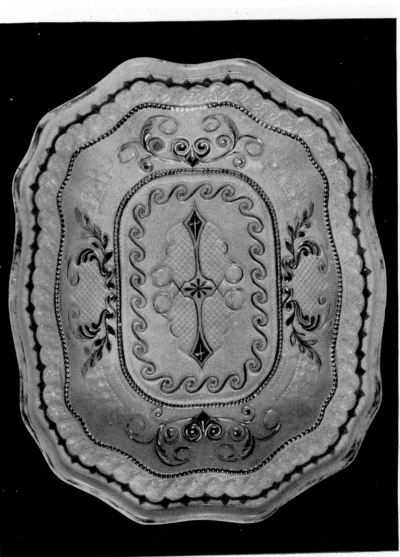

PLATE 152

Porcelain dish bearing Meissen mark of the 1820's from which design on vegetable dish with grape border

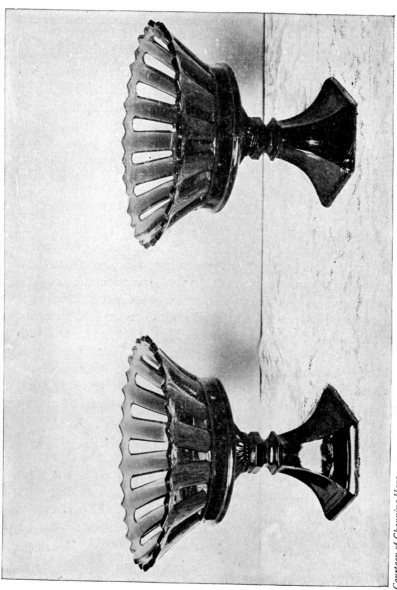

PLATE 153

Pair of extremely rare amethyst compotes.

hollow fluted standard, acanthus leaves in relief on the outside and concentric circles underneath.

A strikingly unusual Peacock Eye bowl is the 6 inch footed one on Plate 150. The rim on the top edge shows that it must have had a cover at one time. On the brim is a grape pattern in relief, a variation I have not seen in any other form of this design. The collared foot is ribbed or fluted on the inside, making a pleasing effect.

Below it is a Heart and Sheaf of Wheat compote, also in a 6 inch size. The base of the bowl has a diamond waffle pattern with four intertwined hearts in the center. The pedestal is clear solid glass with a knob in the center.

Collectors should not be surprised to find that almost any plate or bowl in lacy glass may have any one of the various pedestals illustrated in this book. Many of the footed pieces in the various Heart patterns are not pictured because they are too numerous.

On Plate 150 are shown two of the small lacy miniature tumblers, which may be found in any of the many shades of color used at Sandwich. They are 1¾ inches tall. Little can be told about the cups and saucers on the same page. They appear to be Sandwich but it is not clearly established that they are. There is also some uncertainty about the tall egg glasses. They are 3¼ inches high, with scalloped top and foot and a large Shell pattern. These appear to be Midwestern. For the present it seems fair to give them the benefit of a doubt.

Probably the rarest non-lacy colored compotes of the period 1840–1850 are those with the openwork bowls and hexagonal bases, pictured on Plate 153. They are in a particularly fine shade of deep amethyst. Few perfect examples are known of these large footed dishes, which measure 8¼ inches high and 8¾ inches in diameter. It is a fortunate collector indeed who can add one to his collection, to say nothing of a pair. Lately another one was found in that beautiful shade of peacock-green, sometimes seen in Sandwich glass.

Chapter XX

LACY SUGAR BOWLS AND CREAMERS

Among the choicest of the rare collectibles originated by the Boston & Sandwich Glass Company, both in clear glass and in colors, are the lacy sugar bowls and creamers. For some unascertained reason, fewer different patterns were used in these two useful articles than in anything else. Another curious fact is that so few of them were mates. The nearest approach to a match in the distinctly "lacy" type is the sugar bowl and creamer in the top row of Plate 154. Each is octagonal with a shield-like medallion on the sides containing diamond-shaped ornaments and each has a scalloped foot. The panels are so distinct on the creamer as to make it appear round, at first glance. They are typical of the intensive period of lacy manufacture at Sandwich, and both are scarce items, particularly in anything approaching perfect condition. The creamer is 4 inches high to the top of the lip. It is rare in color but is found in a beautiful opaque powder blue.

On many of the sugar bowls the covers not only do not match the bowl in design but vary even in the knobs, of which the quaintest and perhaps the loveliest are those that resemble open flowers. These were used on the sugar bowls oftener than on other covered pieces, though one may be seen on the cover of the Peacock Eye butter dish illustrated on Plate 138.

An example of the same style of sugar bowl having a different cover is illustrated in the Shield pattern on Plate 154. In the upper row is a pair of bowls, pictured so that the reader may see the pattern on two sides. The bowl in the upper left-hand corner has a lyre-shaped ornament enclosing an acanthus leaf. In the right-hand corner is another view of the reverse side of the same bowl, which has a shield-shaped motif. Acanthus leaves form dividing panels between these ornaments. The knob to the cover is the open flower variety. An example of this sugar bowl is known in a brilliant deep blue.

Below, in the center of Plate 154, is a similar bowl having numerous small points of difference. For example, the foot is not scalloped, the edge where the cover joins is plain instead of ornamented and the cover has acanthus leaves but is without panels or stippling. The plainer cover seems too simple for the more elaborate base but since the rim is straight where the cover joins, instead of being ornamented, like the bowl in the upper row, it is quite evident that they were meant to go together.

The two rarest and most outstanding sugar bowls are on the ends of the lower row of Plate 154. The design of the bowl on the left consists of a basket of flowers resting on a double-headed eagle and shield. The eagle heads are similar to those on the Providence salt, some specimens of which are marked "Providence," and this sugar bowl is often referred to as the "Providence" bowl, though it is not so marked. The cover is stippled, with acanthus leaves in relief, on the outside. The foot is scalloped around the edge and has a dainty design underneath. This rare sugar bowl is impressive with its brilliant elegance. It may be found in a vivid sapphire blue, or opal as well as in clear glass. The colored bowl is shown on Plate 156.

The other outstanding sugar bowl is the oval piece, at the right-hand end of the lower row on Plate 154. A thistle is the chief motif, though there is a pineapple on each of the oval ends of the bowl. The cover matches perfectly, having a large thistle corresponding to the one on the bowl. The foot is unlike any used on the other bases. It is clear, not stippled, and has concentric circle steps, the detail of which may be seen more clearly on the dark blue specimen pictured on Plate 156. The design is on the inside of the cover, which shows through clearly on the clear bowl but is very faint on the colored piece. The Thistle sugar bowl has not been found in any other color than sapphire blue and in clear glass, so

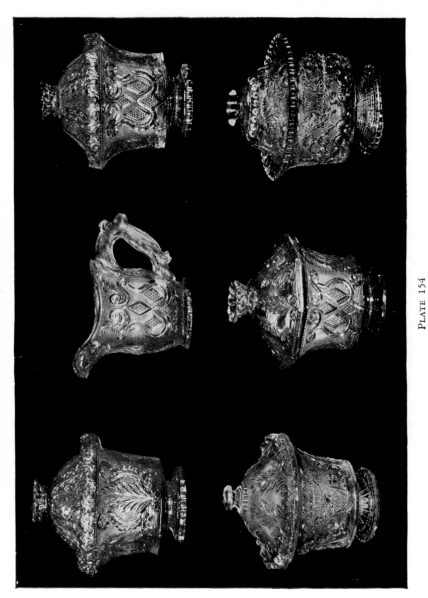

PLATE 154

Rare lacy sugar bowls and creamer.

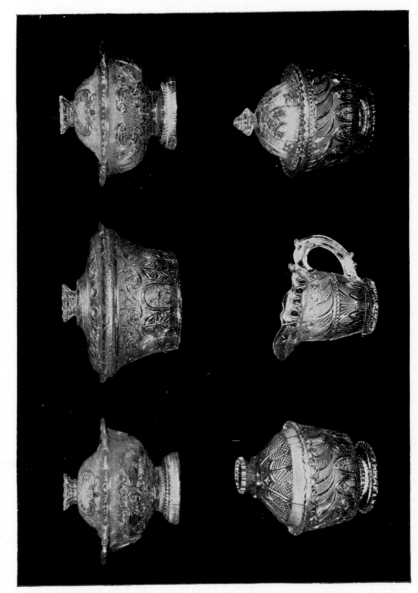

PLATE 155

PLATE 156

Rare colored sugar bowls and creamer. Lower left bowl is Midwestern.

PLATE 157
Lacy creamers.

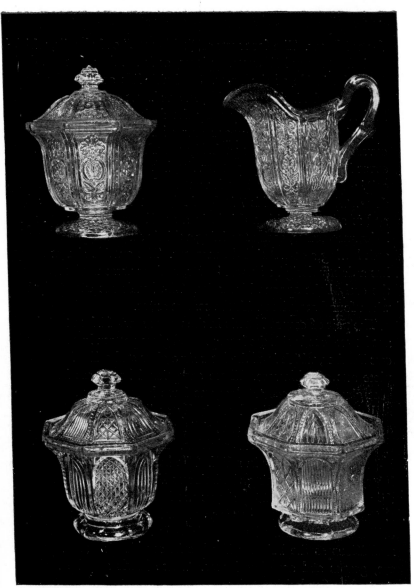

Collection of Mrs. William Greig Walker

PLATE 158

Upper—Sugar bowl and creamer of later period.
Lower—Two sugar bowls. That on the left not positively identified as Sandwich.

far as I know. The foot rests on "table rests" or hobnails, which is typical of many Midwestern pieces, as is the fact that the design is on the inside of the cover. Sandwich lids are found with the pattern on the inside or outside, in an almost equal proportion but Midwestern covers usually carry the design underneath.

In the center of the upper row of Plate 155 is a large deep covered bowl which was probably never intended for sugar. The cover in the Peacock Eye pattern fits, but nevertheless, it is not the original lid. Covers to match were made but it is difficult to find them. The dish itself is 7 inches in diameter and 3½ inches deep, and is stippled, with a thistle in a scroll around the upper part. Below are arches, each containing a thistle alternating with another arch having a conventional ornament. The outside rim at the top has a dainty design of small leaves, such as were used on some of the early light opaque blue salts. The bowls are extremely rare, when found complete with the correct cover.

The pair of covered bowls in the upper row of Plate 155 should not be confused with the later pressed glass pattern known as Princess Feather, which is of the later lime glass and collectible in complete sets of tableware. These exceptional bowls are in a heavy flint glass. They are too large to have been sold as sugar bowls and doubtless were listed originally as "covered nappies." The covers have an open knob, are brilliantly stippled on the inside, and carry the Princess Feather medallion. The upper brim of the bowl has a border of grapes in relief. The bowl itself has three medallions, one of them being the Princess Feather. The first bowl in the upper row (Plate 155) shows another of the medallion decorations. Below the medallions is a narrow band of peacock eyes. The collared base is ribbed underneath. It is unusual to find such medallions as the Princess Feather in combination with peacock eye, grapes and acanthus leaves. These bowls may be included among the Sandwich rarities.

An interesting example of interchangeable covers which may or may not be the originals, is seen in the lower row on Plate 155.

The bowls are exactly the same, with pointed arches below a band of peacock feathers and a scalloped foot. The cover on the right-hand bowl has pointed arches and four-leaf clovers on the inside against a stippled ground. The knob is of solid glass. It appears to be an original cover because there are arches in the bowl too. The sugar bowl cover on the left also has pointed arches which do not match the arches in the bowl nearly as well and there is no stippling. The knob is of the open style. This might very well be the original cover, for it fits, but the combination is not particularly attractive. From Sandwich anything can be expected. Further evidence that interchangeable covers were sold separately at this period, probably due to the amount of breakage incurred in transportation or handling, is supplied by William Stutson's old memo book, listing separate covers for sale.

The Providence Eagle sugar bowl and the Thistle, on Plate 156, have been described but are shown here for the color contrast.

The Roman Rosette bowl in the upper left-hand corner is a sapphire blue. The pattern does not need describing for collectors encounter it so often in honey dishes, sauce dishes, bowls, etc. It is rare in sugar bowl form, especially in this sapphire blue with a purplish tint.

The creamer on Plate 156 is sapphire blue. This is a variation of the Arch with Chain, shown on Plate 157. It may properly be called Peacock Eye with Arch, to identify it more precisely. The upper part of the creamer has a row of peacock eyes, separated from the arches below by a heavy row of beading. Such creamers may be found in clear glass and in colors, though they are rare in color. A fiery opal one was called to my attention lately. The colors seen most often (when at all) in creamers are a dark sapphire blue and an opaque powder blue. Canary yellow or opal are rarer. Amethyst would be extremely rare.

On Plate 157 are the three styles of lacy creamers which Sandwich produced in the greatest quantity. The two on the outside have been described. The creamer in the center is most frequently encountered. It will be noticed that the lower part of its bowl is very similar to the one with peacock eye decoration. Through the center there is a chain effect, with a row of beading directly below it. All of the creamers are large and brilliant, with a rather wide lip. The stippled handles are large, rather clumsy affairs. The bases are invariably scalloped around the edges, with concentric rings in the very center, rayed out to the edge of the foot. Sometimes the opaque blue creamers are also found streaked in a lighter shade of blue or with bright deep opalescent hues. Most of them are from 4 inches to 4¼ inches in height, measured to the top of the lip.

On Plate 158 in the upper row are a sugar bowl and creamer of a slightly later period, which go nicely together, although the designs are not exactly the same. They both have a diamond pattern on the foot, each diamond space enclosing a dot. Many fragments of these bases have been found at Sandwich. The glass is a heavy flint, lacy but not stippled.

The Gothic sugar bowl in the lower right-hand corner is of the lacy period though the design is simpler than that on the others pictured. It is octagonal in form and partly stippled. These are sometimes found in canary yellow and in a number of soft pastel shades of opaque glass, such as light blue, jade green, opal, etc. As usual the colored ones are rarer than the clear glass and command a higher price, particularly when complete with the cover. The covers, naturally enough, suffered most from breakage which is substantiated today by the fact that more odd bases are found than complete specimens with lids. This may be one of the answers to why so many of the covers on the early sugar bowls do not match. A demand for lid replacements may have exhausted the supply of a particular kind, and bowls were sold with covers originally intended to match other types, although it seems reasonable to assume that more lids were made than bowls.

The last sugar bowl on Plate 158 (lower left corner) is of a rather plain pattern, which followed the intensive production of lacy glass. While it is octagonal, there is no stippling. Each panel in the bowl has a pointed arch, one fluted alternating with one filled with diamond point. There are several styles of later sugar bowls which are not pictured here, not only because they do not belong to the lacy period but also because there is no certainty that they were of Sandwich origin.

Chapter XXI

PITTSBURGH VS. SANDWICH

It will require as much study and painstaking research work in connection with the product of Midwestern factories as has been done with that of the East, before we can acquire certain knowledge of their wares prior to 1850. It is true that careful work in this direction is going forward steadily but there is much left undone, particularly in the field of lacy glass. It has been established that lacy cup plates were produced in the Midwest at the Union Glass Works and also by the Fort Pitt Glass Works in Pittsburgh. Evidence points to other sources in the vicinity of Philadelphia and Baltimore, but so far there is no proof available today to show that much if, indeed, any lacy work was done outside of Sandwich in the large pieces. The smaller plates which I attribute to the Midwest show such marked differences in style from the Sandwich output that experienced collectors who for years have studied their specialty with unprejudiced minds, free from wishful thinking, have reached the same conclusion.

When the first edition of this book was written, there appeared to be some doubt in the minds of a few in regard to a lacy creamer, marked "R. B. Curling & Sons, Fort Pitt" on the base. Controversy raged over this piece to the extent that a sense of fairness impelled me to attempt to paint both sides of the picture. The innocent object of the dispute is fully illustrated, front view, side and base, on Plate 159. The question in point was—did R. B. Curling & Son actually produce a creamer which some Sandwich addicts felt must have been made at Sandwich on special order for Curling, because it was so closely similar to many known Cape Cod pieces?

The "Curling" creamer, so-called because of the inscription on the base, is a rare item, since not more than one has come to light

PLATE 159
Creamer marked "R. B. Curling & Sons, Fort Pitt."
The Fort Pitt Glass Works was located in Pittsburgh, Pa.

PLATE 160

Lacy pane of Pittsburgh origin, marked "Curling's & Robertson." This was made by
the Fort Pitt Glass Works.

PLATE 161
Upper: Lacy glass pane, unmarked, found in Pittsburgh.
Lower left: Lacy pane, found in Ohio. Lower right: Small view of marked pane.

since publicity was given it in 1939 in this book. "Fort Pitt" refers to a concern established in Pittsburgh in 1827 by Robert B. Curling and William Price. The latter soon retired from the partnership and Mr. Curling brought his two sons with him into the business which was known as the Fort Pitt Glass Works.

At the time the argument was in full swing, only two marked creamers were known and they were both found in the Midwest. I do not know of any authenticated Sandwich creamers of which a number of specimens cannot be found and usually in New England. No marked Sandwich creamer has ever been discovered. Sandwich wares overshadowed those of all other factories and therefore it was important for the Curling firm to mark their own plainly, if they wished to differentiate it from Sandwich. Besides, there is one other known marked Curling piece. On Plate 160 may be seen a heavily stippled glass pane marked "Curling's & Robertson." In the 1830's the firm became Curling, Robertson & Company, having admitted Morgan Robertson as a member of the concern. Two other lacy panes have emanated from the Midwest which, so far, have not been found in the New England area. One came from Pittsburgh and the other from Ohio. Two of these, both unmarked, may be seen on Plate 161. In years past these would easily have been attributed to Sandwich. Careful study places the stylized leaves tapering into a small flower on the marked pane, to be taken directly from the design in the Oak Leaf bowl, illustrated on Plate 127. Concentric circles with a dot in the center are typical of many Sandwich pieces. This motif, on Plate 161, carries the Midwestern flavor, in the row of bull's eyes surrounding the large diamond-shaped ornament in the center. The third pane, also on Plate 161, bears a striking resemblance in character of design to the large rectangular dish on Plate 133. Evidence seems to point to these panes having embellished early steamboats. Certainly the bright stippled crystal glass would have made handsome decorative panels, as well as being useful for lighting purposes. They were also utilized as ornamental frames for doorways, thus beautifying the entrance and admitting light to dark hallways. The early panes are found in clear glass. Much later types, not illustrated, are seen in several colors.

Marking of pressed glassware began quite early. Two styles of marked Pittsburgh salts are known, each having an anchor design in the base. One has "Pittsburgh" embossed on the stern, while the other is marked "J. Robinson & Son, Pittsburgh." John Robinson came to America from England and built a factory for the making of flint glass in Pittsburgh, during the early 1820's. His company was known as the New Stourbridge Flint Glass Works. A six-inch plate with a vague leaf pattern in the border, definitely not "lacy" in character, may be found marked "T. & J. Robinson Pitts.G." It is quite likely that this plate was produced prior to 1836 since John Robinson died that year. The marked Robinson salt and plate may be safely placed between 1830–1835.

The Curling creamer has a heavily beaded handle unlike any handle of a known Sandwich piece. The basket of flowers shown in the front view of the creamer is like the basket on the "Providence" sugar bowl, only larger. The chain border and beading also are used on Sandwich creamers. Other elements of the design on the Curling creamer are almost identical with upper portion of the Arch with chain creamer pictured in the center of Plate 157. The foot is scalloped, as is the case with all the Sandwich creamers of this period. The chief point which would eliminate the Curling creamer as a Sandwich product is the fact it is marked "R. B. Curling & Sons, Fort Pitt." It remains to be learned only whether the Curling firm was guilty of plagiarism. It would seem unlikely that Sandwich was the copyist, since their lacy wares, both in preponderance of the number of designs and enormous output over a period of years, far surpassed that of any other glass company in this country. R. B. Curling & Sons could well be proud of their marked creamer, which is quite as beautiful as any Sandwich turned out, to say nothing of the added value in interest and historical significance, in the marked base carrying their name. *All* that glitters in lacy glassware is not Sandwich.

Chapter XXII

RARITIES IN LACY GLASS

In every branch of Sandwich collectibles, there are exceptional pieces which are interesting to collectors, either from a standpoint of rarity or historical association. In each chapter the respective rarities are mentioned but there are a few outstanding pieces which for one reason or another are of particular interest and therefore should receive special treatment. Curiously enough, all of the items selected for this group are somewhat miscellaneous in character. There are three large oblong dishes, two trays, two shell-shaped dishes, an oblong covered dish and a jewel casket.

It is well to bear in mind that the word "rarity" does not necessarily connote "beauty," though the selection for consideration here happily combines the two.

The rarest piece in point of the number found to date, is the jewel casket on Plate 162. This was discovered in New Orleans. Curiously, it will be remembered that the New Orleans office and salesroom was one of the first established by the Boston & Sandwich Glass Company prior to 1830. So far, the writer knows of exactly three perfect jewel caskets. Lucky the collector who can add one of these to his collection!

The next rarest and perhaps one of the handsomest pieces ever produced at Sandwich is the large, oblong deep dish with open handles at each end and an open chain border along the sides. A perfect specimen is illustrated on Plate 163. I may add that perfect specimens are few and far between. It is the superlative in lacy Sandwich.

The mold must have been extremely difficult both to make and to manipulate by the glass workers, for it is evident from surviving examples of the dish, that they did not fill readily in the handles.

I have seen several of which the handles failed to meet in the center by one-eighth inch. Other specimens may have one handle perfect and the other partially melted, as if the workman had attempted to make it meet by finishing it by hand. Even a "perfect" piece may show a line where the handle joins, such as a check or crack. Any collector who is fortunate enough to find one of these dishes would do well to ignore these apparent imperfections. While it might not be advisable to pay the perfect specimen value for one with the handles entirely ground off or with a broken chain border, still one would be justified in paying full price for a dish that has one of the blemishes described, which after all are merely indicative of the handicaps encountered in producing glass one hundred years ago. It measures 11½ inches long by 8 inches wide.

The third choice for the rarest and most beautiful Sandwich piece is that pictured on Plate 164. It is fully as rare and exquisite as the chain-bordered dish, but it is in third place only because the former was by far the more difficult mold. Less than a half-dozen perfect specimens are known of this lovely oblong tray which more closely resembles a fine piece of lace than does any other so-called lacy Sandwich dish.

Fourth in importance of those illustrated would be the large oblong vegetable dish pictured on Plate 165. In point of beauty it is not as delicate as the first two but it is almost as rare. It is oblong, with a flat rim, and a scrolled peacock eye outlines the brim. The bowl has a peacock feather design at each end and on the sides a thistle, a lyre and a basket of flowers. Heavy, and brilliantly stippled, this piece measures 10 by 8½ inches and is 2⅛ inches deep.

On Plate 166 are two large and exceptionally beautiful shell-shaped dishes, one with an open handle and the other closed. They are equally rare.

The shell with the closed handle is in the well-known "Hairpin" pattern. It is larger than the photograph would make it appear, being 9½ inches long, by 8 inches wide. Both dishes are exceptionally brilliant and very heavy in weight. Few perfect examples of either one are known.

The shell with the open handle is in the equally well-known Peacock Eye design, except that the "tail" runs straight across the dish, instead of being swirled, as is usually the case. The handle of this dish often has the same hair-line check in the center that is noted in the chain-bordered piece. In size it is approximately the same as the Hairpin dish. Any collector may consider himself fortunate to be able to add this pair of shell dishes to his collection.

Above the shells on Plate 166 is a pair of oblong trays in a design which is called by some collectors "The Pipes of Pan" and by others "Devil dishes." Neither is accurately descriptive, for Pan did not have wings and from all we are told the devil had horns! Such being the case, the result is a dilemma for the author. Since the dish has been known as the "Pipes of Pan" for years, perhaps it would be well enough not to insist on rechristening it to conform with the design. It is a brilliant, lacy tray, and the only one of this period bearing anything like a human form, with the exception of the "Industry" bowl, cup plates, and the Victoria or Victoria and Albert plates. It is interesting for this reason, rather than for its extreme rarity. It measures eight inches long.

A rarity that deserves a place in any museum is the "U. S. F. Constitution" oblong tray shown on Plate 167. It has a full-rigged ship in the base, with twenty-one stars. The border, with its hearts and stars, carries a sentimental appeal. Doubtless this tray was produced at the time of all the agitation about "Old Ironsides" in 1830. It naturally calls to mind Oliver Wendell Holmes' stirring poem about this ship, published that year. Because of its historical association, the tray commands a high price in dollars and a high regard in collectors' hearts. It is difficult to find one in anything approaching perfect condition.

The last in this series of rarities is the oblong covered honey dish and tray. They are photographed separately on Plate 168 so that collectors may have the full benefit of the design on both.

The tray has a border of hearts and stars, as on the Constitution

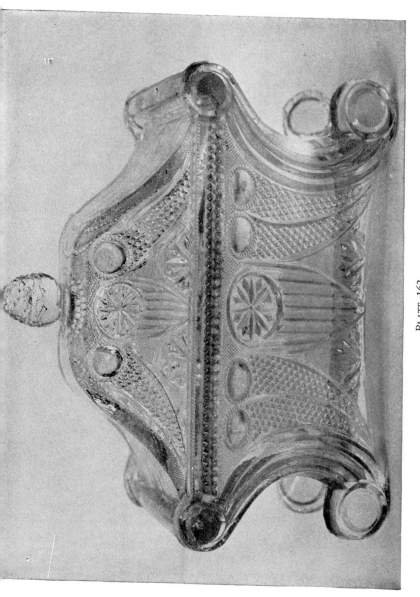

PLATE 162

Extremely rare lacy jewel casket.

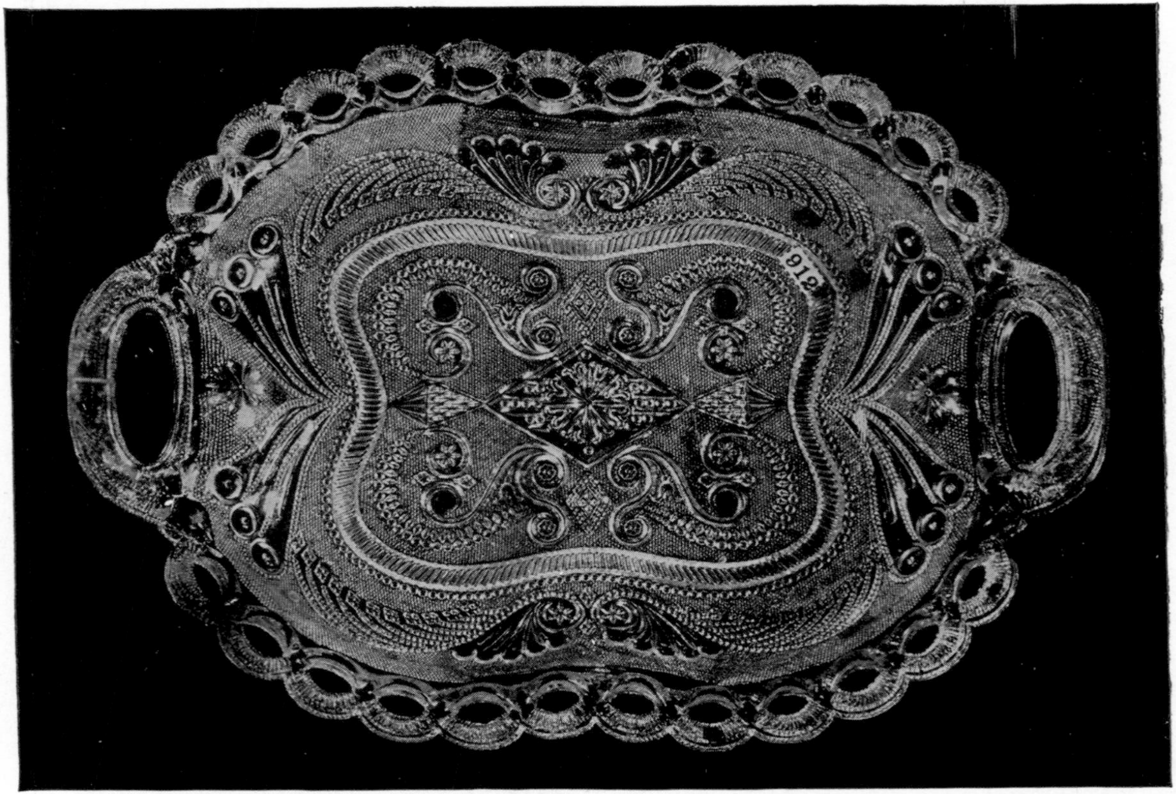

PLATE 163

Extremely rare deep dish with open chain border. Size 11½ x 8 inches.

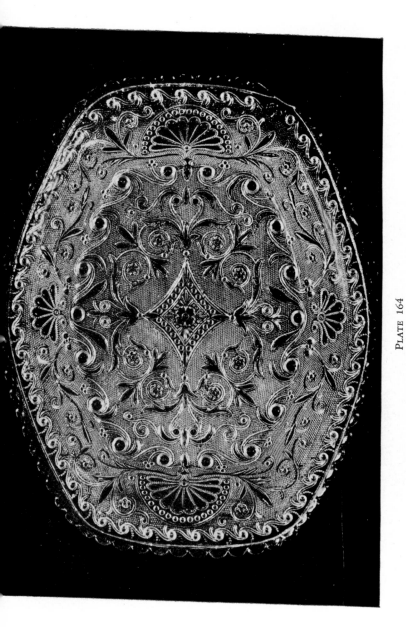

PLATE 164

Extremely rare large shallow tray. One of the most beautiful of all the lacy designs. Size 10¾ by 9 inches.

Plate 165

tray, but the center of the base has a conventional pattern. It is seven inches long. The oblong covered dish which fits on the tray has two styles of covers. Apparently the first style was difficult to make, so a simpler was devised.

The cover design is on the inside, so that it reflects through the thick glass. The first type has a double step in it, as may be seen in the illustration. It has two stars on the inside of the top, on both ends. The same tray and base were used with a second, and plainer cover, which lacks the double step and is very shallow. The top is rounded, whereas the first is square and flat. It has a thistle with leaves on each end of the top, while the first has stars. The corner designs of the covers also vary. The dish itself has Gothic arches with hearts above and between them. Both of these covered dishes are scarce when complete and in good condition.

Of course, there are many other rarities in lacy Sandwich, such as some of the compotes and sugar bowls in color and certain *unusually* large bowls, compotes and covered dishes, but those described in this chapter are all exceptional. As in the case of the "rarest" cup plates, the list is intended as a shining mark for collectors to aim at, since the rarer the piece the greater the joy of possession.

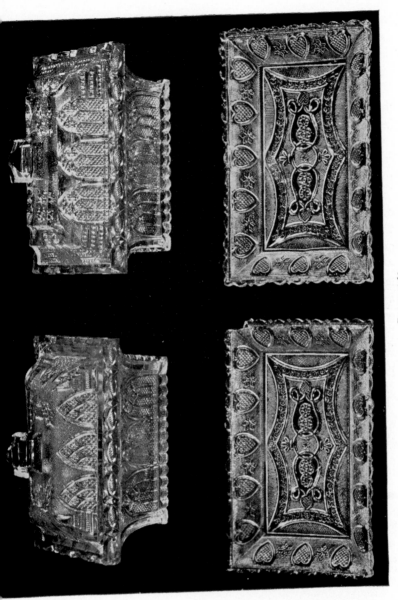

PLATE 168
Covered oblong deep dishes and trays.

PLATE 167

PLATE 166

Upper—Pair of Pipes of Pan oblong dishes.
Lower—Two large shell-shaped dishes.

Chapter XXIII

OCTAGONAL SERIES OF LACY PLATES

When the Midwest has been as thoroughly combed as the East for treasures in the way of old glass and when the same amount of research work has been carried on in that section, we shall acquire much information that is today unobtainable about the origin of certain types of early American glass.

It was not a difficult matter in years past to ascribe to New England certain lacy patterns as well as certain Blown Molded ("three-mold") styles even though there was not much in the way of evidence to confirm or justify the ascription. Naturally, the frequency and quantity of specimens found in a particular locality or section carried weight with collectors. When Mr. Francis Wynn, of Sandwich, Mass., unearthed quantities of lacy and blown glass fragments from beneath a factory which was built in 1849 but was not torn down or, at least, the flooring was not removed, until 1933—much needed evidence was obtained. Additional evidence will undoubtedly be forthcoming in the future, particularly in regard to a series of octagonal and round plates which are usually found in 6 and 7 inch sizes.

To date there have not been found fragments of every type of glassware which we ascribe to Sandwich today but from the similarity of style, pattern, and technique, and knowledge of the history of the particular locality of the findings, we obtain corroboration which cannot be blithely brushed aside by doubting Thomases. There are numerous cup plates which we are certain are not of Eastern manufacture. A few odd pieces, together with the series of octagonal plates are also under suspicion. Up to the present there is no conclusive evidence that any particularly large or handsome lacy pieces are of Midwestern origin. However, glass factories abounded in the Pittsburgh area, and we know that at least some of them produced lacy glass. Some of the finest glass in this country was made by the Bakewells of Pittsburgh, whose concern antedated Sandwich by many years. Evidence points to the Fort Pitt Glass Works of Pittsburgh and to Mulvaney, Ledlie & Company of Pittsburgh, as makers of some lacy glass.

The type of octagonal plate which it seems certain is not of Sandwich origin, is illustrated on Plates 169 and 170. The specimens of this series are related not only in form but in quality of metal and appearance. Nearly all of them, if, indeed, not all, are found in a round as well as in an octagonal form. There is something about the stippling which imparts to most of these plates a white, slightly frosted look rather than the soft, silvery Cape Cod sheen. Probably the most beautiful of the series is the 6 inch plate on Plate 169. It has a basket of flowers in the center and clusters of grapes and leaves in the border. The basket is against a finer stippling than that used on the border. The glass itself is dull and the stippling rather coarse. The somewhat unusual edge is partly stippled and partly dotted with large bull's eyes. All the plates in this series have the same border. The round as well as the octagonal, have bull's eyes, though without the stippling in the edge.

Next to the Basket of Flowers plate is another 6 inch octagonal in a Rose pattern, with a large rose in the center and six of smaller size around it. The border has a shell motif and scrolls. This plate is somewhat more brilliant than the others but the stippling is the same.

In the lower row of Plate 169 may be seen a round and an octagonal form of the same plate. There is a compote with the bowl in a pattern similar to the border of the plate, shown on Plate 144. The base in this 6¾ inch round plate with acorn and oak leaf center is clear, while on the 5 inch octagonal, it is stippled. They all bear the same family resemblance.

The rarest plates in this series are the two pictured on Plate 170. Both are of the 6 inch size but each with a different ship in the

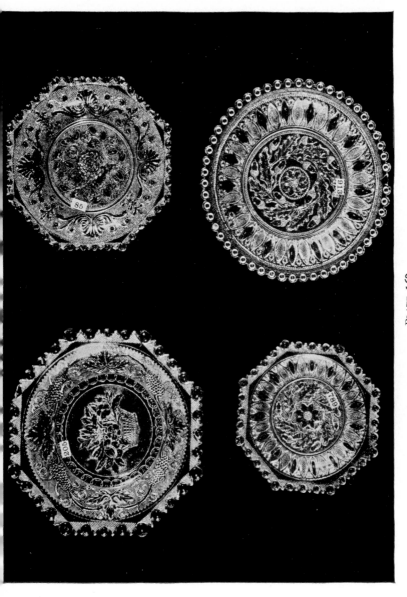

PLATE 169

Group of 6 inch plates, attributed to Midwestern glass district.

PLATE 170

Group of 5 inch plates and oblong tray. Unidentified factory; attributed to Midwest.

center. In the plate at the left is a side-wheel passenger steamboat. It flies two flags, one having nine stars and the other a large star within a circle of thirteen dots. The full-rigged ship in the other plate was probably intended for a frigate. It flies a flag with thirteen stars. Below it is the title: "Union." One plate has a border of shell motifs with a scroll, as on the Rose pattern plate and the other has acanthus leaves.

The side-wheel passenger ship is probably an Ohio River boat. The identity of the frigate is more difficult to determine, for it might be any one of several. I have heard it referred to as the "Constitution" but this is not altogether a logical solution. The agitation over the proposed junking of "Old Ironsides" was at fever pitch in 1830 when Oliver Wendell Holmes dared the Secretary of the Navy to "tear her tattered ensign down," but this plate is obviously of a later period. Captain D. W. Knox of the United States Navy, retired, writes me that the United States had but one ship of war named "Union" prior to the Civil War. It was a steamer of 956 tons with submerged paddles, built in 1842. As was the custom at that time, it also carried sails, to take advantage of favorable winds. Captain Knox, who is the well-known historian of the United States Navy, goes on to say, "During the Revolutionary War there were several privateers named "Union" fitted out at various places to war against the commerce of the enemy." However, that period is obviously much too early to date this plate, since pressed glass was not known in this country until fifty years later.

The thirteen stars about the ship could have no possible Revolutionary meaning. Each star was supposed to signify a state and in this case it would mean the thirteen original states. By Act of Congress of January 13, 1794, the flag was changed to fifteen stripes and fifteen stars, on the admission of Kentucky and Vermont into the Union. But the thirteen stars early became symbolical of our national entity and are utterly unreliable as a dating device.

The ship carries a flag having twelve dots in a circle plus one in the center of the circle. The dots are so small that it is impossible to tell whether they were meant to be stars or not. Stars were arranged in this order in flags until 1777, according to Preble's "History of the American Flag." After that they were placed in rows until 1818 when for a short time the twenty stars were arranged in the form of a five-pointed star. Since it is not likely that the Revolutionary War period is commemorated in this plate, it is possible that it was made by the Union Glass Works, though if this were so why should not the works have used their full title? That it was a commemorative piece is obvious, but "Union" was a favorite invocation with political orators even before Daniel Webster. It makes the date and meaning of "Union" and the ship too elastic to serve in this case.

The oblong dish above it (Plate 170) could be Sandwich, though it lacks that distinctive appearance, which also is true of the series of octagonal plates. The only "different" thing about it is that it has a plain scalloped edge instead of the bull's eye border. The sides have two cornucopias, with a heart in the center and a tulip in each corner. Each end has a shield with twenty stars about it. It is perhaps the rarest of the oblong deep dishes. This would be accounted for if it is, as I suspect, of Midwestern origin.

Chapter XXIV

BACCARAT AND OTHER FOREIGN LACY GLASS

American collectors of glass of an older generation—and also of furniture, silver, paintings or china—were content to confine their acquisitions to plainly labeled foreign antiques. They enthusiastically accumulated Egyptian, Sidonian, Greek, Roman or Venetian glass because their antiquity was beyond question and to a nation aged one century the impact of 2,500 years of existence was terrific. No patriotic thrill was aroused by the possession of glass made in America when the English Colonies had not yet become the United States. But as a nationalistic spirit developed, the collecting of Americana became not merely a patriotic hobby but a social duty. The vogue for glass here, as in England, was later in starting than furniture or china. Glass articles for display in cabinets lacked the element of usefulness but it did not take collectors very long to lose the utilitarian point of view.

At first collecting was merely indiscriminate amassing. Attributions were not questioned by patriots. Since birth certificates were not demanded, oral tradition took on the authority of documented history. It was enough to be assured that the object had belonged to an American-born grandmother. Today this is no longer true. American collectors now demand facts—chapter and verse.

Not many glass collectors realize how much there is to be learned from the study of the development of the glass industry abroad in relatively recent times, as, for example, in France and England, in Bohemia and Germany, during the past two centuries. To be fair, few of the books on the subject, written by recognized authorities, are readily available in English translations. Too many technical terms and overelaborate explanations of methods, a superabundance of mechanical drawings, and excessive concern over artistic and commercial conditions in their own countries make many European treatises difficult reading. The right collecting spirit, which means the appreciation of quality and the realization of the need of wise selection, does not have to be subordinated to overstressed insistence on strict specialization along historical or technical lines. On the other hand, whatever develops anywhere at any time that has a bearing on whatever American collectors hunt is of unquestioned importance. Otherwise, collecting would become a childish game of wishful thinking. It is to the present intelligent demand for accurate information about our most popular collectibles that we owe the increased interest in the design and composition of whatever foreign glass has influenced our own makers and their product. The most chauvinistic collectors of paper-weights ungrudgingly admit today that the palm for the most exquisite workmanship must be awarded to the products not of American but of the French factories, at Clichy, St. Louis and Baccarat. The wisest collectors have gone still farther afield and their researches have extended into other times and other countries —including our own!

It has long been known that lacy glass of the type made at Sandwich was also produced abroad, but for years American collectors either did not know it or flatly denied it, possibly out of a misguided sense of loyalty to the Cape factory or because of the chagrin inseparable from having to admit a mistake in judgment or in attribution. Marked differences of workmanship were not accepted as proofs of non-Sandwichicity. Indeed, at times it has seemed as though proofs were definitely not wanted. Today we know that Sandwich had no lacy monopoly, not even in the United States. This point having been established to the satisfaction of all collectors, excepting the diminishing number of irreconcilables, it seems fitting to print a short account of the history of the world-famous "Compagnie des Cristalleries de Baccarat" for the benefit of those lovers of lacy glass who may wish to learn how to distinguish foreign specimens from those of unquestionable Sandwich origin. In preparing this sketch I have made use of a pamphlet issued by the company in June, 1922, on the occasion of the celebration of their hundredth anniversary. It contains the speeches delivered by Messieurs Adrien Michaut, chairman of the board of directors, Senator Henri Michaut, member of the board of directors (Conseil d'administration) vice president Godard-Desmarest, the curé of Baccarat, the prefect of the Department of Meurthe-et-Moselle, M. Pierre Michaut, the administrative delegate, and Louis Milot, the dean of the workers. From all accounts it was an impressive celebration, held in the old court of the Ste. Anne Glass Works (Verreries de Sainte-Anne) which were started in 1765. The French Government's Honor Medal of Labor was awarded to those workers, male and female, who had a record of thirty years of uninterrupted service.

Many have been the complaints of tourists and even of clients who have sought, in vain, information about the early wares through letters or by visits to the offices of the company in Baccarat and Paris. Perhaps the seekers after Baccarat data did not apply to the right person or in the right manner. To grant requests by mail for copies of the earliest catalogues or for permission to examine old records would require the help of busy officials familiar with the archives of the company, which, fortunately, were not destroyed by German vandals. The complete records exist and may be studied by any properly introduced research worker. They deserve adequate treatment by themselves, for both the New Deal's "economic royalists" and Mr. Lewis' C. I. O. cohorts would find in them much to give them thought in connection with the problems of capital and labor.

The Bishop of Metz, Monseigneur de Montmorency-Laval, seeking a market for the wood of his castelry of Baccarat, formed a partnership with Antoine Renaut, a glassmaker, and M. Leopold, a capitalist, and they started the Ste. Anne glasshouse. There was an abundance of fuel that needed a consumer and good sand within easy reach. On the death of Leopold the Bishop sold his interest to Renaut, who operated the factory alone until the Revolution made it impossible for the average industrialist to remain solvent.

Moreover, he was not a good business man and the confusion of the times and his own ineptitude were too much for him. The works were sold but the new owners also went under. The factory closed down and was again offered for sale, but Napoleon was busy fighting all Europe and business suffered in France as in the rest of the so-called civilized world.

A certain M. d'Artigues was the owner of a glass plant at Vonèche, near Givet, in what was then French territory. In 1815, after the various treaties and dismemberments, Vonèche became a part of Belgium. D'Artigues' chief and, possibly, only market had been in France and his factory was now Belgian. He could no longer sell its wares to his old customers because the import duties made it impossible to compete with French factories. He asked the government of the country of his birth to waive the duties for a short time to enable him to move his stock across the border where he proposed to resume business as a French manufacturer. They agreed and he purchased the property of the abandoned Ste. Anne works, which thereupon became the "Cristallerie de Vonèche-Baccarat." He, d'Artigues, was the first to make lead glass—crystal, so-called—instead of the cruder ordinary product of other works. It won not only commercial success but world-wide recognition for its superb quality. But his health failed. According to M. Adrien Michaut at the Centenary celebration: "Six years later, Pierre Antoine Godard-Desmarest negotiated the purchase, assisted by my great-grandfather, Adrien-Antoine Michaut de Lunéville with whom he had become acquainted through a mutual friend. The Compagnie des Cristalleries de Baccarat was born. There were three associates or partners: MM. Godard, Lolot and Lescuyer. They took possession of the works on December 3, 1822." M. Godard assumed the management and kept it for seventeen years. In 1840 he was succeeded by his son Emile, who in turn was followed, in 1851, by Jean-Baptiste Toussaint, who had been the Vonèche-Baccarat factory's technical director and continued in that position when the Cie. des Cristalleries de Baccarat bought out M. d'Artigues. To Toussaint's technical equipment the company owed much of its material prosperity and to his spirit the greater part of those measures and practices that made the relations between owners and workmen at Baccarat what they have been for over a century. On the death of Toussaint in 1858 M. Godard resumed the management, which he carried on until 1868.

For 117 years Baccarat has been operated and managed by descendants of the organizers of the company. It was a family affair not alone with the owners but with the men, who also were descendants of old Baccarat workers. A man who keeps a job for twenty years without grievances or regrets is a rare phenomenon; but when a man spends his working life with one concern and is followed by his son and the son of his son, who inherit, as it were, the trade, the job, the tradition and the loyalty, we have the solution of the world's greatest problem today. I cannot refrain from quoting here from M. Michaut's speech: "One may erect furnaces and install cutting shops, find places where fuel, raw materials, motive power and labor may be obtainable to greater advantage, commercially. One may even find it possible to recruit workmen as skillful as ours. With all this and with abundant capital it would nevertheless be impossible to make *a Baccarat*, that is to say, a large family of workers, devoted to their chiefs, imbued with the same wholesome traditions, intelligent, industrious and as great sticklers for their *duties* as for their *rights!*"

In his address M. Michaut recounted the mechanical and other obstacles they had to overcome at their works. "The first fifty years of the Company belonged to the Age of Wood [for fuel]. It was the constant concern of the managers to make sure of an adequate supply and to maintain and if possible improve the quality. It became necessary from time to time to purchase new forests or go farther afield for fuel."

They experimented with coal but were unable with that fuel to produce an absolutely clear crystal. The English had been somewhat successful in the use of coal, but their furnaces required too frequent cleaning or replacements to suit the French method of production. In 1862 Baccarat experimented with gas made from wood. Later they employed the famous Siemens to design coal furnaces. Finally one of Siemens' men, a German, Boetius, who had been studying the Baccarat wood-gas furnace, solved the problem. "His first furnace, of twelve pots, built in 1864, succeeded so well that it melted itself," says M. Michaut. "This was changed when they used sixteen pots, instead of twelve." The number was increased to eighteen, then to twenty, then to twenty-two pots. "Fifty-eight years after it was made, the Boetius furnace, very slightly modified, was still the furnace in use in 1922." The rest of M. Michaut's speech told of matters of general rather than of technical interest.

An American at the Centenary celebration, listening to the history of the company, would have found it very easy to understand why Baccarat glassware deserves all the praise that is showered upon it wherever high quality, superb workmanship, and striking beauty are appreciated. I cannot think of a higher compliment than to call Sandwich the Baccarat of America, unless, perhaps, it is to call Baccarat the French Sandwich—the Sandwich of Deming Jarves' heyday.

The temptation to describe in detail the vicissitudes as well as the technological triumphs of the industry at Baccarat is irresistible, because no student of the history of Sandwich can fail to be struck by the striking parallelism with Deming Jarves' experiences and industrial philosophy. The strict adherence to the policy of using the best materials; the stressing of the quality of the metal; the unceasing experimenting in search of better ingredients and methods, the insistence upon the artistic appeal of the product; the clear grasp of the wisdom of having workers who were not only skilled but devoted to the glasshouse—an asset obtainable only by a proper concern of the owner over the welfare of the men —and the recognition of the greater likelihood of success of the industry if it were controlled by one family and successors who would inherit not only a business but an ideal were in Deming Jarves' mind. The product of his factory, his indefatigable pursuit of something better, more beautiful, prove that his interest in excellence was more than that of an owner. From the first days of the factory, indeed, even before the first batch was poured from the first pot, he was guilty of what at first glance might be taken for nepotism. He placed members of his family in key positions and he undoubtedly indulged his dreams of founding a glass dynasty when he endeavored to persuade his sons to follow in his footsteps. Men who accomplish greatly invariably dream of still more splendid triumphs—through their heirs. For them immortality lies in the perpetuation of the family leadership, carrying into the years the magic of the same name and the prestige of achievements under that name. Contemporary acclaim, titles, property, are ephemeral successes to men who not only conquer their enemies in this life but deny that the statute of limitations can apply to future conquests by their flesh and blood.

The identification of foreign lacy pieces is not difficult, once the student becomes thoroughly familiar with our own Sandwich designs, quality of the glass, character of the stippling and other distinguishing qualifications. We may safely assume Deming Jarves decided which patterns were to be used by Sandwich. If for the most part he did not slavishly copy the foreign styles he unquestionably felt their influence. He selected whichever form of ornamentation pleased him, like the Gothic pointed arch of the French, the rose, thistle and shamrock of Great Britain or the tulip of Holland or conventional decoration, whether classic or of the Renaissance, not because they were popular fashions in Europe but because they suited his purpose and possibly also because they had become conventionalized, the world over, by long usage. As a good salesman, he played safe and did not seek to compel his customers to accept a new or revolutionary form of art. The Gothic influence on decoration and ornament naturally was far stronger in countries like France, Germany or England than in America, where the people had not worshipped for centuries in cathedrals like those of Rheims or Cologne or Canterbury. He must have felt that if Gothic designs were not typically American, neither for that matter were hearts, shields or pine trees typically foreign.

In endeavoring to distinguish lacy Baccarat types from lacy Sandwich the collector would do well to bear in mind that Baccarat is usually, though not always, heavier in weight. The metal has a harsh brilliance, whereas Sandwich is characterized by a soft, lustrous, silvery sheen. The quality of the early French should be considered, its depth of clarity and a degree of superb workmanship not found in early Sandwich, which often shows black flecks, bubbles, sand blisters and even specks of sand. French designs are in higher and sharper relief. Moreover, there could not be real decorative kinship between theirs and our own, for each shows the influence of the immediate surroundings as well as the measure of the art education of the two countries. What may be called typical Sandwich motifs are Hearts; Stars; Shields; Pine Trees; Acorns and Oak Leaves; Baskets of Flowers; Cornucopias; Peacock Eyes; Eagles; Medallions such as the familiar Princess Feather; Sheaves of Wheat and such flowers as the Rose, Thistle and Tulip, but if they are not typically American neither are they indicative of a particular period.

French design is on more classical lines. They resorted to the Gothic architectural elements, Renaissance and Rococo ornament "against a granulated or pebbled background." Pazaurek in his *Biedermeirzeit* states: "A similar effect produced by solid high-relief cutting, would have required a fortune. When one reads the catalogues of a leading firm in this particular field, Launay, Hautin & Cie of Paris, one is surprised by the more than abundant fullness of the most elaborate of the molds which towards the end of the 30's were already on the market, although the decorative elements can be traced back to a comparatively few types. Nor could one be less surprised to see how soon technical restraints and obstacles were overcome, when even bottles, carafes and scent bottles were produced with the patterns in sharp relief. Competition finally compelled Austria and Germany to join in the general pressed glass madness. The factory of Johann Mayr of Adolph in the

PLATE 171

Group of Baccarat and other French lacy pieces.

PLATE 172
French lacy glass, circa 1840.

PLATE 176
Large bowls of European origin.

PLATE 175
Baccarat. Period 1840-1860.

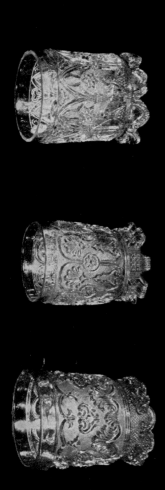
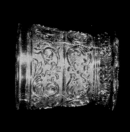

PLATE 174

French lacy glass, circa 1840

PLATE 173
French lacy goblets, circa 1840.

Bohemian Forest, noted for the excellent quality of its crystal glass, exhibited, in an incidental way, to be sure, at the Prague Exposition of 1836, some pressed glass 'with raised Arabesque ornamentation through the manufacture of which the French and Americans threatened our own cut-glass works.' This quotation is from a report of the exposition which went on to say that only in conjunction with fine glass cutting could further prosperous development be expected."

Pazaurek states further, "It was not until the middle of the nineteenth century that the supreme effort, massive poured-in-a-mold productions, making small dull portrait busts mostly mounted on black cut glass pedestals, appeared."

In still another place, speaking of the 1845 period, he says: "The flood of English pressed glass had already thrown their market into confusion and disorder. It led to a drop of 200% in prices in other glass producing countries, as for example, Northern Bohemia. Then this was immediately followed by a flood of pressed glass from France which made matters even worse, if such a thing were possible, because the French were not content with imitating diamond facet or cylinder cutting but added an abundance of relief ornamentation in all currrent styles."

Officials of the company to whom were submitted photographs of Baccarat patterns pictured in this chapter (plate 171) were able to trace the majority of them. Their Paris records show that the concern manufactured some of them during the period of 1840–'45. That type was abandoned a long time ago, they reported, but they were careful to add that there was no technical reason why their manufacture could not be resumed. The company early developed a considerable export trade to all parts of the world. Large shipments were sent to the French and British West Indies, as well as to North and South American countries. Shortly before World War II a Boston antique dealer went to the French West Indies in search of antiques and "French lacy Sandwich"—Baccarat—and found enough to help make the gamble of the trip a success.

Evidently that highly ornate type of glassware appealed to the Creole taste at a time when "there was money in sugar and rum." Very often when a rich planter discovered that his brilliant table sets were incomplete through breakage, he simply asked the local agent, or wrote direct to France, for a fresh supply, and the Baccarat factory cheerfully filled the re-order. The same Boston dealer, encouraged by the success of his West Indian trip, recently went to Brazil where he found more Baccarat ware. Some items bore the well-known paper label showing a decanter and goblet. The Paris office states that this label was first used in 1860. From this it is clear that much of the lacy Baccarat that was picked up in the West Indies and Brazil by the Boston dealer was manufactured at a much later period than 1840. It is perhaps due to this late paper-labeled product, made from the original mold and of the same quality of crystal, that so many Sandwich collectors have insisted that all French lacy was modern—after 1860—and that therefore Sandwich was the sole maker of that type of ware in the 1830's and 1840's. Under the circumstances it is clear that such claims to both priority and exclusive manufacture are not justified.

It is only fair to say that accurate information on this point was not available to American collectors until relatively recent times.

So much for the type of ware (lacy) which was abandoned by the Baccarat Company a long time ago but which could be manufactured again at any time. On Plate 172 is another style of decanter and several patterns of whiskey glasses. Here are the "diamond facet," "Gothic" and "Arabesque" motifs. On Plate 173 are a series of goblets, some of which have been identified in a catalogue of Launay, Hautin et Cie., who were agents for several French concerns. In my collection is a massive goblet in Gothic style, known to be a Baccarat pattern, but of a heavy, deep-red, opaque glass.

It may also be noted that a water tumbler design on Plate 172 is like the decanter and tumbler on Plate 171. Nearly every French goblet has a diamond pattern in the foot, a characteristic of their glass. Many early foreign water tumblers are "footed" or with a collared base, like those illustrated in Plates 172 and 174.

Numerous Baccarat plates have a diamond pattern in the base, with a rosette in the center. One is illustrated on Plate 175. This particular design was used over a long period of years and pieces are sometimes found today with "Baccarat" embossed on the surface. A similar border scroll was used by Sandwich in the old days and there is one manufacturer in this country who is now producing sets of tableware, in a variation of this style of scroll, which has been advertised by some department stores as a true copy of an early Sandwich design. Perhaps fifty years hence new collectors may treasure specimens of this 1939 American-made glass, though students will know, by the quality of the glass itself, that they are "not of the period."

On Plate 175 is also shown a typical Baccarat cup in Gothic design of which the saucer is missing. The other piece on the Plate is a flower vase.

Two large deep lacy dishes of European origin are shown on Plate 176. The upper dish, as someone has observed, "has a French look about it." It is French—and late. A friend of mind has purchased them from an importer. It measures $7\frac{3}{4}$ inches in diameter. The lower bowl is in an $8\frac{3}{4}$ inch size and has an eight-pointed star in the base. In the center of the star are the numerals "$\frac{3}{4}$." What these are intended to signify is beyond even guessing at present.

Evidence that many other factories abroad made lacy types of glass will undoubtedly be presented in due time. Mrs. Mildred Pike has already discovered a cup plate marked "Val St. Lambert/Belgique." She learned, through the American agents of the Cristalleries de Val-Saint-Lambert, that the design on the cup plate was illustrated in the company's *Album,* an illustrated cata·logue of crystal pressed ware issued in 1913, as *Diana* pattern. The factory at which her cup plate was made is situated in Val-Saint-Lambert, Belgium and was founded in 1825, the very year the Boston & Sandwich Glass Company was established. The Val-Saint-Lambert Company issued their first catalogue presenting their

wares in 1829. All Sandwich collectors today must regret that
Deming Jarves did not follow their example. Mrs. Pike was informed by an official of the Belgian company that this catalogue
included pressed ware. It is obvious that the process of pressing
glass was certainly introduced in more than one factory in Europe
within a year or two of its use in this country.

The marked cup plate in question is so similar to many others
I have collected for use in further research and study that it is
apparent that any number of factories, including Sandwich, used
adaptations of the same design. In my collection are ten or twelve
variations, all foreign. But among Sandwich fragments I have
found pieces of similar plates, though they are more flintlike in
character and often are colored. Also in my collection is a large
fragment of a light green cup plate with the identical pattern of
the marked "Belgique" specimen of Mrs. Pike's, illustrated in the
magazine *Antiques* for January 1939, except that the rim the plate
rests on is scalloped, in four wide loose scallops, like a four-leaf
clover or quatrefoil and the stippling is much finer. Even at that
early period it was obviously the practice of factories everywhere
to copy from one another.

Chapter XXV

CANDLESTICKS

Candlestick making began with the early days at Sandwich and lasted almost throughout its glass-making existence. There are many types both in clear glass and in a wide range of colors which can be definitely attributed to that factory. However, it is not always safe to assert that certain types are "positively Sandwich" because so many other glasshouses also made candlesticks. The majority of the dolphin types may be safely ascribed to Sandwich, particularly those with the single and the double square bases. We know too, of course, that Pittsburgh made dolphin candlesticks and compotes.

A M'Kee & Brothers, Pittsburgh, Pa., trade catalogue of the late 50's pictures a dolphin candlestick with a hexagonal base, a style which was not produced to such a large extent in New England. Bakewell, Pears & Co. of Pittsburgh, illustrate in a catalogue, undated but probably of the 60's, dolphin compotes with a shell-shaped bowl and dolphin compotes made in two styles, either with an oblong or a round bowl, in the Ribbon pattern. Sandwich apparently did not have a monopoly of the dolphin candlestick trade.

It is reasonably certain that, fairly early, Pittsburgh made candlesticks in hexagonal form, a type which does not seem to have been quite so popular at Sandwich judging from the number of fragments found in the buried heaps. But Sandwich did make a large number of Crucifix candlesticks, in two sizes. More fragments have been found of these and of the well-known "Petal and Loop" and Dolphin types, than of any others.

One of the rarest of the earlier candlesticks is a lacy type with a ring handle, which was at one time on exhibition in a collection at Yale University. I have never seen or heard of more than two others like it. Indeed, any lacy candlesticks are difficult to find today and become increasingly rare as the years go on.

The small pair at the top of Plate 177 have octagonal bases, stippled underneath with an acanthus leaf design. The standard or column is fluted and the top is decorated with Peacock Eye, the edge having a small scallop. These are 5⅛ inches high.

In the lower row on the same Plate is a single lacy candlestick, which is similar to the pair just described. The stippled base is octagonal, with a leaf design. The top has a dainty, lacy pattern instead of the Peacock Eye. Beside this single one is a pair having a five-step base and stippled top. These were made in two parts and fused together where the top joins the column. They are also 5⅛ inches high. I have seen an early pair which had an ornate scrolled standard and triangular base with paw feet, similar to the pedestals on some of the lacy compotes. The tops were stippled and lacy. These are exceedingly scarce.

The choicest and probably the rarest pair of candlesticks illustrated in this chapter is pictured in the center of Plate 177. The bases are octagonal and elaborate in detail. The bulbous centers are fluted and the tops lacy, with the Peacock Eye pattern. It is to be doubted if six perfect pairs of these candlesticks could be found today, that is, in anything like proof condition. A collector will rarely come upon a finer example of Sandwich glass candlesticks than this particular pair. There are similar styles, with single, double or even five-step bases, but none approach this perfectly proportioned pair in beauty.

Plate 178 illustrates a pair and two odd candlesticks of the same period, with clear bases and stippled lacy cups. The lamp pictured, of the same period, is of the whale oil type. Originally it had a collar which kept one or two wick-holders in place. Probably a pair of snuffers was attached.

The pair of candlesticks on Plate 179 are the same as those on Plate 177, except for the larger detail. Between them is an early Sandwich sand shaker with a pewter top used to dry the ink in the

PLATE 177
Early, rare lacy candlesticks. Period 1830-1835.

PLATE 178
Early lamp and group of candlesticks. Period 1830-1835.

PLATE 179

Upper—Choice pair of lacy candlesticks and sandshaker.
Lower—Group of miscellaneous salts and a cordial glass.

PLATE 180

Early candlesticks, blown and pressed. Period 1830-1835.

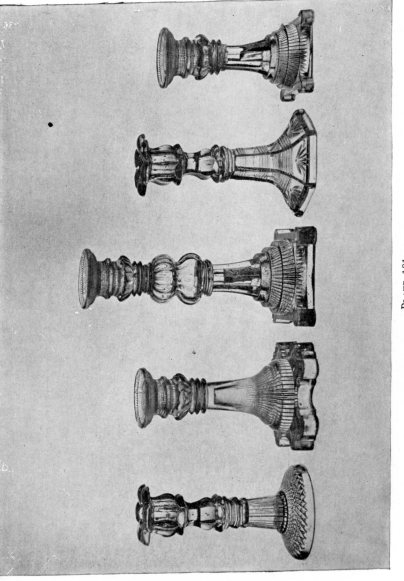

PLATE 181
Early candlesticks. Period 1830-1835.

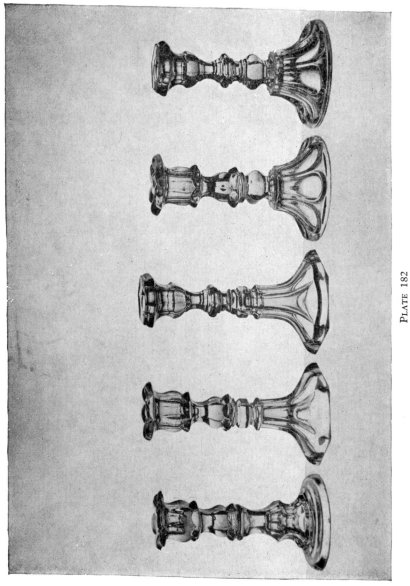

PLATE 182
Early candlesticks. Period 1835-1840.

old days, before blotting paper superseded them. Different styles of sand shakers were produced in a wide range of colors.

A group of very unusual candlesticks, each partly blown and partly pressed, is shown on Plate 180. These would be difficult to match in pairs. It will be noted that the one on the left end has a pattern in the base, somewhat resembling the Peacock Eye.

On Plate 181 is a similar group save for two unusual variations of the Petal and Loop candlestick. The upper part of these two does have the petal top, but from the point at which this type of candlestick was usually fused and joined to the base, the designs are entirely different. Both are rare types and might date from 1830 to 1850.

How many variations there can be of the same candlestick is more fully illustrated on Plate 182. Three of them have Petal tops and two have Loop bases! The most common type of all is the complete "Petal and Loop" pattern shown in the second candlestick from the right. All the others are unusual variations.

Petal and Loop candlesticks were made in a wide color range, opaque as well as clear. Canary yellow and clear glass are the most common. Any other unusual shades would be rare. A clear blue of the shade once popularly known as "Alice Blue" is much sought after. It is very scarce. Peacock green is extremely rare. On Plate 183 may be seen two more variations of petal top candlesticks in opaque glass.

The most unusual combinations are to be found in opaque candlesticks. Here Deming Jarves could play with bright colors to his heart's content. Examples of well-known Sandwich designs in opaque may be seen on Plates 183, 184, 185, 186 and 187. It is not uncommon to find blue or green tops on white bases. Generally speaking the colored section is at the top, but not always. One of the rarest colors is a soft opaque jade green in which dolphin candlesticks all in that same shade may be found. Among the Sandwich fragments of dolphin candlesticks are several pieces in an opaque lavender, so soft that it verges on a mauve. I have never

seen any perfect specimens in this color, but they certainly were made.

Two early pairs of dolphin candlesticks with single square bases are shown on Plate 184. The pair on the right is an exceptionally rare variant. Instead of having the usual petal top, they are ornamented with shells and dolphins.

Among the most dignified of the Sandwich "sticks," as laconic collectors sometimes refer to them, are those shown on Plate 185 with the double square base, fluted column and petal top. These come in a variety of colors, more frequently in opaque than in clear shades. Sometimes the opaques have an almost rough, frosted surface which was the intended finish. One was brought in to me by the owner. It was the same type as shown in the center of Plate 185 in an opaque blue. The man wished to sell it and gave assurances that the "defect" of the rough surface could be corrected by an application of "banana oil"!

On Plate 186 are two more unusual types of clear glass candlesticks. Collectors have come to believe that there is an inexhaustible supply of them. No sooner do they think they are nearing the completion of their collection of "different" designs than a new one is sure to make its appearance and lures them on.

Two sizes of a more ornate opaque white candlestick, with a blue top, are shown on Plate 187. These are a departure from the usual straight lines, for the base, the shaft and the top are all decorated with an attractive scroll and acanthus leaf.

The "draped lady" may or may not be of Sandwich origin. Unquestionably classical figures were made there, but I lack adequate proof in this particular case. The small clear glass candlestick next to it is one from a pair of an early, simple type.

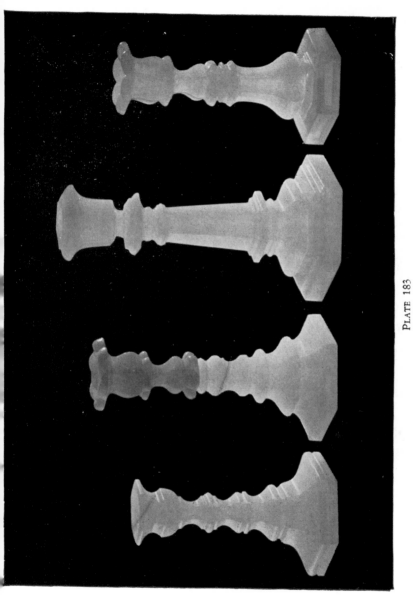

PLATE 183
Opaque candlesticks. Period 1840-1850.

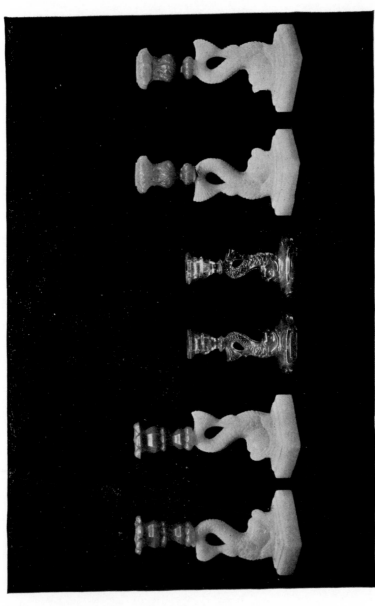

PLATE 184

Dolphin candlesticks, circa 1840. The small pair in the center may be Midwestern.

PLATE 185

Three pairs of candlesticks. Period 1830-1840

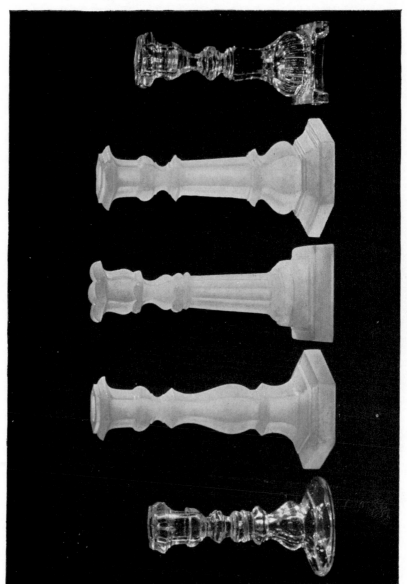

PLATE 186

Early candlesticks, circa 1840.

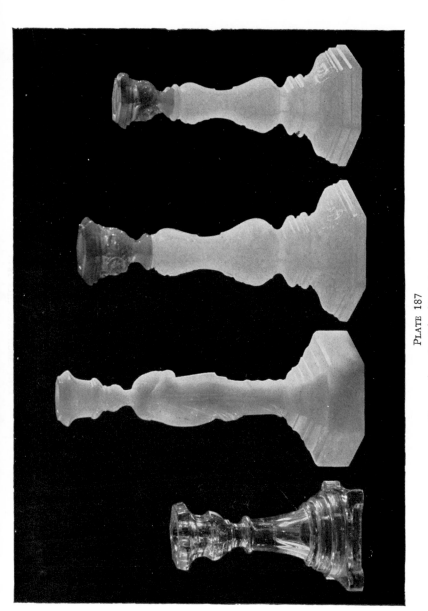

PLATE 187

Group of candlesticks. Period 1840-1850.

Chapter XXVI

LAMPS

The earliest lamps produced at the Sandwich factory were made during its opening year. According to an old account book, on July 30, 1825, they were already making "high blown stem lamps," "lamps on foot," and "peg lamps."

On Plate 188 are two small lamps which may well be among these first types, though it is possible that they do not date before 1827. The one on the right at the end of the line has a base similar to the earliest cup plate, pictured in that chapter. When the cup plate styles were used as a foot for lamps, they were made thicker and the plate was inverted. There is a wide variety of lamps which may still be found today with "cup plate" bases, some in New England types and others in Midwestern patterns.

Those lamps with "step" bases are contemporaneous with the similar styles of candlesticks. Many collectors find there is nothing more fascinating than the collecting of these small, early lamps, for they are quite numerous and widely varied in pattern.

The first lamp on the left on Plate 188 has quite an ornate base, yet it belongs to the same period as the others. Next to it is one with a square, lacy base that probably was not made much before 1830.

As mechanical devices improved and the workmen acquired greater skill, larger and more elaborate lamps were produced. On Plate 189 are some interesting examples of the elongated blown bowl which was attached to a pressed base. "Sperm" or whale oil was used at the time and the lamps became known as sperm oil lamps. Many also refer to them as whale oil lamps to this day. Three of those pictured have lacy bases. The rather plain pressed base of the fourth is often seen on candlesticks of the period.

On Plate 190 is an interesting pair of early blown lamps, with pressed glass bases. A story has been told of a collector who once refused to buy a similar lamp from a dealer because of the bowl's shape. She simply knew that a fraud was being perpetrated on her because the blown bowl of the lamp was nothing more or less than an electric light bulb! They are actually quite similar in shape and almost equally thin, but of course it would not be possible to fuse the end of a modern bulb to an old glass lamp base.

Comparable to the superlative in Sandwich candlesticks as illustrated in Chapter XXV are the glass lamps pictured on Plate 191. The detail is plainly shown, though no photograph can convey adequately the beauty of such a pair of lamps. The bases are pressed, the bulbous hollow part of the stem is cut, as are also the blown bowls. The collars and wick holders are of pewter. Few pairs of such handsome lamps are available today, for most of them are found now only in private collections.

Mentioned in the opening paragraph, which lists items produced at Sandwich in July, 1825, are the peg lamps that appealed to thrifty New Englanders. They were intended to save candles and fulfill the functions of both candlesticks and lamps. A peg lamp is, as the name suggests, a small lamp bowl with a peg at the end that will fit into the socket of a candlestick. When the candles burned low, the peg lamp, filled with whale oil, could be inserted in the candlestick, lighted, and the room would not be left in darkness. Most of the peg lamps originally were very simple. As the nation grew in wealth and required more lavish furnishings, the peg lamp became more ornate. The most elaborate are in the so-called "overlay" glass, a "case" glass which consisted of more than one layer, so that when the lamps were cut, the color of the second layer, or even the third, made the color combination "a thing of beauty."

Patterns in Sandwich vases were used on lamps, as may be seen on Plate 192. All of these would date from the late 30's through the 40's and some as late as the 50's. They were made in many shades of color, sapphire blue being the favorite. Other colors would include yellow, peacock blue, green, amethyst, varying shades of blue and possibly "alabaster" or opal. It is an interesting fact that whale oil was still being used in these lamps. Perfect pairs are obtainable even today, which is remarkable, since many of them are now one hundred years old.

In fact, excellent examples of pairs may be seen on Plate 193. The plain glass ones are complete with the original collars, wick-holders and snuffers. The opaque pair in the center are Sandwich favorites. The bases and standards of this particular pair are in white while the top is blue. Both sections have an acanthus leaf decoration. They were produced in all white, in white with a blue top, in a soft jade green and in a combination of green and white. If other colors were made, they have not come to my attention. The pair is very likely of the 1840 period, when candlesticks and so many other varieties of opaque colored "sticks" were in vogue. For most collectors, this lamp has a strong appeal and they find it one of the most attractive of all.

Kerosene oil after 1859 gradually superseded "burning fluid," "camphene" or sperm oil. It was at this period that overlay lamps became favorites. Their value has increased year by year as they have become scarcer. They were made in comparatively simple styles ranging up to enormous sizes with cut stems which are simply magnificent. The unusually large lamps are seldom seen today except in private collections.

In the simpler styles pictured on Plate 194, both the bases and the bowls vary greatly. One has a double marble base with a brass fluted stem, while the others have different styles of glass standards and bases. The lamp in the lower row on the right is in opaque white glass, decorated with gold, simulating the one next to it with a brass stem and marble base. These lamps, on an average, are from 10 to 14 inches in height.

What lamp collectors crave today, or even collectors who seek choice lamps for use in their living rooms, are those with the stems cut as well as the bowls. Such lamps are usually a bit taller than those shown on Plate 194 and, it might be added, are much more

PLATE 188

Early blown and pressed, whale oil lamps.

PLATE 189

Early blown and pressed whale oil lamps

PLATE 190

Pair of early blown lamps, with pressed lacy foot.

PLATE 191

Pair of large, exceptionally handsome whale oil lamps; blown, cut bowl
and pressed foot.

PLATE 192

Colored glass whale oil lamps. Period 1835-1845.

costly. The double marble base is further embellished with French gilt bands, between the steps and in that portion which connects with the base of the standard or stem. Three are shown on Plate 195.

Two exceptionally large, beautiful overlay lamps, 28 inches high, are pictured on Plate 196. Very few of this size are seen today, since they have been intensively collected for years. But for the coloring, they are an identical pair which makes them even rarer.

On Plate 197 are shown the superlative in overlay lamps, all measuring 38 inches in height. One cannot appreciate how enormous they really are, from the photograph. So far as I know, they are the largest size in this style. It is to be doubted whether the commercial output of these largest-sized lamps was ever very considerable because they were quite expensive for the times.

A considerable amount of overlay work was done abroad during the middle of the nineteenth century, particularly in old Bohemia. The popular trend there was more toward vases and pieces of ornamental character such as urns and covered jars. The influence of this foreign work was undoubtedly felt here but resulted in utilitarian rather than ornamental pieces. A sheet from a Boston & Sandwich Glass Company catalogue pictures a number of the lamps illustrated in this chapter, including those in the largest size. The catalogue is undated but appears to be of the 60's. Popular wares were made over a long period of years so it is not unreasonable to assume that the overlay lamps were produced into the 70's and possibly the 80's. Those shown in the catalogue entitled "Petroleum or Kerosene Lamps and Chandeliers" were fitted with frosted, cut globes. The customer might order whichever style of globe he preferred with the lamp, as some would be more expensive than others. From the catalogue picture, two or three globes appeared to have colored medallions which were engraved or cut. "Flashing" in color was extensively and effectively employed abroad, particularly in Germany. Sandwich also used it to a considerable extent. Thus a frosted, cut lamp globe with amber

PLATE 193

Three pairs of whale oil lamps. Period 1830-1840.

PLATE 194
Choice overlay lamps.

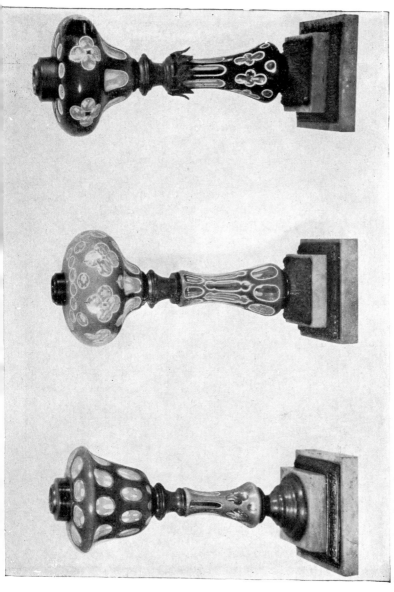

PLATE 195

Rare overlay lamps with cut stems. Height 21 inches.

PLATE 196

Rare overlay lamps in a large size. Height 28 inches.

PLATE 197

Exceptionally rare overlay lamps. Height 38 inches.

medallions either cut or engraved, would make an attractive combination.

Several of the lamps pictured in the catalogue boasted one or even two sets of prisms. The opal pedestals and bases of others were beautifully decorated in gold. The pattern names which accompanied the lamps were as follows:

Cut Punty & Diamond point.

Cut opal Flint art.

Cut Diamond & Punty.

Alabaster gilded.

Opal gilded.

Thus it may be seen that many patterns had descriptive titles at that time just as they do today. The catalogue listed the lamps by number, but the patterns cut on them could be adapted to a suitable lamp style.

Later lamps, not pictured here, were so ornate, particularly in their overly elaborate bronze pedestals that they would be considered quite unattractive and in poor taste, by present-day collectors. These were made during the 80's, or closing years of the factory.

Reproductions of overlay lamps have been flooding the markets here for some years. For the most part, they are small, set on obviously new brass standards, or else the bowls are inserted in old standards in an effort to make the fraud less obvious. In the case of the reproductions the overlay on the bowl is thinner than on the old lamp. In addition the brass collars should be scrutinized to make certain that they are not new ones, carefully treated to give an appearance of age.

Dolphin lamps in at least two different styles were produced at Sandwich, probably during the period when the dolphin candlesticks were in vogue. Collectors may find the lamps in a single dolphin style, often in clear glass, or with three dolphins forming the standard or shaft, resting on a round base. The latter are usually seen in milk white or in a colored opaque glass. Dolphin lamps are exceedingly scarce and therefore are highly prized by those fortunate enough to own them.

Chapter XXVII

VASES

During the 40's the vogue for the earlier products, such as lacy Sandwich and cup plates, was already waning. New forms and fashions were coming into popular favor and the demand grew for colored vases, lamps and candlesticks, as well as for opaque colored ointment and pomade jars, and perfume bottles.

For the benefit of those collectors interested in the early vases, a number of the choicest patterns are illustrated. Incidentally, many of these vases are now at least one hundred years old. The color range included canary yellow, varying shades of blue, emerald green, amethyst, amber and the shade that many refer to as "Peacock," so frequently used at Sandwich. It is an unusual, deep bluish-green. For no apparent reason, the scarcest color in vases appears to be amber. Relatively few were made in clear glass. Color, of course, has always had more appeal in decorative pieces.

A much-favored form was one that collectors today call the "Tulip," which is illustrated by the second vase from the left on Plate 198. It is similar to the pottery vases made at Bennington. Sandwich produced them in glass in deep brilliant hues. Next to the Tulip is an example of the elongated Loop design (with the round base) used on any number of vases, both short and tall. The high, slender vase to the right of the Tulip has a pattern around the bowl resembling the Ashburton. The base is elaborate and of a style which may be noted on some of the early candlesticks. The Punty or large thumbprint pattern pictured at the end of the row is well-known, particularly in New England.

On Plate 199 the Heart pattern vase carries the same motif which Sandwich used on so many of the whale oil lamps. However, it is rare on the vases and also on the perfume bottles. The

Loop vase in the center with a hexagonal pedestal or shaft, also shown on Plate 198, is rarer than those with the round foot. This particular style of vase was sometimes mounted on a marble base, in which case the glass foot was omitted. The draped vase at the right on the same Plate is seen in a number of queer shades, such for example, as a greenish-yellow instead of a canary yellow. The colors appear murky rather than clear as in most of the vases.

Among the most beautiful of the vases are those in a swirled effect, shown on Plate 200. It will be noted that some of the tops are finished with a plain rim while others are fluted or crimped. Again, the foot may be square, round, or hexagonal. Almost any of the bowl patterns illustrated in this chapter may be found combined with the varying tops and types of foot just described.

Further examples of the finished tops may be seen in the smaller pair of vases on Plate 200 in the Punty and Loop pattern. In this instance both of the bases are exactly alike.

Mr. W. Colston Leigh, who makes a practice of collecting only in pairs, is the owner of the two pairs of vases shown on Plate 201 and the heavy flint glass sugar bowl which appears to have been made by a New England factory. Beyond placing the sugar bowl as of the period 1840–50, only a venturesome collector would positively identify it as the product of a particular glass works without documentary proof of some sort. It could just as well be Midwestern.

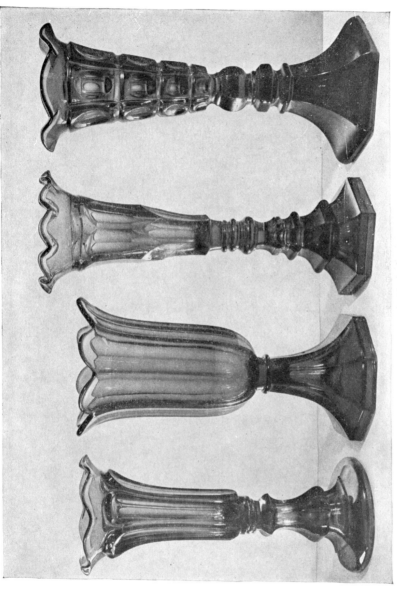

PLATE 198

Sandwich vases in color. Period 1835-1845.

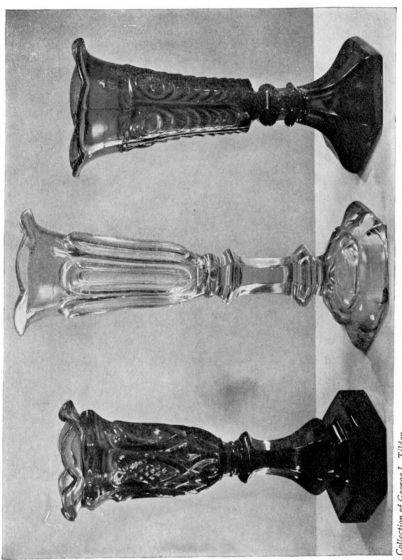

PLATE 199

Sandwich vases in color. Period 1835-1845.

PLATE 200

Sandwich vases in color. Period 1835-1845.

PLATE 201

Sugar bowl and pairs of Sandwich vases in color.

Chapter XXVIII

PAPERWEIGHTS BY NICHOLAS LUTZ

More than one veteran collector of American glass, particularly Sandwich, will be surprised to learn that a workman at the Boston & Sandwich Glass Company made, among other things, artistic glassware of a type that for centuries had been associated with Venetian masterpieces. It is no secret that all our early factories, from Stiegel's to recent times, imported skilled European blowers to ply their trade here and teach native workmen. But for obvious reasons they worked on wares intended for the everyday use of cisatlantic families. There was a greater demand abroad for the more artistic decorative pieces. It took some decades for the same demand to develop here, but from then on the artistic ability of the workers found appreciation and reward.

Among some of the earliest fragments excavated at Sandwich were found many pieces of "striped" glass, the type that inevitably suggests the use of candy cane—such as you see in so many paper-weights. To all appearances they were of Venetian origin, and yet the fragments were so numerous that it was impossible not to conclude that this type of glassware must have been made at Sandwich. Extensive research has established the fact that such ware was the handiwork of one Nicholas Lutz.

Nicholas Lutz was born in St. Louis, Lorraine, France. He began his apprenticeship at the local glass factory (Cristalleries de St. Louis, founded 1767) at the age of ten and continued there until he reached the age to join the colors and serve his four years of required military service.

Later he came to this country and at first settled in White Mills, Pennsylvania, until he was called to the Boston & Sandwich Glass Company. He worked there from 1869 to the closing of the fac-

487

tory in 1888. According to Victor Lutz, a son of Nicholas, now a
resident of Boston, Massachusetts, his father was a master workman in all lines of glassmaking, but specialized in fancy colored
glass, bowls for cutting, chandelier arms and thin glass and stem-
work, meaning by the latter blown glass and goblets, wine glasses,
et cetera. Paperweights were made after hours and were not a
commercial product of the factory.

Victor Lutz asserts that his father brought with him from France
pieces of cane and other decorative material used in forming paperweights. From this it is a fair assumption that he was instructed
in the art of making paperweights while learning his trade at St.
Louis. Some of the choicest paperweights obtainable today were
made there during the 1840's and 1850's. However, it should be
noted that the weights which are in the possession of the Lutz
family today do not bear typically French attributes. They are
quite as characteristic of New England as the sacred cod!

On Plate 203 may be seen a variety of flowers and leaves which
were made by Mr. Lutz for use in paperweights. The six at the
top are red poinsettias. Even though some of the fragile leaves
have been broken away in the course of the years, it may be seen
that the arrangements vary, as well as the center of the flowers.
Some centers contain a single piece of cane, while others have the
effect of a gold-colored bead. The three flowers in the center are
particularly characteristic of Lutz. That at the extreme left is of
a coral-red color, with the center and three lower petals in a white
polka-dot effect. Those flowers having too large plain upper
petals, with three smaller striped petals below, may always be
counted on as specimens of Lutz handiwork. The three flowers
in the lower row (from the left) are white, deep blue, and white,
with petals striped in blue.

Mr. Lutz had a special iron tool with which he pressed the
leaves. Those examples illustrated are so typical that one can be
practically certain of the identification of a Lutz weight, from the
style of these leaves alone.

Plate 204 illustrates some apples, cherries, pears, and carrots,

PLATE 202

Six typical paperweights made by Nicholas Lutz at Sandwich.

PLATE 203
FLOWERS AND LEAVES FOR PAPERWEIGHTS
These were all made by Lutz for insertion in his paperweights. Leaf sprays were done with a special hand tool.

PLATE 204

Above: An Apple Paperweight by Lutz, and a flower knob.

Below: Apples, pears, cherries and carrots in various colors, for insertion in weights. Composition bouquets, to be silvered before being encased in paperweights.

which Mr. Lutz made up in different colors for insertion in his paperweights. All the fruit and vegetables appear much larger in the paperweights because they are greatly magnified by the gatherings of glass which cover them. One member of the Lutz family owns a pair of vases having paperweight bases, containing a group of the colored vegetables.

It would appear that Mr. Lutz took patriotic motifs quite seriously, for I find a number of examples of his work in red, white and blue. Of course, this trinity belongs also to the French flag but Lutz was working in America. The first weight at the left in the top row of Plate 202 is an example of those colorings. The smaller weight in the center has white petals in the flower, dotted in bright blue. The numerous leaves are in his usual style, in green. The third weight, or that at the right end of the upper row is in a brilliant deep blue with green leaves. The cane in the center of the flower is like a white rose, with red heart.

The cherry weight at the lower left is typical of Lutz workmanship. The center weight in the bottom row is a bright purplish-blue. It is not well formed, being somewhat irregular. The third paperweight, at the right end of the row, is a red cross decorated with cane and has two green leaves. It will be noted that one of the leaves is attached backward, difficult to explain for a man known to have performed the most skillful work.

In the upper row of Plate 204 is by all odds one of the most beautiful of the apple paperweights that I have ever seen. It is a beautiful yellowish-green in color with a streak of orange shading across the center. (The white spot on top is merely a reflection from one of the photographer's lights.) Of all the paperweights remaining in the hands of the Lutz family, this one is an outstanding example of fine workmanship.

At the upper right is a curious paperweight knob, having a large hollow stem. It looks as though it might have been made as a stopper for a large cologne bottle. Mr. Lutz remembers that at one time there were two of them, one at each end of a rod, so it may have been designed as a door-knob.

wich glass, is little short of amazing. Each and every individual bottle has its own peculiar beauty.

A collection confined to the various forms of early ointment and pomade jars produced at Sandwich is a hobby in itself. They are scarce enough today to intrigue any collector, so rare indeed that they are seldom seen in antique shops, even in attic-ransacked New England.

The little bear jars are particularly interesting because there are more varieties of them than one would suppose. Mr. Shaw discovered, in his systematic research, that there were four sizes of the "muzzled" bear and two of the "chained" bear, shown on Plate 207. The best known of the series is the smallest size, which was made in black glass, opaque blue, milk white, etc. In this size and variety, Mr. Shaw found one made of pottery, finished with a grayish-blue glaze. It bore a British registry mark on the base showing the date of manufacture as 1854. It is quite possible that Sandwich may have copied this marked specimen, for the British and the Sandwich bears are almost identical, though, of course, Sandwich did not make them in pottery. Deeming Jarves, with his eye for form and color, must have instantly grasped the possibility of a market for these little animals in glass.

Collectors have found the bears in different colors marked on the base with names that at first glance would seem to raise some doubt as to their being a Sandwich product. But they are exactly like the authenticated Sandwich pieces, and it is more likely that they were made to order at the Cape factory. It was a common practice to make molds with a removable plate for lettering. The name of the firm for which they were made probably required no extra expense. One bear was found with "X Bazin-Philada" embossed on the base and still another was marked "Phalon & Son, N. Y."

The line was increased from the original size to four sizes and variations were introduced in time. For instance, one bear is found muzzled and another without a muzzle. The models were probably European, since tame bears were the chief attraction of itinerant showmen in Europe for centuries. The chained bear, which is the

most realistic, is seen in the bottom row of Plate 207. These bears were assembled by Mr. Shaw from discarded pieces unearthed at the site of the Sandwich factory. Some were cracked and ruined in annealing.

Another fascinating small figure is the "Little Cavalier" shown in the second row on Plate 207. These are rarer than the bears, but when found at all they are usually in opaque glass, white or colored.

Some of the ointment jars were probably made in the 40's such as the paneled piece with an oval punty mark, in line 1, Plate 207. Beside it is one in a different style which appears to be threaded. The rounded type that looks polished is in smooth opaque glass. All of these pieces are particularly rare. The Basket Weave jars may be found in two sizes and are probably a later product. They are scarce enough, but are met with more frequently than the first three types mentioned.

At first glance, even experienced collectors might be tempted to pronounce some of the bottles in the illustrations as unmistakably "Bristol" and others to be of French manufacture. There is no question about their foreign appearance. European stylistic influence was felt here and in certain instances we undoubtedly copied some Continental types, the chief difference in our products being in the colors employed. We know that a few fragments of foreign lacy have been excavated at Sandwich and it is difficult to explain these away unless they were from objects that were utilized at the factory to study or copy. We had much to learn from Europe, and glass from abroad carried with it a distinct appeal as something "different." The daughter of a designer for a Pittsburgh concern, who worked in the glass industry for seventy-six years, told me that she remembered going to the factory as a girl and seeing a piece of Baccarat that her father was using as a model from which to copy.

Among puzzling fragments found at Sandwich are those of a stippled jar of a type familiar to workers who have examined quantities of fragments. Almost invariably a piece or two in the jar pattern will be unearthed from among a quantity of fragments,

PLATE 205

Group of interesting toilet bottles.

PLATE 206

Group of interesting toilet bottles.

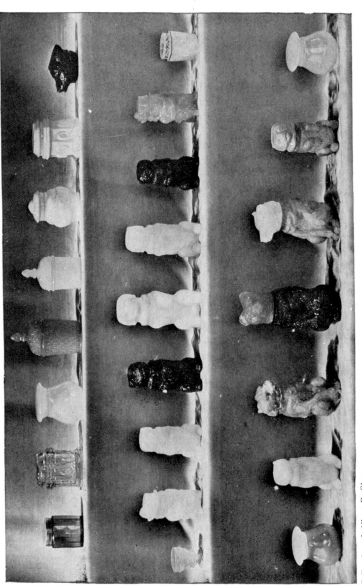

PLATE 207

Bear and "Little Cavalier" ointment jars and other pomade jars.

usually in colored opaque glass, with a heavily beaded edge and a design of acorns and oak leaves against a stippled ground. Lately an antique dealer who was interested in this particular jar, because she owned a fragment of it, came across a specimen somewhat nicked but still whole, in "vaseline" color, that is, a yellowish-green. She examined her fragment, which was in frosted glass and crackled, as from faulty annealing, which would be a logical reason for its having been discarded. On comparing the fragment with the yellowish-green jar, in the bright sunlight, it became apparent that the color was far too green for the usual Sandwich "canary" yellow. The dealer was also impressed by the strong similarity of the bright shade of color to some West-Indian importations of foreign lacy which she had handled. There was the unmistakable mirror-like hardness in the surface reflection to be noted so often in much of the foreign colored glass of the lacy period. Close examination of this yellowish-green jar revealed the lettering "Baccarat" on the inside of the jar cover. On further comparison of the jar with a perfume bottle brought from France, it was found that the metal of the two matched. The Sandwich jar is smaller than the foreign, but the similarity of design is unmistakable.

There has never been much doubt that Deming Jarves and his master moldmakers evolved many patterns which are typical of the Sandwich factory and nowhere else. Nevertheless, the fact remains that in the glass industry there was a vast amount of pattern and design copying, and Jarves lived and worked at a time when such practices were merely routine business. It may have been felt that it was a far easier matter to beguile one's conscience by imitating foreign importations rather than running the risk of suits or trade condemnation by copying home patterns.

Certain types of perfume bottles made here decidedly suggest English designing, such as the two in the middle of the bottom row in Plate 205 and the bottle immediately above. Travelers returning from England have brought back with them precisely such bottles, definitely known to be Bristol. On the other hand, a quantity of fragments of the same style bottle have been excavated at Sandwich in jade green, pale canary yellow, dark opaque yellow and a dark opaque blue. Corresponding stopper fragments were found in jade green and dense turquoise blue. Also unearthed were two stoppers (with the petals broken off) in the same colors, but showing evidence of never having been fitted to a bottle, as the mold marks carried right down the sides of the plug. They had never been ground to fit any bottle. Moreover, it was discovered that the tray which may be seen with the toilet bottle in the lower row of Plate 205, and believed to be Sandwich, had deep indentations or deep scallops in the edge, whereas the known English specimen had a lightly scalloped edge.

There is so much unclassifiable glass among the Sandwich fragments that it is impossible to arrive at a completely satisfactory answer. Some of it may be junked cullet.

It is known that Baccarat or another of the French factories produced perfume bottles similar to the second in the top row of Plate 207. But Sandwich also made them, since corresponding fragments in corroborative quantities have been found. Further research may find the correct answers to many questions that cannot be answered today.

On the following pages is an identification key to all the various items pictured.

IDENTIFICATION TO PLATE 205

Top row:

1. Hexagonal, cut and polished, deep ruby glass. Excellent quality of metal. Stopper a very definite Sandwich pattern.
2. Very thin, blown, canary yellow. Lightest in weight of any illustrated. Common type stopper which is hollow blown, cut hexagonally and pointed at the top. This type of bottle has been found in light blue, ruby and canary yellow.
3. Milk white hexagonal bottle with narrow oval crossed with horizontal lines on each side. Stopper is hollow blown but has been left natural (uncut). Both stopper and bottle are decorated, stopper with gilt only. Bottle has gilt stripes with scroll

decoration around the shoulder, in color. The small match holder on Plate 205 has same pattern of decoration. Colors: Yellow; light amber; deep amber; dark blue; milk white.

4. Deep canary yellow bottle with hexagonal stopper. No fragments of this style, but from pattern and colors seen believe it to be Sandwich.

5. Opaque white with blown hobnail pattern, having original factory decoration in green and gold. Colors: Canary; yellowish-green; clear glass, all without decoration. Also, in translucent white without decorations. Identified bottle fragments in white, crystal and yellow. Stopper fragments in yellow and in white.

6. Dense robin's egg blue, same type as Number 4. Stopper has not been cut.

7. Yellow thumbprint pattern. Hexagonal cut stopper.

8. Deep rich amber bottle with gilt decorations. Original stopper. Small, flattened diamond pattern. This type appears to be English, but a whole part of one bottle was recovered from excavation at Sandwich.

Center row:

9. Amber, hexagonal, with vine decoration in relief. Fragments of this bottle in smaller size. Note same type of tall stopper in bottle Number 25. Colors: Amber; green.

10. Yellowish-green bottle, design of arched panels, flat across base, in relief. This motif has been found in many fragments. Hollow blown stopper such as is used in Numbers 1, 12 and 14. These bottles were made in several sizes.

11. Deep canary yellow, heavy bottle with diamond-shaped indentations. Stopper is cut, hexagonal in shape with flat top.

12. Canary yellow, unusual bottle with original pointed stopper. Typical Sandwich type, usually found in New England.

13. Greenish-yellow (sometimes referred to as "Vaseline") bottle. The body is like Numbers 21 and 22 but the neck and flange are finished like Numbers 7 and 11. The original stopper is a conventionalized closed flower. The saucer tray which matches it was acquired separately.

14. Honey amber, similar to Number 12.

15. Rare, greenish-yellow bottle with original stopper. Design appears to be the heart pattern used for lamp bowls, inverted. The stopper is a flat topped, four-sided design with corners cut. Many fragments of the stoppers in various sizes.

16. Clear glass, star and punty pattern. Same pattern used on lamp bowls and spill or taper holders. Stopper is solid, cut hexagonal with flat top. Colors: Green; opaque white; canary; opaque blue; crystal.

17. Olive-green, in the same shape as Number 1, though the original stopper in this bottle is in a different design.

Bottom row:

18. Deep yellow Loop pattern, typical of Sandwich. Has also been found in deep sapphire blue.

19. Deep yellow, star and punty pattern. Heavy bottle, with solid, cut stopper.

20. Hexagonal, green, squatty bottle, similar to Numbers 12 and 14.

21. Rare opaque-blue bottle with a white flower open stopper and white tray. Trays were made for these bottles.

22. Like above, in a greenish-yellow having a slightly opalescent appearance. The tray which came with it is somewhat more yellowish-white in color. Bottles or fragments have been found in the following colors: Opaque blue with white stoppers and white trays; canary yellow, slightly opalescent; jade green; dense turquoise blue; powder blue; opaque yellow; yellowish-green. Also, varying shades of blue.

23. Typical Sandwich bottle in yellow, with the typical hollow-blown cut hexagonal stopper. This pattern, inverted, is found on many whale oil lamps. It is labeled "typical" because the design is so much more familiar to collectors than most of the others illustrated.

24. Yellow hexagonal bottle having a lyre in each panel. Hollow-blown, cut, hexagonal stopper with flat top. Usually found in either crystal or yellow. The Lyre motif was in use early at Sandwich, particularly on small footed salts.

25. A crystal clear flint glass bottle in the well-known Sandwich Loop pattern.

IDENTIFICATION TO PLATE 206

Top row:

1. Small blown hobnail perfume bottle in yellow, with original stopper. Many corresponding fragments.
2. Small yellow perfume bottle, hexagonal with long oval in each panel. Fragments of stopper.
3. Blown threaded bottle with horizontal ribs. Purple with white threads.
4. Opaque white hobnail pattern, like Number 5 in Plate 205, but without painted decoration.
5. Pink threaded bottle, engraved with monogram "A. H." Considerable "threaded" work was done at Sandwich.
6. Yellow threaded bottle. Also found in jade green. Fragments of both stoppers and bottles were recovered from Sandwich dumps.
7. Bottle in excellent quality of flint glass, with open flower stopper. Similar type was made by New England Glass Company but with a different style stopper. Fragments of this bottle are in Mr. Shaw's possession.
8. One from a pair of small, crystal bottles. Hexagonal with elongated oval in each panel.

Center row:

9. Green bottle, not so dark as it appears in photograph. Has a stopper of a type found at Sandwich.
10. Square crystal bottle similar in size and design to one known to have been produced by New England Glass Company, except this has paneled sides, with a pressed-in flower design within an oval, on each side. There is a different flower spray in each panel, and the panel is frosted. The stopper is original to the bottle and is a common cut Sandwich design.
11. Yellow hexagonal bottle with elongated ovals in each panel, having a band of vertical threads across each panel.
12. Same as above, deep amber.
13. Sandwich overlay bottle. Crystal body cased in blue and white, cut in attractive design. Open stopper. Fragments in attractive

design. Open stopper. Fragments of this bottle found at Sandwich.

14. Sapphire blue, same as Number 11.

15. Deep yellow bottle in hexagonal shape with elongated ovals in each panel. New England Glass Company made similar type but the top of the ovals on the N. E. bottle have flatter surface than on the Sandwich, which are more rounded. Colors: Yellow; amber, decorated in gold.

16. The same bottle as Number 10 except that the flower panels are not frosted. Fragments of these bottles in two sizes, have been found at Sandwich.

17. Unusual purple bottle in an off-shade. Acorn stopper.

Bottom row:

18. Small perfume bottle in light blue with hexagonal stopper to match.

19. Small bottle in deep green. Style of bottle and stopper appear to be definitely Sandwich though no fragments to match have been found to date.

20. Unusual bottle in apple green with tall open stopper. A number of examples in this style have been seen in a number of colors, including green, canary and crystal. Some examples have gilded decoration.

21. Same type as Number 14 on Plate 205.

22. Unusual bright deep green, in same style as many Sandwich types, though no corresponding fragments have been recovered so far.

23. Same type as Number 11 on Plate 1.

24. Same design as bottle Number 4 on Plate 205 except this is in a bright dark blue with cut stopper.

25. A crystal clear bottle with interesting tall stopper, of a type made at Sandwich.

PLATE 207

Top row:

1. A twelve-sided amethyst jar with pewter cover.

2. A crystal glass jar with glass cover. Paneled, with an elongated

oval in each panel. Mr. Shaw has fragments of both the jar and cover. Colors: Opalescent; dense white; pale blue; clear glass.

3. Translucent white covered jar with smooth surface. Found in two sizes. Colors: Jade green; opaque white; clear glass. Corresponding fragments for the jar and cover.

4. Basket weave jar in jade green. Produced in two sizes. This is the larger and rarer size.

5. Same as above, usual size. Made in at least 15 varieties of color.

6. A dense white covered jar. Fragments have been found in three colors and in a different size, which is a similar but somewhat changed design.

7. Same as Number 2 except for slight differences in the molding.

8. A bear's head in black glass. This is a fourth and largest size of the muzzled bear jar.

Center row:

9. Small footed receptacle, with two rows of horizontal ribbing. Definitely Sandwich and occurs in many colors.

10. Little Cavalier covered jar, in translucent white. These are extremely scarce today.

11. Smallest size muzzled bear, in translucent white.

12. The second size muzzled bear in black glass.

13. The third size muzzled bear in opalescent white.

14. The second size muzzled bear in translucent white.

15. Smallest size muzzled bear in black glass.

16. The "Little Cavalier" jar in a translucent blue glass.

17. The toothpick holder in white glass that matches bottle Number 3 of Plate 205.

Bottom row:

18. A jade green jar pictured with a white cover, both of which were recovered from the Sandwich dumps.

19. Smallest muzzled bear jar in opalescent white glass.

20. An opaque blue "chained" bear jar. Both jar and bear's head came from the Sandwich dumps. They were cracked and ruined in the annealing. Note the difference in posture.

21. A second size chained bear. They are mismatched here as to

color only but this is the true size. These two parts were purchased in shops.

22. This is the smaller sized chained bear jar. Both parts were injured in the annealing and so were discarded, but were recovered among other Sandwich fragments. The body is an opaque blue and the head a "clam-water" or milky-white.
23. Small muzzled bear jar in opalescent blue. The head shows more opalescent coloring than the body, though this difference is more marked in the picture than in reality.
24. Smaller size of Number 3 in this illustration. Translucent white.

Chapter XXX

PATTERN GLASS

For nearly twenty-five years the Boston & Sandwich Glass Company had been going through a notable period of experimentation and improvements in methods and machinery. The works had produced everything from pharmaceutical supplies to tableware for the White House. Blown glass, pressed glass, cut and engraved glass, lanterns, lamps, candlesticks, paperweights and novelties without end indicate the character of the Sandwich output. To enumerate every article produced at this factory would be an utter impossibility. There is not available enough detailed information to enable us today to compile a complete record.

During the 40's were produced glass whale oil lamps with bowls in patterns familiar to collectors today. Spillholders or taper holders were often made to match the lamp bowls. The spillholders were thick, heavy flint glass affairs with very short stems. Sometimes they also served a double duty as cigar holders. Today collectors find them to be just the right size for short-stemmed flowers. Groups are shown on Plates 208, 209 and 210.

The spills were made of strips of dry wood or paper and served to light the candles, of which many were required for adequate illumination. The flame of the spills lasted longer and burned more steadily than matches and so was more satisfactory, especially for lighting lamps, since they took somewhat longer to light. The paper spills were sometimes made of colored paper strips rolled spirally or folded lengthwise, and in the literature of the period we read of the skill displayed by housewives in making them not only useful but ornamental. Some of them were cut to resemble feathers. The holders were called spill boxes, spill cases, spill pots, or spill holders, and were made in a variety of designs and materials. A wide-awake manufacturer like Jarves must have realized how readily glass spillholders made to match the lamp bowls would sell. Matches were poor, scarce, and expensive in those days. The first friction matches were made in England in 1827. The old "lucifers" did not ignite as rapidly as they do today, but they improved and came into general use. Nevertheless, the thrifty spills survived a long time, for they could be lighted from the fire in the stove or the fireplace and cost next to nothing.

These early spillholders are the forerunners of the later spoonholders. In the course of time they increased in size. The spoonholder is taller, with a longer stem, and is almost invariably scalloped on the upper edge of the bowl. On Plate 210 are two opaque white spillholders, together with an opaque green spoonholder in the Cable pattern. Spoonholders in the early patterns in color, which were largely produced during the 50's, are rare today.

During the late 40's what is today widely known as pattern glass came into being. There is a record of a shipment of the Ashburton pattern to California during the gold rush in 1849. No one can positively assert today that this was the first pattern made in complete sets of tableware, although it may well have been. It is a plain, simple pattern in heavy flint glass. A wide range of articles was made, from cordials to large thick flip or toddy glasses. It is not likely that the entire line was produced at once. Prudent manufacturers would try out a few pieces, and if they "took" with the public the line was built up.

The Ashburton pattern was made by almost every factory producing tableware, for in the 40's and 50's, imitation and copying were not capital crimes any more than they are in these copyrighted days. There would be slight variations, which is one reason why collectors find it more difficult to match pieces in Ashburton than in almost any other. This pattern enjoyed a longer life than most, for the known period of its manufacture extends over many years. Fashion was less fickle in those horse-and-buggy days, when a change meant improvement, than in the automobile age when what is sought in changing is difference; a new but not necessarily a better or more artistic article. During the late 40's and early 50's, the vogue for pattern glass was definitely established. Besides Ashburton, Sandwich made other designs, the keynote of which was simplicity, in keeping with the times, such as Flute, Bigler, Loop, Argus, Pillar, etc. These early patterns were in demand before the novelty of six-inch plates made its appearance.

Sometimes "table sets" were made, even though the line was limited to four pieces—the sugar bowl, creamer, spoonholder and butter dish. An early line which was never fully completed, for example, is the Rayed, with Loop border, illustrated on Plate 211. The six-inch plates, sauce dishes and butter dishes are seen more frequently than other items in the set, which includes a small oval pin tray similar in shape to earlier ones produced in lacy glass.

Another early design in heavy flint-glass seldom seen outside New England is the Smocking, shown on Plate 209. The goblet is particularly scarce. The footed pieces in the Smocking are all scalloped, which is an indication of its early age, for scalloped feet are seldom seen in pressed glass, though frequently on blown.

As the country grew in population and wealth, the variety of patterns of pressed glass kept pace with it, and more elaborate designs appeared. The lozenge pattern was extremely popular. Specimens are found ranging in size from a small diamond point to a large "Diamond Mitre," as one of them was originally termed. Examples of a few fragments of these diamond or lozenge patterns excavated at Sandwich are illustrated on Plate 212. One of the earliest was the Diamond Thumbprint, so well known to collectors today. A wide variety of footed bowls and large compotes came in this pattern, as well as handsome celery vases and divers other pieces. The goblets are extremely rare. The normal breakage in these was greater than in the more carefully handled larger items.

Following Diamond Thumbprint during the 50's came such familiar patterns as Horn of Plenty, Cable, Bellflower, Fine Rib, Ribbed Palm, Ivy, Comet, etc. This may be called the intensive period for these early lines, even though they continued well into the 60's.

PLATE 208
Group of interesting early spillholders.

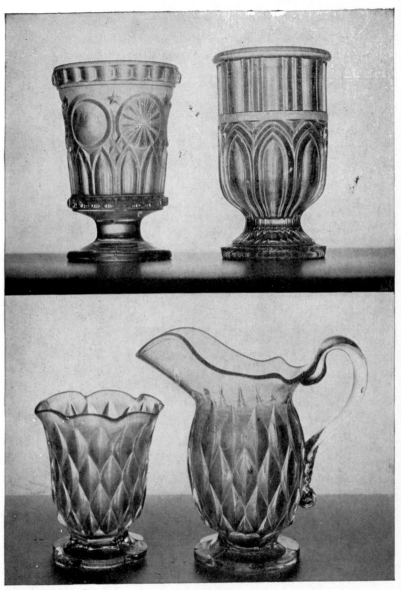

PLATE 209

Upper—Spillholders.
Lower—Smocking pattern.

PLATE 210

Upper—Rare oblong Horn of Plenty honey dish.
Lower—Two opaque spillholders and a Cable spoonholder.

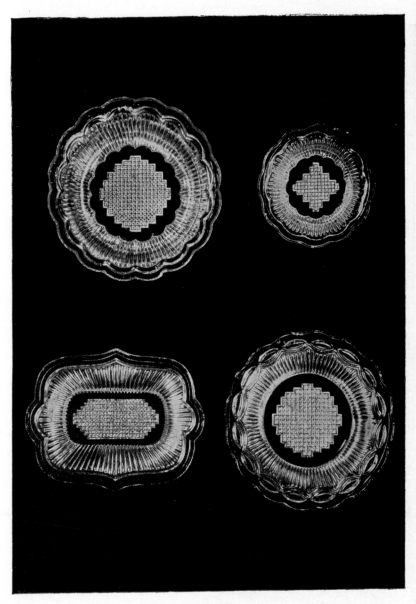

PLATE 211
Group in Rayed, with Loop border.

PLATE 212

Fragments of Diamond patterns excavated at Sandwich.

There are a few designs of pressed glass which apparently were
not produced by other factories than Sandwich, even at the time
when the glassmakers stole or copied whatever promised to be a
good seller. One is the Comet. It was my good fortune to find a
goblet in a brilliant sapphire blue. Colors in early pattern glass are
rare and desirable. I adhere to the belief that such colored specimens were all made either at Sandwich or by Deming Jarves in his
Cape Cod factory, which he built after he severed his connections
with the Boston & Sandwich Glass Company in 1858. Stray colored pieces may be occasionally found by collectors in any of the
early flint-glass patterns which were made up to the time of the
Civil War. I have seen Ashburton sugar bowls in opalescent and
in yellow; Ashburton egg cups in opalescent and in dense white;
Bellflower spoonholders in varying brilliant shades of blue; Bellflower syrup pitchers in opalescent, milk white and dark blue;
Bellflower egg cups in opalescent and in amber; Waffle and Thumbprint in opaque white and in yellow; Ribbed Grape in a brilliant
deep blue and in a peacock shade; Horn of Plenty spoonholders in
yellow, in opaque white and in crystal with an amber band at the
upper edge. Cable spoonholders have been found in numerous
opaque shades, such as deep blue, green, etc. Waffle was made in
canary yellow and other colors. Bull's Eye pieces may be found
occasionally in color, chiefly yellow or opaque white. A few fragments in the Hamilton pattern have been picked up in blue, though
I have never seen whole specimens in color. Tree of Life was made
in colors and the Sandwich "overshot" glass was sometimes
"flashed" with color. The outer coating of the glass would be rose
on top, as well as the lining with clear glass between, as a fragment
reveals.

Other patterns than Comet that were produced only at Sandwich,
so far as we know today, include Waffle; Sandwich Star; Cable;
Bull's Eye with Fleur-de-Lys; Bull's Eye and Bar; Flowered Oval;
Flat Diamond and Panel; Morning Glory; Beaded Circle; Bradford Blackberry; Divided Heart; Rayed, with Loop border and

Chrysanthemum Leaf. There may be still others, but these are the outstanding patterns.

In the early 60's came the Hamilton, Morning Glory, Sandwich "overshot" glass and others which were produced just before the beginning of the most highly commercialized era of glassmaking in this country, which began after the Civil War. There was a reason for the change in the industry.

To begin with, methods of pressing glass had been greatly improved long before the Civil War. Toward the close of the conflict an important discovery was made which again revolutionized the glass industry. A cheaper substitute was found for lead, which was expensive, in lime, which gave a certain amount of brilliancy to the metal, though not the weight nor resonant "ring" which came when a piece was tapped. As a result, the production of tableware increased by leaps and bounds since nearly all the factories were quick to adopt the new method. During the late 60's, pressed tableware was being made in complete sets which were attractive enough to sell readily in large volume but lacked the beauty, weight and particularly the resonance of the earlier ware.

During the 70's and 80's the manufacture of glass tableware in more complete sets was in its intensive period. Whereas in the earlier ware it was all of clear flint glass, now colored sets were introduced, particularly in the Midwest. Sandwich apparently did little of it, if we may be guided by the fragment findings. The competition from factories in the Pittsburgh area, of which already there were twenty in that district alone, was altogether too active to disregard. Apparently Sandwich continued flint patterns, just as the New England Glass Company did, long after other factories had gone into the cheaper line. The rock-ribbed New England conservatism held to its ideals. Both New England companies undoubtedly felt the inroads of the lower priced Midwestern wares into their trade, for the Pittsburgh factories were doing an enormous volume of business. Just as Sandwich held the upper hand during the lacy glass period, the Midwest now held it in the cheaper pattern glass. A vogue for colored ware developed to which we owe those designs so eagerly sought by collectors today, such as Wildflower, Thousand Eye, Fine Cut, Cathedral, and others.

Sandwich did produce a small amount of the later milk white glass (besides the earlier Opal, Alabaster, etc.), as well as some of the later patterns but not many in color, with the possible exception of Daisy and Button. Of the late designs (1870's) might be included Tree of Life (different from the Portland Glass Company product) Magnet and Grape with stippled leaf, Grape and Festoon (clear and stippled) Arched Grape, Powder and Shot, Leaf and Dart, Drapery, etc. A complete list will be found toward the close of this chapter.

The outstanding favorite in New England today of all Sandwich patterns is the Morning Glory. A group is pictured on Plate 213. It is eagerly sought after not alone because it is scarce but because of its beauty of design. Apparently it could not have been produced in large quantities over a long period of time or more of it would be available today.

Rarities in the Ivy pattern are shown on Plate 214. Covered 6 inch sweetmeat dishes in any of the earlier designs are rare and desirable. The same holds true of berry bowls, which are true bowls and not footed. Covered salts are found in Ivy but it is difficult to find them complete with the covers. The rarest of all covered salts belonging to this period is the Bellflower.

The Tree of Life pattern was produced by the Portland Glass Company, by Sandwich and by one or more Pittsburgh factories. The Sandwich type is shown on Plate 215. The Portland variety has more merit than any of the others, both in quality of the metal and in form.

"Overshot" glass differs from the Tree of Life more than is apparent from the picture (Plate 215). It has a rough, sharp surface but lacks a design. A glassmaker's explanation is that the surface effect was produced by rolling the glass while it was still very hot in "ice" or small particles of crushed glass, which melted into the surface.

A Horn of Plenty covered oblong deep dish is shown in Plate 210. Very few specimens of this rare honey dish are known.

Besides the Morning Glory, another favorite with New England collectors today is the Sandwich Star, pictured on Plate 216. It was not made in many forms, but one can find huge compotes, decanters, lamps with the star bowls and spillholders much more readily than the goblets.

On Plate 217 are shown four other typical Sandwich patterns. The Bull's Eye and Bar is of an excellent quality of flint glass, and was made in a few forms only. The Flute with Diamond Border goblet, also of flint glass, is a short, rather squat type. I have not seen many other forms in it, though they may exist. The Beaded Circle, shown in the goblet on Plate 217, is a later glass without the lead content. Apparently it was made in sets of tableware, as I have seen goblets, celery vases, sugar bowls and several other pieces. Chrysanthemum Leaf is said to have been the last new pattern made in sets before the factory closed.

A grape band pattern was produced at Sandwich, which varies from grape designs found elsewhere. An egg cup is shown on Plate 218. The grape band is said to have been copied from a Wedgwood piece. It certainly has a more "classical" appearance than any other grape pattern.

On Plate 218 are pictured ten Sandwich patterns, authenticated on the basis of fragment findings. Only one of the group is shown in *Early American Pressed Glass* because not enough forms in the others were found before the book was completed to justify the belief that they were made in complete sets of tableware.

The Bradford Blackberry pattern was first called to my attention several years ago by the late Emma Fitts Bradford, whose interest in pattern glass never faltered, and so it was named for her at that time. The goblet is paneled and has a vine-like stem encircling the bowl, with leaves and a large berry (or it might be taken for a cluster of grapes) pendent from the stem. It is a heavy flint glass pattern of decided appeal.

Next to it on Plate 218 is a Scalloped Lines goblet. It is a late pattern of no particular appeal.

Stippled Fuchsia was pictured among the odd goblets in *Early American Pressed Glass*. Considerable confusion has been caused by calling it "Fuchsia" because there is a still later Midwestern pattern having a large fuchsia against a clear background. Many collectors believed the latter to be the "Sandwich" fuchsia merely because they had heard it said that the Cape factory produced such a design. The Midwestern Fuchsia was made during the 80's in sets of tableware which were square in form, whereas the Stippled Fuchsia from Sandwich was neither square nor produced in complete sets of tableware, though many more pieces have been discovered than were known at the time this book first appeared.

The Ripple pattern in the top line of Plate 218 appears to be one of the very late Sandwich products, probably of the 80's, or shortly before the closing days. Midwestern competition in cheap tableware had to be met. It was made in fairly complete sets.

The "Dickinson" design, next to the Ripple, is a flint glass pattern of considerable merit. It was named a number of years ago for May Dickinson Kimball, the well-known founder of Mothercraft, of Amherst, Mass. It may be found in a variety of pieces.

In the lower row of Plate 218 is an egg cup in the Flowered Oval. It is also a flint glass pattern, probably produced in the 60's or early 70's.

Next to the Flowered Oval egg cup is a Grape Band Variant egg cup, already described on a preceding page as having been copied from a Wedgwood grape design.

In the center of the lower row of Plate 218 is a Beaded Mirror spoonholder. Mrs. Emma Fitts Bradford christened it some years ago. It was made in complete sers, including 6 inch plates.

The Divided Heart is a well-known pattern in New England, where it is seen more frequently than elsewhere. It is collectible in a number of forms, including goblets, compotes, egg cups and sauce dishes.

The last piece in the lower row of Plate 218 is a Beaded Acorn champagne. Similar designs carrying grapes in the clear beaded space were first made in the Midwest, so it would appear that Sandwich was making an effort to compete with them, as it would quite naturally have to do. The Beaded Grape medallion of the Midwest was produced in such large quantities that it is not difficult to find today, but the Beaded Mirror and Beaded Acorn are comparatively scarce.

While Deming Jarves ruled at Sandwich, any number of covered egg cups were produced, not alone in clear glass but in those soft opaque shades of color of which he was so fond. There have been many collectors of egg cups and their most prized specimens are those which have covers and are in colors. They have been found in opaque jade green, opaque yellow, mauve and many shades of violet and blue. Two are illustrated on Plate 216.

Western competition was keenly felt when Deming Jarves built the Cape Cod Glass Works and it was easy to foresee still more serious rivalry for Sandwich. The Midwest had advantages in the way of cheaper fuel from the nearby coal fields and exceptional transportation facilities, not only by railroad but by water. There are no records to show exactly what was being produced at Sandwich during the late 1850's, but the works must have catered to the demands of customers in their steadily contracting territory, notably for lamps and lamp chimneys, a certain amount of pattern glass, etched and engraved ware, decorated toilet sets, barber bottles, gas globes, drug store counter jars, etc.

In a section like New England, where tradition is held sacred, both spiritually and materially, iconoclasts are not wanted and myths conveying a sense of superiority in morals and in manufactures are cherished. Sandwich produced much excellent glass of various types, but they did not make all of the glassware in America. For example, they never produced the Westward-Ho pat-

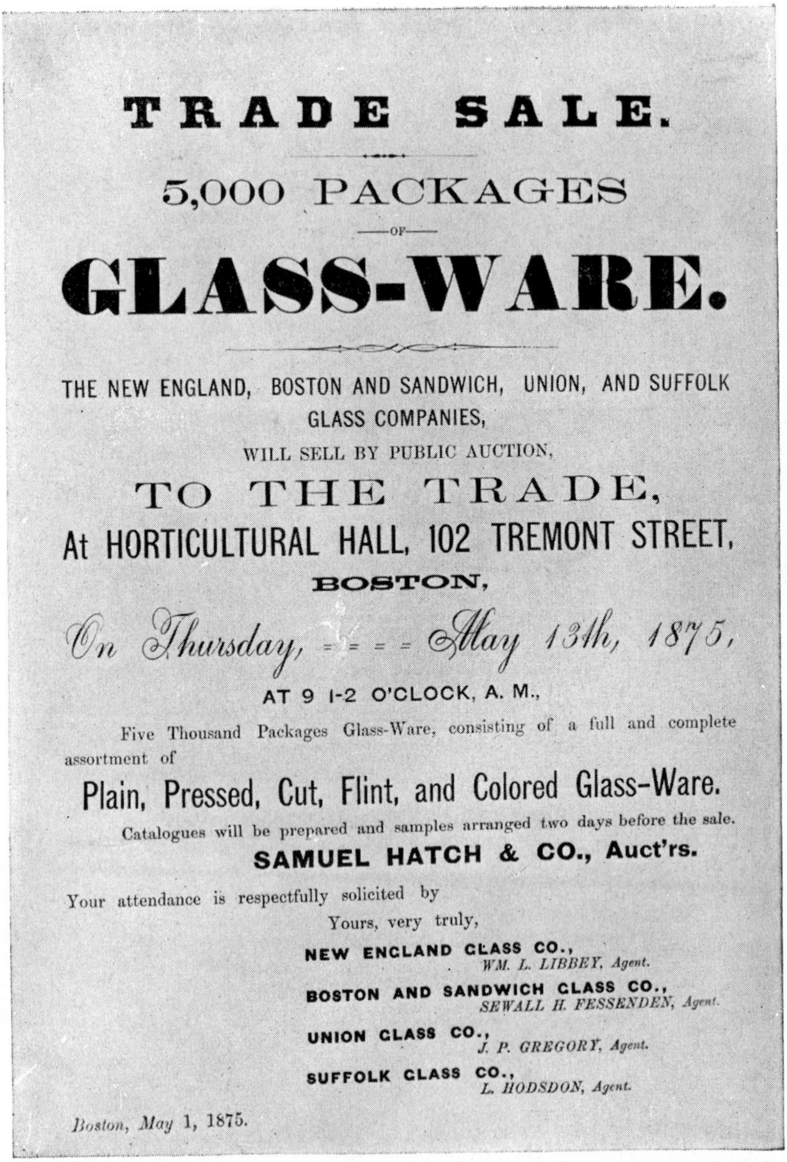

TRADE SALE.

5,000 PACKAGES

—OF—

GLASS-WARE.

THE NEW ENGLAND, BOSTON AND SANDWICH, UNION, AND SUFFOLK
GLASS COMPANIES,

WILL SELL BY PUBLIC AUCTION,

TO THE TRADE,

At HORTICULTURAL HALL, 102 TREMONT STREET,

BOSTON,

On Thursday, = = = May 13th, 1875,

AT 9 1-2 O'CLOCK, A. M.,

Five Thousand Packages Glass-Ware, consisting of a full and complete
assortment of

Plain, Pressed, Cut, Flint, and Colored Glass-Ware.

Catalogues will be prepared and samples arranged two days before the sale.

SAMUEL HATCH & CO., Auct'rs.

Your attendance is respectfully solicited by

Yours, very truly,

NEW ENGLAND GLASS CO.,
WM. L. LIBBEY, Agent.

BOSTON AND SANDWICH GLASS CO.,
SEWALL H. FESSENDEN, Agent.

UNION GLASS CO.,
J. P. GREGORY, Agent.

SUFFOLK GLASS CO.,
L. HODSDON, Agent.

Boston, May 1, 1875.

Collection of the author

PLATE 219
Poster Notice of a Trade Sale of Packages of Glass.

PLATE 218—AUTHENTICATED SANDWICH PATTERNS

Upper—Bradford Blackberry; Scalloped Lines; Stippled Fuchsia; Ripple; Dickinson.
Lower—Flowered Oval; Grape Band Variant; Beaded Mirror; Divided Heart; Beaded Acorn.

PLATE 217—FOUR AUTHENTICATED SANDWICH PATTERNS

Upper—Bull's Eye and Bar goblet. Flute with Diamond border goblet.
Lower—Beaded Circle goblet. Chrysanthemum Leaf sherbet cup.

PLATE 216

Upper—Opaque covered egg cups. Cable; Bull's Eye and Bar.
Lower—Two goblets. Flat Diamond and Panel; Sandwich Star.

PLATE 215

Tree of Life goblet and footed glass. Sandwich "Overshot" plate and tumbler.

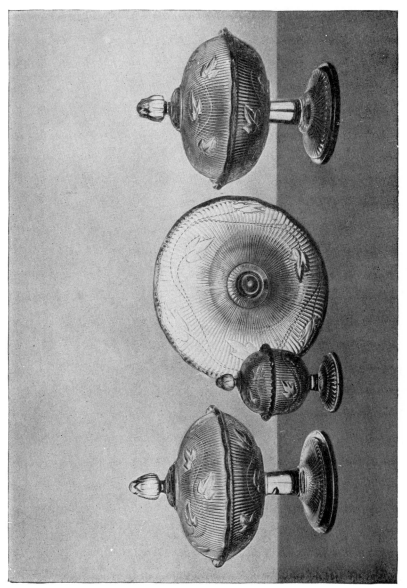

PLATE 214

Group of rarities in the Ivy pattern.

PLATE 213

Morning Glory goblet, champagne glass and egg cup.

tern and there is incontrovertible evidence to prove this. Neither did they ever make Lion or Classic, all three of these patterns being products of Gillinder & Sons of Philadelphia. Sandwich never made Rose in Snow, which was an old Adams & Company design of Pittsburgh, nor Three Face, which was a pattern of George Duncan & Sons, also of Pittsburgh, Pa. Even myths that date back only a few years are hard to break down. But when pattern glass collecting enlisted thousands of enthusiasts and attributions were demanded, the line of least resistance was in the direction of Sandwich. The label was popular and profitable and it stuck, in defiance of proofs of its false character. There is no evidence among fragment findings that Sandwich ever produced milk white or black plates to any extent nor the milk white hen dishes. Mr. West of the Westmoreland Glass Company in Grapeville, Pa., told me that he built up his fortune making the 5 inch hen dishes which he sold in carload lots, filled with prepared mustard, at ten cents each. I have in my possession one of these hen dishes with the original label of the Westmoreland Specialty Company still on it and the somewhat aged mustard within it. Animal dishes were a late Midwestern specialty. The only fragment of an animal dish from the Sandwich dumps to my knowledge was a piece from a dish having a dog on the cover, resembling a King Charles spaniel. A single fragment cannot be accepted as adequate proof. Any glass manufacturer today will cheerfully admit that there are many items in his plant which he did not make. Every company is anxious to know what his competitors are making and that rule held in the old days as well as now.

Included in my list of Sandwich patterns are only those of which enough fragments have been found to justify the ascription. Those patterns of which only a very few fragments have been found are listed as "doubtful." It is not fair to include in the list of designs all the innumerable odd sauce dishes, for no one could ever be sure that all had been listed. It is not always possible to say "positively Sandwich" of many patterns, since the greater part of them were produced by more than one company. For instance, Sandwich made Beliflower, Ribbed Palm and Horn of Plenty. So did M'Kee & Brothers, of Pittsburgh. An old trade catalogue of the M'Kees, of the late 50's, pictures all three of them. No one can tell today which of the two houses was guilty of copying. Collectors will find two distinct sizes in Horn of Plenty goblets but the difference gives no clue and it is impossible to determine which was the Sandwich and which M'Kees'. In the Ribbed Palm there are even more noticeable differences. In one the rib is convex and in the other, concave.

Of the later Sandwich patterns belonging to the early group, in such designs as Hamilton and Morning Glory, it may be noted that while they have a lead content, it is not so great as in those produced during the 40's and 50's.

Old memoranda merely listing patterns by the trade names by which they were originally known, tell us little today unless accompanied by sketches which alone could identify them. I have had access to one that belonged to William Stutson. It is marked "Memo" on the cover and dated "1859." Inside the cover, in his handwriting, is: "Presented to Mr. G. L. Fessenden by Wm. Stutson, 1865." It contains much information of value, such as a "List of numbers to be [—illegible word] pr moves and weight, per dozen." A list of the patterns follow, some of which are familiar to us because their original labels clung to them. The book also lists "Valuations of Houses belonging to the B. & S. Glass Company, February 1859." The rest of the memo is devoted to glass formulas, the colors of which are reprinted here as a matter of interest to present-day manufacturers. The patterns listed are those which we know were being produced during the 50's. I have seen one bill of sale listing the Cable pattern in 1859. It would be interesting to know which was the "Jenny Lind" design mentioned as used in sugar bowls and creamers. Special interest attaches as well to the listing of the "Bee Hive 9 inch plates" at that fairly late date. The "Boston Ship" doubtless refers to tumblers made for use on ships.

From William Stutson's Memo.

List of numbers to be (illegible word) pr. moves & weight per doz. tumblers. (Mr. Stutson's spelling, punctuation, etc., have been retained.)

Qt. Concave Mead
Pt. 6 Arch Flute Havana
Pt. 12 Edge Flute Havana
Pt. 16 Edge Flute Taper
Pt. 6 . . . . . . Flute Ale
Pt. 6 . . . . . . Flute McCoy
Pt. 8 Flute Taper
Pt. Gothic Taper
Pt. Ashburton Taper
⅓ Qt. 6 Arch Flute
⅓ Qt. N. Y. 8 Flute Taper
⅓ Qt. Gothic
⅓ Qt. N. Orleans
⅓ Qt. Short Flute Taper
⅓ Qt. Marsterson Shep
⅓ Qt. American
⅓ Qt. Dble. Ashburton
⅓ Qt. 8 Flute Shep
⅓ Qt. Tulip 6 Dble. Flute
⅓ Qt. Concave Flute
⅓ Qt. 4 Flute
Pt. Tulip 8 Flute 8 Edge
Tulip Punty
Revere Ship
Double Ashburton
Art Union
Flute & Hoop
Star & Punty
Oval Punty & Split
Large Jenny Lind
Small Jenney Lind
Ashburton Bar
Bedford Bar

Boston Bar
Philadelphia Bar
N. York Bar
Mussey Bar
Taper Bar
Hotel Bar
Revere Flute Bar
N. York tall 8 Flute
Boston Ship
Revere Flute Ship
Pt. Tall 9 Flute Ship
Large Grove Ship
Small Grove Ship
18 Edge Flute
Worcester & Mussey
Light Revere Flute
Gothic Ship
No. 1 California
No. 2 California
4 Flute
⅓ Pt. Ashburton Bar
Keystone Bar
8 Flute Bar
Plain Bar
Gothic
7 Flute Havana
French Bar
Ashburton
Punty & Split
Jenney Lind
8 Flute Ship
6 Flute Ship
6 Flute Taper
6 Flute Pillar

Sugars

Jenney Lind
Punty & Star
Ashburton
Concave on Foot
Concave off Foot

Celerys

Sandwich
Jenney Lind

Jugs

Great Jugs
3 Pint
Pint Jug unshape formed

Jars

Gallon
½ gallon
9 gallon

Lamps

All No. 1
All No. 2
Rochester
Bedford
Boston & Otis
No. 1 Handle
No. 2 Handle
No. 3 Handle
Hotel night

Candlesticks

Concave foot 6 Ball
No. 2 Dolphin
Large foot

Creamers

Ashburton
Jenney Lind
Punty & Star

References are made to other items but without pattern names. These include cup plates: Bee Hive 9″ Nappy (probably means deep plate) 5, 6 and 7 inch plates, caster bottles, wines and egg cups, bowls on foot, spoon holders, decanters, goblets, beer mugs and bitters bottles.

The "memo" further itemizes the coal consumption in each furnace per week, giving the total amount used in the Upper and Lower house. It lists the valuation of 21 houses belonging to the Boston & Sandwich Glass Company in February, 1859. Included are single houses, a block of five tenements, double houses and three tenements. The total estimated value was $9,600. The value of the single houses averaged $400 each.

The balance of the book is made up of glass formulas, with instructions for certain preparations. One is labeled "Mixture for silvering. To make Nitrate Silver." Another is headed "Preparation for purple Cassus for making ruby glass." Still another reads:

"Preparation of the gold." There are formulas for the following: Flint glass for coating. Best Flint. Moorland Flint. Blue for coating. Canary. Opal. Dark blue. White agate. Amber. Amethyst. Purple. Light purple. Dark purple. Red jasper. Olive green No. 3. Light green. Turquoise. Black. Flint crystal glass.

Another privately owned notebook was prepared in 1865 and 1866, apparently by a secret agent sent out to investigate a number of factories with a view to listing their output, prevailing scale of wages, etc. If, as has been suggested, he was a professional "snooper" he assuredly did a good piece of work, for he covered the Union Glass Company of Somerville, Mass.; the Boston & Sandwich Glass Company of Sandwich, Mass.; the New England Glass Company of Cambridge, Mass.; the Portland Glass Company of Portland, Maine; the St. Lawrence Glass Works, Montreal, Canada (January 1868) ; and Wm. T. Gillinder's (1870).

He lists the names of workmen at the various factories and their pay, including those at the Mount Washington Glass Company at South Boston; the Suffolk Glass Works at South Boston; the Phenix at South Boston; Cape Cod Glass Works (Feb. 6, 1866), Sandwich, Mass.; Bay State Glass Works; Constitution Glass Works, Brooklyn, N. Y. (Oct. 1865) ; Excelsior Glass Works, Leich & Sneider, Williamsburgh, Va.; Lafayette Glass Works; Concord St. Glass Works, Brooklyn, N. Y.; Marrets, South Ferry, Brooklyn, N. Y. Note on Corning Glass Works, Corning, N. Y.

He goes into detail with the utmost care, quoting sizes of furnaces, number of pots set per year, average loss of pots, amount of glass made into glassware, etc., and he states that from March 31 to December 24, 1873 (39 weeks) the New England Glass Company used a total of 893,400 lbs., average 22,908 lbs. per week or 4,582 per five-day week. Figuring the cost at 20 cents per lb., this equalled $178,681.80, or $4,581.51 average per week. There seemed to be nothing the man did not know. Since all this was painstakingly entered in a small notebook accompanied in parts by pen-line drawings, it can be reasonably assumed that he was employed by some wide-awake Midwestern factory.

Below are listed all the articles he noted as being made at Sandwich in 1865. It is interesting to know that even at that time many of the early patterns were still popular; for instance, Ashburton, Comet, Star and Punty and Huber. It has been said that the manufacture of Ashburton continued well into the 70's, which accounts for its being so plentiful today, and also explains why some of it is found in a decidedly inferior metal. The New England Glass Company lists many patterns by the same names that were used at Sandwich, though Sandwich is the only company to call egg cups "egg cups," all the others referring to them as "egg glasses." Of particular interest is the fact that sugar covers were ordered separately, breakage being responsible for the greater demand for them than for the bases. The following items and patterns were produced at Sandwich in the year 1865.

Goblets

Ashburton
Comet
Flute & Split
Finger & diamond
Mirror
Huber
Old Colony
Db. Large
    Small
St. Lawrence
Mt. Vernon
Mt. Washington
Zouave

Nappies

4 inch
6 inch
7 .. C. H.
8 .. C. H.

Washington 3 inch
            4 inch
            6 inch
            7 inch
Nappie Tops

Beer Mugs

Hoop & slave
Pony
Short 9 flute
Pony
Patch

Bottles

O & G Bottles
6 Flute
⅓ qrt ......
½ pt. Acorn
½ pt. Washington
⅓ pt. finger Taper

Beer Mugs

½ pt. finger diamond
Finger ship
6 flute
Short 9 flute
½ pt. flute & split
French flute
½ pt. Ash ......
⅓ pt. Ash
½ pt. No. 200
pt.
⅓ Qrt. plain Albion
Balloon
½ pt. Pillar Ship
pt. pillar Ship
Barrel
204 Bar
Gill
Toy

Sugars

Washington
Zouave

Sugar Covers
Creamers

Mt. Washington
Zouave
Huber

Spoon Holders

Star & Punty
Mirror
Oyster pepper
Chimneys
Mustard Tops
Mt. Vernon Plates

Champaignes

Huber
Finger Bowl

Mirror
Mirror
Mt. Washington
Zouave

Wines

Ashburton
Mirror
Finger & Diamond
Huber
Mt. Washington
Zouave

Tumblers

Knob Ale Tumblers
½ pt. Revere flute
3 pt. ....
½ .. Rd. bottom
⅓ Pillar
½ pt. Worcester
½   Gem
Mt. Washington
Zouave

Lamp Feet

Salts
Darby
Cone rope bt
Mt. Washington
Lincoln
Sandwich
Sqr. Ind. Salts
Round

Egg Cups

Huber
Mt. Washington

Lemonades

Mt. Washington
Toy

Lamps

Ring Handle
Hotel—night—1 lower
                2 lower

Melon Hand
Plain Melon
Hand
Fount
Fount

Patterns produced at Sandwich, as identified by fragment findings of Francis Wynn, when found in sufficient quantities to justify the attributions. Patterns in which goblets were not made are marked by an asterisk. Odd items, such as sauce dishes not belonging to sets, are not included.

PATTERNS IDENTIFIED FROM SANDWICH FRAGMENTS

Argus
Arched Grape
Ashburton

Banded Buckle
Barberry
Beaded Acorn
Beaded Circle (clear or milk white)
Beaded Grape Medallion (one type)
Beaded Mirror
Bellflower
Bigler
Blackberry (one type, not such fine
    detail as Wheeling product)
Block with Thumbprint
Bleeding Heart
Bradford Blackberry
Buckle
Bull's Eye
Bull's Eye and Fleur-de-Lys
Bull's Eye and Bar

Cable
* Cable with ring
Colonial

Chrysanthemum Leaf
Comet
Crystal (one type)
Cube

Daisy and Button (very little made
    at Sandwich)
Diamond Thumbprint
Diamond Point
* Diamond Quilted with Bull's Eye
    border
Dickinson
Divided Heart
Drapery

Fine Rib
Flat Diamond and Panel
Flute
Flute with Diamond border
Frosted Leaf
Flowered Oval

Gothic
Grape and Festoon (clear back-
    ground

Grape and Festoon (stippled background)
Grape Band Variant
Gooseberry (clear or milk white)

Hamilton (2 fragments in blue)
Hamilton with leaf
Hobnail (one type)
Horn of Plenty
Huber

* Inverted Heart (sauce dishes, honey dishes, bowls, etc.)
Inverted Fern
Inverted Thumbprint (very little made at Sandwich)
Ivy

Leaf and Dart
Lincoln Drape
Loop
Loop and Dart
Loop and Dart, round ornament
Loop and Dart, diamond ornament
Lyre

Magnet and Grape, frosted leaf
Magnet and Grape, stippled leaf

New England Pineapple

Open Rose
* Overshot glass

* Petal and Loop
Pillar
Powder and Shot
Pressed Block
Prism
Prism and Diamond Point
Pressed Leaf

* Rayed, with loop border
* Ribbed Acorn
Ribbed Grape
Ripple
Roman Key (clear or frosted)

Sandwich Star
Sawtooth
Scalloped Lines
Smocking
Star and Punty
Stippled Band
Stippled Fuchsia
Stippled Star
Strawberry

Thumbprint (one type, not the earliest)
Tree of Life

Variation of the Pillar

Waffle
Waffle and Thumbprint

A few fragments of the following well-known Midwestern patterns were found at Sandwich, but not in sufficient quantity to justify their being listed as positively Sandwich.

1. Eugenie sugar bowl cover
2. Ray pattern. Very few pieces

3. Holly
4. Cord and Tassel
5. Cabbage Rose
6. Thistle—very few
7. Currant, a few, with cable cord
8. Marquisette, one piece
9. Milk white "Wheat." Very few
10. Very slight amount of marble glass, all light in color
11. Princess Feather.

Not a fragment of the so-called "Cape Cod" pattern was found nor any Lincoln Drape with Tassel, though we know Lincoln Drape was produced. The Eugenie pattern was made by M'Kee & Brothers of Pittsburgh, in the 50's. The knob of the sugar bowl was in the form of a dolphin, which must have attracted the attention of some member of the Sandwich concern, since they made so many dolphin candlesticks.

The Star and Punty was among the Sandwich patterns listed at an early date and should not be confused with the Moon and Star pattern made by Adams & Co. of Pittsburgh, in 1888. There is no evidence that Sandwich ever produced any pattern under the latter name. Star and Punty is illustrated in the chapter in this book dealing with perfume bottles, jars, etc. It was not made in a wide variety of forms but only in spill or taper holders, lamp bowls, perfume bottles, hand lamps and other small pieces.

Hobnail was not made to any extent, except in early perfume bottles and in these the hobnails were blown and thus were hollow on the inside.

Literally tons of fragments have been removed from the Sandwich factory grounds in the years since the plant shut down, by souvenir hunters as well as by well-meaning persons who love the glass. Colored pieces, in which the dumps abounded, have been utilized in the making of artistic jewelry by a local resident. A manufacturer of stained-glass windows used brilliantly colored fragments in making window plaques. Fortunately for historians, a quantity of the earliest and most revealing fragments were protected from the relic hunters because they were buried beneath the "Upper House" which was built in 1849 and was not torn down until 1920. Even then the fragments were preserved still longer because the foundation, with its brick flooring, was not removed until 1933. At that time Mr. Francis Wynn, a native of Sandwich, who had always been intensely interested in the history of the factory, began excavating on his own to see if the ground beneath this building might not reveal something of interest. It was here that he discovered the earliest of the Blown Molded glass and the earliest of the lacy fragments. The Heart and Sheaf of Wheat pattern was located four feet below the surface. The largest and best pieces had been previously removed as cullet and what was left was simply dumped. The majority of these fragments are now owned by Francis Wynn, the Sandwich Historical Society, the Massachusetts Institute of Technology and the author.

The original Sandwich factory, which was a wooden structure built in 1825, was absorbed in the 1849 building, which was of brick construction. The site was marshy and most of the land was "made." As the factory grew, more and more "made land" was used. There was no common dumping ground. The discarded glass was thrown wherever it was most convenient. To some extent the fragment findings shed an interesting light on the growth of the industry. As stated before, the Blown Molded and early lacy fragments were found underneath the 1849 building. The early pattern glass, such as Horn of Plenty, New England Pineapple, Pillar, Ashburton, Cable, Waffle, and Waffle with Thumbprint were found under another portion of the same building where the third leer had stood.

The Blown Molded ("three mold") dark glass inkwell fragments in Keene and Coventry types were not found with the other early fragments. They began to appear, as Mr. Wynn excavated, in a portion of the filled land which was created after the 1849 period. Whole specimens, as well as a large number of fragments, were discovered not only in this spot but also close to the bank of the creek and alongside the Lower House (1871). Their appearance cannot be explained, for practically all of the fragments of bases show base wear. The patterns are well established as having been produced by Keene and Coventry. At some future date it is to be hoped that adequate proof of Sandwich origin, or an explanation of why so many Keene and Coventry fragments came to be dumped where they were found, may be offered. It has been suggested that they came with cullet bought by Sandwich and thrown away because of their undesirable color.

In the marshland, not far from the cooper shop, was found a quantity of late pattern glass fragments as well as some in Morning Glory. Alongside the Lower House there were found also some of the early patterns such as Hamilton and Morning Glory. Bellflower and other ribbed pattern pieces were in an entirely different location, near where a horse-drawn "bogy" carried goods from the factory to the outer wharf.

Lacy glass was still made in quantity after 1849 because fragments were found all over the yard. Acorn stoppers, which we know were popular, were recovered in large numbers. Other curious objects came to light, such as old Irish pipes, decorated with roses and shamrocks.

A small quantity of lacy glass fragments was also discovered alongside the 1871 building. Several fragments of an unidentified Eagle-Masonic flask came from beneath the building built in 1849 along with the rest of the early material, in a peculiar soft jade green. More may be learned about them later on. Mr. Wynn did not attach much importance to them, knowing that few of the old glassworkers were teetotalers, which would readily account for any quantity of the flask fragments.

Many unidentified patterns were unearthed, one being in a design similar to that known as Cane, which resembles the cane seat of a chair. Another fragment has a diamond pattern, one clear diamond alternating with a stippled, each being outlined in small beading. There were fragments of a variety of Acorn with oak leaves, heavy bowls in Oval Mitre, and a thick, flint glass design known to some New England collectors as Bradford Blackberry. The last-named has wide panels, with large bunches of pendent blackberries and leaves. Doubtless other designs used in complete sets of tableware may be identified from time to time, though it is more than probable that all of the best known patterns are already familiar to collectors. To identify every odd piece ever produced at Sandwich would be an utter impossibility; to attempt it, an absurdity.

Chapter XXXI

SANDWICH ENGRAVED, CUT, AND
DECORATED WARES

The history of glassmaking at Sandwich would be incomplete without some comments on their cutting and engraving departments, as well as their decorated wares. Among the notes in the old company ledgers are many references to the cutting department, which was the most profitable one left during the closing years. From time to time as the plant prospered, the space was enlarged, which could only indicate that the volume of sales was great enough to warrant the increased space. During the late 1860's and early 1870's as many as fifty of the best glass cutters in the country worked in the cutting shop, as did a number of engravers.

Many special orders were executed in addition to their regular commercial output. The finest of flint glass stemware was blown at Sandwich, often on special order, engraved with the initials of the owner.

The illustrations in this chapter, with one exception, are taken from a catalogue of the Boston & Sandwich Glass Company; it is undated but pictures wares they produced over a period of years. There was not the demand for incessant change in the old days, so articles could be and were carried on for many years and they still found a ready market. There was good and bad taste in the past and we still have good and bad taste, so my readers can judge for themselves whether the articles pictured, dating from the 1860's and some from the 1870's and 1880's, are deserving of a place of honor in their homes.

Plate 220 pictures blown pieces delicately engraved. Many such dishes may be found in the cupboards of New England homes today, where they are treasured. In the bottom row center is what appears to be a covered Toddy jar with accompanying tray. It is engraved with large cool-looking fern leaves. Most of the items in the lower row carry the same or a similar design, with the exception of the center pitcher at the left, which engraving appears to have been influenced by the type of early decoration such as is found on Stiegel pieces. Noteworthy are the two styles of pitchers in tankard and bulbous styles; a covered cheese dish; compotes, open and covered; decanters, a "water bottle and tumble-up," and one lone goblet.

Plate 221 illustrates Sandwich favorites of Victorian style. The dolphin epergne is a rarity today. The stem that holds the upper engraved flowerholder is of spun glass. Beside the epergne are two classical figures with a frosted, or satin finish, supporting bowls, one of which is cut and the other engraved or acid etched. All three pieces appear to date in the 1870's, when objects partly frosted were in great demand. Candlesticks were made in a similar style to the stems supporting the bowls, but try to find any of them! They were produced in color and one or two pairs appeared in a collection sold at the Parke-Bernet Galleries a few years ago, where they brought a high figure. In fact, the bidding on these candlesticks became almost as spirited as at the sale of the famous Morgan "Peach-blow" vase.

Plate 222 illustrates more elaborate types of engraved epergnes, which may well have been the work of Nicholas Lutz. Thin blown work was one of his specialties—the engraving being done in another department.

The painted and decorated wares are probably among the least known of all the Sandwich products. That it was not considered unimportant during the factory's heyday is established by the fact that just one of my old catalogues pictures fourteen full pages. Two of these are shown on Plates 223 and 224. There are tall round vases decorated with flowers, butterflies, birds and conventional designs. There are epergnes, flowerpots, light globes and all manner of articles. Many of the pieces were probably inspired by contemporary English glass, popularly attributed to Bristol for lack of any more authentic information.

Plate 225 illustrates some of the plainer footed tableware. The ribbed feet are typical of much Midwestern glass, so Sandwich appears to have borrowed the idea, since they had need of meeting keen competition from that section of the country. It is quite likely that the bowls of many of the pieces pictured may have been made in color, and the feet applied in crystal. The Lutz family have in their possession some ruby-colored glass having plain crystal stems and feet, known to have been made in Sandwich.

There is not room in this volume to picture all of the decorative glassware produced at Sandwich. There are many ornamental epergnes, some decorated with cutting or engraving; dolphins supporting fish bowls, the globes being either plain or engraved with fish and seaweed; candlesticks; and an almost endless amount of cut and engraved ware of all sorts. The blown and delicately cut tableware is greatly admired by enthusiastic collectors today.

No mortal can hope to live long enough to list and authenticate all the blown, cut, engraved, and decorated pieces made at Sandwich. All that appears feasible is to point out some of the most interesting types, which have been neglected up to this time for lack of documentary evidence concerning them.

PLATE 223

This type of decorated glassware is not usually associated with Sandwich but as documented by old catalogues, was

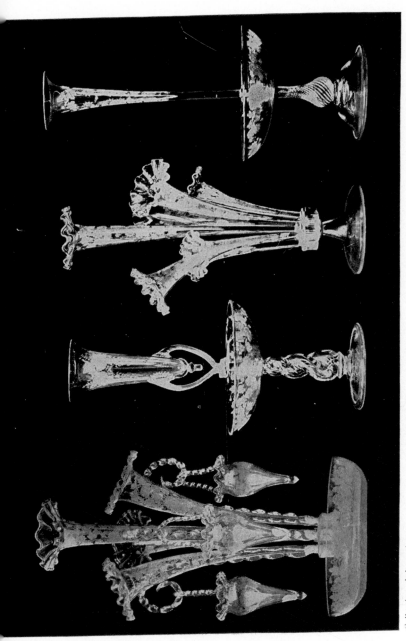

PLATE 222

Ornate blown and engraved epergnes, as shown in a Boston & Sandwich Glass Company catalogue.

PLATE 221

Dolphin epergne and two frosted glass classical figures supporting bowls which are engraved. Taken from a Boston

PLATE 220

Engraved ware, as shown in a Boston & Sandwich Glass Company catalogue.

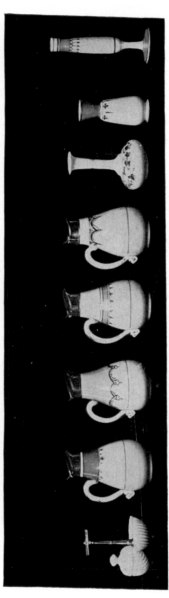

PLATE 224

Page from an old Boston & Sandwich Glass Company catalogue. The water bottles with inverted tumblers seen at the upper right were known as "water bottles with tumble-ups."

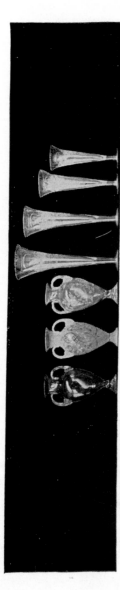
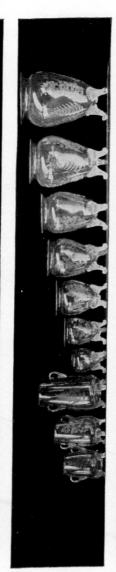
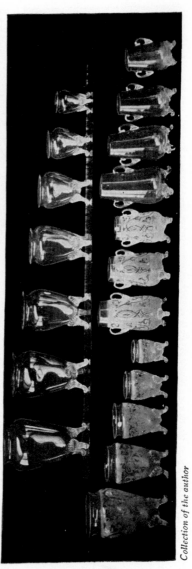

PLATE 225

Vases with applied ribbed feet were among items produced by the Boston & Sandwich Glass Company in the large

Chapter XXXII

CLOSING DAYS

While Deming Jarves severed his connection with the Boston & Sandwich Glass Company in 1858, it is reasonable to assume that his influence did not disappear entirely with his departure from that factory. Mr. Sewell H. Fessenden succeeded Jarves as General Manager and ran into difficult times soon after. Later, the Civil War took away many of the older men and business in general suffered when the South seceded. It is well to bear in mind that at the time the Boston & Sandwich Glass Company was formed there were only two really important glass companies operating in the United States. They perforce were the most formidable competitors of Sandwich for a generation—the New England Glass Company of Cambridge, Mass., and Bakewell, Pears & Company of Pittsburgh, Pa. But by 1858 when Jarves resigned from the Sandwich Company, glass factories had begun to spring up like mushrooms over the Midwest. Their proximity to the coal fields, and cheaper transportation by river, gave them almost a monopoly of the Western and Southern business. Naturally their activities multiplied. In the 1860's the Western makers found in lime a cheap substitute for lead. The newer Midwestern factories, with no such traditions of quality to maintain as the New England companies or Bakewells, were quick to adopt the new process. They knew that it would mean an inferior product, but with costs lower there would follow larger sales and greater profits. The two conservative New England producers at that time deemed it incompatible with their standards to lower the quality of their wares. Their trade was accustomed to the best. The New England Glass Company therefore decided to continue making lead glass, and so did Sandwich. And, of course, so did Jarves in his new venture, the Cape Cod

Glass Works. By 1870 every factory in the old Pittsburgh glass district was producing cheap tableware in volume and was competing vigorously with the East. No one can tell what Deming Jarves might have done had he continued at the helm at Sandwich. He was now an old man, and even if he had tried, he would not have been able to stem the tide. Times had changed and the industry with them, but Jarves had unshakable convictions about the sort of glass to make. The desire to buy as cheaply as possible began when humanity took to trading instead of stealing, but the attitude of the American public was beginning to change. We were developing a national buying-policy which was to consider the price first and quality second. It was still called thrift, the great Benjamin Franklin virtue. Lime glass helped to expedite the change and, of course, so did improved technological methods and high pressure salesmanship.

Sandwich bowed to the inevitable to the extent of producing pressed lime glass tableware in sets to meet the Midwestern competition. Before long twenty factories were operating in the Pittsburgh area alone, and they were flooding the market with their products, particularly in the West and South, and in Canada. The New England Glass Company, like Sandwich, suffered grievously from the falling off in the demand for quality, but it did not lower its standards, at least not radically. During the 1870's that Company specialized in cut and engraved ware, so fine in quality as to earn the praise of discriminating buyers both at home and abroad. Sandwich also had a large cutting shop and an engraving department where special orders were taken and filled for dinner services and testimonial pieces. The two companies could and did supply the New England trade with fine glassware. By the beginning of the 80's, however, both companies were on their way out. Their most prosperous era had passed, never to return. Energetic high-pressure Western salesmen were successfully at work in the once exclusive territory. The competition had grown steadily from the day in 1870 when Pittsburgh glass manufacturers established an office on Milk Street in Boston. Two years later another Western company also established a Boston office, where orders were taken for their products. It was not carrying coals to Newcastle but over-stressing the virtue of thrift as demonstrated by the wisdom of buying something that was not so good but was much cheaper.

A period of prosperity had followed the abatement of the business disturbances and industrial uncertainties that prevailed during the Civil War, and it was under the Fessenden management that the Sandwich factory reached the height of its financial prosperity, during the 70's. Not even the panic of 1873 could put an end to it. But by 1880 the effects of Western competition were alarming. It was not alone the steadily increasing pressure of that competition that wrote the last chapter of the story of Sandwich, where for two generations the Sandwich workmen had been a contented lot and, as a whole, well paid.

Sandwich had had its day. For sixty years its story could be read in the streamers of smoke rising into the sky. Today the reader of it looks into the cabinets containing some of the most beautiful glass ever made in America. Perhaps Deming Jarves would not have asked for more, for it is the early Sandwich, the Deming Jarves Sandwich, that is enshrined in cultured homes.

It has been variously claimed that the arrogance of the Directors of the Company was chiefly responsible for the fatal strike; that Midwestern manufacturers had encouraged delegations of their unionized men to go to Sandwich, not so much to organize the Easterners as to foment trouble. Or that since the works was obviously on its last legs, the Company cheerfully welcomed an excuse to enable them to cease operating at a loss without incurring the odium of abruptly depriving thousands of men of work. Another source places the blame on certain absentee owners and asserts that but for the sudden and unexpected death of Mr. Nathaniel J. Bradlee of Boston, a leading Director of the Company who was respected by the men for his fairness and tact, the troubles would have been adjusted.

Instead of the conjecture and the conflicting rumors which attend the decline of an industrial enterprise as manifested above, it is possible now to substitute documented facts. Along with isolated facts of general interest, the chain of events which led to the final closing of the plant will be detailed here.

In 1882 Henry Spurr became the new Superintendent and, in the early part of 1883, he was able to cause the resignation of Sewell Fessenden as Agent of the Company. Shortly thereafter, Spurr accepted the position of general manager. At about the same time, the National Flint and Lime Glass Association sent out a circular to every flint and lime glass manufacturer, sounding each out with regard to voluntarily shutting down during the months of July and August. The object was to attempt to relieve the surplus that existed and keep prices up. The Boston & Sandwich Glass Company inventories revealed a tremendous stock of glassware on hand. The marked tendency of American industry to "get in on a good thing," flood the market and then find itself out on a limb, was present even in those days.

Henry Spurr, who was not averse to blowing his own horn, had some interesting comments. He said it was with great pleasure that he presented the affairs of the Company for 1883, considering the unfavorable reports from many other corporations! Spurr spoke of his opal glass, in quality equal to any in this or any other country. He retained a proof from every pot of opal glass produced since the first batch under his supervision, April 20, 1882, "and, as everyone remarks, not a change since the first in any way whatever." Spurr laid claim to producing the best coating ruby ever made in the factory, even to supplying other manufacturers with ruby goods for etching purposes. He mentioned turning out what is called "pot ruby" which some other factories had made for a long time. Sandwich endeavored to produce it at great expense in 1876 and failed. Manufacturing and selling more rich cut goods than ever before was another feather in Spurr's cap. The modest Mr. Spurr also spoke of producing with two furnaces in 1882 and 1883 more goods than had been manufactured for years.

During the following year, 1885, the Sandwich Glass Company notified its landlord that it would "quit and deliver up the premises

at 164 Devonshire St. and 21 Federal St. in the city of Boston."—
This was symptomatic of the "beginning of the end."

Business had fallen off badly. In 1886 it was less by $47,000
than the preceding year and represented an actual operating loss
of $11,175.74. The statement for that year charged this off in part
to a strike which cut off one month's production with all other
expenses still going on. Another contributing factor was the Company's altered financial position whereby they had become bor-
rowers of money instead of lenders. In March of 1886, a month
after the publication of the foregoing statement, the Directors state
that "In addition to the excessive dullness of trade, the fierce competition of Western as well as foreign manufacturers has largely
diminished our sales and reduced prices painfully and, with these,
we have had a share of labor troubles in common with other large
employers of labor. A strike of the glassmakers at our works which
lasted for five weeks plus an unusual shutdown of four weeks during the summer months made nine weeks during which the manufacture of glass was entirely suspended, while the other expenses of
the cutting shop and other departments of the factory were running
on as usual. Then too, the moving of the warehouse and the fitting
of the new quarters entailed an expense of about $2,000, without
estimating the very considerable loss felt by consequent delays and
hindrances; so, in short, the year 1885 closed, showing a positive
loss in our manufacture of upwards of $11,000. In former years,
the Company had been able to hold a considerable sum of ready
cash which usually earned a handsome sum in the way of interest.
This year the interest account stands debited at $620. In the neces-
sary conservation of our property and in the preparedness for a
business which did not come, we expended the sum of $8,083.28
and were not able with all our efforts to escape bad debts. There
is a change for the worse in indebtedness to $26,000. To offset this
uncomfortable statement, we have only to say that our stock of
glass was large, brilliant and varied. It appears to be larger by
$12,000 than a year ago. Works and tenements are in better condi-
tion and better shape to earn money if there is any to be earned."

Of great significance in the closing chapter of the Boston & Sandwich Glass Company is the sixty-first annual report, submitted on March 28, 1888, to the stockholders, quoted here in its entirety:

We can take no pleasure in presenting such an unsatisfactory report of the last year's business as we are obliged to present for your consideration today. During the year we have been called upon to mourn the loss of your late president and largest stockholder, Mr. John D. Parker, who died on the second day of February last. Mr. Parker took a deep interest in the affairs of the company, and gave it much of his personal attention. He had undoubted faith in its ultimate success and at the time of his death was the owner of four hundred and twenty-four shares, representing over one-sixth of its capital stock. As he had such a large interest and such strong convictions as to its success, your directors relied largely on his judgment. After his death it was unanimously decided to be for the best interest of the company to put out the fires and reduce expenses to the lowest judicious limit, as we were of the opinion, that it would be impossible to give you a fair return for your investments and accede to the demands of the workmen employed. While this state of affairs exists, it is best to stop manufacturing, to sell from the large stock of manufactured goods now on hand, to pay off the debt of the company, and to keep the surplus for your future action.

When a manufacturer cannot control the workmen employed, and the men assume the right to fix the amount of work to be performed, the wages to be paid, and say who shall be employed, and who discharged, it is then impossible to continue manufacturing successfully. The question of labor which is causing so much trouble throughout the country, together with the competition among the glass manufacturers, especially at the West, where fuel is so cheap or natural gas is used, thus giving them great advantages, require us, in order to be successful to use the greatest economy in manufacturing, and to employ only those who are willing to work for its success, and until we can accomplish this, it will be useless for us to start the works again.

It is self-evident to your Directors that the workmen have had all the benefit of running the works for the past few years, and now the question for you to decide is as to what is best to be done—whether to authorize the Board of Directors whom you may elect to-day to wind up its affairs, or to give them such power if they in their judgment deem it best to do so.

We have no doubt that if the workmen would forsake their Association and work only for the success of the manufactory, the Company would again be able to return to you a fair compensation for your investment, and it has been suggested, that some plan might be devised on a cooperative basis, by which a fixed dividend should be paid to the stockholders and any surplus over said agreed dividend should be equally divided between the employees and the stockholders.

You will have in the report of the Examining Committee and Auditor a full statement of the affairs of the Company. In this statement the manufactured goods are taken at 25% discount from jobbing prices and the consigned goods at the same valuation.

In the account of the cost of manufacturing, it will be seen that the sales have amounted to $209,859.45 and the cost of the goods sold was $189,653. 42, showing a gross profit of $20,206.03; the sales therefore show that there has been a profit of $10^{65}/_{100}\%$ on the cost, but the expenses of selling have been $34,902.15 which is $18\frac{2}{5}\%$ of the cost, and if we include the repairs of real estate and of tools and machinery, together with the worthless accounts, the total expense has been $45,307.34; against this is the profit on the sales of flour and house rents amounting to $2,260.25 and reducing the expense to $43,047.09 showing an actual loss for the year of $22,841.06.

The sales as they appear credited on the manufacturer's account amount to $235,644.69 but the goods returned, allowances, and discounts made reduce the amount to $209,859.45. The amount paid for labor during the past year was $10,582.99 more than the previous year, and the amount of sales $8,030.43 less, but we have $6,998.62 more glass on hand than a year ago.

The amount of outstanding notes of the Company on January 1 was $35,000. This amount has been reduced to $10,000 since the closing of our accounts by the sale of glass and from accounts receivable. Having now given you a full statement of the affairs of the Company it is for you to decide what action shall be taken. Respectfully submitted, Nathaniel J. Bradlee, President.

Following the ominous import of Mr. Bradlee's letter, we find only sporadic items of interest relating to the intermittent production of the factory, such as the following: "Among the items being made, as listed in January 1888 at Sandwich, were opal squat gas globes; ten inch dome shades; nutmeg lamps; founts. [These could have been lamp founts and probably were]; 14″ dome shades; 14″ cone shades; plaques; columns; salts for decorating; lanterns; gas shades for etching and cutting." Apparently unnecessary expense was incurred by poor workmanship because mention is made of blown glass by Mr. Mathews, Mr. Louvet and Mr. Lutz, saying, "The above work made by Mr. Mathews, Mr. Louvet and Mr. Lutz is mostly for cutting and very little. of the losses occasioned by bad work."

For April 1888, Mr. Lapham made a detailed report of the list of the employees at Sandwich respective of duties and their wages. He concluded: "One man makes the patterns on the articles for cutting, gets out new designs and does the most difficult work in the cutting. The hands that are cutting glass are paying a good profit and are cutting goods that are wanted and do the best of work. Since the above hands have been employed over at the Veneer Works, Feb. 20, 1888, we have finished and sent off over $1,000 worth of cutware and have a quantity underway."

Under date of April 1, 1888, there is a highly significant report of the glass on hand at Sandwich. Glasses are mentioned first. The pattern names are not revealed. The list goes through bar bottles, bitters bottles, clarets, creamers, caster bottles, candlesticks, cigar globes and dishes. There are decanters, egg cups, electric globes and shades, flower trays, finger bowls, fish globes, gas globes, etc. There are hot whiskeys, inks and ink tops, ice cream plates, jars, kerosene globes with edge cut or crimped, and so on. Lamps are assorted and include small prisms and large prisms. There are also nappies, pomades, port lights for ships, lanterns, many types of shades, sponge cups, smoke shades, smoke bells, spoonholders, salts, tumblers, wines. In open stock they list a capping room, foot room, graphite room, left-over etching room, passageway, cutting shop, decorating room. Total amount of glass in these departments amounted to $23,783.

In May 1888 the roster of workers had dwindled to: C. R. Swift, day watchman; Philip Shevlin—night watchman; William Eaton —P.M. to 1 o'clock—extra watchman; John O'Donnell, extra watchman; S. W. Hunt, in charge of the packing room, who had more or less to do each day according to the goods sent away; Owen Carraway, who looked after and kept in order, as far as possible, everything around the premises; J. Buckley, responsible for the care of the horses; H. F. Spurr, Jr., who entered orders in ecah department, keeping account of work made in glasshouse, when working; H. F. Spurr, general manager; B. H. Lapham, paymaster, in charge of the glass-cutting department in absence of the manager in full charge. In addition there were five men in the cutting room. Mr. Lockwood marked the patterns on articles for cutting, got out new designs and did the most difficult part of the cutting.

Apparently several people decided the works could be put back in full operation. Included was one Edward J. Swann. Under date of July 17, 1888, he wrote the Directors:

Gentlemen:—Your return of the 16th I have received. I regret very much to note therein that which amounts almost to a decision to permanently close the works. You say in speaking of the rules of the Association, "Which are fatal to any successful operation of the manufacturer." The fact that all that are manufacturing successfully notwithstanding said rules are everywhere in operation would seem to indicate some inability to manage the men here employed. You also say, "Our directors were not willing to try any more experiments and you could give no guarantee." Glassmaking is not an experiment in Sandwich. It can still be successful down here. I say this fully believing that if given full control of the operations (I do not desire such control or in any other direction) I can with your cooperation make you a paying business. When I say your cooperation, I mean all that the word implies. No one can or will, who is worth considering in connection with this matter, give a guarantee to run a business like yours successfully. The best assurance anyone can give is that he has a knowledge of the business to be done, has seen wherein it has gone wrong and has the ability and a just and full confidence that he can and will make a success of it. I know I can manage the men. They are elsewhere; they can be here. I am chiefly anxious to see the works in operation again. I shall be just as well, yes, better satisfied, if some other man of whom you are more confident, is put in management and success results. What guarantee from me would satisfy the Directors? In what way would they expect me to warrant the success of the work? They can have assurance and recommendations from the best men of the town, who have known the workings of the factory for many years. Yours with respect.

He received a reply as follows:

I see very little prospect of the Sandwich Glass Co. ever starting again. A majority of the Directors as well as the stockholders would vote to close up the concern at any time when called together for the purpose. In fact, the directors now have full power to do so and have only delayed action in the belief that the workmen might see what was for their interest as well as that of the town of Sandwich and give up their association with outsiders who have no real interest with them or with the town. In regard to your case, as to what guarantee the directors would require, I can not say, but suppose they would require bond equal to 6% of the stock at least. Very truly yours, Nathaniel Bradlee.

Rather belatedly, on Sept. 20, 1888, the workmen came across with an amendment to their agreement as to what conditions they would work under:

"Rule 1. We agree to work for your Company at the list of wages and numbers adopted by the joint meeting of manufacturers and workers, held in Brooklyn in August last." Some two years before, a petition of Robert Mathews and 63 other employees of Sandwich called for an investigation of the operation, and evinced a willingness to provide a committee to assist wherever possible. Ironically enough the policies which the Union members had pursued contributed substantially to the downfall of the Company and indirectly to their own undoing. Their growing realization of this fact apparently began with the petition and increased with their willingness to come to more reasonable terms in 1888. It was a little late in the day, however.

The Sixty-Second Annual Report of the Directors of the Boston & Sandwich Glass Company for March 27, 1889 gives virtually all of the details of the end of the Company. Because of its great value to the continuity of the story, it is quoted fully.

No goods having been manufactured at your works for twelve months, the report we make to-day, consequently, can be only as to what assets have been sold, what debts have been paid, and what property is left.

Such a report cannot be pleasing, but simply interesting.

That my predecessor as President, Nathaniel J. Bradlee, whose death occurred on December 17th, 1888, should have been taken away the very next year after the decease of his predecessor, Mr. Parker, is singular. To many of our stockholders the loss to this community of so valuable a citizen is keenly brought to mind; especially, because of his very sudden death in the prime of his great usefulness and of his many varied responsibilities. For fifteen years this Company had the benefit of his well-known good services, which we all appreciate the more, now that he has gone.

Beyond paying our debt, reducing expenses and the stock of goods on hand, our problem has been—which and what to do first and how to do it.

The books have been made up for thirteen months, to show the Company's condition, as near as possible, to this day. Therefore the accounts cover the period from 1st. January 1888 to 1st. February 1889.

On the 1st. January 1888 we owed $35,000.

The last of this indebtedness was paid off on the 24th. May 1888.

On the 1st. January 1888 we had on hand manufactured goods, after deducting 25% from wholesale jobbing prices, $106,943.35. On the 1st. February 1889 this was reduced (by sales with large discounts, and taking balance on hand at 40% discount) to $24,-682.23.

By the "statement of affairs" to be submitted to you to-day you will find:

Cash Assets	$32,925.94
Glass Ware at 40% off	24,682.23
Materials at 25% off	18,962.28
Showing available personal property	$73,570.43
Real Estate and Machinery	25,000.00
	$101,570.43
Balance of Profit and Loss showing impairment of capital	98,429.57
Amount of Capital Stock	$200,000.00

It was deemed expedient early in the year to change our Boston Salesroom (where we were paying rent and taxes of about $5,000 per annum) to a less expensive place.

From the 1st. July last we underleased our Franklin Street store to the United States Express Company for a bonus of $1,000 per annum for the balance of our lease (twenty-one months); and secured our present location, 13 Federal Street, at a rent of $2,000 per annum, without taxes, for one, or three years, at our option.

The lease of our New York store having but a few months to run, it was difficult to dispose of it, and we decided to continue business there until that lease expired.

We have now no office in New York, and our Agent and employees there have been discharged. We have dispensed with the services of our General Manager, thereby making a saving of his salary,—and in our Boston store have reduced our working force by one salesman and one clerk.

At Sandwich our property is in charge of our former Paymaster, with one assistant and five day and night watchmen, as required by the Insurance Companies.—One of these watchmen was our former assistant engineer, who has especial charge of the Engine Room and all other machinery.

The occupants of many of our houses at Sandwich, having been delinquent in paying their rent, your Directors employed an attorney, who has arranged amicably with them, and we are now getting a moderate income from those occupied.

We have been in treaty with these several parties for the sale or lease of the Real Estate at Sandwich, but although, on the part of your Directors, two different offers were made to each, all of them were declined, and neither party made any definite proposition.

The Town of Sandwich Tax bill for 1888 has not yet been paid—the valuation on which their bill was made was the same as in previous years, when the works were running full.—To this we demurred, and have made two applications for abatement, both of which have been refused;—this we consider an injustice on the part of the authorities toward a Corporation, who for half a century has been a large tax-payer and the life of the Town.—We have now appealed to the County Commissioners, as our redress, who have appointed a hearing in April.

Several months since some of the leading and most influential citizens of Sandwich, realizing the importance to the Town's prosperity of our Factory being again in operation, took energetic measures to reconcile the differences between the Employees and our Board, and taking the refusal of a large block of the stock of our Company, raised a popular subscription for its purchase; but their efforts were crushed by a conference between your Directors and a high official of the Glass Makers' Union, who objected to the workmen signing certain rules submitted by us, which they were willing to do.

Thus you will see that your Directors have had constantly in mind your wishes as expressed at your last annual meeting, and have endeavored in every possible way to diminish the expenses of the Corporation, to press the sales of the stock of goods on hand, to lease or to sell the property at Sandwich and to perfect some proper arrangement by which the Factory could be reopened and the industry made profitable.

It is now for you to say whether you wish further efforts made to start the works again, or to instruct your Directors to realize, as fast as practicable, from all the Company's assets, and to divide the Proceeds among the Stockholders.

Respectfully submitted,

CHAS. M. SEAVER, President.

In October, 1889, there were three watchmen left, plus Mr. Lapham who had general charge of the property. The Sandwich factory was sold October 17, 1889 to the Electrical Glass Corporation. It was sold for $20,000 cash, the agreement saying that at the time of transfer papers must be in within 30 days from the date of the sale for all of the real estate and personal property of the Boston & Sandwich Glass Company in Sandwich.

The final balancing of the books came on March 1, 1891, the sum being $4,833.05. All stockholders paid, all debts paid.

The New England Glass Company also closed down in 1888 due to labor strife and was moved to Toledo, Ohio, where it carried on successfully under the name of the Libbey Glass Company, and that ended the careers of the two largest glass industries in New England. The great Midwest had taken over.

Several attempts were made to reopen glass companies in the old Boston & Sandwich Glass Company buildings, but without success. The last attempt was in the middle of the summer, in the year 1904, when a few glassworkers from Monaca, Pa., and Rochester, Pa., headed by William Swansey, William Burgess and Charles Schrader went to Sandwich, Mass., with the intention of starting up the old Boston & Sandwich Glass Company's factory. One of the glassmakers who participated has contributed the following account:

"The undertaking was incorporated under the laws of Massachusetts in the old name: The Boston and Sandwich Glass Company. Mr. George T. McLaughlin and Mr. J. W. Dalton, both natives of Sandwich, were chosen president and secretary respectively. The capital stock was $75,000 and the shares, $100 par value.

"They planned to make it a cooperative enterprise. Every employee, including laborers, was to purchase stock. A percentage of the wages was to be held back to pay for stock for those who had no ready cash.

"It was believed that with $15,000 the plant could be started and run until the returns came in for glass sold. However, at the last minute some of the pledgers backed out, so instead of $15,000 they began operations with scarcely $7,000. Most of it went for getting the plant in shape. The factory had not been run since

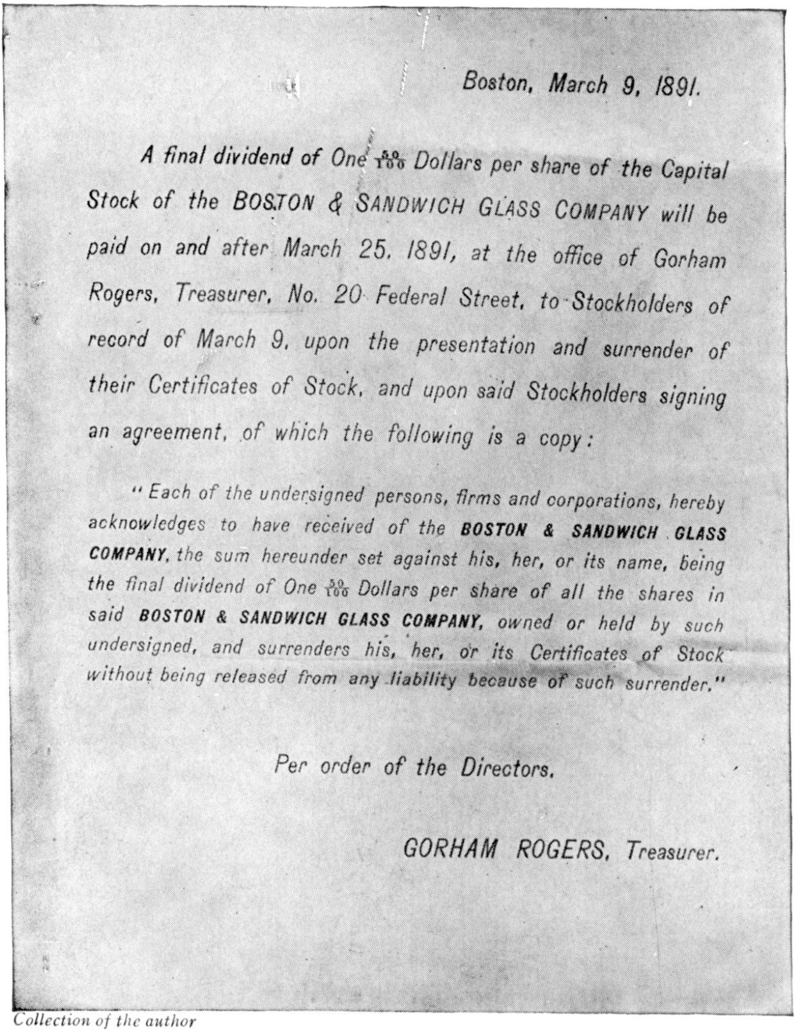

Boston, March 9, 1891.

A final dividend of One 50/100 Dollars per share of the Capital Stock of the BOSTON & SANDWICH GLASS COMPANY will be paid on and after March 25, 1891, at the office of Gorham Rogers, Treasurer, No. 20 Federal Street, to Stockholders of record of March 9, upon the presentation and surrender of their Certificates of Stock, and upon said Stockholders signing an agreement, of which the following is a copy :

"Each of the undersigned persons, firms and corporations, hereby acknowledges to have received of the **BOSTON & SANDWICH GLASS COMPANY**, the sum hereunder set against his, her, or its name, being the final dividend of One 50/100 Dollars per share of all the shares in said **BOSTON & SANDWICH GLASS COMPANY**, owned or held by such undersigned, and surrenders his, her, or its Certificates of Stock without being released from any liability because of such surrender."

Per order of the Directors.

GORHAM ROGERS, Treasurer.

PLATE 226

Final Dividend Notice of the Boston & Sandwich Glass Company. This printed notice of a dollar and a half a share and surrender of the stock is dated March 9, 1891, three years after the fires at the Sandwich plant had been extinguished.

PLATE 227

All that remains standing today of the Boston & Sandwich Glass Company.

about 1890 and during the intervening years rain and snow had worked havoc with the woodwork. It had to be replaced and this took more money and labor than had been anticipated. In a measure this was offset by the low price paid for molds, blowing pipes, pot setting tools and other tools obtained from an idle plant in Elwood City, Pa.

"After much arduous work the place was ready and glass made in September. The line produced consisted of: Electric bulbs, offhand shades and globes, paste and iron mold globes and blanks for cutting. Much difficulty ensued from not being able to bring the furnace up hot enough to melt the glass regularly. This persisted more or less during the entire time the plant was run. The furnace was a low eye coal furnace with the firing place from the factory floor. There were days of waiting between the melts. There was a lack of adequate machinery and facilities and no money. Some of the men became discouraged and left, and nobody took their places. A sympathizing neighbor advanced $1,000 for materials and pots. When this was gone, without money or credit the plant was forced to close down and a receiver appointed in April 1905.

"Some of the men were not discouraged by the failure and began to look about for ways and means to start up again because at the time of the shut-down there were considerable orders on the books. A man from New York by the name of Barnard and his son-in-law became interested. In April 1906, another start was made. But the furnace was again causing trouble and it was decided to change from coal to oil. An oil tank was bought and installed to pipe the oil to the furnace. It was successful for a short time but none of the workers knew much about the workings of the oil system and it ran until the oil and steam, striking the crown, ate a hole in it. An immense gloryhole was hurriedly converted into a furnace to be used while the cap in the other furnace was repaired.

"For some time the work went on spasmodically. But so many things were needed to get the place in good condition for running right that Mr. Barnard decided to withdraw, stating that life was too short to bother with it. Unable to carry on without his support the factory closed down in October 1906. In May 1907, still another start was made to operate it by a Philadelphia man by the name of McCarthy. After a few weeks the factory closed down never again to open."

INDEX